NEWNES
PICTORIAL KNOWLEDGE

VOLUME ONE

United Kingdom
GEORGE NEWNES LTD.
LONDON : 15-17, LONG ACRE, LONDON, W.C.2

Australia
GEORGE NEWNES (AUSTRALIA) PTY., LTD.

ADELAIDE :   S.A.A.C.C. HOUSE, 32, HINDMARSH SQUARE
BRISBANE :   ROUBIN BUILDING, 117, QUEEN STREET
MELBOURNE : PRUDENTIAL BUILDING, 150, QUEEN STREET
PERTH :   N.M.L.A. BUILDING, 81, ST. GEORGE'S TERRACE
SYDNEY :   NEWNES HOUSE, 20-22, MARGARET STREET

NEWNES

PICTORIAL

KNOWLEDGE

General Editor:
PETER FINCH, M.A.

Associate Editors:
WALTER SHEPHERD
CEDRIC DOVER

VOLUME 1

GEORGE NEWNES LIMITED
15–17 LONG ACRE
LONDON, W.C. 2

PRINTED IN GREAT BRITAIN
BY THE WHITEFRIARS PRESS LTD., LONDON AND TONBRIDGE, AND
BOUND BY HAZELL, WATSON & VINEY LTD., AYLESBURY AND LONDON
N.P.K. 1037760.   W.P. 1220.

FOREWORD

THESE volumes are the key which will open the door for you to an enchanting world of knowledge. As you turn over the pages you will find in words and in pictures the fascinating story of our progress from the distant past, when our earliest ancestors were making their first discoveries, right down to our own times, when new marvels are still being revealed by the work of our scientists.

The men who are carrying out their great tasks to-day were inspired when they were young by the stories they read of what others had done before them. So, somewhere in the many pages of these books, you too may find the inspiration to guide you to the work which will interest you all your life and be of value to others. These volumes will tell you of inventors, of great artists and famous writers, poets, and musicians, of explorers and scientists, and of how the work they did and are still doing has taught and influenced others; and always there are pictures to bring everything clearly before you.

In these pages you will travel to the countries of the world and see the people who live in them at work and at play. As you read, you will go with the daring pioneers and adventurers who first opened up new lands by cutting through forest, bush and jungle, or ventured across the seas to find the unknown, or learned the secrets of the frozen wastes around the North and South Poles. The wonders of the heavens are explained; there are the enthralling stories of how great industries have grown and so made possible the building of mighty ships, of locomotives and motor cars, and of aeroplanes that fly above the continents and oceans.

You will read, too, how the familiar things of everyday life are made; of film-making, and of the way in which radio and television have been developed in this present century from the dreams of men who scarcely foresaw the far-reaching results of their experiments. The myths and legends of ancient Greece and Rome are re-told as well as the story of the earliest civilisations. But you will also learn how we are governed to-day, and of the part you can play as a good citizen.

These wonderful volumes have been created for YOU. You will read them with untiring interest and enthusiasm, and in so doing you will gain that knowledge and understanding which will be your treasured possession now and in the days to come.

THE EDITORS.

v

CONTENTS OF VOLUME ONE

Colour Plates

Special Colour Supplement

Special Transart Supplement

Photo=tone Supplements

LONDON'S RIVER AS IT IS TO-DAY

Graphic Photo Union.

The River Thames in England and the valley through which it flows have seen many strange changes since those far-off days when the valley was the hunting-ground for enormous animals. Something of the wonderful story which has been gradually revealed in the course of excavations in this and other parts of the world is told in the pages that follow.

WHEN THE EARTH WAS YOUNG

MORE than a century ago the famous historian, Lord Macaulay, wrote of a time in the far distant future " when some traveller from New Zealand shall, in the midst of a vast solitude, take his stand on a broken arch of London Bridge to sketch the ruins of St. Paul's."

In those far-off times when such great changes as these may have taken place in Britain the scientists from other parts of the earth may visit the ancient lands of Europe, seeking to discover what kind of people lived in the once-great city of London. By digging below the soil they will unearth the relics of a bygone age and slowly piece together the story of the past.

It is in this way that our scientists of yesterday and to-day have learned the story not only of how the people of the bygone cities of Egypt, Babylon, Greece and Rome lived and worked in the days of long ago, but have learned, too, of the great changes that have taken place in the formation of the earth itself and of the strange animals that roamed the plains and forests in the days before Man had appeared.

There was a time when crocodiles and other reptiles even more gigantic, as well as animals bigger than the elephant, wandered at large in the English valley through which the River Thames still runs. We know this because these great creatures have left behind them records of their existence—not in writing but in the earth itself. These records have been discovered by the simple process of digging.

Concealed Beneath City Streets

It is not often that an opportunity is afforded of digging in this way in a comparatively modern city such as London, but there have been occasions when it has been possible. The bombing of London from the air during the war of 1939–45 destroyed many buildings and left great craters, and the archæologists

Ellison Hawks.

FOSSILS OF FISH

Here is a wonderfully clear picture of fossilised fish. The slab of stone in which the fish are embedded was found in South Africa, where in all probability it rested undisturbed for millions of years. In very many cases fossils are imperfect or incomplete, and scientists must then employ their knowledge and skill to build up a picture of what the creatures looked like when alive. Here, however, the fossils are so perfect that even the novice may trace their outlines as readily as he could those of living fish in an aquarium.

took the opportunity of searching still deeper to add to their knowledge. Under the uppermost relics of quite recent date have been found traces of the Anglo-Saxon and Danish people who at one time occupied the country. Below these have been discovered remains of the Roman and Celtic inhabitants at the beginning of the Christian era. Even lower, relics of the races that inhabited Britain in prehistoric times have been unearthed.

Among these last remains have been found enormous bones that could not possibly have belonged to any kind of creature now in existence. These bones form a record that has been preserved for us through countless ages. Slowly and laboriously scientists have fitted these bones together to form complete skeletons, from which we are able to reconstruct with a considerable degree of accuracy the appearance of these long-vanished creatures.

The story of the Thames Basin is wonderfully interesting, although it is one of the newest parts of our country. Variations in the successive layers of rock show us that for ages the land alternately rose and fell—now buried beneath the advancing sea and then emerging and rising to a considerable height.

The Temple beneath the Waves

On the whole, the movement of the land was very slow, seldom more than a few inches in a century. This gradual rise and fall continues even to-day, and is particularly marked in certain parts of the world. A remarkable example is provided by the history of a Roman temple on the shores of the Bay of Naples. Nearly 2,000 years ago this temple was well above sea-level, but the gradual sinking of the land brought it lower and lower until at last it was submerged, its roof destroyed, and its floor buried under several feet of sand and mud. To-day the temple—or what remains of it—stands at a height above sea-level almost as great as when it was built, showing that the fall of the land has been succeeded by a rise of almost equal extent.

Several of the larger pillars that supported the roof of this temple have survived the change of conditions, and they clearly tell the story of their experiences. When they were submerged their bases were protected by the mud, and consequently they are well preserved. Above them is a section that contains countless little round holes bored by marine creatures, showing that this portion of the pillars stood in sea-water. The tops of the columns, however, are merely worn by the weather, for even when the land was at its lowest level they stood above the surface of the water.

A Country that behaves like a See-Saw

Sweden provides us with a very interesting case of movement, and one that has been carefully measured. In the extreme north the country has risen at the rate of between 3 feet and 5 feet

WHY WE HAVE COAL MINES TO-DAY

Three hundred million years ago the earth was in the *Carboniferous* (Coal-bearing) Period, and the country covered with rich vegetation. Trees, shrubs and smaller plant-life grew thickly, and some specimens, such as the branching club-mosses shown in the centre of the picture, reached a height of over a hundred feet. As time went on this vegetation died, and from its remains deep peat bogs were formed. Gradually the peat bogs sank and newer layers of soil formed above them, so that they underwent pressure and chemical change, until in the course of time they became seams of the coal which is of such value to us all.

MILLIONS OF YEARS AGO

GRAVEL AND RIVER MUD. FIRST WRITINGS
FIRST TRACE OF IMPLEMENTS
SANDS AND LOAM. FIRST REMAINS OF MAN
MEDITERRANEAN ROCKS. FIRST MAN-LIKE APES
SAND AND CHALK. SANDS, CLAY AND PEBBLES. FIRST APES
LAST OF THE GIANT REPTILES
CLAY AND LIMESTONE. FIRST BIRDS
PEBBLE BEDS AND LIMESTONE
SANDSTONE. FIRST OF THE PRE-HISTORIC
MONSTER ANIMALS. FIRST CONE-BEARING TREES
COAL-BEARING. NOTE THAT THE STRATA
HAVE "FAULTED" THROUGH EARTH TREMORS
OLD RED SANDSTONE. FIRST FISH WITH BACKBONES
SHALE AND LIMESTONE. FIRST AIR-BREATHING CREATURES
MUDSTONES. FIRST FISH APPEAR
THE CAMBRIAN LAYER
YIELDING FLAGSTONES AND SLATES

This is a helpful key to the wonderful pictorial diagram which appears on the opposite page. It explains the different layers or strata of which much of the earth's surface is composed. Note particularly that the coal-bearing layer has slipped at one point owing to some mighty underground upheaval. This movement is called a "fault." It is of the utmost interest to realise that beneath us, as we walk along a street or across a meadow, are remains of creatures which lived and died many millions of years ago. Our diagram should be read in an upward direction.

4

THE EARTH'S TALE TOLD BY ROCKS

If you could take a portion of the earth and cut it like a piece of cake, this pictorial diagram shows what you would find. Layer by layer, and stratum by stratum, marble and slate rocks, limestone, coal, chalk, clay, sand, gravel and soil have been laid upon the earth's surface by the influence of rushing water and other great forces of Nature. Moreover, in these rock and other layers we can find fossilised remains, bones, shells and other lasting substances which tell us plainly as the printed word the story of evolution from primitive prehistoric creatures down to Man. A key to this picture on the preceding page will enable you to unlock its mysteries.

5

a century; but at Malmö, in the south, the land has sunk 5 feet during the past 140 years. Sweden is, in fact, swaying up and down like a see-saw, with its centre at Stockholm, where there is practically no movement at all. The rate at which parts of Sweden are rising or falling is extremely rapid compared with the rates at which similar movements are taking place in other parts of the world.

Although, as we have seen, earth movements are usually extremely slow, there appear to have been occasions when the land has sunk so suddenly that many creatures had no time to escape to higher ground and were drowned. The bones of numerous small animals have been found mingled with those of fish in what are known as " bone-beds." These bone-beds are discovered in many parts of Europe, and probably they are to be explained only as being the result of sudden and violent inrushes of water.

One of the periods when the land was beneath the sea came in what is now called the Age of Reptiles. It is so named because of the fact that during this period reptiles reached their highest development in regard to size and numbers ; and, in fact, dominated all other creatures then living. The land continued to sink until all that was left of Britain was a series of unconnected islands. The climate at that time was probably tropical, and life of many kinds flourished abundantly.

The Weald Formation

Towards the close of the Age of Reptiles, the land rose to form a vast

London Museum.

THE THAMES IN PREHISTORIC TIMES

Here we see Britain's greatest river, the Thames, as it appeared when, in the days before the dawn of history, it first settled down into its present course. These banks, with their forests and marshes, centuries later, were to witness the rise of London, one of the mightiest cities ever built by the hand of man.

London Museum.

THE THAMES IN THE DAYS OF THE ROMANS

Here again we see the Thames from the same viewpoint as in the picture on the opposite page. The forests have been cleared, the marshes drained, and the walled Roman city has taken the place of the riverside settlements which abounded along the wooded banks of an earlier day. A bridge spans the river at a point near where the Tower Bridge now stands.

plain that was very little above the level of the sea. The climate continued to be warm and palm trees flourished. At that time south-east England was under shallow water, and a great river entered the sea near the present position of the Isle of Wight. This river built up a large and complicated delta, and the sludge it washed down formed a deposit that grew until it reached a thickness of more than 1,000 feet. This deposit is now called the Wealden Formation. The Weald Clay—formed millions of years ago—makes the surface soil sticky and slippery in the districts in which it comes to the surface.

In this great delta there survived a few large reptiles, known as dinosaurs, the largest of which—a huge creature called the Iguanodon—attained a height

of from 15 feet to 20 feet. There were also crocodiles and turtles, which basked on the mud banks that separated the streams of the delta, and hundreds of different insects and various kinds of birds. Among the insects was a dragon-fly of extraordinary size, measuring no less than 28 inches across its outspread wings.

Rivers in Prehistoric Times

It is interesting to realise that river conditions at that time in southern England greatly resembled those existing to-day in the lower course of the Mississippi in America. When this great river is in flood, tree trunks and branches are carried away by its furious waters. At awkward bends in its course they jam and are buried by the mud that is carried down in enormous quantities,

It is evident that exactly the same thing occurred in the far-off days of which we are writing, for log jam of prehistoric times has been found in the Isle of Wight and at many other places.

Once more the land sank, and the shore line crept westward until the site of London became a peninsula separating two seas. At this time a reddish sand with occasional greenish bands began to accumulate on wide shallow shores, and this formed the sandstone called " Greensand."

Where the Chalk Came From

Yet another rise was followed by another subsidence, and as the land once again sank below sea level the change was very marked. The whole of the Thames Valley and indeed practically the whole of the British Isles became submerged to a great depth, in some places probably several hundreds of feet. In this clear sea Chalk was formed on such a vast scale that the period has been named the Age of Chalk. Subsequently the land rose and the vast mass of Chalk emerged from the sea.

An examination of the chalk of the North and South Downs, and of the chalk everywhere from Dorset to Yorkshire, tells us plainly of the time when the whole of England was at the bottom of the sea. At one time this soft white limestone was thought to be the remains of innumerable shells of tiny marine animals which accumulated on the sea-floor. Nowadays scientists think that the chalk was formed by the agency of microbes on the sea floor which deposited vast masses of carbonate of lime. At many places— including the Chiltern Hills, Salisbury Plain, the Downs, and the cliffs of Dover —the chalk comes to the surface and is easily examined.

Sharks and Crocodiles in London !

When the land rose again England was covered with a great sheet of chalk, which probably formed downs and wolds all the way from Ireland to the North Sea, for in the west England was joined to both Ireland and France by dry land, and there was no English Channel. The sea lay to the east, for the North Sea was much larger than it is now, and at its southern end it formed a great lagoon which covered south-east England. The London area, Kent, Sussex and Hampshire were all under water except for a long narrow island of chalk hills in the middle of Kent and Sussex.

Into this shallow sea a great river flowed from the west, bringing sand and clay in enormous quantities. In the neighbourhood of Reading these deposits are of the kind dropped in the mouths of rivers, but farther east, at Woolwich, they are of the sort found on the bottoms of shallow seas. The land rose and fell slightly several times during this period, for sometimes the river-deposits spread much farther eastwards, and sometimes they retreat to the

Geological Survey and Museum.

A TELL-TALE ROCK

A slab of sandstone, cracked by the sun and covered with the footprints of an extinct animal. Long ago this slab was part of a soft sandy deposit in which footprints were made as easily as we make them to-day on the sand of the seashore. The deposit, baked by the sun's rays, became firm, and the footprints were thus preserved for millions of years.

EIGHTY MILLION YEARS AGO

In this picture some of the giant crocodiles (*Phobosuchus hatcheri*), which flourished some 80 million years ago, are seen. They were 45 feet or more in length, and with their powerful jaws and teeth for attack, and the armour plate of thick, bony scales for defence, were well adapted to hunt and destroy giant prey such as the dinosaurs seen in the background. The skull of one of these crocodiles is in the British Museum (Natural History) and this drawing was made by the artist with the co-operation of Dr. W. E. Swinton at the Museum. Crocodiles are no longer found in Europe but still flourish in Africa, South Asia, tropical America, and Northern Australia.

9

west even beyond Reading. The sea finally advanced right across England to the line of the Cotswold Hills, covering Wiltshire and Dorset as well as Hampshire, and over the whole of this area there was laid down a great thickness of stiff blue clay.

To-day this clay is known as the "London Clay," and London's underground railway tunnels run through it. When exposed to the weather it turns brown, and sometimes the fossilised remains of extinct creatures are found in it. Shells and sharks' teeth abound, and there are fossil crabs and turtles. We know that crocodiles and hippopotami swam in this old sea, and that tropical palm-trees grew on its shores.

Birds like the ibis, the flamingo and the heron built their nests in the marshes, and a great bird resembling a modern albatross flew overhead. The remains of a bird as big as an ostrich have also been found, but giant reptiles known as dinosaurs were by now completely extinct.

How the Thames Began

The rivers now began to bring down enough sand and mud to force the sea slowly back, and at the same time the land began to rise in the middle of the area, raising the island to a great height. Presently the sea was right back at the position of the North Sea to-day, and then even the southern half of this "North Sea" became dry land. A great river—the Rhine—flowed out of Germany and Holland northwards in pursuit of the retreating sea, and into this river there ran a small tributary from England—the Thames.

At about this time the climate began to grow very cold, and the cap of ice and snow which always covers the North Pole began to spread until it covered the whole of Britain as far south as the valley of the Thames. This was the beginning of the great Ice Age, which lasted altogether about a million years though it was broken by three warmer spells.

During this period the huge, shaggy mammoth and the woolly rhinoceros roamed over the London area, and were hunted by prehistoric man. But the most dangerous enemies of man were the frightful sabre-toothed tiger and the monstrous cave-bear, both now extinct.

When the cold period was over and the ice had all melted, the Thames valley became a broad, flat marsh, filled with millions of tons of mud and gravel which the river had brought down. It was still very much in this state when English history began, and when the Romans invaded Britain. By that time, however, the land had sunk enough for the North Sea and English Channel to link up through the Strait of Dover and make Britain an island.

Were We Joined to Canada?

The geological story of Britain is full of interest, but one remarkable point often escapes notice. It is that for almost the whole of the story there was no Atlantic Ocean. We find the sea invading the land from the east, and sometimes from the south, but in the west the signs have nearly always indicated a vast continent of land.

For a long time it was thought that the Atlantic Ocean must have been formed by this huge western continent sinking beneath the sea, but the modern explanation is much simpler. It is that the lost continent was really only Canada, and that there was no Atlantic Ocean because North America was then jammed up tight against Europe! It was probably about twenty million years ago that the great split which gradually widened to form the Atlantic first appeared.

Deep down in the earth it is so hot that the rocks are never far from their melting-point. From time to time they probably do melt, and then the continents are able to drift slowly about like rafts. Your atlas shows you how the two sides of the Atlantic Ocean fit into each other, and the mountains, rocks and minerals on both sides match up so well that it is difficult to believe that they were not once joined together.

ANIMAL LIFE APPEARS ON THE EARTH

FOSSILS OF SMALL MARINE CREATURES *Ellison Hawks.*

Fossils have become the great clue which enables the geologist to read the story of the earth's changes in the distant past. The fossils of the shells of small marine creatures, such as those seen in the photograph above, show that at one period the ground in which they were found was covered by the sea. These fossils include those of the molluscs such as the extinct cockle, the first in the upper row, and the ammonite, next to the cockle, which became extinct sixty million years ago.

WE have already referred to the evidence that has come down to us of the existence in prehistoric times of strange and weird creatures in the shape of bones and footprints. Impressions of remains of this kind preserved in the rocks are known as fossils.

What the Rocks tell us

It is quite clear that only the remains of certain animals could be preserved in this manner. For instance, soft animals, such as jelly fish, are obviously of a kind that could very rarely leave permanent traces of themselves. The creatures of which we may expect to find the best preserved relics are those that had bony structures, or were covered with hard scales or shells. Except in a few rare instances, the softer portions of these creatures have left no trace of themselves, but hard parts of their bodily structures have

been preserved in a large number of cases. There must be millions of teeth waiting to be discovered in various layers of the rocks, for teeth are the most indestructible parts of an animal's skeleton.

The rare instances in which an entire animal has been preserved are the result of the action of very low temperatures. In the ice-bound wastes of Northern Siberia, entire carcases of the mammoth and woolly rhinoceros have been discovered, and were in such excellent condition that the hair was still attached to the skin. Even the flesh was fit to eat and was relished by dogs. These carcases have, in fact, been preserved in exactly the same manner that meat is kept in good condition by cold storage. Such cases are, however, the exception.

The fossilised skeletons of many animals have been preserved under accumulations of sand and dust blown over them by the wind. Others have been protected by being covered by mud brought down by the rivers. In both cases the protecting material has preserved the bones from injury, while allowing the flesh to decompose. Gradually this material has been replaced by minerals, and to-day the remains are dug out of quarries, or brought to light by the wearing away of the cliffs on the seashore.

The sea bed provided the most favourable conditions for the preservation of an enormous variety of fossils, for in deep waters huge numbers of dead fish accumulated and were buried by the sediments continually washed down by rivers. Lakes, too, afforded good conditions for accumulating and preserving the remains of animal life. These animals were caught in the mud or quicksand as they came down to the shores to drink, and became buried either by sinking through the mud or by the accumulation above them of vegetable refuse and successive layers of mud and gravel. It is, in fact, in the sand and clays laid down millions of years ago that the greatest number of buried bones of giant reptiles and mammals have been discovered along with those of fish, and—more rarely —birds.

The Age of Fish

The earliest extinct animals known to us through their fossils include the graptolites (so-named from their resemblance to writing on the slates in which they are found) and the trilobites. The trilobites looked like very large wood-lice, and are so named from the three divisions that extend from front to back of their jointed horny coat or " shell." But unlike wood-lice trilobites were not crustaceans. They flourished in enormous numbers in very early times. This age of Trilobites was succeeded by the Age of Fish.

At this point it may be well to explain that in saying that one particular Age was succeeded by another, we do not mean that the creatures of the earlier Age came to an end suddenly and were immediately succeeded by others. What actually took place was that during a defined period certain creatures came into prominence and developed to such an extent, either in size or number, that for the time being they were predominant in the world. This state of affairs reached its climax, and then these creatures began slowly to decrease in number and importance.

During this period of decay other creatures, which previously had been comparatively insignificant, began to develop, and ultimately became the predominant animals and succeeded those of the previous period. The important point to remember is that the change was exceedingly slow—so slow in fact, that if there had been human beings living at that time to the age of a hundred years they would not have been aware that any change was taking place.

Geological Survey and Museum.

A TRILOBITE

This curious little creature was one of the most ancient of the seashore animals. He lived with others of his kind in a large crowd or group and frequented muddy waters. Some trilobites were of minute size whilst others reached a length of eighteen inches. They have no direct descendants living to-day.

Strange Sea Dwellers

The amazing creatures, the bones of which have been found in the rocks of the Age of Fish, would scarcely be regarded as real if they were met with to-day. They were mostly fish, but among them were scorpion-like creatures of such size that even the lobsters

In the period known as the *Devonian*, hundreds of thousands of years ago, fish had developed sufficiently to bear some resemblance to those we know to-day. The big fish in the centre of the picture might have measured anything from two feet to five feet in length. He was a primitive kind of shark. The fish at the top of the picture belonged to the group known as *Ganoids*. They were so called on account of their glistening scales.

of to-day would be insignificant beside them. We must compare them with lobsters, because the present-day scorpions do not live in the water. These prehistoric creatures were very probably more than 4 feet in length, and covered by a very strong shield of armour.

Most of the fish of this period were utterly unlike the creatures to be seen in an aquarium; and, generally speaking, they would have been really hideous to look at. Modern fish have their bones covered with skin or scales, but many creatures of the Age of Fish had no such covering, the bare bones being protected only by a layer of shiny enamel. Their heads were covered with large bony plates, inside which were probably nourishing blood vessels.

One strange fish of these early days

MARINE LIFE (2)

The Old Red Sandstone Period produced fish some of which looked like warriors in armour plate. One peculiar little fellow, with a name which few could spell at a first attempt—*Pterichthys*—had his eyes set well to the front of his face. He was heavily armoured, and you will see him towards the bottom of the picture.

MARINE LIFE (1)

Here we see some of the tiny creatures that flourished in one of the earliest Ages or Periods. In the bottom left-hand corner are various types of Trilobite. The fragile star-like creature near the right-hand edge is a Graptolite, and in the right-hand top corner are graceful floating Sea-lilies.

carried an enormous head shield or buckler—a great bony plate with a rounded front edge, and with its rear drawn out into spines. The eyes of this fish were close together and situated on the top of its head, and its body was covered with row upon row of large angular plates of bone. Curiously enough this fish had no teeth.

Even more extraordinary was a fish that had " wings "—or what looked very much like wings. Its body resembled that of a small turtle and was encased in heavy plates of bone, the outer surface of which was roughened and warty in appearance. Its eyes were even closer together than those of the buckler fish just described. It had two fins or paddles, placed well forward, but these could not have been of much

MARINE LIFE (3)

Here we have " fish-lizards " or *Ichthyosaurs*. The Ichthyosaur was somewhat whale-like in appearance. He was a long-jawed creature and was armed with sharp teeth. In the picture a pair of Ichthyosaurs are hunting *Belemnites*, small, dart-like creatures, with straight and tapering shells.

assistance to it in swimming and probably were used to enable it to shuffle along the sandy shore when it became stranded at low water.

A Fossil Mystery

There is a very curious mystery about one fish of this type. Thousands of fossilised remains of it have been discovered in the North of Scotland, and their appearance undoubtedly points to some sudden disaster that overtook the creatures in an area extending over about 10,000 square miles. Practically every fossil of this fish discovered between the Orkney Islands and Cromarty shows plainly that the creatures were killed suddenly and violently. Their figures are strangely curved and contracted, and their fins spread out to the full.

What was the nature of the catas-

trophe that overtook the animals that lived in the sea in those regions is unknown, and probably never will be known. It has been suggested that there may have been a sudden eruption of lime or similar material from some distant volcano. Whatever the cause may have been, there is no doubt that a moment before the catastrophe took place the sea was calm and peaceful. We know this because the scales of the dead fish have been scattered over a distance of only a few inches.

Many of the fish of these ancient times were of enormous size. One wonderful creature grew to as much as 8 feet in length, and the armour in which it was encased was of sufficient weight and thickness to protect a modern crocodile or alligator of far greater size. This fish was distinguished

MARINE LIFE (4)

In this illustration we see for the first time creatures of the lobster group. Some of these closely resemble lobsters of our own time. The lobsters shown here belonged to what we call the *Cretaceous* Period, and marine life during this stage showed considerable development.

by having two rows of teeth, one taking the place of the lips of an ordinary fish, the other and more formidable row being behind the first, and consisting of teeth of enormous size.

Most of the fish that inhabit present-day waters are of quite recent origin, and resemble the ancient fish only in a general way. But in quite recent times a living fish was caught off the South African coast and identified as a Coelacanth (*pron.* " seelacanth "). This 5-foot long fish is a direct descendant of a group which zoologists believed existed 300 million years ago. In fact, the *youngest* fossil evidence of it occurs in the chalk formations of 100 million years ago.

A second specimen of the Coelacanth was caught in December, 1952, off an island west of Madagascar, and a third specimen was caught in September, 1953. The only explanation of the survival of this prehistoric fish is that the species found a world of their own at great depths of the ocean, and there the Coelacanth has continued to exist through millions of years.

The only other fish now living that show any real resemblance to the inhabitants of the old-time seas and lakes are the sturgeon, the gar-pike, the Australian lungfish, the Port Jackson shark, and the Dawson River salmon.

The Coming of the Reptiles

During the Age of Fish there appeared a few small reptiles, and as the fish started to die out these reptiles began to develop in number and size. Subsequently they dominated the earth to such an extent that a period of its history, which must have endured for millions of years, is known as the Age of Reptiles.

This Age of Reptiles comes into the middle division of geological time. It was in this stage of the world's story that the first mammals began to appear, while the earliest species of birds developed from their reptilian life and discovered how to fly.

A LIVING LINK WITH PREHISTORIC TIMES

One of the most remarkable and exciting catches of fish that ever happened was the capture with hook and line of a living specimen of the Coelacanth group of fishes, off Anjouan island, west of Madagascar, in December, 1952. Other specimens have been caught since, and one measures 5 feet long and weighs 100 pounds. The species is known to have existed at least 100 million years ago, though the group is believed to go back 300 million years. The Coelacanth is a surviving link with the days before man existed.

THE AGE OF REPTILES

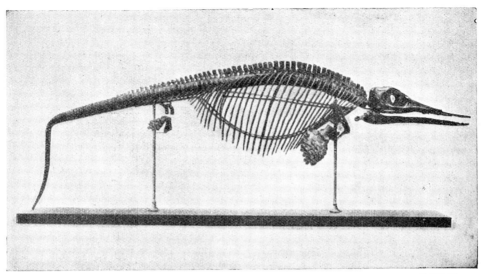

British Museum

FOSSIL OF AN ICHTHYOSAURUS

Long extinct, the Ichthyosaurus must have existed at one time in large numbers in European seas. The skeleton of one of these fish-like reptiles seen above is 13 feet long.

A RAMBLE through one of the dense and strange-looking forests of the Age of Reptiles would have been a very interesting but decidedly dangerous experience. Perhaps the first thing to be noticed would be footprints of various shapes and sizes, among which would probably be a line of tracks, each of which covered an area of a square yard—clearly made by a very large animal. If the tracks were followed it might have been found that they had been made by a giant dinosaur, known as the *Brontosaurus* or " thunder lizard."

The " Thunder Lizard "

This enormous reptile, which was 80 feet in length, must have weighed somewhere about 30 tons. Strangely enough, in spite of its terrifying aspect and the ease with which it could raise itself on its hind legs and peer over the top of the forest trees, there would have been very little need to be afraid of it. It had no thick hide to protect it from the onslaughts of more energetic neighbours, and it pos-sessed no means of attack. It could not even look ferocious if it tried, for the head at the end of its long neck was out of all proportion to its body; and, in fact, looked little larger than the head of an outsize cow!

In all probability the " thunder lizard " lived on aquatic plants, and no doubt it often became caught in morasses and quicksands while search-ing for its favourite food. It is prob-ably because of this that so many fossils of it are still in existence, for its huge weight would cause the animal to sink into the marshy land, where its bones would be covered and protected from disturbance and decay. No doubt also many " thunder lizards " came to an end in this manner when trying to escape from smaller but more ferocious members of the dinosaur tribe.

Huge Bodies but Tiny Brains

Although many of the herbivorous— or " browsing "—dinosaurs had the bulk of a large elephant, their dis-tinguishing feature seems to have been meekness. Even that massive giant, the

ANIMALS OF THE WORLD OF LONG AGO

Vernon Edwards.

The Uintatheres flourished in America about fifty million years ago. Massive, ponderous creatures, they had long dagger-like teeth for fighting but lived on the soft juicy vegetation found in
the vast forests where they roamed.

This quaint-looking creature, which closely resembles the dragon at a Christmas pantomime, was
one of the dinosaurs. A vegetarian, he was probably quite a harmless beast when unmolested.
The length of these creatures ranged up to 30 feet.

Ellison Hawks.

One of the last of the dinosaurs and most fantastic in appearance was Triceratops, the " three-horned." The ruff or fringe round its neck was a continuation of the bone of the skull. When fully grown its total length was about 25 feet.

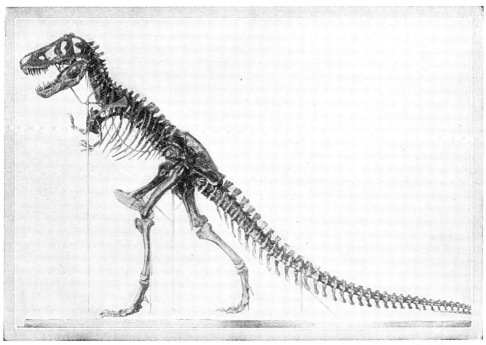

H. J. Shepstone.

A skeleton of the Tyrannosaurus, probably the largest of the flesh-eating creatures, is seen here. The skeleton, as mounted, is exhibited at a New York Museum. In America, the dinosaurs, of which the Tyrannosaurus was one, attained their largest size.

RECORDS OF PREHISTORIC TIMES

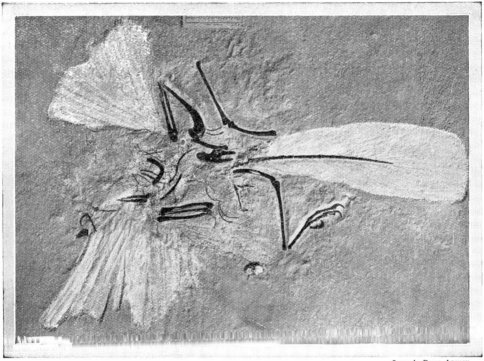

The Archæopteryx was a long-tailed bird which had teeth like the flying lizards but feathers like the birds of to-day. It was about the size of a crow and lived in Europe.

The greatest care must be exercised in digging for bones and fossils and here we see an expert uncovering the remains of a Dinosaurus.

Flying lizards or *Pterodactyls*, remains of which have been found in Bavaria, were not unlike great bats in appearance. They were provided with teeth and probably lived on fish and the larger insects. Some were no bigger than a sparrow, whilst others reached the size of a heron. The long tails which some of the specimens are known to have possessed, and which are shown above, gradually disappeared in the process of evolution.

ON THE SHORES OF THE WEALDEN LAKE

Crown Copyright.

The part of south-east England lying between the North and South Downs and having Tunbridge Wells near its centre is known as the Weald. Many geologists have studied this area very thoroughly and the picture above gives a reconstruction of a scene on the shores of the great Wealden Lake in that far distant past before man had appeared and the different types of the Dinosaur land reptiles were the dominant forms of animal life.

Atlantosaurus, which lived in what is now America, was an inoffensive creature in spite of its length of 90 feet. It also had a very small head and was slow-moving and stupid, for its brain had not developed in proportion to its body. If a smaller, but more active dinosaur had seized an atlantosaur by the tip of the tail, quite an appreciable time would have been taken for the sensation to travel along the latter's enormous neck in order to reach its tiny brain. An even greater length of time must then have elapsed before it could have set its huge body in motion in order to deal with its assailant.

Creatures such as these must have been almost entirely at the mercy of smaller animals that were quicker in movement and had more developed brains. There is some ground for thinking that the head of the atlantosaur was not large enough to hold even the small amount of brain that the creature possessed, and it is believed that there was a second centre of intelligence somewhere in the rear part of the animal. This was probably a ganglion or nerve centre, rather than a thinking organ.

Although the gigantic reptiles we have described were harmless, there were others that were distinctly dangerous roaming in the tropical forests that in these far-off days clothed Southern England. These were the flesh-eating dinosaurs—terrible creatures with large and powerful teeth. They had bigger heads than the browsing dinosaurs, and were more crafty and determined. One of them had a tremendously long and powerful horn

MONSTERS OF SEA AND RIVER

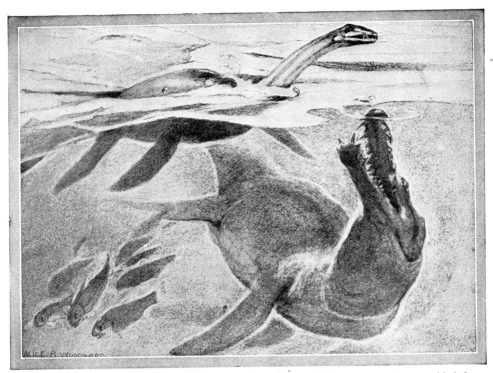

The *Plesiosaurus*, which measured some 15 feet from tip to tail, in some respects resembled the turtle. Another member of the same family, *Pliosaurus*, was a much more formidable creature. He is seen in the lower half of the picture. *Pliosaurus* reached a length of 30 feet.

Here we see the prehistoric creatures which were the forerunners of the crocodiles existing to-day. Remains of these crocodiles have been found in the Oxford clay at Peterborough. You will notice that their feet have been modified into paddles for expeditions to the sea.

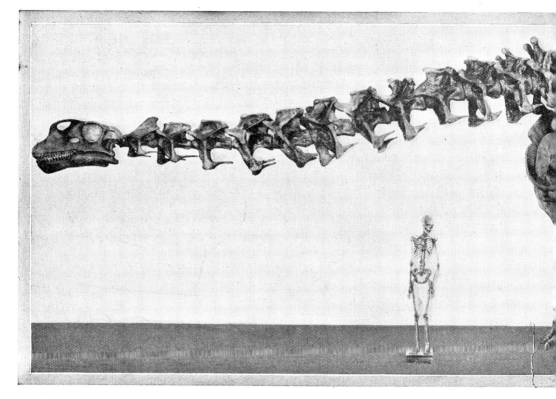

A HUMAN SKELETON COMPARED WITH

One of the largest of the dinosaurs, the Brontosaurus, measured 80 feet from his snout to his tail. The Brontosaurus fed mainly on water plants, particularly the bed herbage of lakes and rivers. Its about in fairly deep water. No remains of the Brontosaurus

on its skull. This beast was 20 feet in length, and stood over 12 feet in height. As it raised itself on its hind legs, it might well have served for a model of the fearful dragons of our old legends and fairy tales.

To complete the nightmare aspect of a forest of the Age of Reptiles there were gigantic and uncouth creatures that flew. These were not birds, but true flying lizards that supported themselves in the air on membranes outstretched between their bodies and a finger that had been extended until it was longer than the creatures' bodies. One at least of these lizards appears to have measured thirty feet across the wings.

There seems no doubt that these lizards really did fly, and that they did not merely take great leaps as flying squirrels do. As is the case with birds,

they had hollow bones, and a keel on the breastbone to which the muscles used in flying were attached. They are best described as giant bats, and the discovery of their bones in olden times probably gave rise to the legends of flying dragons.

Even these did not exhaust the surprises that awaited anyone who might have been bold enough to ramble through the haunts of these prehistoric animals. While running away from a ferocious flesh-eating dinosaur or creeping along under the vegetation to avoid the downward swoop of a flying lizard, one might be pulled up suddenly by the side of an armour-plated monster that would be ideal for a modern pantomime scene. This was a plated lizard or Stegosaurus, an amazing animal that walked on all four feet, although its

American Museum of Natural History.

THAT OF THE BRONTOSAURUS

The skeleton is a massive affair and many times greater in bulk than that of a full-grown man. long neck must have been of great service in searching for food, enabling the creature to probe have been discovered outside the United States of America.

hind legs were much longer than its fore legs, thus giving it a curiously unbalanced appearance. It was a huge creature, but even its heavy defensive armour did not give it adequate protection from its more agile enemies. As was the case with so many of the giant lizards, it had an exceptionally small head, was unwieldy, and very slow in action.

The skin of the Stegosaur was covered with bony plates, but perhaps the most astonishing feature that it presented was a series of huge plates that stood upright along the line running down the centre of its back. The plates in the head and the tail were small, but those in the middle of its back were of an enormous size. Britain was one of the countries in which this armour-plated reptile lived, and its remains

have been found at Swindon among other places.

Rulers of the Ocean

The prehistoric marine reptiles were even more remarkable than their land relatives. In those days the rulers of the ocean were the whale-shaped Ichthyosaurs and the long-necked Plesiosaurs, and a voyage in a small boat would have been distinctly exciting.

The Ichthyosaurus attained a length of some 40 feet, and the smaller marine creatures learned to dread its formidable pointed teeth and the sight of its long snout. Its enormous eyes gave it excellent vision, and it had a third eye in the top of its head. Though in course of time its limbs had lost their toes and developed into swimming paddles, it was strictly a reptile. Remains of this creature have been found in practically every part of the earth from the Arctic zone to Australia and New Zealand, and are plentiful in Great Britain. The largest complete skeleton found in Britain is 28 feet in length, and 8 feet in width across the paddles.

A Prehistoric Sea Dragon

The fossilised remains of an Ichthyosaurus were found within quite recent times at Harbury in Warwickshire. Another remarkable discovery which was made in a quarry at Harbury was the remains of a Plesiosaurus. It was an exceptionally big and complete specimen, measuring 16 feet from tip to tail. This sea dragon had lived and died millions of years ago when England was at the bottom of the sea.

The sea dragon or Plesiosaurus was not as long as the Ichthyosaurus, but was broader. Its remains have been found in great number at Lyme Regis,

Whitby, Peterborough, Weymouth, and other places. The paddles with which the Plesiosaurus was equipped show that it was an aquatic reptile, and certain resemblances to the turtle suggest that occasionally it visited land, although on land it could have moved only in a very awkward manner. Probably even at sea it was not absolutely at home and was by no means so well adapted to life in the ocean as the Ichthyosaurus.

Extensive as are the remains of extinct reptiles found in Great Britain, they are small in comparison with those in many other countries. In Colorado in the United States, for instance, great numbers of fossilised reptiles have been found almost exactly in the positions in which they died. Over a distance of more than 500 miles on the eastern side of the Rocky Mountains are beds of rock that have been called the " Atlantosaur Beds " on account of the enormous number of the remains of these

H. J. Shepstone.

WHEN THE EARTH WAS YOUNG

This photograph, taken in a famous Continental Zoo, gives some idea of what might have been seen in the early days of this world's history. These life-size figures are reconstructions in stone of one of the last of the great land reptiles which roamed the earth long before mankind had appeared. The Triceratops was about 25 feet long, and had a collar of spikes, or spines, around its neck.

H. J. *Shepstone.*

THE DIPLODOCUS AT HOME

This stone model shows a reconstruction of the Diplodocus, a gigantic North American land reptile, with abnormally long neck and tail. It measured from 60 to 80 feet long, and was nearly 20 feet high. When alive it would weigh from 25 to 30 tons. These creatures were unarmoured, and spent much of their time in water browsing on aquatic plants. Fossilised remains of these lizard-footed reptiles have been found mainly in Colorado and Wyoming, U.S.A.

dinosaurs that have been found in them.

Extraordinary discoveries of dinosaurs have been made also in Tanganyika Territory by expeditions sent out for the special purpose of unearthing the fossilised remains there. In the days when these creatures flourished the Tanganyika Territory consisted of flat, wet plains covered with a forest of enormous fern-like plants in which the creatures found a congenial home. Here they developed to an enormous size, the remains of one of these creatures showing that it had a neck nearly 40 feet in length!

The Preparation of Fossil Bones

Before the work of unearthing the dinosaurs that once inhabited the swampy forests of Tanganyika Territory has been completed, it is probable that the remains of new and even larger creatures will be discovered. Progress

in this direction must necessarily be slow, however, for the work of extracting the fossilised bones and setting them up each in its proper place is not one that can be hurried. The bones are extremely fragile and the utmost caution is necessary, for a single misguided blow from a pick may cause damage beyond all hope of repair.

When the bones are unearthed they have to be swathed in silk paper and covered with plaster, in order to protect them from injury during the long journey to the place where they are to be studied. The task of removing these protecting wrappings must be done with the greatest care, and then follow the delicate tasks of cleaning the bones, hardening them with various chemical solutions, identifying and mounting them. Some idea of the time taken by these various processes may be gained from the fact that a

CREATURES THAT MAN NEVER KNEW

Among the last of its kind was the Duck-billed Dinosaur, Edmontosaurus, which lived on this Earth over seventy million years ago, long before Man had appeared. A specimen was acquired by the British Museum (Natural History) from Canada towards the end of 1950. The Edmontosaurus was an amphibious, herb-eating creature, some 30 feet in length, with webbed fingers and toes, and a broad duck-bill as shown in the reconstructions on this page.

Illustrated London News.

The fossil remains of the Edmontosaurus were the first ever received in Britain and came in twelve sections which had taken two years to assemble and prepare for exhibition. Work began first on the tail section and the way in which this is carried out is seen on another page. An impression of the pattern of the scaly skin was revealed when working on the fossil.

MOUNTING THE BONES OF A DINOSAUR

The Times.

Mounting the limbs of a giant fossil dinosaur such as the Edmontosaurus is a task for the expert. In this picture is seen a plaster model, made from an original in Canada, and the expert is seen comparing one of the fossilised remains, mentioned on the previous page, before proceeding with the task of assembling the fossilised sections sent from Canada to the Natural History Museum in London.

huge Canadian dinosaur, discovered in 1915, was not ready to be placed on view until ten years later.

In recent times many striking results have been obtained by the experts in this branch of science now known as palæontology—the study of animals and plants which lived during the past ages of the earth's history. Some twenty-five dinosaur eggs, the first of their kind to be discovered, were brought to light during explorations in Mongolia in Central Asia.

The Earliest Birds

Judging from the remains that have been found, true birds first appeared during the Age of Reptiles, but it is possible that they were in existence a good deal earlier. The most ancient birds resemble reptiles in many respects, and differ greatly from present-day birds, particularly in regard to the head and the tail.

With the disappearance of favourable conditions the great reptile family began to deteriorate, and one form after another died out. Some of them persisted for a very long period, but they gradually became larger and more unwieldy and more soft. As they were unable to adapt themselves to their changed surroundings they ultimately passed out of existence.

The only reptiles that have survived to the present day are small creatures in comparison with the monsters of the past. They include crocodiles, turtles, lizards and snakes, our only living reminders of the Age of Reptiles.

Planet News.

CLEARING AWAY THE SANDSTONE FROM A FOSSIL TAIL

A portion of the fossil remains of the Edmontosaurus, of which a reconstruction is seen on an earlier page, is being dealt with by an expert at the British Museum (Natural History). The sandstone in which it was embedded is being cleared away from the tail portion. This fossil was unearthed in the Calgary district of Canada where this dinosaur lived long ages ago.

THE FIRST MAMMALS

THE WOOLLY RHINOCEROS

The extreme cold of the Ice Age drove the Woolly Rhinoceros from Siberia. It lived in the same period as the Mammoth and for a time it roamed in Europe, but later returned to its old haunts. In the end the severe weather conditions led to its extinction.

WHEN the Age of Reptiles came to an end and the gigantic lizards died out, they were followed by a race of creatures of quite different type. These were the mammals, which subsequently became as dominant as the reptiles had been previously. Mammals were not entirely absent during the Age of Reptiles, but the representatives of the class were creatures of the size of rats or opossums. These now began to develop in size and in various other respects.

Hoofed animals, such as deer and antelopes, came into existence; the earliest specimens of the horse appeared; and finally there developed flesh-eating animals similar to wolves, foxes and cats, that followed the ancestors of the rhinoceros, the hippopotamus and the elephant. Whales made their appearance in the sea and true birds in the air.

It is remarkable that the ancestors of some animals that are quite big to-day were originally very small. For instance, the earliest horse was a curious little creature, no larger than a cat; and instead of the familiar hoof it had five toes on each foot. At a later stage it lost some of its toes, and one well-known early type had four toes on the fore feet and three on the hind feet. As it continued to develop the number of its active toes became gradually reduced. A later representative was about the size of a sheep and had three toes; and, finally, after millions of years of slow development, nature produced the single-toed animal that for thousands of years has been man's willing helper.

The Elephant's Tiny Ancestor

Another similar instance is that of the elephant. To-day this is one of

British Museum.

BRITISH PREHISTORIC MAMMALS (1)

The skull of a mammoth which was found in brick-earth at Ilford, in Essex. The tusks are 10 feet 6 inches in length.

the biggest of all animals, but the earliest elephant of which we have any knowledge was a tiny creature, the remains of which have been found in Egypt. In addition to its extremely small size it was very un-elephant-like because it had no trunk! In every other respect it had all the characteristics of the elephant of to-day, with a snout that in the course of ages length-ened into the trunk and also large teeth that ultimately developed into tusks.

The evolution of the elephant appears to have gone forward very rapidly, and in the suc-cessive pages of the story written in the rocks may be seen even larger creatures of the

elephant tribe, ending at last in the mastodons and mammoths. These enormous prehistoric creatures would easily be recognised as elephants, for they have the bulldog skull, the appear-ance of which suggests that it has been pushed in in front, the mighty tusks, and the long prehensile trunk that distinguish the type.

Last of the Mammoths

The mammoth was covered with hair, an indication that it lived and flourished in cold regions. It is there-fore not surprising to learn that its remains have been discovered in the greatest number in northern Europe. At one time it lived in large numbers in our own country, and about the time that primitive men inhabited the land it sported itself in the forests in the valley of the Thames. Its teeth are frequently found in ancient gravels, and in a brickyard at Ilford an entire skull, still furnished with enormous tusks, has been dug up.

As the numbers of this animal gradually decreased it appears to have withdrawn to Siberia, and there is little doubt that it was in that country

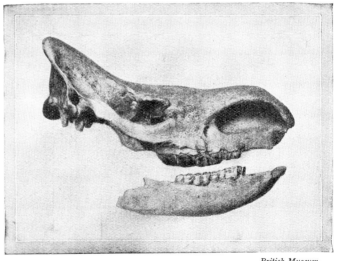

British Museum.

BRITISH PREHISTORIC MAMMALS (2)

The skull of a Woolly Rhinoceros which was dug up from peaty mud under Whitefriars Street, London. It is 27 inches in length.

ANIMALS OF PREHISTORIC TIMES—Plate 1

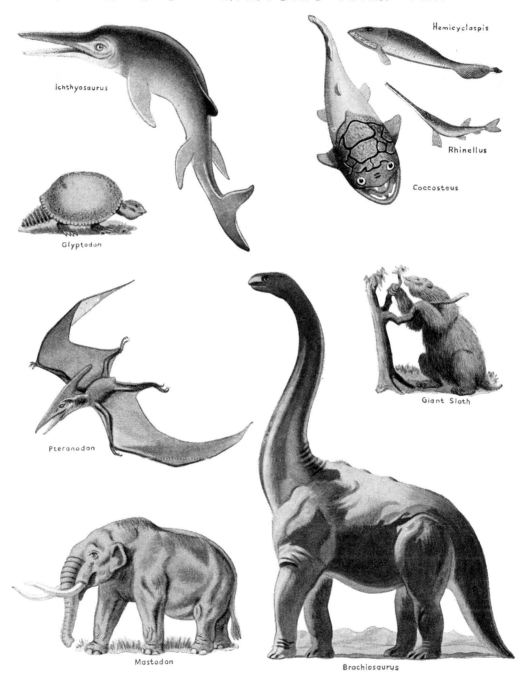

Ichthyosaurus

Hemicyclaspis

Rhinellus

Coccosteus

Glyptodon

Pteranodon

Giant Sloth

Mastodon

Brachiosaurus

Long before Man appeared, the world was populated with other forms of animal life. When the primitive trilobites were becoming extinct, the first real fish were beginning to appear, of which the three seen in the yellow panel are examples. Fish-like reptiles such as the Ichthyosaurus came next and were accompanied by the great land reptiles, the Dinosaurs, of which the Brachiosaurus is shown here. One type of reptile, the Pterodactyls, developed wings, and a member of this family, the Pteranodon, is seen above. Long after these creatures came such curious mammals as the Glyptodon, an early armadillo about 9 feet long, and the Giant Sloth or Megatherium, which measured over 20 feet. The Mastodon, as will be observed, was not unlike the elephant, and brings us almost to modern times.

Moa

Archæopteryx

Stegosourus

Great Cave Bear

Baluchitherium

Woolly Rhinoceros

Titanothere

Mammoth

In the yellow panel are seen two of the birds that appeared in prehistoric days : the Archæopteryx, the oldest real bird known, in size rather smaller than a crow; the Moa, a much later bird, was similar to the ostrich and could not actually fly. Among the earliest Dinosaurs was the Stegosaurus or plated lizard. The Megatherium or Giant Sloth and the Baluchitherium were later mammals. When the Ice Age overwhelmed a great part of the earth it destroyed large numbers of animals, among them the Titanothere, as well as the Mammoth, the Great Cave Bear and the Woolly Rhinoceros, which roamed in big herds over the vast steppes of the northern part of Europe.

that the last of the great mammoths lived and died. Many of them were trapped in the swamps, and their huge weight caused them to sink and be completely covered up. In most countries their flesh would have decayed, leaving only the bones; but, as we have already seen, the effect of the low temperature has been to preserve the entire carcase of the animal in many places.

Other enormous mammals that developed along with the elephant were different forms of rhinoceros, one of which—known as the Dinoceras—had three pairs of horns. It was a tremendous creature but appears to have possessed a very small brain, for although it was much bigger than the largest rhinoceros of to-day, the space occupied by its brain was only one-eighth of that of its modern descendant.

The most wonderful feature of the time during which mammals have ruled the earth has been the amazing variety of animal life that has been produced. To describe in detail the extinct members of the enormous number of kinds of mammals known would be an unduly long task, and the only one of these that really calls for

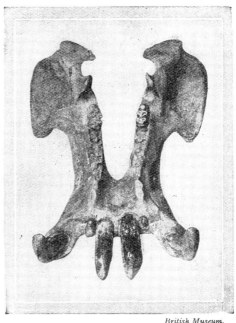

British Museum.

BRITISH PREHISTORIC MAMMALS (4)

The lower jaw of a Hippopotamus which was found at Barrington, Cambridgeshire. The width of the jaw at the widest part is 2 feet.

special notice is the great cat tribe, of which the lion and the tiger are to-day the best-known representatives.

The Sabre-toothed Tiger

The most ferocious of the prehistoric cats was the sabre-toothed tiger, which was one of the terrors of our own country during the period when the mammoth and the rhinoceros still lived here. It was of formidable appearance, for its upper jaw bore two downward-pointing tusks, like enormous daggers. Even the huge mammoth was no match for this terrible beast. The nearest approach to the sabre-toothed tiger that may be seen to-day is the

British Museum.

BRITISH PREHISTORIC MAMMALS (3)

The skull of a Cave Lion recovered from brick-earth at Crayford, in Kent. This skull is 16 inches in length.

ANIMALS ONCE COMMON IN EUROPE

James's Press Agency.

Through many ages the flesh-eating " Sabre-toothed " tigers, so called from their two formidable tusk-like teeth, flourished exceedingly. They preyed chiefly upon elephants and rhinoceroses. In the end their teeth grew so long that it became difficult for the animals to eat and they probably died of starvation in the midst of plenty.

James's Press Agency.

This magnificent creature existed in large numbers in Ireland after the first Ice Age. Its horns in some cases measured 12 feet across and weighed over a hundredweight. Deer have adapted themselves to widely different conditions of life in many parts of the world.

FORBEARS OF THE ELEPHANT

James's Press Agency.

The Mastodon was at one time plentiful in both Europe and Asia. In appearance it looked like an elephant, but it was not a true elephant in the shape of the head, the neck and the tusks. It was a more primitive type than the Mammoth.

James's Press Agency.

Once common in Europe, the Mammoth was noted for its long curling tusks. It stood 12 feet to 13 feet high and was covered with a warm coat of hair and under-fur. Many specimens have been discovered in the Arctic, and remains were found during excavations in London in 1921.

Siberian tiger that continues to inhabit the eastern portion of that country.

We have seen how one type of creature has developed on an enormous scale and dominated the earth, and how it has subsequently decreased in numbers and strength and been replaced by creatures of another type. The only living creatures that do not appear to be doomed to extinction sooner or later are the lowest and simplest forms. An interesting example of this is a mollusc-like animal called the *Lingula*, a shell-fish with an astonishingly long history. The present-day representatives of this race burrow in the sand, instinct prompting them to retire quickly within their holes when danger of any kind threatens. It is this simple mode of life that has enabled this lowly animal to survive the amazing changes that have occurred on the earth since the creature's first appearance four hundred million years ago.

On the other hand, the bigger creatures appear to have so many natural enemies that in the struggle for existence which is going on all the time they fail to hold their own. Even to-day the larger wild animals, driven further and further from their haunts by man, are becoming fewer in number, facing an extinction that seems inevitable.

But we should always remember that there are two kinds of extinct creatures— those which were the ancestors of modern animals, into which they have slowly changed, and those which were really exterminated and left no descendants. The first kind presents us with a pretty puzzle, for while they are undoubtedly extinct it is also quite clear that they have never died out—they have only changed !

E. N. A.

WHEN THE BRONTOSAURUS LIVED

One of the most gigantic of prehistoric creatures was the Brontosaurus, a member of the Dinosaur family of lizards. Some 80 feet long and weighing 30 tons, it was four-footed but spent most of its time in shallow waters. On land it moved slowly and clumsily. The food of the Brontosaurus was entirely vegetable and consisted largely of water plants that grew by the lakeside.

WHERE THE EARTH'S STORY IS WRITTEN

FORMING A NATURAL SAND BARRIER

Sand dunes frequently give the land protection against further encroachment by the sea. In this photograph can be seen the tufts of bent-grass which arrest the drifting sand, binding it with tangled roots, and so prevent the wind from blowing the sand still farther away.

THE accounts of the great events of history that have come down to us have been written by men who witnessed these events, or who have collected the stories of those who were present, and have combined them into one complete account. The events in the history of the earth itself have not been recorded by human witnesses, but by the actual forces that brought about these happenings. The science that deals with the story of the earth is called geology, and it has taught us how to read the records that exist in the rocks all about us.

Although in many respects the conditions that existed on the earth millions of years ago were very different from those of to-day, yet the forces that were at work then are still in action. For this reason the best method of learning to read the records of the rocks is to look round us and see exactly what is taking place on the surface of the earth.

The land surface of the earth appears to be fixed and permanent, yet it is undergoing ceaseless change and, in fact, is gradually being destroyed in some places and built up in others. This destruction is being brought about by what might be called nature's weapons. There are several of these, and although they operate in quite distinct ways they are all engaged in the same task—that of breaking up the surface of the land.

What Rain does

One of the greatest of these weapons is rain. Even in the gentlest shower each of the tiny drops tends to wash out of position a correspondingly tiny portion of the ground on which it falls. If the rain is heavy, and particularly if it falls on sloping ground, the effect is very much more noticeable. If we examine the surface of a country road after heavy rain we shall notice how the raindrops have collected into miniature streams; and, following a downward slope, have washed with them sand and any light substances, such as leaves, that may have been lying on the surface of the road. This process takes place on all unprotected land whenever rain falls. If the nature of the ground is very porous the rain will quickly be absorbed and disappear, but in other cases it will run along for some distance, forming little streams and then bigger ones, and finally carrying its burden of mud into some permanent stream or river. The river then plays its part by transporting this material to the sea.

Although the amount of material washed away in a week or a month by rain in this manner is very small, yet it will be realised that when the process goes on for hundreds and thousands of years the effect must be very great.

During recent years careful measurements have been made of the amount of material carried away into the sea every year by certain big rivers. The Mississippi, for instance, carries into the Gulf of Mexico every year over 500 million tons of matter!

Influence of the Wind

Another of nature's weapons, of much greater importance than we might imagine, is the wind. Except when the air is quite still there is always a certain amount of dust being transported from one place to another, and a large proportion of this moving dust finds its way ultimately into rivers, and so to the sea. The surface of the land may be changed very rapidly in districts where there are strong winds blowing mostly in one direction. At the seaside, for instance, most of the

Australian Geographical Society.

A REMARKABLE ROCK FORMATION IN AUSTRALIA

The great mass of the Earth consists largely of rocks, and from those near the surface much of the geological history of our planet can be read. In this aerial photograph is shown an unusual formation in part of the desolate MacDonnell Range in Australia. This shows that at one time these rocks were under the sea, and, later, under compression, they became the folded structures seen here. The MacDonnell Range is in the Northern Territory and its elevation causes rainfall which is drained away by many streams, most of them ending abruptly in the dry lowland.

H. J. Shepstone.

A GLACIER IN ALASKA

The Mendelhall Glacier near Juneau, Alaska, belongs to what is known as the Piedmont type.
This type of glacier consists of a number of valley glaciers which meet to form a wide area of
nearly stagnant ice.

strong winds blow in from the sea and bring with them sand, which they carry continually farther inland. In this manner are formed the long lines of sand hills or sand dunes that are found along many parts of the coast.

The sand hills thus formed do not remain stationary, but travel inland at a really surprising speed, and means have to be taken to check their progress, otherwise there would be a danger of whole villages being overwhelmed. In some parts of the world this has actually happened. One of the most usual methods of checking the progress of a line of sand hills is to plant in it a kind of rush called starr-grass. This extraordinary plant appears to like a dry home of this nature. It sends its roots down through the sand and helps to combine it together, while the parts of the plant above the sand act as barriers to the further progress of the sand grains.

Nature's Stone-breakers

Changes of temperature play a large part in disintegrating the land surface. The heat of the sun during the day causes the surface of rocks to expand, while at night contraction takes place. The result is that the surface of the rock is in a state of constant strain, and sooner or later it begins to crumble, and is thus in a condition to be removed easily by wind and rain. This process is, of course, most rapid in countries where fierce heat during the day is succeeded by very cold nights.

Frost works also in another way. Water penetrates into all the tiny cracks and crevices in the surface of rocks; and in winter, when the temperature falls sufficiently low, this water freezes. As everybody knows, water expands during the freezing process, and the result is that it exerts strong pressure on the sides of the crack and tends to push them apart. This process also causes the rock to crumble and decay.

The great glaciers or ice rivers that exist on the slopes of very high mountains are further agents of destruction. They scour away the rock face over which they slowly move forward, and in addition carry along on their surface

Geological Survey and Museum.

CLIFFS ON THE WELSH COAST

The force of the sea in many an angry storm has beaten off great masses of rock from the cliffs. One stack of rock which formerly was part of the mainland now stands alone surrounded by water. The cliff face is seamed by the layers or strata of rock and at the foot of the cliff are piles of broken rock which will eventually be ground into pebbles by the waves.

large quantities of rock fragments that have fallen from the cliff sides.

Finally, there is the greatest of all destroying agents the sea. We are all familiar with the manner in which the great waves gradually undermine and break down the coast and penetrate farther inland. Although this process is naturally most rapid where the coast consists of soft material, yet even the hardest cliffs are not proof against the battering of the sea, and bit by bit they are worn away.

The sea has special weapons of its own. In the first place it picks up rock fragments and hurls them forward in a fierce bombardment against the cliffs. The blows struck by these rock fragments are very heavy, and their constant repetition has a very serious effect upon the cliff face. The sea also makes use of compressed air. As a great storm wave strikes against the cliff face it drives back the air with terrific force into every nook and cranny, and when the wave retires, the air escapes with almost explosive violence and does considerable damage to the rock. Quite apart from the rock battering rams and compressed air, the biggest storm waves are capable of

doing enormous damage on their own account, especially if they can find extensive joints or cracks, or sections of rock that are softer than the rest.

The combined result of all these agents is to wear down the surface of the land and carry the *débris* into the sea. If this process continued for a very long period without anything to counterbalance it the land would become worn down into a vast level plain, and the sea would be completely master of the situation. Nature has provided various checks upon this crumbling process, however, the most important of which is that of vertical movements of the earth.

New Land for Old

As we have seen, some of these movements are upward and others downward ; but the final result after countless thousands of years has been to preserve the land surface, or rather to replace old land surfaces by new ones. Vast deposits of materials that have been washed down into the sea and have collected on the sea floor for long periods, during which they have become compressed into rock, are raised again by these mysterious earth

ROCK LAYERS IN A CLIFF FACE

Geological Survey and Museum.

An example of stratified rocks arranged in layers or beds. If this picture is compared with those on pages 40 and 42 it will be noticed that the beds shown here do not seem to have been affected by earth movements. They are fairly regular and horizontal. In the other pictures referred to above, particularly those on page 42, the strata lines are twisted into the most fantastic curves.

Geological Survey and Museum.

A CURIOUS EFFECT

This remarkable example of folded rock strata may be seen at Saundersfoot, Pembrokeshire. The strata have been bent into the form of an arch which at one time extended to the front of the picture. The sea has gradually worn the rock away, but the remains are clearly visible.

movements, and so form a new land surface. Immediately this takes place the old process of destruction commences again; wind, frost and rain set to work, and rivers are formed that carve out valleys for themselves on their way down to the sea.

Of course, a check on the wearing of the surface of the land is provided by the grass that forms a protective covering for the loose soil. Forests also have a similar and even more marked protective effect. The removal of sediment to the sea is also checked by lakes, which receive streams muddy with the burden they are carrying, and by slowing them down cause them to

release the sediment, so that they emerge from the lake as clear streams.

How Rocks are Formed

The material that is washed down to the sea is deposited upon the sea floor in a series of layers, which are still visible when the material has been compressed into solid rock and raised above sea level. Rocks that show these layers are known as stratified rocks, and many of them, such as sandstone, are familiar to everybody. The strata or layers are not always horizontal, but are often tilted. Sometimes also, as the result of earth movements and pressure, the layers are

Geological Survey and Museum.

STAGES IN MOUNTAIN BUILDING

This picture shows in a striking manner how the layers of rock in the earth's crust have been folded into humps or ridges. The same thing happening on a very much larger scale has been the means of forming ranges of hills.

HOW ROCKS HAVE GROWN

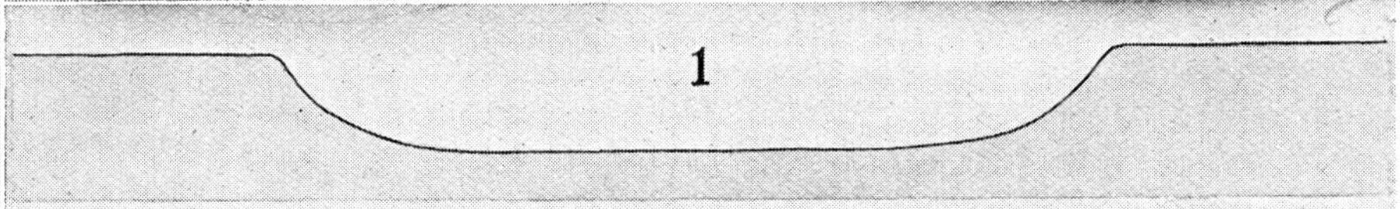

1

1. This section represents an enormously broad valley in the earth's surface under the sea in the very earliest ages. Imagine it filled with water.

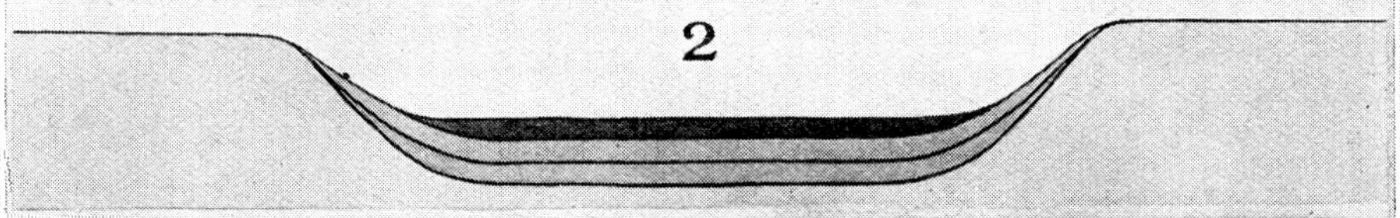

2

2. Rivers, or the rush of mighty waters, have carried down sand or other materials in the form of sediment and with them partly filled the valley with layers.

3

3. Under such pressure as we cannot calculate, these particles became welded into layered or stratified rocks, and other forces then folded the strata.

4

4 and 5. The layers of rock may become squeezed into very sharp folds, which may presently slip out of line and begin to slide over one another.

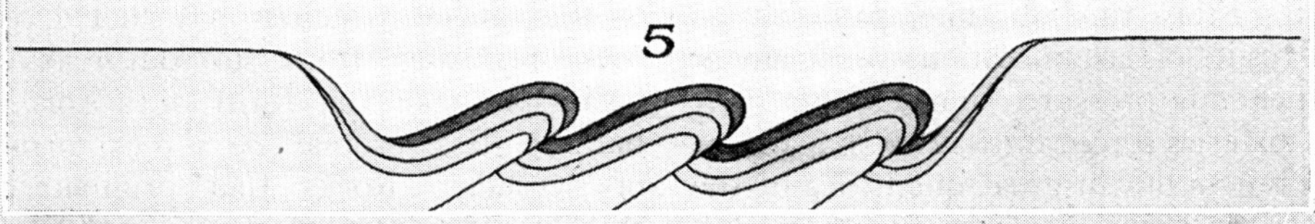

5

When next you visit the seaside or an inland place where rocks are fully exposed to view you may apply the above diagram to the scene before you. Look specially for the layers or strata of the rocks. Millions of years ago these layers were formed of particles of sediment and put under such terrific pressure that they became solid stone. Followed then some great upheaval which brought the earth's surface above the level of the sea. The story of our world is told in rocks.

H. J. Shepstone.

A LAVA FIELD

A good example of a lava field in one of the islands of Hawaii near the volcano of Kilauea. Lava, or igneous rock—which means rock produced by volcanic action—is divided into two classes, acid and basic. Basic lava is more fluid than acid lava and flows further from the volcano.

bent into the most remarkable curves so that the rock appears to be, and indeed is, contorted. Rocks that have been formed from sediments laid down in the bed of the sea or in that of a lake are known as sedimentary rocks, and they form a very large proportion of the land surface.

There are other rocks that have an entirely different origin. The interior of the earth is intensely hot, and it contains enormous reservoirs of molten rock. From time to time, probably as the result of accumulations of steam at tremendous pressure, some of this molten material forces its way to the surface and bursts out in great quantities of the material known as lava, together with ashes and other matter. The great mountains that we call volcanoes are almost entirely composed of lava and ashes, and they are simply gigantic heaps of material that have been ejected by a

series of eruptions. During a big eruption enormous quantities of lava are poured forth, and they cover large areas of country. Subsequent eruptions continue the process, and in time the lava sheet becomes of immense thickness.

The Story of Lava

If we examine a piece of lava we see that it is not in the least like sandstone or other sedimentary rock, for it has no trace of the familiar layers. According to the rate at which it has cooled, the rock resulting from an outbreak of lava may take the form of a sort of natural glass, or may be a rock formed of crystals. Rocks that originate in this manner from materials within the earth are known as igneous rocks.

Igneous rock is extremely hard, but nevertheless it is worn away in time by the various natural forces we have mentioned, and thus provides material

THE VOLCANO THAT BURIED POMPEII

E. N. A.

One of the most interesting volcanoes in the world, Vesuvius, rises to a height of 4,000 feet above the Bay of Naples. At one time it was probably twice this height, but in A.D. 79 a tremendous eruption blew off the top of the mountain and the ashes which were belched from the crater brought ruin and desolation to Pompeii and other towns. Further eruptions have taken place since then, but the mountain did not pour forth lava until 1066. The picture shows smoke coming from the central cone, with part of the crater in the foreground.

for the formation of new rock of the sedimentary type.

From a very early period in the history of the earth these processes have been going on. Land surfaces have been destroyed and their materials distributed over the sea floor to form vast thicknesses of sedimentary rock; long ages afterwards this rock has been raised above sea level to form a new land surface, which in turn has been destroyed; and so the process has gone on through millions of years.

The earth movements that have resulted in the raising or lowering of the land level have varied in speed at different periods, and possibly from time to time have ceased altogether for a while. There have also been periods of abnormal volcanic activity during which sheets of lava of enormous extent and thickness have been formed. Outbursts of this kind appear to have decreased in intensity as the ages have passed, and at the present time the earth is comparatively quiet in this respect.

When we come across a series of rocks lying one upon another we should naturally expect the lowest rocks to be the oldest. This would always be the case if nothing had happened to disturb the order, and it is fortunate for us that such disturbances have taken place, for otherwise we should never have been able to in-

H. J. Shepstone.

THE LAVA CONE
One of the many curious effects produced by a succession of outflows of molten lava.

vestigate the earliest, and therefore the lowest, rocks. In many places earth movements of various kinds have pushed the layers of rock one over the other, with the result that it is possible to find the original order completely reversed, with the oldest rocks at the top. It is frequently the case that some particular rock formation is only to be found in a certain part of the world, and this is because it is only in that region that earth movements have brought these rocks to the surface.

What Fossils Teach us

In previous sections we have referred to the fossil remains of animals, and have shown how these have enabled us to understand the kind of creatures that lived on the earth millions of years ago. Fossils serve also another very important purpose—that of enabling us to decide the relative ages of rocks found in different districts or different countries.

Fossils have enabled geologists to arrange the different rock formations in a definite series according to the typical fossils that they contain. The oldest rocks that have been found do not contain any recognisable fossils. Next come rocks in which are found traces of the very simplest forms of animal life, and the fossils of each successive younger generation show how the animal life of the world has developed.

LIONESS AND LION

W. S. Berridge.

With his majestic head and bushy mane, the lion seems to deserve his title " King of Beasts,"
yet neither in weight nor courage does the African lion match the Indian tiger. Even so his
strength is such that he can fell an ox with one blow of his paw.

THE GREAT CATS OF THE JUNGLE

TWO ROYAL ANIMALS—THE LION AND THE TIGER

THE Lion is the King of Beasts, and the glossy, black-striped Tiger is his cousin. Both are splendid animals, handsome and strong. The tiger is the braver of the two, but he is not quite so magnificent because he has no mane. He looks like a very large cat.

Both these animals belong to the Cat Family; and, like your cat at home, have eyes that see very well at night, sharp claws that can be drawn in or out, rough tongues that can scrape every bit of flesh from bones, and teeth that can rend and tear.

The lion lives in Africa and Persia. He can also be found in India, but there he does not wear his splendid mane. He is so strong that he can fell an ox

with a blow of his paw, and drag it away easily.

His light yellow hair makes it difficult for him to be seen, for it is so like the colour of his surroundings. He hunts at night-time, and during the day sleeps in a thicket, or in a reed-bed near the river. When darkness comes he awakes and roars loudly, frightening all the animals near and far.

When he roars he puts his head close to the ground, and then it is impossible to tell exactly where the sound is coming from. Many animals, in their fear, run straight into the lion's path and are killed with one blow.

The tiger is found in all parts of Asia. His legs are shorter than the lion's, and because he has no mane he looks smaller. It is very difficult to see him as he stalks through the jungle,

F. W. Bond.

BENGAL TIGER

Except that a tiger's weight is between 400 and 500 pounds, while that of a cat rarely exceeds 15 pounds, there is not much difference between the two animals. With its short ears, sleepy eyes and stiff whiskers, there is something both cunning and cruel in the expression of this magnificent Bengal tiger. Yet a tiger in its prime never attacks man unless shot at. It is only the old, toothless, mangy tiger that turns man-eater.

golden yellow sunshine.

He is very strong indeed, stronger even than the lion, and he is bolder and braver, especially when he becomes a man-eater. Then he is a terror to all the natives, and has to be killed as soon as possible.

A Tiger Hunt

A tiger hunt is very exciting. Sometimes the tiger is driven into a small clump of jungle. The natives then or lies hidden in a bamboo thicket, for the black stripes on his coat and the bright orange colour of his fur are so like the black shadows of the bamboo stems and the

F. W. Bond.

THE KING OF BEASTS

Like the tiger, the lion, when old, sometimes turns man-eater, but the one you see in this picture is never likely to do so, for he lives in a famous Zoo where he is well fed every day of his life,

From the painting by Scott Langley.

BRITAIN'S NATIVE RED SQUIRREL

Everyone's favourite is the red squirrel of our countryside, now so quickly diminishing in numbers before the advance of its grey American cousin. The native squirrel is golden-red in the sunlight as he sits on a branch high in a tree and peers down to see what is taking place below. It is indeed one of the squirrel's characteristics that he is always interested in the movement of birds, rabbits and other creatures who share with him the hours spent in a woodland world.

THE STOAT CHANGES INTO ITS ERMINE COAT

In this picture we see the ordinary stoat when it has changed into its winter coat of white and become a beautiful ermine whose fur is regarded as being fit for kings to wear. The specimen here painted still retains some of the summer brown about its head, for stoats in our country often fail to complete the change to snow-white all over their bodies. Even then, the ermine must be regarded as a very lovely creature blending well into a wintry scene.

A LIONESS TAKES HER OWN PHOTOGRAPH

Major A. Radcliffe Dugmore.

This fine lioness was never in a Zoo and is probably still roaming her native jungles in East Africa. The photograph was taken by flash-light by the well-known African explorer, Major Dugmore. Or, to be more correct, the lioness was made to photograph herself by a trip-string connected with a camera. As she touched the string the light blazed up recording the above picture on the film of the hidden camera.

Neville Kingston.

LEOPARD

Leopards are found in Africa and throughout Asia. They are smaller than the tiger but no less ferocious. The leopard hunts by night; and, being an agile beast and an excellent climber of trees, he lies in wait on some overhanging bough for any unfortunate antelope or goat which may pass beneath. He possesses a beautifully marked coat.

quickly surround this with strong netting. When the tiger tries to get out, and shows himself anywhere near the net, the men throw spears at him. It is not long before he is killed.

Another favourite way of catching tigers is to set up a trap, and at the back of it fix a large mirror. This is placed in the daily path of the tiger. When the great animal comes along, he catches sight of himself in the mirror and at once thinks that another tiger is coming towards him.

He swings his tail angrily from side to side, and shows his great teeth in a snarl. His reflection does the same, and this infuriates the tiger so much that he leaps at the mirror in anger. He jumps right into the trap, which shuts fast behind him. He is caught!

Both lions and tigers have fascinating little cubs. They are delightful play-things when they are small, but they soon grow, and then must be put behind bars. In their own wild life they hunt with their fathers and mothers until they are old enough to look after themselves ; then they leave their parents, and live their own lives.

THE LION'S COUSINS

THE Lion has some smaller, but very fierce, cousins. The Leopard, one of the largest, is a beautiful animal, and is most powerful. In India it is called a Panther. It is more difficult to hunt than a Tiger because it is much more watchful and alert. If you could watch a panther padding through a jungle, you would see that it not only looked from side to side, but also upwards, into the trees, in case any enemy was hidden there.

Neville Kingston.

This lion cub is evidently greatly interested in the photographer and his camera. Lion cubs are docile little creatures and easily tamed, in which they differ greatly from their cousins the tigers. The tiger, almost from babyhood, is treacherous, and keepers and others who have to look after **young tigers must always keep a watchful eye on their** charges.

The Leopard

The leopard has a beautiful coat. His fur is a bright yellow, tinged with red, and is white underneath. Black ring-shaped spots are splashed over his body, each spot enclosing a patch of yellow. You will perhaps be able to guess the reason for these spots. They are so like the mixture of sunshine and ring-shaped leaf-shadows that an enemy or a victim finds it very difficult to see the leopard, when he crouches down to the ground, or slinks silently along.

The leopard can climb trees, and often does so to catch his prey. He waits in the branches until a deer or some other succulent animal passes below, and then he hurls himself down. He kills his prey, eats what he wants, and then takes the rest of the carcase up into a tree, and hangs it on a branch out of reach of jackals.

A beautiful leopard, called the Ounce or Snow-Leopard, lives in Central Asia. His coat is white, clouded with grey, and is marked with irregular black rosette-like spots. He has a thick, bushy tail.

There are Black Leopards too; and, at first, you might think they had no spots, but in a good light they can be quite clearly seen. Black leopards are savage beasts, and practically impossible to tame.

Another cousin of the lion is the Jaguar, who lives in Central and South America. He is rather like the leopard, but his spots have one or two small patches of dark brown fur in the middle. He also wears a few black streaks across his chest, and has a shorter tail.

He loves climbing, and his chief food

F. W. Bond.

PUMA

The puma is found in both North and South America, where it does a great deal of damage on farms and ranches, stealing cattle, dogs and even horses. Curiously enough it appears almost friendly to man himself and will follow him without attempting harm.

A WELL-TRAINED TEAM

H. J. Shepstone.

For as long as there is any history lions have always been regarded as the Kings of Beasts, and exhibited for the amusement and interest of people. This was certainly the case in Bible days and also at the time of the Great Roman Empire. In the picture above a lion tamer is shown with his charges.

Neville Kingston.

THE SAVAGE CARACAL

This cat-like creature, who wears a bright, red-brown coat and has jet-black ears, lives chiefly
in India, though found in some parts of Africa. It is incredibly ferocious and almost impossible
to tame. Its body is usually about 2 feet in length and the tail 10 inches. The animal is
reputed to follow lions and devour such food as they leave.

is monkeys and birds, which he easily finds in the trees.

The Puma, or Mountain Lion, is another member of the Cat family, and lives in nearly all parts of the American Continent. He is smaller than the Jaguar, tawny brown, with no markings at all. The puma does not attack man,

but causes great distress to farmers by carrying off sheep and killing horses and cattle.

One of the handsomest of the smaller cats is the Ocelot of tropical America. He is grey and his coat is marked with spots, blotches and streaks of fawn. He climbs well, and lives mainly upon

THE CAT WITH THE TUFTED EARS

Neville Kingston.

This member of the cat family, the Lynx, is distinguished by the tufts of hair at the tips of his ears. Like the leopard, he is an expert climber of trees and displays all the ferocity of both leopard and tiger. In prehistoric times lynxes were found in England, and they still exist in parts of Europe, notably in Russia and Scandinavia, and in Tibet and North America. The Lynx measures about 3 feet in length excluding the rather short tail, and for his food he favours chiefly birds and small animals, at the catching of which he is an adept.

birds. He is a bold and blood-thirsty animal, but can be tamed in captivity.

The oddest looking cousin of the lion is the Lynx, with long, pointed grey ears, tufted with hair, and a great pair of bushy whiskers hanging below its chin. It has a grey coat, marked with spots, and is still to be found in Europe.

A very savage cat is the Caracal. It is a bright red-brown, with jet-black ears. It lives in India and Arabia and can climb skilfully. It feeds chiefly on small deer and birds, and will sometimes leap into the air and catch a bird as it flies past.

THE STORY OF TIBBY THE CAT

TIBBY the Cat sits before the fire, blinking her eyes lazily. She is a house pet, but we do not love her as much as we love the dog. Neither does she love us as much as the dog does. She is a very self-possessed creature, with good manners and pretty ways, but she does not try to please us as do dogs.

Perhaps you think you know all about your Tibby at home, and could write a story about her and her ways yourself, but I wonder if you know how it is that she can " see in the dark " ?

Neville Kingston.

THE HEAD OF A JAGUAR

We count the Jaguar a cousin to the lion, and he is certainly not unlike the leopard, though his spots have patches of dark brown fur in the middle. In addition, there are black streaks across his chest and his tail is not so long. The jaguar is at home in Central and South America and is noted for his prowess as a climber.

A FAMILY GROUP AND AN OUTLAW

C. Reid.

This family of kittens seems to enjoy facing the camera. Cats have been domestic pets from time out of mind, and the common word " Puss " has come down to us from the Egyptian word for cat. A healthy cat can live for more than fifteen years, but often when it is about eleven or twelve years old, a cat will lose its hearing or eyesight, and it is sometimes kinder to have it " put to sleep."

F. W. Bond.

Observe the savage expression on the face of this Scottish wild cat. This is one of the few creatures which are utterly untamable. Wild cats still exist in the Highlands of Scotland in remote places, but they are very seldom seen by anyone other than local inhabitants, who know their ways and their haunts.

Like all the cat family, she can expand the black centres of her eyes at night, so that they take in every scrap of light there is. In the daytime the black pupils of her eyes narrow to tiny slits. Since Puss goes hunting in the dark she needs very keen sight, and this she has, for as long as there is the faintest light about she can see well enough to catch her prey.

But if you put Tibby in a completely dark room she could not see at all, because there would not be the smallest ray of light available to help her.

She would use her fine whiskers then, for they are very sensitive to touch. She could run through a room crowded with furniture in the pitch dark, and yet never bump her head. As soon as her sensitive whisker-ends touch a chair leg or stool they warn her not to go that way, and she turns in another direction.

Have you watched her eating? You must have noticed how slow she is over her food. Even if you have a dog who will gobble up Tibby's food if she isn't quick, she will not hurry.

This is because she has always been a solitary animal, one that hunted by herself and not in a pack. She always had plenty of time to eat her meals slowly and in peace, and her age-old habit remains to this day. Half a dozen dogs will not make her gobble her food—she must eat daintily and slowly.

A Rough Tongue

Her tongue is very rough, and this is so that she may rasp all the flesh off bones. Even a kitten's tongue is rough, as you may have felt when it licked you. The cat cannot crunch up bones as a dog can, because her teeth are not made to do that, so she makes up for it by having a very useful tongue. If you could examine it under a magnifying glass you would see a great number of little horn-like projections on it pointing back towards her throat. It is these that rasp the meat from the bones.

How is it that Puss runs so quietly after her prey? She has soft pads under her paws, so velvety that not a bird hears her coming; and pulled back by a strong muscle are her sharp claws, curved and cruel. She keeps them withdrawn when she walks or runs, for she does not want them to become blunted. She needs

SIAMESE CAT   *F. W. Bond.*

Even people who do not like ordinary cats become fond of the Siamese cat, which is the handsomest and by far the most intelligent of its tribe. It has a dark face, black ears and feet, blue eyes, and a most peculiar voice quite different from that of its European cousins.

Neville Kingston.

A KITTEN IN STRANGE COMPANY

It is not often you see such an assorted party enjoying a meal from one dish. On the right is an ordinary domestic kitten, who seems quite unperturbed. In the centre is a fox cub, looking around him mistrustfully; while on the left is a very young timber wolf—who will probably not be so docile as he grows older!

them for climbing and for scratching her enemies.

For hundreds and hundreds of years the cat has been domesticated, but we have not succeeded in teaching her to love us and be loyal to us as we have the dog. We cannot blame her for this, because she has always been a lonely animal in her wild state, and has never learnt to love or to be loyal to the leader of a pack or to comrades.

Her kittens are charming. They play delightfully, and there is a good reason behind all their pretty play. They will pounce on a cotton reel drawn along by a string, or throw a paper ball into the air, or stalk a flying leaf. All these things are preparing them for their grown-up life when they will pounce on rats and mice, throw them into the air, stalk birds, and so on. They learn in their play all the things they will do when they are fully grown.

Our Wild Cat, or Cat-a-Mountain, lives in the Highlands of Scotland. It is a savage, fierce beast, quite untamable, and very handsome. Sometimes our own home cats become tired of their stay-at-home lives and go off on their own to poach in the woods. Then we hear of wild cats being found here, or discovered there, but they are not the real Cat-a-Mountain. They are, in fact, just poor imitations, and usually it is not long before they are shot by a gamekeeper.

ANIMALS AND THEIR YOUNG (1)

F. W. Bond.

Here is a zoo picture of a zebra and her baby. Young zebras resemble young horses in having very long legs so that they can keep up with the herd. Zebras are found only in Africa.

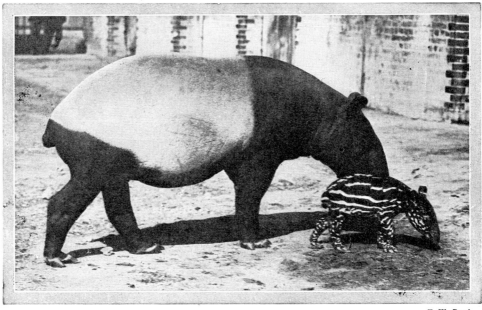

F. W. Bond.

The mother and baby depicted in this second zoo photograph are Malayan Tapirs. These queer creatures, which exist mainly on vegetable fare, sugar cane, and so on, are easily tamed.

Zoological Society of London.

The Giraffe has such a long neck because it browses from the tops of trees. Despite its awkward shape it is fleet of foot and when galloping brings its hind hoofs outside the front ones. Giraffes are found only in Central and S. Africa.

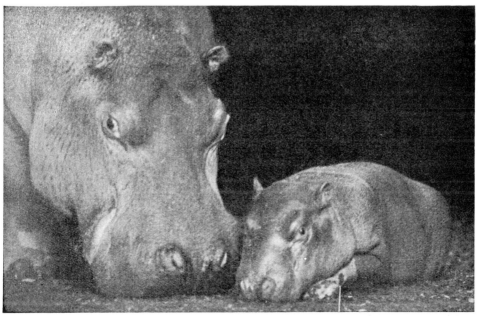

F. W. Bond.

The common Hippopotamus is the largest of land mammals excluding the Elephant. It attains a length of 14 feet and a height of about 4 feet at the shoulder. Found only in Central Africa in these days, it spends most of its time in water and is a fairly rapid swimmer though slow and clumsy on land.

THE OLD MAN IN THE FUR COAT

POLAR BEAR CUBS

Will. F. Taylor.

Taken on the edge of the Arctic Ocean, this photograph shows two Polar bear cubs captured by Eskimo hunters and kept on leash like dogs. Eskimo hunters will tackle a Polar Bear single-handed, and armed only with a knife. In the olden days no Eskimo thought of using a rifle in hunting the bear. He employed a dog to follow up the trail of the bear and fought it, when he found it, with knife or spear.

DO you know who "the old man in the fur coat" is? It is the Polar Bear! The hunters give him that name when they seek for him in the Arctic regions where he lives.

His coat is creamy yellow, and is difficult to see against the white snow. This helps him when he is hunting for food, for it makes it easier for him to catch his prey. He is a very good swimmer, and spends a great deal of his time in the water.

"But doesn't he get very cold?" you will say. No, he doesn't, because his coat is very thick, and is so oily that the cold water cannot get through it. When he walks on the ice he does not feel the cold either, for underneath each foot he has long thick hairs, and these keep his feet warm, and also prevent him from slipping and sliding to and fro.

He has a small head on a long neck, which makes it easy for him to swim fast in the water. If he had a big head he could not move nearly so rapidly and would find it difficult to catch porpoises and seals.

Sometimes he catches seals in a cunning way. He finds their breathing-hole, and lies down by it, keeping quite still and quiet. When a seal comes up to breathe, the bear strikes him quickly with his paw, and then drags the stunned animal out of the water to devour him.

Baby bears are reared in a nursery under the snow. This sounds very cold and bleak, but the little bears are warm and snug there. When they are old enough, the parent bears take them out on the ice, and teach them to hunt. They do not take a great while to learn how to catch seals and fish, and are soon able to care for themselves.

The Brown Bear

The Brown Bear is a coloured cousin of the Polar Bear. He lives in Europe

TWO MEMBERS OF THE BEAR FAMILY

Photos: Sport and General.

Two young members of the Bear family are seen here. The Brown Bear lived in Britain at one time and is still found in Europe, Asia and North America.

Here are the twin cubs, Jack and Daphne, again. In the wilds they seek honey; at the London Zoo their keeper, knowing their love of sweet things, is feeding them with syrup.

Topical Press.

Polar Bears are among the largest of bears, attaining a height of 4 feet and up to 9 feet in length. A Polar Bear which achieved tremendous popularity was Brumas, seen above with its mother, Ivy, taking a walk at their home in the London Zoo.

THE GIANT PANDA

G. P. A.

Though everyone has heard of the Giant Panda, he is one of the world's rarest animals and makes his home exclusively in bamboo forests in south-west China. He wears a coat of black and white but does not belong to the bear family.

and Asia, and once upon a time used to live in Britain.

He loves honey, and if he can find a nest of wild bees he is delighted. He climbs the tree to reach it, and then eats up the honey, comb and all, never heeding the angry bees that swarm round him and sting his nose. He likes fruit, too, and roots, and will turn over stones to find beetles and earwigs.

He becomes very fat in the autumn; and, when the cold weather comes, finds a hollow tree, or a cave, and curls up there to sleep the winter away. He is very thin when he wakes up in the spring, but after a few good meals he soon fills out again.

The Grizzly Bear is very big, strong and savage. He lives in North America among the Rocky Mountains, and sometimes grows to a length of 9 feet. The hunters call him " Old Ephraim."

He likes honey, too, but his chief prey is deer. He likes to kill one, and bury it in the ground, returning to dig it up and eat it when he is hungry.

He sometimes has a feast of acorns, and it is said that he will climb a tree and shake the branches in order to feast on the hundreds that tumble to the ground.

There are other bears, such as the queer sloth bear and the mischievous black bear; but, though he is so much like a toy " Teddy Bear " we must not, strictly speaking, include the Giant Panda in the bear family at all.

It was in 1869 that the very first wild panda was discovered by a French missionary-explorer and it was decided that the quaint creature was a mammal of an entirely new family. The only homes of pandas are in the bamboo forests of Szechwan in south-west China and these creatures eat nothing but bamboo shoots. They are really carnivores (*i.e.*, flesh eaters) who have turned vegetarians.

Mondiale.

MALAY BEAR

Distinctly smaller than most of its relatives, the Malay bear has a very short coat, usually black in colour except for the muzzle and the light band on the chest.

GIANTS OF THE ANIMAL WORLD

F. W. Bond.

INDIAN ELEPHANTS AT THE ZOO

In size the Elephant is the largest of all land animals and is found only in Asia and Africa. Our photograph shows an Indian elephant with her baby taking a bath at their home in the London Zoo. Compared with the African type the Indian elephant has a more massive head, smaller ears, and one finger-like lip at the end of its trunk instead of two.

THE Elephant is the giant of the land animals, and a very strange-looking and ponderous beast he is. His pedestal-like legs, grey wrinkled skin, large ears and swinging trunk are known by everybody, and no child could possibly mistake the elephant for any other animal.

His trunk is like a very useful hand. Have you seen it being used? The elephant can pluck bunches of leaves from trees with it, and can pick up even such a small thing as a half-penny from the ground. He puts his food into his mouth with his trunk, and when he wants a drink he fills his trunk with water, and then squirts it down his throat.

Sometimes, when the weather is hot, the elephant squirts water over his back to cool himself! He finds his trunk very useful indeed, and since he would certainly starve without it, he carefully rolls it up whenever danger is near.

As you look at an elephant you wonder how his legs can support so huge a body. The bones, however, rest directly upon one another, so that each leg is like a pillar.

Elephants come from India and from Africa. Do you know the difference between the two? The Indian elephant has not such large ears as his African cousin, and at the end of his trunk he has only one little finger-like projection, instead of two. He is more intelligent than the African elephant, and is easier to tame.

Those who tame and train elephants must be kind and patient with them to be successful. An elephant never forgives a cruel deed. He remembers it for years, and when he meets the man who ill-treated him, perhaps ten or twenty years later, he has his revenge on him. He never forgets.

How Elephants Work

The Indian elephant is very useful. He helps in pulling teak logs from place to place, and will pile them up neatly and carefully. He is so strong that a heavy tree trunk is nothing to him. He can lift it easily with his trunk, and carry it to some other place.

In his natural life the elephant uses his trunk to feed himself. He reaches up to the fruit or young leaves he wants and pulls them down. If he cannot reach them he tears up the tree by the roots, using his strong ivory tusks. He can uproot a tree easily ; then he strips the branches of their leaves and enjoys a good meal.

Elephants live in herds. When they pass through a forest they make little noise, for they put their big feet down very silently. When they are frightened they stampede, and then they do a great deal of harm, for they crush everything over which they pass.

We hunt elephants for the sake of their fine ivory tusks, which are very valuable. Sometimes these grow to a length of 9 feet or 10 feet and weigh over 200 pounds. We use the ivory for many things, from billiard balls to piano keys.

The elephants which carry children have to be very carefully trained before they are fit for such work. Zoos which

F. W. Bond.

THE ELEPHANT GOES TO WORK

Elephants are so immensely strong and also so intelligent that they make splendid workers once they have been properly trained. Burma is the great country in which to see these huge animals employed, and in this photograph you observe one lifting with ease a trunk of teak which he is about to place on the stack.

STRONG AND WILLING WORKERS

E. N. A.

Here is another elephant earning its living by hard work in the timber yards near Rangoon. The animals work strictly to hours, and cease their labour when the knocking-off signal sounds.

Topical.

While the African elephant is valued for its ivory the Indian elephant, which has a less savage disposition, is appreciated for its qualities as a draught animal. This picture comes from Ceylon.

5—2

WHERE A TRUNK IS INDISPENSABLE!

Herbert G. Ponting, F.R.G.S.

In some cases the animal may carry the load, or he may be ordered to pull it. In this case, as the teak log came from the river, he was ordered to push it towards the stackyard instead of pulling or carrying. Maybe this particular tree was very smooth, and as easy to push as to pull! In any event, the elephant makes very light work of the job, thanks to the great muscular strength of his massive trunk.

THE GIRAFFE

I EXPECT you have heard the story of the old lady who went to the Zoo and saw a giraffe for the first time. She looked at the tall creature for a minute or two, and then said: " Well, I don't believe it. That animal can't be true."

AFRICAN ELEPHANT

These two photographs show plainly the great difference between the African and Asiatic elephants. This top one is the African. Notice its sloping forehead, immense ears and huge tusks. It was always supposed that the African elephant could not be tamed, but this has been proved a mistake, and in East Africa native elephants are now being used for farm work. There are still a few wild elephants in the Cape Peninsula.

keep them are glad when an elephant can earn his living in this way, for his food costs a great deal, as you can imagine.

In the springtime all elephants in captivity are spring-cleaned. The keeper brushes their hides with oil, and this keeps the wrinkled skin from cracking and becoming sore. It is a funny sight to see the great creatures being oiled in this way.

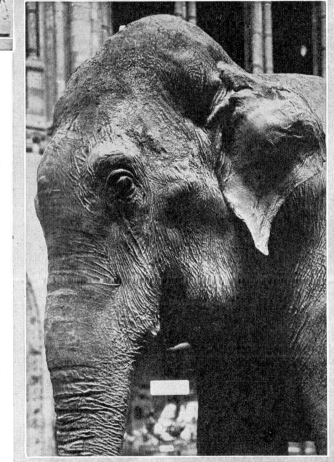

INDIAN ELEPHANT   *James's Press Agency.*

In Asia elephants are found in India, Ceylon and Further India. Even the wild ones are very strictly protected, so there is no chance of the largest of land animals being wiped out.

Perhaps you felt like that the first time *you* saw the quaint giraffe. He really is a peculiar-looking beast, with his long thin legs, very long neck, funny little horns, and great brown eyes.

Do you know why he has such a long neck? It is because his food grows high up on trees. He likes the new shoots and the fresh young leaves for his meals, and needs a long neck to reach them. He plucks the leaves with his long slender tongue, curling it round them, and pulling them from the branch. He uses his upper lip, too, to draw his food into his mouth.

The giraffe can run very fast, as fast as a galloping horse. He looks queer when running, for he puts his back legs in front of and outside his fore-legs, while his long neck rocks up and down in a most comical manner. But he is really a very graceful animal, and delightful to watch as he wanders along, looking for young leaves.

Why the Giraffe's Coat is Spotted

Can you guess why a giraffe's coat is dappled with spots? You might think that the dark brown markings make the giraffe easy to see, but they don't, for they are very like the spots of shadow made by the moving leaves overhead. When a giraffe stands still beneath the trees he can hardly be seen. His spotted coat tones in so well with the spots of sunlight and shadow that you would find it hard to tell any animal was standing there.

When the giraffe drinks he has to place his front legs wide apart in order to get his head down to the water. It

Paul Popper.

QUENCHING HIS THIRST

Although giraffes have long necks, they have to spread out their legs and bend their knees to reach water or to pick up anything from the ground. This picture comes from the Kruger National Park, which is probably the most famous game reserve in southern Africa.

is said that he can go for months without drinking, but as he gets plenty of moisture from the young leaves he eats this is not very wonderful.

The giraffe is our very tallest animal, and even if you stood two elephants one above the other, the giraffe could still see over the top of them both. He grows to a height of 19 feet or 20 feet, and, like the elephant, lives in herds.

He is not as gentle as he looks. He can be very fierce indeed, and when he is frightened or angry will use his hoofs or head for attack or defence.

At the London Zoo there is a giraffe's stall which has a small square of plate-glass placed over a hole in the wood. This hole was made by an angry giraffe which one day tried to strike at his keeper with his head. The keeper dodged—and the giraffe struck the wood and made a hole in it! He must have been very much annoyed!

TWO ANIMAL GIANTS

THE rhinoceros and the hippopotamus were both going to the river, and they met on its bank.

"What are you going to do?" asked the rhinoceros.

"I am going to walk about on the bottom of the river to find some growing plants to eat," said the hippo. "I can stay beneath the water for quite ten minutes, so I have plenty of time to eat my dinner. My long name means river horse, you know. What are *you* going to do?"

Nigel Watt.

A GIRAFFE IN NORTHERN RHODESIA

Tallest of all animals, the giraffe is a native of Africa, and is found in the savannas or tropical grasslands south of the Equator. This one was photographed in the Livingstone Game Park, Northern Rhodesia, and the two admiring girls give a good idea of its height, as well as justifying its reputation as a harmless, inoffensive creature, though it can offer stout resistance if attacked.

"I am going to take a mud-bath," said the rhinoceros. "Do you see how my skin hangs in folds? Well, although it looks so thick, inside the folds it is thin and tender, and the flies creep in there and bite me."

"But how can you prevent them by taking a mud-bath?" asked the hippopotamus in surprise.

"Just watch!" said the rhinoceros. He flopped into the river, and made his

THE HAPPY HIPPOPOTAMI!

Paul Popper

Hippopotamus is Greek for river-horse, but the hippo is much more like a pig than a horse. This great beast lives mainly on grasses and weeds, and is harmless. Yet if attacked it becomes a terrible enemy, for its mouth is armed with tremendous tusks. Note the two egrets perched on this one's back. The hippopotami like to have these birds, which peck irritating insects off their skins

Paul Popper.

Here are some hippos basking in the sunshine on a mud-bank in mid-stream. Each of them weighs about three tons, and they find it difficult to move quickly when out of water.

way to where it was muddy and marshy. Then he rolled over and over, and covered himself with mud. Soon he came out and stood in the hot sun.

" Why, the mud is drying, and making you a nice hard coat! " cried the hippo.

" Yes," said the rhinoceros. " Now the flies cannot bite me, you see. So for a little while I shall have peace. But as soon as I move and the mud coat cracks, the flies will torment me again."

" I shouldn't move, then," said the hippo.

" I shall have to when I am hungry," said the rhinoceros, yawning, and showing his teeth. " I shall soon go and rip up the trunk of a tree with my horn and feast on the woody fibres. I use my horn for attacking my enemies, too, and it is a dangerous weapon, I can tell you, for I lower my head, and then strike upwards with the horn.

THE RHINO

Paul Popper.

The rhinoceros's trumpet-shaped ears are held erect to catch the slightest sound, and are of much more use to him than his small eyes. Like all the really large land animals the rhino feeds chiefly on grass and leaves!

But I am rather a timid animal, and prefer to run away. I can run very fast, although you might not think it when you look at my long heavy body! "

The " Tearing Teeth " of the Hippo

" I have no horn," said the hippopotamus, glancing at his companion out of his little, bulging eyes, " but I have strong teeth and tusks. Look ! "

He opened his mouth so wide that it seemed as if it had split in half. Inside were huge teeth. Two of them, the tearing teeth, were like tusks.

" That is not a pleasant sight," said the rhinoceros, and he ran off in disgust. With him went some birds, who had been perching on his back, listening to the conversation. The rhinoceros did not mind them, for they picked off many of the flies that annoyed him.

The hippopotamus looked round for her little one who was near her.

" Climb on to my back," she said. " I am going into the river."

So the baby hippo climbed on to the mother's back, and soon the two were down at the bottom of the river,

THE COW RHINO AT HOME

Major A. Radcliffe Dugmore.

The photographer has here been so fortunate as to catch a fully-grown female or "cow" rhinoceros at home in Kenya, East Africa. The rhino's skin is enormously thick and, in the case of the African species, is smooth. The thinner, more tender parts are often tormented by flies. To overcome this annoyance the monster animal wallows in mud, allowing the coating to dry hard in the sun and so defeat the object of the insect pests.

A BULL RHINO STANDS AT BAY!

Major A. Radcliffe Dugmore.

This huge African rhinoceros is getting ready to charge, and woe betide any creature which stands in the way of his 3 tons of massive flesh and bone! His sight is very poor, but his power of scent extremely good, and if the wind brings him a whiff of man-smell that is quite enough to upset his extremely short and crusty temper. In spite of his vast bulk he can travel for a short distance at very great speed, and it takes more than one bullet to stop him, for his hide is tremendously thick in places and tough as well.

Paul Popper.

A RHINO FAMILY

The rhinos are on the prowl all night, and for them " bedtime " comes soon after seven o'clock in the morning. They make a light supper of salty earth, and have a little romp in the open while the dew is still on the grass. Then they file off into the thick bush to sleep all day, " father " leading the way. His two wives seem to hesitate, but soon they too will be out of sight in the gloom of the forest.

Both the hippopotamus and the rhinoceros are giant animals. The Indian rhinoceros has its skin in folds, and owns but one horn, whilst its brother in Africa has no folds in its skin, and grows two horns. When wounded they are terrible foes, and use their horns mercilessly. The horns of a rhinoceros are not made of bone but of the same material as hair, and they grow on its skin.

When a hunter is attacked by a rhino he slips off his jacket and throws it on the ground in front of the charging animal. The rhino stops to examine the coat, and is so short-sighted that the hunter has no difficulty in slipping away.

There are altogether five different kinds of rhinoceroses. The largest is the very rare white rhinoceros of South Africa, which stands nearly 7 feet high at the shoulder and has two terrible horns, the front one being about a yard long. The smallest rhino lives in south-east Asia and is only 4 feet high. It has two horns, but unlike the other rhinoceroses it is covered with reddish-brown hair.

THE SHIP OF THE DESERT

THE Camel is the Ship of the Desert, for he can travel for miles across a waterless waste, carrying his master safely. He needs very little food—perhaps a handful of dates, or a few bits of dry thorns—and can go without water for weeks if need be.

How can any animal travel across a sandy desert, with the wind blowing burning sand around him, and go without food or water for so long ?

" I can do that easily," says the camel, " for I have all sorts of things to help me ! "

He can pad along over the soft sand far better than a horse, for a horse's hoofs would sink down and

HOW NOMADS TRAVEL

This camel was photographed in the northern Sudan and is one of the many used by the nomadic tribes in this part of Africa for their journeys across the desert lands. On its back is an enclosed tent in which womenfolk travel. Camels can move across the desert more easily than most animals because their widely-spread toes (two on each foot) are linked by skin and do not sink in the soft sand. When they are lying down camels rest on the hard, protective pads of skin on their chests, knees and ankles.

he would soon be tired. But the camel has two toes with a leathery sole joining them on each foot, and finds it easy to travel over the desert without sinking into the sand.

When the wind blows the hot sand into his face he closes up his nostrils so that none shall fly up. His thick eyelashes protect his eyes from the blazing sun, and he cares nothing for the heat. For he is well equipped for hot and dusty climates.

A Storehouse of Food

His hump is very useful to him. It is made up of fat, and whilst the animal is travelling over the desert, getting little or nothing to eat, he uses the fat in his hump as food. The fat passes from the hump into other parts of the camel's body, and feeds them just as well as if the animal had eaten a good meal.

But this means that the hump becomes smaller. As the days go by, and the camel travels many miles over the sandy wastes, his hump gets slacker and slacker; and, at last, at the journey's end, it is nothing but an empty bag of skin. Then the camel is tired out, and can do no more work for some weeks. When he has had a good rest and plenty of food his hump fills out again, and the camel is ready for his next journey.

His Own Water Supply

Not only does he carry his own food about with him, but his own water too. In his stomach are a number of deep

W. S. Berridge.

MOTHER AND CHILD

This is a Bactrian camel and her fourteen-day-old calf. Notice the immensely long legs of the young creature. This is a provision of Nature to enable the baby to keep up with its parent and the herd. Young colts and calves are born with similarly long legs, a relic of the time when wild horses and cattle were constantly hunted by wolves. The large, leathery feet of the camel are well adapted for travelling on soft sand. The Bactrian camel has two humps whereas the Arabian camel has only one.

Polar Photos.

JOURNEYING OVER THE SAHARA

These camels are Dromedaries, the lightest and fastest breed of Arabian camel. The Sahara, where this photograph was taken, is a vast desert in North Africa and has an area of more than three million square miles. Notice the oasis, with its date palms, in the background.

cells, and whenever he can take a drink he fills up all these with water. Then, when he is in the desert and can find no pool from which to drink, he simply opens some of his water cells, and lets the liquid run out into his body, which uses it as if the camel had drunk it down through mouth and throat.

An Unwilling Worker

The camel can carry heavy loads, and will take them forty or fifty miles a day, travelling about two or three miles an hour. He hates being loaded, for he has to kneel down to have the pack strapped to him, and he does not like that. He grumbles and tries to bite, for he is a bad-tempered beast. He has hard flesh on knees and chest so that he may rest in comfort.

The Bactrian Camel

Some camels, the Arabian ones, have only one hump, whilst others, the Bactrian, have two. The Bactrian camel is stronger than the Arabian, but is not so tall. It has a thick coat to protect it from the cold when it lives in hilly districts. Arabian camels have sandy-coloured coats, but the coat of the Bactrian is reddish-brown or even black.

Riding camels are called Dromedaries. They can go four or five times as fast as ordinary camels. Riding a camel is quite different from riding a horse, because the camel moves both the legs on one side of its body at once, instead of alternately, like a horse, and this causes the animal to sway in a queer manner. Many people do not like it, for it makes them feel as if they were on board ship in very rough weather!

THE KANGAROO

THE Kangaroos were all feeding together peacefully. Many tiny ones were hopping over the grass. They used their long hind-legs and tail just as their parents did.

"I have been told that we look rather like big hares," said a mother kangaroo, "but we do not run like hares. We take enormous leaps instead. Our thick, strong tails help us to leap, and we use them for balancing, too."

"What are those two great claws for on your hind feet?" asked a baby kangaroo, hopping up. "Mine are not as long as yours yet."

"We use them for defence," said the big kangaroo. "Sometimes we are hunted by swift and powerful dogs. Then, if they get us into a corner, we have to turn and face them. We find our great claws very useful then, for we strike out with our hind feet and kill the dog at one blow."

"Another thing we do when we are hunted is to go to a river," said a second kangaroo. "I did that some time ago. There were many dogs after me, so I entered the water and turned to face them."

"What did you do next?" asked the baby kangaroo.

"I waited until the foremost dog came swimming up to me and then I took hold of him with my short, strong fore-legs and pulled him under the water," said the kangaroo. "Then I took the next one and drowned him too. So I saved myself from death. Remember that trick, little kangaroo, for it may be useful to you some day."

Just then the sound of barking dogs was heard in the distance. In a trice each of the mother kangaroos leapt to where her baby was playing and took hold of him. She stuffed him into a pouch

THE POUCH OF THE KANGAROO

Mondiale.

Mother kangaroos have deep, roomy pouches or pockets which serve as cradles for their babies, these young animals being known in Australia as "Joeys." Here you see a kangaroo baby peeping out from its mother's pouch.

THE BOXING KANGAROOS

The kangaroo is not what you might call a brainy animal, yet it has been found possible to train kangaroos to box. But that is not the way in which they fight in their wild state. The kangaroo's hind legs are enormously strong and provided with long and powerful claws, and these are the weapons he uses in a real battle, kicking forward and cutting his enemy open.

on the under part of her body, and sprang off with him to safety.

The Kangaroo's Pouch

The babies—or Joeys, as they are called by the Australians—were quite used to being stuffed into their mothers' pockets. As soon as they could they poked their heads out to see what was happening. Their mothers were leaping along at a great rate, for they were afraid of the barking dogs.

Soon they were safe, and the Joeys scrambled out of the pouches again. They looked very funny as they popped their heads out, and then hopped down on to the grass.

A Giant Bird

Among the giants of the animal kingdom we must include the African Ostrich, which stands nearly 8 feet high and lays cream-coloured eggs weighing 3 or 4 lb. each! It is much too heavy to fly, but is a very swift runner and can easily outstrip a horse or antelope.

W. G. Davis.

AN AFRICAN OSTRICH

The Ostrich is an odd creature in more than its size and shape. It eats nearly anything from mice, snakes and fruit to stones, bones and metal objects like nails. It always runs in circles, and when it doesn't want to be seen it buries its head in the sand. The cock bird (shown here) hatches out the huge eggs laid by the hen.

THE WOLF AND HIS BROTHERS

IT was winter, and the snow lay thick upon the ground. A bitter wind blew, and all men stayed by the fire and listened to the wind howling—and something else howling, too—the wolves!

The dogs in the yard sniffed with their noses to the wind.

" I can smell wolf," said one of them. " The pack is getting hungry and more daring. They will be coming near the towns soon."

" I hate them," said another dog fiercely. " They belong to the dog family, but they are not like us. They are wild and savage and would eat our masters if we did not protect them."

The wolves came nearer, and their howling grew louder. They were very hungry. For days they had not had anything to eat. They had hunted the country in great packs, but except for a small rabbit or two, had found nothing. Now they dared to draw near to the towns, where they could smell horses, cattle and men.

" If only we could see a sleigh starting off with people inside! " said the leader of the wolves, a great grey fellow. " We might kill the horses and then fall upon the people ! "

Suddenly there came a jingle of sleigh bells and a sleigh came through the forest, drawn by six horses. The wolves ran after it, hoping to find a meal at last. But one of the men in the sleigh was on the watch.

" I am not going to lose my horses! " he cried to the wolves. " Keep away, or I shall shoot! "

But the wolves were too hungry to fear the gun. They came loping up like long, grey shadows, getting nearer and nearer to the sleigh.

It was not the first time the grey old leader had had an experience like this.

F. W. Bond.

WOLF

At first sight you might take this for the head of a big dog, but it is actually a picture of the common wolf. Wolves are extinct in the British Isles, but still live in France, Germany and most parts of Europe, especially in Russia.

The prowling animals lived in Russia and most of the year spent their time in forest and woodland, finding little difficulty in obtaining food. Snow, however, cut off their supplies. They became first hungry and then ravenous, and their terrible plight bade them forsake the wilds and for once seek the haunts of human beings.

" Shoot! " cried the man who was driving. " They will pounce on the horses in a moment ! "

" Crack! " The gun spoke and a wolf fell. The whole pack gathered round eagerly, forgetting to follow the sleigh.

What were they going to do ? Were they going to help their wounded comrade ? No, they were going to eat him, for wolves are merciless and

THE HYÆNA   *W. S. Berridge.*

Cowardly, ill-smelling, treacherous, the hyæna is no man's friend. It lives on carrion and possesses the most powerful jaws of any living animal. It is a fact that the hyæna can crack the leg-bone of an ox to extract the marrow.

show no kindness to any beast even though it may be their own brother.

"We are safe!" said the driver, looking back. "By the time they have finished their horrid meal we shall be in the town!"

They raced onwards to the sound of jingling bells. When they entered the town in safety they heard afar off the mournful sound of the pack of wolves, hunting once again for their prey.

THE ANIMAL DUST-MAN

"GRR - RR - RR - RR!" said the lion, showing his great teeth, as he placed his front paw on the deer he had killed. "This is *my* dinner! Nobody else must touch it!"

He tore off big pieces of meat and swallowed them. When he had eaten as much as he wanted he went to a thick bush, curled up under it, and fell asleep.

"I shall finish eating that deer when I awake," he thought.

But whilst he was asleep the animal dustmen came creeping out from behind trees and under bushes. They were the jackals, who had been following the lion for many nights, hoping that he would kill something.

"Then we will wait until the lion is asleep, and feast on what he has left!" they said. "We are the animal dustmen! We leave nothing to decay; we clear it all up!"

They fell upon the remains of the deer, and were soon crunching up the bones and tearing off the meat that the lion had left. They ate quickly, for they were afraid that he might wake and find them.

"If he sees what we are doing he will be angry and catch one of us," they

F. W. Bond.
JACKAL

Jackals of different species are found in Africa and Asia. They are night-roaming animals and live largely by their wits.

said. "Do you remember how he caught a jackal last time, and bit off its paws as a warning to us not to steal his dinner again?"

When they had eaten all they could they stole off. There was nothing left of the deer except the largest bones of all, which the jackals could not finish, for their teeth were not strong enough. When the lion awoke he went to eat what he had left of his dinner—and it was all gone except the few big bones. He was angry, and roared so loudly that every beast near and far crouched and trembled.

The hyænas heard him roaring, and guessed that he was angry because the jackals had finished up his dinner.

"Let us go and see if they have left anything!" they cried. So off they ran, great ugly creatures, with their hindquarters sloping downwards like those of a dog who fears to be whipped. They soon came to where the lion had killed the deer. The great maned beast was still there, trying to crunch up the large bones that the jackals had left. But he could not, for even his teeth, sharp and powerful as they were, were not sufficiently strong.

The Strong Teeth of the Hyæna

When he had glided away, swishing his tail in fury, the hyænas crept up. In a trice they had the large, thick bones between their teeth; and, with one crunch, ground them to pieces. Soon there was not a sign of the dead deer left. The animal dustmen had cleared away everything.

"Our teeth are stronger than those of any other animal!" said the hyænas as they slunk away. "We can crunch bones an inch thick, and even bite through tins of meat if we find them!"

"But you are cowards!" cried a monkey, sitting safely up in a tree,

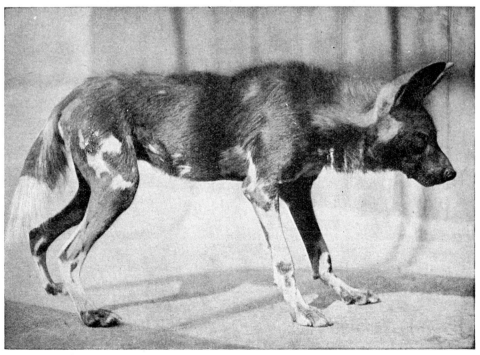

Neville Kingston.

A HUNTING DOG OF AFRICA

This queer-looking member of the canine race is the somewhat rare Hunting Dog of Africa. He is perfectly wild and roams about in packs. His scent is amazingly keen, and he will follow human beings on trek for days in the hope of snatching some of the foodstuff they carry.

" You will never fight if you are caught! Ho, ho, what did I see the other day ? One of you was snared by an Arab, and he was so scornful of you all that he threw a handful of mud in its face, dragged it along by its hind legs, and gave it to his women to stone! You are all cowards! "

" That may be so," said the hyænas, " but we are artful. We often pretend to be dead when we are caught, and we lie quite still. Then, when we see our chance, we leap up and run away."

" You are cowards, and I do not like you! " cried the monkey, hurling a nut at the hyænas.

The mischievous monkey was quite right. All the hyænas are cowardly, slinking creatures. There are three kinds, the striped, the brown and the spotted. The spotted one is often called the laughing hyæna, because of the horrible laughing sounds it makes.

REYNARD THE FOX

REYNARD the Fox was hungry. He put his head out of his hole, or " earth," as it is called, and sniffed the wind.

" I smell Rabbit ! " he said, and slipped out of his earth into the field. Then he ran to where some rabbits were playing, and stopped nearby. He began to chase his own tail round and

Neville Kingston.

THE SLENDER DOG OF THE ARGENTINE

A curious, fox-like creature is the Slender Dog of that huge South American Republic known as the Argentine. Dogs in a perfectly wild state are found in nearly every part of the world, and of this class the Australian " dingo " is probably the best known. Almost all the wild dogs hunt in packs. Some of them make one think of foxes and others of hyænas and jackals. In certain countries they do much damage, and in others serve as useful scavengers of garbage.

AN ALERT LITTLE FOX CUB

Miss Onslow.

This is a fox cub, a kit fox as country folk say. Caught young, the fox is easily tamed. Yet there is a great difference between the face of this cub and that of a dog puppy. The eyes have a watchful gleam and the whole expression of the little animal is alert as if he would be up and off at the first hint of danger. The common fox of the countryside is a native British animal.

round and round, keeping one eye on the rabbits all the time.

"Oh look!" said a baby rabbit in surprise. "What is that funny creature doing? He is going round and round. Do let us go and watch him."

"Come back!" cried a big rabbit sharply. "It is an old trick of the fox. As soon as you are near enough he will pounce on you and eat you."

The rabbits all ran off in a fright, and the fox saw their little white scuts disappearing down the burrows.

"No rabbits for dinner to-night," he said. "What about Farmer Giles's hens? I'll see if I can get into the hen-roost and snap up a chicken."

He ran quietly down to the farm and squeezed himself through a small hole in the fence. But the watchdog smelt him, and began to bark, so that the farmer looked out of the window.

"You wretch!" said the fox to the dog. "You and I both belong to the dog family and yet you give me away like this. I will be even with you one day."

"Rubbish!" said the dog. "I wish I were loose, then I would chase you."

"I should go too fast," said the fox.

"Ah, but I should get you in the end," said the dog. "I chase you by scent, for you have some little scent-glands at the root of your tail, and the grease that comes from them has such a strong smell that you can easily be traced by it."

"I can always trick you," said the fox with a laugh, and ran hurriedly off as the farmer came out with his gun.

Many a time had Reynard tricked the hounds that hunted him. He knew quite well that they chased him by scent, and he had all kinds of dodges to put them off. He would double back on his own track, and then jump sideways off it. The dogs would follow it, and find that it came suddenly to an end. They did not know that he had gone back again and jumped off it in the middle.

Sometimes Reynard would run along by a wall, and then jump to the top of it. He would run along the top for some distance, and then jump down again. The dogs did not know that he had jumped up on the wall, and would be puzzled because the scent suddenly ended at the foot.

The fox spoke truly when he told the dog that both of them belonged to the same family. The fox is really a beautiful wild dog, very clever and very destructive to the farmer's poultry. If he were not kept for hunting he would soon be extinct in this country, for the farmers would trap and shoot him mercilessly.

He lives in an old burrow belonging to a rabbit or badger, or sometimes will make an earth for himself. His wife makes a very good mother to the charming little cubs, and teaches them all they

Frances Pitt.

BRER FOX

This pretty study of a dog fox shows clearly the pointed nose, white waistcoat and dark legs of the animal. The fox is noted for speed and endurance, as well as cunning.

should know before she turns them away at five or six months old to seek their own fortune.

OUR DOGS

WE all love our dogs, for they are such good friends, always ready for a game and willing to die for us if need be. They are anxious to please us, delighted to be with us, and eager to love and be loved.

They are very different from cats. For one thing, a dog will not put out his claws and scratch you if you anger him. He cannot do that, for he has no muscles to pull his claws in and out as a cat has. They are not sharp, but blunt, for he continually wears them down as he runs about. His pads, too, are not soft and velvety, but rough and hard. He prefers them to be hard.

He cannot see in the dark as a cat can. The pupils of his eyes do not contract like Tibby's. Neither is his tongue as rough as hers.

Sport and General.

A CLEVER ALSATIAN FAMILY
Very alert and intelligent are Alsatians, which are really the sheep dogs of Northern France. They very much resemble the wolf in appearance. Properly trained, the Alsatian makes an excellent guard and house dog, but is apt to prove dangerous if not well managed.

"Scrape meat off a bone with my *tongue!*" we can imagine him saying scornfully. "Of course not! I crunch up meat, bones and all, with my strong teeth."

A dog's world is more of a smell-world than a world of seeing and hearing. He can smell things from a long distance, and uses his nose to find things much more often than his eyes. Because he likes to snuffle along the ground so much, his muzzle is long and pointed, for this helps him in his sniffing.

Unlike the cat, the dog always bolts his

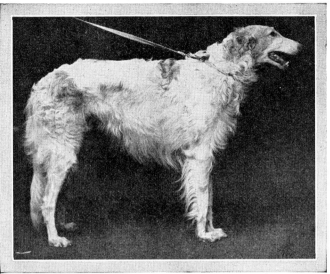

THE BORZOI   *Sport and General.*

Here is a Borzoi or Russian hound, one of the handsomest of all dogs, very powerful and very fast, but not blessed with any great amount of intelligence. The jaw power is very great and a Borzoi is said to be a match for a wolf.

food, and even if there is no other animal near, and he has plenty of time in which to eat it, it makes no difference. He bolts it just the same. This habit is centuries old, and comes from the time when the dog was a wild animal and hunted in a pack.

When a kill was made the hungry animals crowded round to eat. Those who ate slowly got little. Those who ate quickly got much. So the custom among dog packs was to gulp meat down quickly in order to get as much as possible, and the habit remains to this day.

Why Dogs turn round before resting

Another curious custom of the dog is one you have probably noticed when he is just about to lie down; he turns himself round and round and round before he finally settles. Why is this?

This habit also dates from long ago when the dog went to rest in a bed of wild reeds. Before he could lie down

BLOODHOUNDS   *Sport and General.*

Three bloodhounds are shown here with a retriever. Clever dogs are bloodhounds, with marvellous powers of scent; and, in spite of their rather formidable appearance, kindly creatures. The bloodhound that formerly used to hunt runaway slaves was the Cuban variety, a different and more ferocious dog.

THE IRISH SETTER   *Sport and General.*

Beautiful dogs are Irish setters, most useful to sportsmen because they mark down game. There are five distinct breeds of setter dogs. The Irish kind is not the largest, and you will always know him by his glistening red coat. He is distantly related to the spaniel.

other dog does the same and in a trice they are gambolling round one another, all their fear gone.

When a dog wags his tail it is the same thing as a smile. Animals never smile, for that means baring the teeth, which to them is a preparation for a fight. The wagging tail is a very useful signal, and the dog uses it a great deal.

A dog's eagerness for games, its hatred of being left alone, or of being lost, its loyalty and comradeship, all come from its old habit of living in a pack with scores of other dogs.

comfortably he had to bend the reeds over, and to do this he turned round and round, so making a nice flat place on which to lie. Our domesticated dog still does this, although there is no need for it. He cannot get out of the habit!

Do you know why a dog wags its tail when it wants to make friends? Watch two dogs walking up to one another. Do you see how stiff they make themselves, how the hackles rise on their backs, how alert they are in case the other is going to fight? Perhaps they want to be friends, but how can they show it? Their whole bodies are stiff and tense; only their tails are free to show what they feel. Then one dog begins to wag his tail, the signal of friendship. The

Let us be sure to treat our dog well, and give him clean water, good food, and a warm kennel. Such a true and loving comrade should have the best we can afford.

TERRIER   *Sport and General.*

The terrier is the most English of dogs. The one in this picture is of the wire-haired variety. The terrier is the best of all house dogs, the best ratter and the best companion.

MAN'S FRIEND—THE HORSE

Keystone.

A ROUND-UP OF WILD PONIES

In England ponies roam wild in the New Forest and over the rugged open spaces of Dartmoor and Exmoor. During early autumn they are rounded-up and the best of them sold. These ponies are on their way to a village in the New Forest where they are kept until the sales.

NO one really knows when the horse became one of the helpers of man. The dog, we think, was his earliest friend. Most likely the horse was his second animal friend.

The real home of the horse, long long ago, is said to have been the grass-lands of Central Asia. As we know he is a grazing and browsing animal, we can understand why he has no claws or talons like the lion or cat. He does not have to kill that he may eat, or to rend and tear his food apart. His strong horny hoofs are just right for getting about where there is sweet grass, and herbage, and the young growth of trees and shrubs.

He was well adapted for the wild life he had to live long ago. His strong long legs, with which he gallops so swiftly, soon took him out of danger. His eyes look in a sideways direction and not forward; for danger was most likely to threaten from right or left as he walked along the rough ground

searching for good grass. He might be attacked by a crouching tiger or other member of the great cat family. Our horses to-day still shy at some abrupt movement on their right or left, or a rustling near their feet, and we give them blinkers to wear to prevent them from seeing sideways and being fright-ened. Shying is an inborn habit formed long ago. Another interesting fact about the horse is that, without turning his head in any way, he can move the trumpets of his ears so that he can locate correctly some sudden sound.

The wandering tribes of the grass-lands must have soon seen the value of the horse. He never attacked them. They could attract the little foals to them by offering them fresh grass or shoots of young shrubs that they especi-ally liked. Tame horses must soon have proved very useful. They carried to the primitive home the spoils of the chase, the heavy carcase of a bear or other game. When the family moved,

92

WILLING WORKERS!

The horse has been used for thousands of years for pulling vehicles on wheels. At the turn of the present century horses provided the main means of transport in this country. Nowadays their work is made lighter by the smooth roads, which also permit the use of wheels small enough to carry rubber tyres, better for quiet running. However, horse traffic is not very common to-day, for it has been replaced by the motor vehicle.

Photos : Fox Photos.

Horses have also been used in past ages for turning wheels which pump water, particularly in the hot countries of Asia where water is often difficult to obtain. This horse is working a cider-press at Prestbury, in Gloucestershire. The vertical wheel crushes the apples, from the juice of which is made delicious cider. Donkeys are also used for work of this kind and, in spite of their characteristic obstinacy, make very useful workers.

Miles Bros.

WORKING HORSES OF THE ENGLISH SHIRES

These powerful-looking animals are descended from the war-horses of the Middle Ages when they were ridden by knights in heavy armour. To-day these heavy draught-horses are known as Shires. In Scotland the Clydesdale takes the place of the Shire, whilst in East Anglia there is a chestnut breed known as the Suffolk Punch.

they helped to carry the household goods, skins, baskets, pots and other simple home-made things. Perhaps they carried the children. Man probably soon learnt to ride on horseback, and the swift horse helped him in his hunting or fighting. But we can only guess how the friendship between man and the horse began. However, we may be sure children had some part in it. They must at an early age have climbed or been lifted on the horse's back and enjoyed their high position and a ride.

From central Asia the horse travelled with its masters south to Media, Persia, Babylonia, Assyria, Syria, Asia Minor and Egypt. The Persians became famous horsemen. In these lands, perhaps because of its gracefulness, beautiful walk and gallop, it never became a beast of burden; it drew the chariots of kings and great people, or war chariots.

The tame horse first appeared in history in Babylonia about two thousand years before the birth of Christ (2100 B.C.), and in Egypt about 1700 B.C.

Huge carvings on the stone walls of the Temple of Karnak made about 1580 B.C. can still be seen among the ruins. They show the figure of Pharaoh as he stands in his war chariot scattering his enemy before his plunging horses.

The horse has a wonderful past. From the time he became the friend of man until to-day his history has been one of progress, as we shall see.

The Arab horse is the most famous horse in history. He is a descendant of the Asiatic wild horse and the horses of Babylonia, Assyria, Asia Minor and

Egypt. It is strange that the Arabs, who were at first camel riders only, should care so much for the horse. Perhaps it was because the camel so often grumbled and the horse became a loving, patient friend. In any case, by the sixth century of our era—about A.D. 520—the Arabs were in possession of a breed of horses that they loved and spoke of with great reverence as though they were a precious gift from the past, as indeed they were. We have all read stories of the devotion of the Arab to his steed.

The Arab horse, perhaps because of his master's care, was a magnificent animal, the swiftest of all horses. He came to Europe when the Arabs invaded Spain in the eighth and ninth centuries. The Crusaders also may have brought some Arab horses from the East. It is said there is Arab blood in our race-horses to-day, and it is this strain that has helped us to breed the swiftest horse the world has known, the British Thoroughbred.

Able to do Hard Work

The history of our great horses, horses that pull heavy weights, heavy draught-horses (draught means drawing; draught-horses are horses for drawing carts, ploughs, etc.), dray-horses (dray, a low brewer's cart without sides, for heavy loads), is very interesting. These big horses date from the Middle Ages. In the Middle Ages the swift Arab horses were not always suitable, for it was the time when knights wore heavy armour, and the weight of this armour was very great indeed. Therefore, a breed of big war-horses came into being, massive creatures with thick necks, broad shoulders and stout legs. They

Topical.

TAKING A JUMP IN PERFECT FASHION

From the earliest periods of history the horse was domesticated and trained in agriculture, travel, warfare and sport, and has been the most valuable of animals to man. Our picture shows a fine example of the trained horse of to-day, the famous " Foxhunter " taking a jump at the International Horse Show in London.

were truly noble creatures, these mighty war-horses, and we can see their descendants in our hard-working farm-horses of the English shires, known as Shires, our Clydesdales in Scotland, and other breeds of sturdy horses such as the Suffolk Punch and the London dray-horse.

Horses more like the Arab horses that we use to-day are hunters, racers and saddle-horses for ordinary riding. It is interesting to keep one's eyes open and make a list of horses that work for us or give us pleasure to-day.

Wild Horses To-day

There are some wild horses in the world to-day, but they are probably not the descendants of the first wild horses of the grasslands of Central Asia but the descendants of tame horses that have "run wild" again in lonely places. The most numerous and best known of the "wild" horses of to-day

are the mustangs that roam the prairies of North America and the pampas of South America. They owe their origin solely to Spanish adventurers of long ago, who brought the horse to the Americas. Many of these adventurers died of hunger or were killed in fights, but their horses survived them. They were able to find grass on the prairies and plains, where they lived a free life.

The nearest approach to the wild horses of long ago are those found on the rolling uplands of Mongolia and the steppes of Asia. The wild horses of the steppes are called tarpans. They are smaller in size than the wild horses of Mongolia. The tarpans may be the descendants of the original wild horses of Central Asia or descendants of tame horses that strayed from travellers' caravans.

Ponies

The nearest approach to "wild" horses in our islands are our ponies. The Shetland pony, a native of the Shetland Islands, is perhaps the smallest and may be only 36 inches in height. It is a hardy, obedient little horse, allowed to run nearly wild and find food for itself. In winter it grows a much longer coat as a protection against damp and cold. On Exmoor and Dartmoor and in the New Forest there are half-wild ponies living their own lives and finding their own food. In stormy weather their good sense leads them to find protection behind high hedges or thickets, and in the case of heavy snow they do not hesitate to visit farms and homesteads. In the autumn the moorsmen round them up and the best of them are sold.

Fox Photos.

THE OBEDIENT DONKEY

A humble member of the horse family is the donkey. From earliest times this animal's powers of endurance and obedience has made it highly useful to mankind. In tropical climates the donkey can carry heavy loads without distress.

Country Life.

PONIES AND THEIR RIDERS AT THE SHOW

The pony is the oldest breed of domesticated horse, a small type ranging from 8 to 14 hands in height (a hand measures 4 inches). Our picture shows three children's ponies, not exceeding 12·2 hands, awaiting the verdict of the judges in the final test at the International Horse Show in London.

Various breeds of ponies are used in the game of polo, but the most popular are the English-bred New Forest, Dartmoor, Exmoor and Welsh ponies.

The Donkey or Ass

Another member of the horse family is the donkey, a hardy little animal with a thicker and warmer coat than that of the horse. He is, too, far better able to live where green-stuff is scanty than the horse. He differs from the horse in having a tuft of hair at the end of his tail, long ears and an upright mane. His original home was in North Africa, where he once roamed wild in Nubia. He had a dark streak down the back from the mane to the tail, and sometimes a dark band across the shoulders.

It is said that the donkey became the friend of man before the horse. In any case donkeys were used in Egypt at a very early date, and before the horse.

Egyptian merchants used them for carrying goods because of their strength, power of endurance and obedience. They were quite willing to jog along for great distances with heavy loads. They often carried new products from Nubia to Egypt. Donkey caravans often went from Egypt into Asia, travelling along the coast of Canaan to Syria and the East. In Bible days the Hebrew race always rode upon donkeys and not horses, perhaps because the horse was associated with war. If a white donkey were reared, as sometimes happened, it was kept for the use of very great people.

We do not know when the donkey first came to the British Isles. They are mentioned in the reign of Queen Elizabeth as though they were introduced then. They were never well cared for in our islands as the horse was, and so never became popular. This was a pity, as they might have

WHAT THE QUAGGA LOOKED LIKE

Allied to the zebras, the quagga once roamed happily and in considerable numbers in the northern parts of Cape Province. It had no stripes on its legs or hinder parts and was small in size. This animal has been extinct since about 1880.

In Asia the wild asses, like those of Africa, live in the waste places. They are found in the poor grasslands, the wind-swept steppes, the semi-deserts and high mountain plateaux throughout Asia, from Syria to Persia and Western India and northwards through the dryer parts of Central Asia and Mongolia. These wild asses are fleet of foot and enduring like those of Africa. They live in small families of four or five, though they sometimes congregate in herds. Their food too is the same : grasses of various kinds in the lower parts of their range, but woody plants on the high mountain plateaux.

become really fine animals in Britain. To see what a fine animal a donkey can be we must go to Egypt, Arabia, Syria, Italy, Malta or the United States.

Wild Donkeys of To-day

Not many people know that the wild donkey of long ago still exists to-day in Africa and Asia.

In Africa the wild ass is found in the desert regions of the north-eastern portion of this continent—Abyssinia, Somaliland, the Sudan and the dry districts bordering the Red Sea. Wild asses are very fine animals, so fleet and enduring that they cannot be overtaken even by a well-mounted horseman. Although the grass is scanty, they always seem in good condition. They like to drink regularly and will often travel long distances at night to get water. A herd of wild asses consists of only four or five—just a small family. Their bray is said to be the same as the bray of our domesticated asses.

The flesh of the wild ass is eaten by the natives of the Sudan.

Some of the asses have special names. On the high mountain plateaux of Tibet and Mongolia lives the *kiang*, the largest and most horse-like of the wild asses of Asia. He is dark reddish-brown in colour with a very narrow stripe along his back. He is said to be a more confiding animal than most wild asses, and very curious, so that he will often approach to within a short distance of any unfamiliar object, such as a sportsman engaged in stalking other game. In Western India and in Baluchistan lives the *onager*, a slightly smaller animal than the kiang and lighter in colour, with a broader stripe running along his back. In Persia and Syria very similar wild asses are to be found. They are said to be very wary and difficult to approach.

When we see our fat little donkeys at the seaside, we must think of the brave wild donkeys far away, donkeys that are the perfection of activity and courage.

THE TRUE ZEBRA

W. S. Berridge.

Zebras are donkey-like animals, mostly native to South Africa, and there are at least three distinct types. The one depicted above is the true zebra and his bold pattern of stripes is a study in plain black and white. Zebras can be seen in zoos in many parts of the world.

The Mule

The mule is the offspring of a male donkey and a mare. Mules have longer ears and smaller hoofs than the horse, and their weather-proof coats are less sensitive. They are especially valuable because they are as sure-footed as goats and have a wonderful ability for picking their way over rough places. They are therefore much used in mountainous lands where roads are few and far between and the direct routes from place to place merely boulder-strewn tracks leading up hill and down dale. As a rule they are extremely hardy and free from disease, so they have a long life of usefulness; they can also live on the sparsest fare. We can think therefore of many countries where they will be needed — all countries with bad roads, or where food is scarce, or where extremes of weather have to be faced. In many places mules are used as pack-animals, carrying heavy loads slung on either side of their backs. It is an interesting sight to see a long line of pack-mules proceeding snake-like in single file, following their leader. The *one* man in charge of a train of mules is called a muleteer.

It must be remembered that mules were used from very early times. Long ago merchants' caravans in the East were composed of pack-mules. The Greeks and Romans valued them and used them to draw carriages. In Britain, when roads were bad and industries and trade increasing, trains of pack-mules were sometimes used as well as pack-horses. In modern

THE ONAGER, ONE OF THE WILD DONKEYS

This sure-footed, hardy creature is a native of Syria, Persia and certain parts of India. It is somewhat the colour of sand and has a darker stripe running down its back. Very swift in its movements, it is by no means easy to catch.

times they have been largely employed for military transport.

" As stubborn as a mule " is not altogether a true saying. They are most intelligent animals as well as very handsome. The saying should more truthfully be " as intelligent as a mule."

The principal mule countries in Europe are the south of France, Spain, Portugal and Italy. Fine mules are bred to be used in carriages. The mules of Asia Minor, Syria, Cyprus, Egypt and Algeria are good. In the Punjab provinces of India excellent mules are reared, and in North and South Armenia. But the finest and handsomest mules are said to be bred in Spain, the United States and North-west India.

The Zebra

The zebras are very like donkeys, but they differ from them because of their beautifully striped skins. Both donkeys and zebras have short erect manes, the upper part of the tail is free from long hairs, and the ears longer than those of the horse. They are natives chiefly of the southern and eastern parts of Africa. There are at least three types of zebras, differing only in their stripes. First there is the *mountain zebra*, a true zebra. Its black stripes are beautifully arranged on a white background. Its native home is the mountainous region of Cape Province and the great Drakensberg Range, but not many of these lovely animals now roam freely in these parts.

The second type of zebra is perhaps the largest and handsomest of all the zebras and most graceful in its movements. Its stripes are very narrow, numerous and deep black in colour, and are separated by equally narrow white bands. It is plentiful in East Africa, especially between Mount Kenya and Lake Rudolf.

The third type of zebra is the most numerous and best known of the zebras. It is a strong muscular animal but smaller than the second type, though not

Oscar Marcus.

A SHETLAND PONY AND HER FOAL

The smallest British breed of horses comes from the Shetland Isles, Scotland, and is believed to be the direct descendants from the British horse of prehistoric times. A fully-grown Shetland may be only a yard (9 hands) in height. Our photograph was taken on the island of Yell in the Shetlands.

as small as the mountain zebra. It has a pale yellow ground colour and broad black or dark brown stripes. Colts of this type are easily caught and become very tame and confiding; but they are not easy to break in like the horse and have no wish to be ridden by man, though willing to be friendly with him. Indeed, the zebra is rather too spectacular for everyday life. One cannot imagine anyone riding or hunting on a zebra! Moreover, the zebras are so fleet of foot that, if one bolted with his rider, it would not be pleasant for the rider!

Miles Bros.

A PERFECT THOROUGHBRED

This slim, graceful creature is a good example of the racehorse, and its lines should be compared with those of the Shire horses on a previous page. The horse seen above is "Sheila's Cottage," a winner of the Grand National.

Perhaps they serve us best by letting us enjoy their beauty at the Zoo or in the grasslands of Africa. This third type is plentiful in East Africa from the plains north of the Orange River to Lake Rudolf. It is often called the *quagga* because it is like a type of zebra called the quagga, which is now extinct. In size, build and general appearance the two are alike, but the real quagga was not so beautifully marked as its handsome relation. Both have the same barking neigh, "quā-hā-hā, quā-hā-hā." The word "quagga" is pronounced in South Africa "quā-hā" and is of Hottentot origin. It is an imitation of the animals' neighing call. To-day these zebras of the third type are always called "quā-hās" by both Dutch and British.

The grasslands of South and East Africa were the happy feeding lands of all types of zebras until the coming of the white man rapidly reduced their numbers. To-day, however, they are again on the increase because they are protected by the government. They are allowed to lead their natural lives in vast areas of grasslands specially set aside for them.

A herd of zebras peacefully feeding in their own wild pastures is a wonderful sight. It is still more wonderful to see with what tremendous speed they gallop off if they see or hear the slightest cause for alarm. The little colts keep up with their parents because of their long legs. The young of all members of the horse tribe are born with unusually long legs. We have all noticed the length of leg of a very young colt in a field with his mother. The reason for the length is clear—the foal must never drop behind if danger threatens. It is interesting when one goes to a Zoo to notice the stripes on the zebras there, and see if one can pick out a quagga of to-day, a mountain zebra, or one with very narrow stripes.

We will end with some thought-provoking words about the horse by Sir William Flower: "If we were not so habituated to the sight of the horse as hardly ever to consider its structure, we should greatly marvel at being told of an animal so strongly constructed that it had but a single toe on each extremity, on the end of the nail of which it walked or galloped. Such a conformation is without parallel in the vertebrate series."

APES AND THE MONKEY FOLK

A MEETING OF THE RHESUS FAMILY

Fox Photos.

The Rhesus monkeys, seen above, belong to a family found abundantly in northern India and China. They are among the best-known of all monkeys, and no species has been more closely studied.

THE Gorilla is the biggest of the apes. It is a strange-looking beast, very ugly and fierce. Its home is in dense forests, near the equator, and not many have been seen by travellers. Occasionally young ones are brought to the zoos to be shown, but they do not live very long in captivity.

In its native home the young gorilla lives in trees, springing easily from branch to branch. At night time the father gorilla keeps guard over his family. They sleep in the tree-tops, but he stands down below, ready to attack if any danger approaches.

In the morning the family set off to find food. They like fruit, sugar cane, honey, the eggs of birds, and will also catch and eat insects. It would be a marvellous sight if we could see the family setting off on their daily search for food. All three of them—father, mother and youngster—go through the trees, leaping and swinging for miles in this way. If the father sees anything on the ground that he wants he thinks nothing of leaping from his perch 30 feet or more above the ground, down to the earth below. He never hurts himself when he lands, for he knows exactly how to fall.

When it rains the little family sit down and cover their heads with their arms, which are very hairy indeed. The hairs grow downwards from the shoulder to the elbow, and upwards from the wrist to the elbow, so the rain simply runs down the two sets of hairs and drips off at the elbow point ! Look at your own arms, and you will see that the down or hair there grows in just the same way.

One curious point about the gorilla is that it does not seem to talk and chatter as do some other members of the big monkey family. Father Gorilla can bark sharply in anger and roar when he is attacking, and the mother will scream. Beyond this and the pitiful cry of a lost baby gorilla, the animals appear to have no voices.

We should not like to meet the

A BABOON AND A GORILLA

The animal here depicted is the Gelada, a member of the baboon family found in Abyssinia and Arabia. Geladas live together in large groups. Their nostrils are set at the side of their muzzles and dark hair grows profusely above the eyes. The males wear a cape of hair over the shoulders.

Photos: F. W. Bond.

Here is a typical gorilla. These creatures are the largest of man-like apes and are immensely strong. Dark in colour, a gorilla possesses enormous hands with strong fingers, though his thumbs are shorter than those of human beings. As a rule he walks on all fours, and it is unusual to see him erect on his hind legs.

BABY ORANG-UTAN *F. W. Bond.*
It is an odd fact that the young of the great apes are quite intelligent. This baby orang-utan was most amusing and affectionate. But after about two years the skull closes down and the whole nature of the animal changes for the worse.

gorilla family, for all of them are very ugly. Their arms and jaws are big and powerful. Their heads are large, and they have a huge, gaping mouth set with great teeth. Their eyes are small, and deep set, and under their chin grows a ruff of hair. They have black skin, and short, dark grey hair growing all over their body.

They do not walk as we do, for although they can stand upright, they prefer to walk on all fours. Their hands are not placed flat upon the ground, but the fingers are bent inwards, so that they really walk upon their knuckles. They use the soles of their hind feet as we do.

The Chimpanzee

Another ape is the Chimpanzee. Perhaps you have seen the chimpanzees' tea party at the London Zoo. All the chimpanzees at the party have been taught to drink milk from a mug, and

to eat from a plate. One of them will even hand the dish of fruit very politely to another! They sit on chairs, and behave very nicely indeed.

The chimpanzee lives in the same kind of hot forest as the gorilla. He likes to build a nest of tree boughs, and here his family sleep, whilst he rests near by to guard them.

The Orang-utan also lives in the trees, where he finds his long arms very useful for swinging himself about. They are so long that when he stands upright and hangs them by his side they reach the ground!

But he does not often come to the ground, for his food grows in the trees. He loves to feast on fruit and leaves. When he is frightened and swings himself through the branches he can get along just as fast as a man running on the ground below.

ORANG FULLY GROWN *F. W. Bond.*
Compare the baby orang with this monster, with its savage little deep-set eyes and terrific arms. With its bare fingers this great ape ripped the steel netting covering its cage and escaped into a tree in the Zoo, giving the keepers tremendous trouble to recapture it.

MISCHIEVOUS MONKEYS

DO you like watching monkeys? I expect you do! They are so mischievous and comical and they seem so human when they use their little hand-paws for holding nuts or bananas.

But they cannot use their hind-paws for walking as we use our feet. A monkey has really four hands, instead of two feet and two hands, so he walks clumsily when he is on the ground; but when

F. W. Bond.
SPIDER MONKEY
This sad-looking spider monkey is an inhabitant of North and South America and the only one of its kind which lives as far north as Mexico. It gains its name from its immensely long arms and legs.

Zoological Society of London.
LANGUR WITH BABY
India is a great country for monkeys, and since the Hindus hold them to be sacred animals they are amazingly tame. This picture shows a female Langur, with her bald-headed baby clasped in her arms.

he is in the trees, how useful his four hands are then!

There are many monkeys. Some are called "the dog-faced monkeys"; they are the Baboons, and if you look at the picture of them you will know why they have that name. They do not live in the trees as the monkeys do, but run about on the ground. They have four feet-like hands, instead of four hand-like feet.

They like to live together in bands,

F. W. Bond.

ONE OF THE MACAQUES

Macaque monkeys are found in India, parts of China and Japan, whilst one group of these animals lives on the Rock of Gibraltar.

Monkeys, the commonest kind there is. You will see them in every zoo.

Monkeys of the New and Old Worlds

Did you know that the American or New World monkeys are different from the Old World monkeys of Africa and Asia? You might think that from wherever a monkey came he would be just the same as every other monkey in the world. But that is not so.

The New World monkeys have no cheek-pouches, so they cannot put nuts into their cheeks, as you may have seen Old World monkeys doing. Another big difference is that they have no proper thumbs on their hands, as the Old World monkeys have.

The third difference is that New World monkeys never have the bare or brightly coloured hindquarters seen in the monkeys of the Old World.

One of the prettiest of New World monkeys is the Marmoset. It is just about as big as our squirrel.

and do a great deal of damage to crops, for they can spoil a whole field in a single night. They always set one of their number as sentinel, and he keeps watch whilst they feed. If he barks it means " Danger! Run away! " and off they all scamper helter-skelter to the hills.

The brightly-coloured Mandrill Baboon is a strange-looking beast. Someone once said that he showed a sunrise in front and a sunset behind! His face has purple and blue markings, and his nose is tipped with bright scarlet. He wears an orange beard, and a crest of black hair. His hindquarters are a very bright scarlet indeed. He is quite the strangest of all the monkeys.

Have you ever seen an organ grinder with a little monkey sitting on top of the barrel organ, perhaps holding out an old cap for pennies? These little street monkeys are usually Green

W. S. Berridge.

THE WHITE-THIGHED COLOBUS

This monkey, which is also known as the Guereza, makes its home in Abyssinia, where it lives in small families in tall trees.

THE STORY OF THE DEER

Universal Photographic Press.

STAGS PUTTING THEIR ANTLERS TO THE TEST
In this photograph we see a battle between two red stags. Heads down, they struggle desperately.
Sometimes their antlers, which are elastic, become interlocked, and if there is no one to help,
the fighters perish from starvation.

THE deer was talking to the antelope, who was staring at him in surprise.

"Where have your antlers gone?" asked the antelope. "Last time I saw you, you had fine spreading antlers, and now you have none!"

"That is nothing," said the deer. "You keep your hollow horns all your life, and never part with them. But I grow my solid antlers anew every year, and each time they are bigger than before."

Of course, this statement by the deer was perfectly true. Almost all the males of this interesting family are provided with horns or antlers, one set being dropped every year and another set grown. You can indeed tell with accuracy the age of a stag by counting the number of branches on his antlers.

"But how do you do that?" asked the antelope.

"Do you see these two knobs on the top of my head?" said the deer, bending his neck down. "Well, they are my new antlers just beginning to grow. If you could feel them you would find that they were very warm."

"I see them," said the antelope. "They are red and inflamed. Do you mean to tell me that those little knobs will grow into great antlers?"

"That is so," answered the deer. "Watch them during the next few weeks, and you will see that I am speaking the truth."

What "Velvet" Means

The antelope watched. He saw the knobby swellings rise into a soft pulpy mass covered with a mossy coat of hair.

"That mossy stuff is called 'velvet,' you know," said the deer. "It feels very soft."

Day by day the knobs grew larger, and soon the antlers began to develop from them and branch out. They became very tall and splendid-looking, and the deer was proud of them.

"They are fully-grown now," he said. "I shall rub off the 'velvet' against a tree. Come and see me do it."

The antelope watched him rub off the mossy "velvet," and admired the deer's fine branching antlers.

"I wish my little horns would fall off, and that I could grow antlers every year like you," he said.

"It is rather a nuisance whilst they are growing," said the deer. "You see, I use my antlers to fight with, and when I have none I have to hide myself away until they grow again. But now that they are grown, I shall go to find

107

a little doe for a wife. Perhaps I shall have to fight another stag like myself for her, and we shall use our horns."

" Don't get them locked together," said the antelope. " I once saw two stags fighting, and they interlocked their horns so that they could not get away from one another. Then, of course, they could not feed, so they slowly starved to death."

" I shall be careful about that! " said the deer, and he ran lightly away.

The Reindeer

He was a reindeer, and in the winter and spring time he lived in the forest with his brothers. But when the summer came the gadflies began to bite, and the deer had to get away from the tormenting insects. So he and his friends went up into the cool hills, where there were no gadflies, and stayed there until the winter.

When snow covered the ground it was difficult to find food. The reindeer looked for reindeer moss, which often grew beneath the snow. Then they had to scrape away the snow with their hoofs to get at the moss underneath.

The Elk is the biggest of the deer family, and wears enormous antlers. We have three different kinds of deer in our own country, the red deer, the fallow deer and the roebuck. You may see them in many of our parks, and perhaps be lucky enough to catch a glimpse of the baby fawns; they are shy, pretty little creatures, soft-eyed and graceful.

Major A. Radcliffe Dugmore.

A CARIBOU OF THE SNOWLANDS

The caribou s a near relative of the reindeer, but you find the latter only in the Arctic, whilst the former roams in the vast woodlands of Canada. Our picture shows a stag, about three years old, making his way through the undergrowth which is just powdered with the first snows of the long, hard winter. You may see members of the caribou family in most zoological gardens.

THE TALE OF THE STAG'S ANTLERS

(1) Stags drop their horns or antlers every year and grow a fresh set.

(2) In the spring you would see only two knobs on the animal's cranium.

(3) Very hot and feverish these knobs would be, for they are filled with blood.

(4) Growing quickly, the horns form like plants, branching out as they develop.

(5) At this stage they are covered with fine hair and the animal is " in velvet."

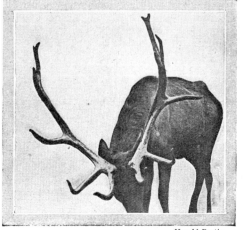

Harold Bastin.

(6) Once the antlers are complete the proud stag chooses his wife and fights for her.

"HIGH O'ER THE FENCE!—"

G. P. A.

The curious animal here illustrated is the Gerenuk, which hails from East Africa. Its extra-ordinary attitude in the picture can only mean that it is trying to show off its height. The creature's neck is so long that it makes one think instinctively of the giraffe, yet the animal is really a member of the large antelope family. The gerenuk lives upon leaves and the soft young twigs of trees. In colour it is a reddish fawn, but it wears a dark band down its back.

THE GRACEFUL ANTELOPE

Africa abounds in antelopes of all kinds, from small creatures no bigger than dogs to huge beasts as large as cattle. This picture shows a group of Impala in the Kruger National Park, South Africa. The bulls have curly horns, the young males short horns, and the females no horns. These are said to be the swiftest and most graceful members of the antelope family.

Here are two fine Waterbuck, inhabitants of the African bushveldt. Their horns may measure 30 inches or more, and they have coarse brown hair. They seldom form herds of more than twenty animals, and are of little use to man. Though named from their love of marshes and water-meadows, in some parts they prefer steep, rocky hillsides, where they are very sure-footed.

SOME WATER-LOVERS

Capt. E. Mills Joyce.

SEAL HUNTING 'MIDST ICE AND SNOW

Our photograph gives you an excellent idea of the conditions under which seals and sea lions are hunted in the Arctic. Some victims of the hunter lie dead in the snow, and you will notice that the sleigh is drawn by " huskies," as these draught-dogs of the ice regions are called. Seals are said to be far fewer in number than they were at the beginning of the century.

I AM sure you have seen Seals and Sea Lions at a zoo or menagerie. They are water-lovers, and are never so happy as when they are gambolling about on the surface, or diving down below to swim under water.

They are not fish, of course, for they are warm-blooded, and have no scales as fish have. Neither have they fins or gills.

The seal manages to keep himself quite warm in the icy waters in which he swims. He has a double coat of hair, and a thick layer of fat. This is the true, or earless hair seal.

The seal keeps his coat well oiled, so that it acts like a macintosh, and does not let the water in to wet his body. The oil oozes out from hundreds of tiny bags in his skin, and as fast as he uses it up more is made.

When he swims, his nose is always closed up tightly to keep the water out. He can get along very fast indeed, using his two back flippers like oars, turning and twisting whatever way he wills. Few fish escape him when he sets out to chase them.

Another interesting point about seals is that they do not go very far from the coast. This is because they love to come ashore and bask in the sun on a rocky ledge. When moving on land they arch their backs like caterpillars and draw forward the hind legs.

Sea Lions or Fur Seals

The sea lions are often called the Fur Seals, because they have a coat of close woolly fur under the outer coat of long hairs. They do not look at all like lions, nor do they act like them. These sea lions have sharper muzzles and also

MONKEYS AND THEIR WAYS

F. W. Bond

The Monkeys are probably the most interesting of all animals, for the simple reason that they resemble human beings more closely than any other creatures. The pair seen above are both chimpanzees and they came from West Africa, though the tribe ranges over most of tropical Africa. As a general rule, these apes travel in parties, using all four limbs when running on the ground, but swinging from branch to branch whilst in the trees. They are as active, agile and graceful as any member of the monkey race.

CATCHES BIRDS ON THE WING

The creature depicted above is the smallest of the man-like apes and is known as the Silvery Gibbon. It makes its home in Malaya and other parts of the Far East and is able to readily to walk upright on its hind legs. It spends most of its life in trees, however, and is so quick with its long arms that it can catch birds as they fly past.

Photos: F. W. Bond

This docile and happy little animal is a Mangabey Monkey, a native of the great Congo district of Africa. If you look closely, you will see he has white eyelids. These monkeys are long-tailed, and because they are so easily tamed have made themselves popular as pets.

A BABOON AND A BABY GORILLA

Topical Press

It is in Africa and the countries bordering on the Red Sea that the true Baboons are found, and they are among the ugliest and most ferocious of the monkey tribes, though the one in our picture appears in a thoughtful mood. The arms and legs of the baboon are nearly equal in length so that they run on all fours with ease.

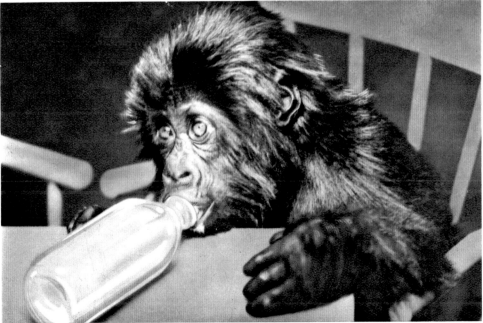

Fox Photos

Gorillas are the largest of the man-like apes, but in this picture we have a baby gorilla which was presented to the London Zoo and had to be taught how to feed itself. Here it is seen drinking milk from a bottle. In addition, numerous oranges and grapefruit formed its diet.

A BRUSH-UP FOR THE ORANG-UTAN

The name Orang-utan is a Malay word meaning "man of the woods," and it needs care to keep them happy in captivity till old age. Their main characteristic, distinguishing them from the chimpanzee and gorilla, is the greater length of their arms, plainly noticeable in the photograph above. When fully grown the orang-utan stands rather more than 4 ft. in height.

Fox Photos

The Chimpanzee is the most human of all the apes and is the one which best imitates the ways of man. Generally speaking, the chimpanzees are gentle, affectionate and intelligent. Our picture shows a chimpanzee, having warned off other chimpanzees and succeeded in turning the barrow upside down, now contentedly turning the wheel and studying the effect.

SING-HI AND SING-LO FROM CHINA

Graphic Photo Union

Monkeys have long been popular as pets on account of their almost human ways and amusing antics. "Mischievous as a monkey" is a popular saying which has sound basis in fact. Our picture above shows two stump-tailed monkeys, aptly named Sing-Hi and Sing-Lo, shortly after their arrival from China. This performance at their new quarters in a famous Zoo suggests that they had settled down quite happily in their new home.

FROM SOUTH AMERICA, AFRICA AND INDIA

M. W. Maginn

This is Humboldt's Woolly Monkey. It comes from South America and possesses a prehensile tail; that is, a tail that can be used for grasping or seizing purposes.

Neville Kingston

A native of West Africa, the Diana monkey has a long white beard and a curious crescent of white above its eyes. The body is about 18 ins. in length and the tail fairly long.

Neville Kingston

Here is another of the African Diana monkeys, Roloway's type. In a dense, leafy forest it is very difficult to see these animals, which are only about 2 ft. in length.

F. W. Bond

This monkey is the Rhesus, quite common in the northern parts of India. It is about 2 ft. in length with a tail nearly half as long again, whilst its brown fur has a greenish tinge.

ON THE HORIZONTAL BAR

This youthful orang-utan has become mixed-up between the supporting ropes and the horizontal bar. The orang, as you will observe, has most curiously-shaped legs and enormously powerful arms, the limbs designed for the purposes of the life it leads among the trees. Upon the ground an orang is an awkward creature, as unsteady as a toddling child.

Photos: F. W. Bond

The intelligent animals depicted above are chimpanzees from West Africa. They make their homes almost entirely in trees and for their sleeping place construct a platform consisting of branches and twigs. These swaying beds are far above ground level to afford some measure of safety against their natural enemies in the forests and jungles of Africa.

F. W. Bond

The animal in this picture is a typical member of the gorilla family. These creatures are the largest of
the man-like apes and in a wild state are formidable opponents, being ponderous, powerful fighters.
In hue a gorilla is jet-black and his hands are of immense size, with enormously thick, strong fingers.
His thumb is much shorter than yours or mine and he does not, as a general rule, walk on his hind
legs, preferring to proceed on all fours.   In height he exceeds 5 ft.

BASKING IN THE SUN

E. N. A.

A Weddell seal in the Antarctic Ocean. At one time these seals were very common on the islands of the South Atlantic, but they are now much rarer. The pups of the Weddell seal grow very rapidly, putting on as much as seven pounds' weight per day!

Copyright.

These sea-elephants were photographed on the shore of Atlas Cove, in the Heard Islands of the Antarctic Ocean. The sea-elephant is the " monster " of the seal family and, unlike the sea-lions, is classed as a true seal because it does not have external ears. Two species are known, one found in the Antarctic, the other on the Californian coast of the Pacific. Note that the tails consist of a pair of paddles.

MORNING SWIM AND TEA=TIME DIVE

Fox Photos.

Several kinds of true seal can be seen on and around the coasts of Britain, but it is not often the camera-man has an opportunity of photographing one in its natural haunts. Here is a young seal, born in the Scilly Isles, enjoying a swim in a pool on one of the little Westward Islands.

News Chronicle.

Among the popular attractions at the London Zoo the sea-lion seen in this picture is always sure of a good audience at tea-time when fish such as cod or whiting is thrown to him. In appearance the sea-lions, or fur seals, differ from true seals in having sharper muzzles and they use their hind limbs when moving on land.

LIKE A SILVERY STREAK!

Topical Press.

The porpoise has a strange habit of leaping right out of the water and then suddenly diving far into the depths. This most remarkable nature photograph shows a porpoise in the very act of leaving the water as though it were a streak of living silver. The wonderful snapshot was taken from the bows of the steamship *Belgenland* in mid-ocean. Porpoises are fond of swimming in a long, straight line and in this form make you think of the imaginary sea-serpent wriggling through the water at tremendous speed.

8—2

THE COMMON SEAL *W. S. Berridge.*

Seals are found in seas of all the cold and temperate parts of the world. They are warm-blooded animals which have taken to the water, and their principal food is fish. This is the Common Seal, one of the two species found round British coasts.

small external ears, which the true seal lacks. The hind limbs are free from the tail and are used when moving on land.

Sea lions make a barking noise that sounds rather like " Aark-aark-aark," and when excited they are very noisy indeed. Perhaps you have seen and heard them. When they are in captivity and are being fed they are most amusing to watch, for they love to catch the fish that the keeper throws to them. They are as clever at swimming as are the seals, and race along through the water in a beautiful and graceful manner.

They are clever creatures, and can be taught many tricks. They are especially good at balancing things. One sea lion was taught to balance a pole on his nose, with a fish on the end of it. He had to waddle across the stage, and then throw the pole into the air and

catch the fish as it fell. He always got the fish, you may be sure.

The Walrus

The Walrus or Whale Horse, is another water-lover. He is a strange-looking animal, 12 feet or 13 feet long, with great tusks growing from his mouth, often 2 feet in length.

He uses his tusks for many things. He digs in the mud with them when he seeks for shell-fish, and uses them when he wants to cut lumps of flesh off any dead animal he finds. He uses them to raise himself from the water when he goes ashore.

Porpoises love the water too. You may have seen them somewhere off the British coasts, gambolling about merrily. They swim in a queer manner, leaping out of the water, and then diving below it. When porpoises swim in a straight line they look rather like a sea serpent, wriggling along in the sea at a great rate.

SEA LION *F. W. Bond.*

Here is a pretty picture of the seal called the Sea Lion with her baby. Notice that the little thing is covered with wool which is shed as it grows older. Young seals are born on the rocks, and do not learn to swim until a few weeks old.

SIXTY MILES AN HOUR

R. Cartier.

Here we have a fine photograph of two Dolphins travelling at top speed. Notice their curious beaked heads. The dolphin, though it does not grow to a length of more than 8 feet, is actually a member of the whale family; that is, a warm-blooded creature and not a fish. It feeds on small fish, and is one of the fastest swimming of all sea denizens.

THE STORY OF THE WHALE

E. N. A.

OUT OF ITS ELEMENT

This monster whale drifted ashore at a port in the United States of America, and the picture
gives you a splendid idea of its tremendous size. Compare its height with that of the man in
the foreground, who is standing on an oil keg. You should note as well the curious markings
in the skin—great, deep ridges whose purpose can only be guessed. They certainly enable the
thick skin to bend more easily, but they often harbour barnacles and seaweeds

THE biggest animal in the world is
that giant of the sea, the Whale.
Its mouth can quite comfortably
take in a small boat, while with one
stroke of its powerful tail it can smash
a little vessel to pieces.

The whale does not belong to the
fishes, for it has no scales and neither is
it cold-blooded. Its tail, too, is set on
its body differently from that of a fish,
for it is crosswise instead of upright.
The two wings of its tail are called
" flukes."

The creature lives in the cold northern
waters and often swims amid ice. How
can it keep itself warm, for it has no
fine fur coat as the seal has ?

Underneath its skin is a layer of fat—
the blubber—a foot or more in thickness. This keeps it very warm, even in
the coldest waters.

Why the Whale comes to the Surface

I expect you have heard of a whale
" spouting," and have seen pictures of
one blowing what looks like water a

great height into the air. The whale
does not do this for play. It has a
good reason for its " spouting."

It breathes air as we do, and has no
gills as fish have. But as it likes to
spend much of its time below the water,
where it cannot breathe, it has to find
some way of taking in enough air to
last it for some time.

So it fills its lungs full, and then dives
below. It can stay under the surface
for an hour or more if it wishes. Then
it must come up to breathe again, for it
has used up all the good air in its lungs.

When it rises to the surface it blows
out the used-up air from its nostrils or
blow-holes. You know what your breath
looks like in cold weather, don't you ?
You can see it puffing out like steam.
Well, the whale, because it lives in such
cold regions, sends its breath out in a
kind of misty spray, and this is called
" spouting "; or, if you like, " blowing."

The spout rises high into the air, and
the whale can be heard " spouting " a
great distance away. Perhaps it will

STRANDED IN SHALLOW WATER

These Pilot Whales or Blackfish are about 20 feet long and swim in " schools," blindly following their leader. If the leader enters shallow water when the tide is ebbing, the whole school may get stranded and death may be the result for a large number of the school. This is what occurred above in Mounts Bay, Cornwall. Other names for this animal are the grindwal and the ca'ing whale.

Photos: Paul Popper.

Like the pilot-whale, the Killer Whale is really a dolphin and a member of the toothed whale family. It feeds on warm-blooded animals, catching seals, porpoises and sea-birds, as well as eating fish. Although the Killer Whale is only about 25 feet in length, it will sometimes attack other whales; in fact, several killers can worry a sperm whale, which is often as much as 60 feet long, to death. Killer Whales are recognised by their triangular dorsal fin and black and white colouring.

THE WORK OF THE WHALER

The whalers described this collection of blue whales as " a small catch," but its total weight exceeded 1,000 tons. It will all be dealt with in the floating whale factory on the left. The blue whale is one of the " whalebone species," often 100 feet long and the largest known mammal in existence. In spite of its great size, it is toothless and can only feed on small crustaceans and molluscs. This picture was taken in the Antarctic, and in the background is the Great Ice Barrier.

These two cheerful whale workers are standing inside a fin whale's mouth, looking out between the strips of whalebone or baleen. In their hands they hold the great " flensing " knives, with which they cut up the blubber. Oil from the blubber, a thick layer of fat surrounding the body, is used in making soap, glycerine and margarine.

ON A FLOATING WHALE FACTORY

Paul Popper.

This is the Fin Whale or Rorqual, the second largest living animal, the blue whale (which may be 100 feet long) being slightly larger. You can see the whalebone " strainer " in the open jaws of this fin whale, as it is being hauled up the ramp into the whale factory ship

"blow" for fifty or sixty times in succession before it dives below once more. It is a curious sight to see.

Upon what does the whale feed? Is it a terrible enemy of fish, seals, and other creatures? You might think it was, but it is not, and I am sure you will be astonished to hear that, although a whale has such an enormous mouth, its throat is very, very small, so small that it cannot swallow any fish larger than a herring!

It feeds on tiny shellfish and other small creatures that float about in millions in the sea. When the whale comes to a shoal of these it opens its great mouth and swims slowly through them. In this way it makes a good meal.

All About Whalebone

There are two kinds of whales, those that have teeth, and those that have whalebone instead. Whalebone is not really bone, but a curious horny substance that hangs down from the roof of the mouth in long, fringed plates, like skins hanging from the ceiling of a room. In this whalebone are caught the tiny creatures on which the whale feeds; it acts like a sieve, letting the water through, but catching the jelly fish, shrimps or shellfish.

Whalebone comes mostly from the Greenland Whale, which, when caught, may be worth £3,000 or £4,000, for the blubber is very valuable, too.

The whale is a good mother and feeds her baby on her own milk, just as a cow feeds her calf. The great creatures go about in "schools," and although they are so huge, they can leap freely in the water and turn and twist as easily as seals. They love to gambol on the surface, and to see a whole school of whales playing is one of the strangest sights in the world.

E. N. A.

A SPOUTING WHALE SEEN FROM A MAORI BOAT

Although it is the biggest of all creatures that live in the sea the whale is not a fish but an animal, breathing in air as other animals do. It can, however, remain under water for an hour or more, but then comes to the surface to blow out the used-up air and breathe again. In the remarkable photograph above, taken off the New Zealand coast, a whale has just surfaced and the air from its nostrils or blow-holes can be seen as it forms into a misty vapour in the cold air.

ANIMALS IN ARMOUR

ALLIGATORS OF THE AMERICAN RIVERS

Zoological Society of London.

The Alligator is a member of the crocodile family but has a slightly different formation of the teeth. Largest of the species are found in the rivers of the southern states of North America. They feed mainly on fish though they take full toll of any animals that come to the river to drink. Clumsy creatures on land, they can swim with remarkable speed in the river.

A GREAT many animals have weapons which they use when they are attacked, or when they themselves wish to attack another creature. Claws, hoofs, teeth, all these may be weapons. Other animals have *armour* too—thick, tough coats, spiny quills, or hard shells. Let us imagine that some of these armour-clad creatures are talking together, and hear what they say.

The Crocodile was talking to the Tortoise and the Turtle.

" You are proud of your hard shells," said he, " but just look at *my* coat! Did you ever see such a tough one? Even a bullet can hardly pierce through my hard scales! "

" You are not a very pleasant looking creature," said the tortoise, observing him closely. " I don't like your long, pointed head and snout, and as for your teeth, they are very cruel-looking. Do you live on land, or in the water? "

" I don't mind which I live on," said the crocodile. " I can live on the land quite well, but I think I prefer the water. What I like to do is to lie quite still by a shallow ford where animals and men cross day by day. I look just like an old log, but as soon as any one comes near to me—you should just *see* me pounce on him! "

The crocodile is, of course, a reptile, and comes to a great extent from the family of some of those extinct monsters of which you will read in other parts of this work. Right at the end of his snout is a sort of valve to prevent water from entering his nostrils when he is submerged. He is found in most of the hot countries of the world in the neighbourhood of rivers, lakes and marshes.

Although they spend most of their time lying on the mud flats or partially submerged in water, crocodiles are capable of rapid movement and swim with surprising speed when roused.

123

TWO EXTREMELY UGLY COUSINS!

F. W. Bond.

Above is a remarkably realistic photograph. It portrays an alligator in the very act of consuming a frog, and there seems a leer of horrible triumph on the creature's face. Alligators have thick hides so covered with hard scales that a bullet can only pierce some vulnerable point.

Felix Kopstein. (*By courtesy of " Asia " Magazine, New York.*)

The crocodile is a cousin to the alligator and no more presentable. It may surprise you to know that crocodiles are hatched from eggs, much as happens with chicks and ducklings, and the photographer in this case was sufficiently fortunate to obtain a snapshot of a baby crocodile at the very moment when it thrust its head from the shell. Crocodiles nest on river banks.

DIFFERENT KINDS OF SCALES

The alligator is the largest reptile in the world to-day and often reaches 15 or 20 feet in length. It is found in the Mississippi, in South America and in China. Fully-grown alligators are dangerous, though they can be taught to come for food when called, but baby alligators are very tame and friendly and people sometimes keep them for pets. This one is only about 7 inches long and loves a ride on its mistress's hand!

Photos: Paul Popper.

Unlike the Alligator, and the Tortoise, which are reptiles, the Pangolin (or Scaly Ant-eater) is an animal. Its scales are composed of the horny material of hair, and they continue underneath its tail except at the tip, where the bare skin is very sensitive to " touch " or " feel." Its food is mainly ants. The Pangolin comes from Asia and West and South Africa.

"You are a horrid reptile," said the tortoise; "I don't like you or your cousin, the Alligator. You are both cruel, dangerous animals. I and the turtle are harmless. I eat green food, and the turtle likes seaweed. Do you see our hard shells? We can draw our heads and legs underneath them, and then our enemies cannot hurt us."

"Sometimes people turn me over on to my back," said the turtle. "Then I am helpless. Isn't that a shame! The natives use my great shell for all kinds of things, baths for their children, roofs for their huts, and sometimes boats in which to go on the water."

"Do you live in the sea or on land?" asked the crocodile, looking at the curious flippers that the turtle had instead of legs.

"In the sea," said the turtle, "but I come out on the shore to lay my eggs. I dig holes in the sand and put them there for the sun to hatch."

Where Tortoiseshell comes from

The crocodile turned to the tortoise, and looked at his hard shell.

"Is tortoiseshell made from your shell?" he asked.

The tortoise shivered at the thought.

"No," he said. "Tortoiseshell is really turtleshell. It comes from the Hawksbill Turtle. But please don't let us talk about that."

"Did you know that our shells are made from our flattened backbone joints and ribs?" asked the turtle proudly.

The crocodile yawned and showed his great teeth. The tortoise looked into his mouth in surprise.

"Why, you haven't a tongue!" he cried. "What a queer thing! You *do* look strange without one."

The crocodile was annoyed and did not answer. He *had* got a tongue, but it was fixed to the bottom of his mouth and he could not move it.

"Look!" said the tortoise. "Here

GIANT TORTOISES

Will. F. Taylor.

Turtles and tortoises are near relatives, but the former exist in the water, and the latter on land. Slow moving and slow growing, they live to an immense age, probably longer than any other creature. Their shells, natural armour plate, protect them from all enemies except man. The largest of this tribe are the giant tortoises of the Galapagos Islands, which sometimes attain to the astonishing weight of nearly a quarter of a ton.

Paul Popper.

THE SPINY ANT-EATER

This Australian " Echidna " catches ants and other insects with its long, sticky tongue. It is covered with spines, like a hedgehog, and burrows into sandy soil or hides in rock crevices.

come two more armoured animals—the Porcupine and the Scaly Ant-eater! Aren't they queer creatures! And whoever is that behind them ? "

" That's the Armadillo of South America," said the turtle. " You wouldn't think such a clumsy-looking animal could go so fast, would you ? "

The porcupine was a strange animal. He had two sets of quills growing in his back. One set was long and slender and easily bent. The other set was

E.N.A.

THE PORCUPINE

The body of the European and African Porcupine has short, sharp quills hidden among long, slender, soft ones. Its tail bears short hollow quills which rattle when it moves. It is a vegetarian.

Topical Press

THE ARMADILLO

This creature, which looks as if it came out of " Alice in Wonderland," is really a small kind of armadillo. Its home is in South America, where it lives in holes burrowed deeply in the ground. Its coat of flexible mail protects it from most enemies, but Indians eat it.

stiffer. The stiff, hard quills were the ones he used to attack an enemy.

" Good - day," said the tortoise politely, as the three animals came up. " I hope your armour is all safe and sound ? "

" Quite, thank you," said the armadillo. " Look at mine! It is made of bony plates growing in my skin, fastened together by bony rings. Watch me roll myself up into a ball. Can you see a gap anywhere ? "

He suddenly rolled himself up into a ball, and all the other creatures looked carefully at him. But nowhere could they find a single gap into which an enemy might put claws or teeth.

" Very clever," said the ant-eater. " But you are not very pretty, armadillo, are you ! "

The armadillo was angry, and he glared at the ant-eater. " Nor are you,

with your body covered with pointed scales," he said. " And I wish you wouldn't eat so many ants. You leave very few for me."

" They are very nice to eat," said the ant-eater. " I love to break down the ants' nests and lick them up with my long tongue. When I am frightened I do as you do, armadillo, and roll myself up into a ball."

" Are you any relation to the Great Ant-eater ? " asked the turtle.

" Yes," said the scaly ant-eater, " we both belong to the toothless family. So does the armadillo. But the great ant-eater does not look at all like me. He has hair instead of scales, and his tail is enormous, almost as big as himself. His head is drawn out into a sort of long, narrow beak, and his tongue is very long and very sticky, so that he can pick up hundreds of ants at a time."

" One of your quills is sticking into me," said the turtle to the porcupine. Do you mind moving ? "

" It can't hurt you, you have such a fine shell," said the porcupine, grunting like a pig.

" You sound like a pig! " cried the ant-eater. " Are you one, or do you belong to the insect-eaters ? "

" My name means ' spiny pig,' " said the porcupine. " I am a gnawing animal, and like to eat roots, bark and leaves. Please don't think I am any relation to the hedgehog. *He* is an insect-eater, and I am not."

Just then the armadillo trod on the porcupine's paw, and at once all his quills bristled. He turned away from the armadillo, and then suddenly ran backwards at him, with all his sharp quills pointing towards him, for the porcupine always runs backwards on his enemy, and hopes that some of his sharp quills will stick into him.

But, of course, he could not hurt the armoured armadillo, and every one laughed.

" It's of no use any of us fighting one another," said the tortoise. " We have all got our armour on ! "

THE CLEVER BEAVER

W. S. Berridge.

BEAVER

The beaver once lived in England, for its fossilised bones have been found. The animals are fairly common in Russia and Siberia, but this one is a North American native. They live in colonies, swim and dive like water rats, and are very intelligent. Their teeth resemble those of the rat, but are of course much larger, and with them they can cut through the stems of trees a foot in diameter.

ONE of the cleverest animals in the world is the beaver. It lives in the northern parts of Europe, Asia and America. It used to live in Britain, too, and its numbers were much greater at that time than they are to-day; but because of its valuable coat of thick, soft, chestnut-coloured fur, it has been very much hunted.

The baby beaver is born in a dome-shaped hut, built near a pool or river. His mother looks after him well until he is old enough to join her in her work of building, for all beavers are fond of building, and pass most of their time in damming up rivers to make a quiet pool in which they can swim.

"Come with me," said the mother beaver one day to her little one. "You shall see how we use our sharp teeth to cut down trees. There is a swift river flowing near here, and we want to dam it up."

The little beaver was glad to follow his mother, and leave the hut, or lodge, as the beaver's home is called. She took him down a long passage that ran to the river side. It opened into the river itself, 2 feet or 3 feet below the surface of the water.

"Come along," said the big beaver. "Glide into the water. You will soon find how easy it is to swim. No one will see you, for we always make the entrances to our passages below the water, then we can enter and leave unseen."

The two beavers slid into the water, and the mother swam swiftly to the nearest bank. The little one followed, and both of them clambered out. There were many other beavers about, and all of them were busy. Some were gnawing at the base of young trees, and others were cutting up logs into lengths of 2 feet to 5 feet.

Felling a Tree

"Now see if your teeth are getting sharp!" said the mother beaver, running to a young tree nearby. "This tree must be felled and cut into short lengths. Come and help me."

She set to work, gnawing at the foot of the tree with her white, gleaming teeth. The little one tried to help her, but he was so interested in all that was going on that he soon stopped, and began to watch the other beavers.

His mother worked hard. She gnawed without ceasing, and after a time another beaver came to help her. Between them they gnawed the trunk right through. Crash! The tree fell to the ground, making the little beaver jump in fright.

"There!" said his mother, pleased. "Now we must gnaw off the branches and cut up the trunk neatly."

Day after day she took her little one to see the work that was going on. Soon the tree was cut up into logs of 4 feet or 5 feet, and the branches were stripped of their bark. Then the busy beavers dragged the logs to the river, and placed them in position there, for they wanted to dam it up.

"Now we must heap stones and mud around the logs to keep them in place," said the beaver. The little one did his best to help. He watched his mother plaster mud around the logs and seal up any cracks and crevices between them, and he tried to do the same. Soon the dam was half made, and the river began to flow past more sluggishly.

"This is rather a swift river," said the leader. "We must build the dam in the form of a curve, and then the current will not break the logs down."

So this was done. Week after week the work went on. More and more trees were cut down and piled into place. Soon a curving wall of logs, stones and mud ran right across the water. It was 15 feet thick at the bottom and 6 feet high. It stretched for 300 feet across the river, and was so

HOW THE BEAVER FELLS A TREE *New York Zoological Society.*

This photograph gives an excellent idea of the way in which a beaver fells a tree. The job is a long one and requires much patience, but often two or more beavers work together. The chisel-like teeth are specially adapted for this work, and they never wear out because they keep on growing. Beavers kept in captivity must have wood to gnaw on, or their teeth will grow out of all bounds. When this tree has been felled the beaver will cut off every branch.

Mondiale.

THE BEAVER PLANS A NEW "LODGE"

A beaver's home is called a "lodge," and is made by laying down a number of tree logs, plastering them over with clay and then digging out the earth beneath to form the dwelling proper. Here you see a beaver actually cutting down a tree. Afterwards he will gnaw away the branches and then cut up the trunk into suitable lengths to meet his needs. If the beaver is interrupted whilst working on a tree he may abandon his task and seek another elsewhere.

well built that the water could not force itself past.

"Isn't that fine!" said the mother beaver when the work was finished. "Now see what will happen, little one. The river will swell out into a broad shallow pool behind the dam, and no matter how hot the weather is, the pool won't dry up, so we shall have cool water to swim in and to drink all the summer through."

The river swelled out into a pool just as the beaver had said, and all through the hot days the little beaver played there with his companions. He swam well, for his hind feet were webbed and he could use them like oars. His tail was very broad and flat, and it was useful as a rudder.

"I am going to build a new lodge for the winter time," said his mother one day. "You must help me, for you are getting big now."

9—2

How the Lodge was made

So the little beaver and his mother, and four other big beavers, all built a lodge for themselves. They piled up a large number of logs which they cut from the trees they felled. Then they plastered them over with clay to keep out the cold, the wet and the wind.

"Now we must dig out the earth underneath the logs," said the chief beaver. So they all dug hard, and in a short time there was enough room below the logs to make a fine dwelling place for all six of them. The walls were very thick indeed, too thick for enemies to come and disturb the beavers once they were safe inside.

From the lodge ran several underground passages, all leading to the river, entering the water below the surface. The only way to enter the hut was by these passages, and the beavers knew that they were safe, for no animal would dive below the water to look for these entrances.

The little beaver loved the lodge he had helped to make. He carried wood chips and grass into it to form his bed, and all the other beavers did the same. Each of them slept on his own bed, and very cosy and warm they were in the well-built lodge.

When winter came they did not mind the cold in the least, for their hut was so thick-walled that they kept as warm as could be. They had been wise enough to store up a pile of logs and branches, and made many good meals off the bark when they were hungry.

When the warm spring days came the beavers rejoiced. They swam through the quiet pool, and played merrily.

"A beaver's life is a fine one!" they said. "Work and play, play and work—who could ask for anything better!"

WHEN THE BEAVER BUILDS ITS LODGE   *H. J. Shepstone.*

In Europe the beaver generally lives in a burrow but his American cousin, similar in appearance and habits, has other ideas about his home and prefers a house or lodge. The lodges are constructed of logs of wood, odds and ends from the river side, and a certain amount of mud. The beaver is in danger of becoming extinct in Europe and even in America its numbers have dwindled rapidly.

OUR COUNTRYSIDE FRIENDS

James's Press.

THE BADGER

The badger is rarely seen, for he moves abroad only at night. Yet he is much less uncommon than people suppose, and is still to be found quite near to London.

BROCK THE BADGER

BROCK the Badger came out from his burrow—or "set," as we call it—and sniffed the air to learn if any enemy were about.

"Come along, my dear," he called to his wife. "Bring the cubs out for an airing. The moon is full, and it is a lovely night. We will try to find some dinner, and teach the cubs a few lessons."

Brock's wife came out of the set, and after her came a file of little silvery-grey cubs, all very much excited to think that they were going to be taught

their first lessons in woodcraft. Their mother had reared them in a cosy nursery underground, and had kept them very clean indeed.

"We badgers are clean animals," she said to her listening cubs. "We hate dirty, smelly sets, and if our bedding of bracken and moss begins to smell nasty we take it out and get fresh bedding. You must be sure to be clean when you grow up."

The badgers looked rather like small bears as they went out on the hillside. They were thick-set creatures, round-backed, with coats of rough, thick hair, reddish-grey above

Barbara Brook.

LEAVING HIS SET

Nearly 3 feet in length and grey in colour, the badger has a white head striped with black.

and black below. Their white faces had two black stripes running through their eyes to their small round ears.

" Our black stripes may make us look a little queer," said the father badger to his children, " but in the moonlight they are a fine protection. The black lines break up the whiteness of our faces and make us very difficult to see. Now just keep close to your mother, and watch how we get our dinner. We don't mind what it is—it may be rabbits, roots, frogs, snakes, birds, fruit or insects."

In the Badger's Set

All night long the little family roamed the countryside, keeping well-hidden in ditches and under hedges. Brock caught a rabbit and his wife two frogs. One clever baby badger found a nest of eggs, which he shared with his brothers and sisters.

When dawn was near the family went back to the set to spend the day in sleep. The set was 9 feet underground, and had a back door and a front door. It was lined warmly with bracken and dead leaves.

" No badger fears the cold or frost when he has a set like mine," said Brock. " Here I can sleep the winter through and never feel the cold. On warm days I wake up and poke my nose outside to see if there is any chance of a meal. But now it is summer and there is plenty of sunshine and food. Learn all you can, little cubs, while the warm days are with us, for winter will come round all too quickly."

" It is a pity we are killed when men see us," said the mother badger, sighing. " We are sensible, good-tempered creatures, and do no harm, and there are few of us left now. Once we were so many that towns were named after us! "

She spoke the truth. Whenever you hear of a town with the word Brock in its name you will know that badgers once lived there in great numbers. At Brockham they lived, at Brockley, and at Brockenhurst, too. In the days when cruel sports were allowed in this country the badger was caught and used to amuse the sportsmen of those days in what was known as badger baiting, for when he is attacked the badger is a fierce and courageous fighter.

A. R. Thompson.

THE OTTER SWIMS AWAY

Usually about 2 feet long, with a tail measuring 18 inches long, and having a coat of thick brown fur, the Otter, like the badger, is one of the distinctive members of the Weasel family. It lives in a burrow on the river bank but often goes down to the sea where it feeds upon molluscs and fish. Our photograph shows an otter which, having been surprised by the camera man, took to the water and swam away.

THE SAVAGE LITTLE STOAT

Eric Hosking.

One of the most savage of flesh-eating animals, the stoat is about 10 inches long, with a tail of 4½ inches, the female being 2 or 3 inches smaller. In cold climates, the stoat's reddish-brown coat changes to pure white or yellowish-white in winter and it is then known as the ermine, greatly valued for its fur.

THE OTTER AND HIS FAMILY

COME and see how the Otters teach their family of cubs to swim and catch fish. We must go to the river side to find their lair, for the otter likes to bring up his family in a hole in the river bank.

There it is, under the root of that tree. You can hardly see the front entrance, for it is below the water. There is a back door, too, that leads up to the land.

Listen! Can you hear a pretty, flute-like whistle? That is the otter calling. It is sunset now, and he is coming out to hunt fish.

Here he comes, slipping out of his lair like a dusty-brown shadow. See how gracefully he swims in the water, darting this way and that, his sleek body glistening. He does not get wet, for he wears two coats. One is made of long, glossy hairs, and the other is an undercoat of fine, soft fur. The undercoat does not get wet, for the longer hairs keep it dry.

Look at his short, powerful legs, ending in five-toed feet, all webbed to help him in his swimming. You can see that he is made for the water, for his head is broad and flat, and he has a long, thick tail, flattened from the sides so that it makes a fine rudder. He loves the water, and spends most of his time in it, but he can go long distances on the land, too.

Here comes the mother otter, and after her tumble the little cubs. They have to learn to swim, and they do not take long to do so. They cannot chase fish until they can swim, so the big otters take them into the water as soon as they are old enough.

Now watch the mother chasing a trout! See how she twists and turns after the fish, which is trying hard to get away. But it is of no use. She

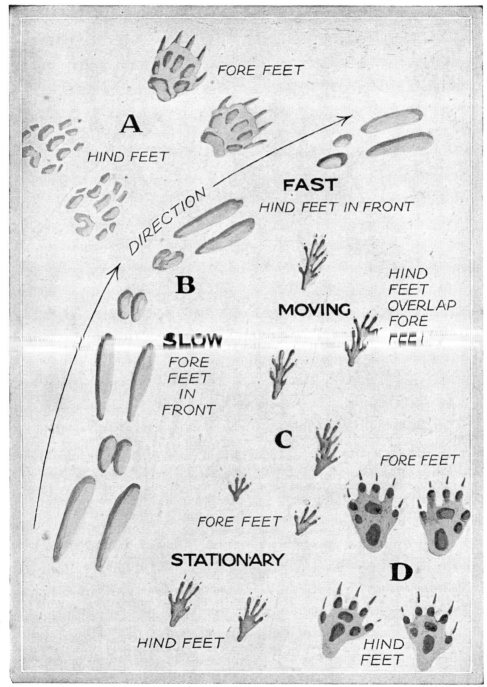

FORE FEET

A

HIND FEET

DIRECTION

FAST

HIND FEET IN FRONT

B

MOVING

HIND FEET OVERLAP FORE FEET

SLOW

FORE FEET IN FRONT

C

FORE FEET

FORE FEET

STATIONARY

D

HIND FEET

HIND FEET

Can you tell the tracks of animals and birds on soft ground ? or, better still, upon the snow ? This is one of the great accomplishments of true woodcraft, and the pictures will help you. Group A. above is the spoor of the badger, showing both hind and fore feet. B. is that of the common rabbit, going slowly at first and then more rapidly. You can tell his speed by the position of the footmarks. C. depicts the tracks of the pretty water vole, sometimes in error called the water rat. The splodges marked D. are made by the curious feet of the hedgehog.

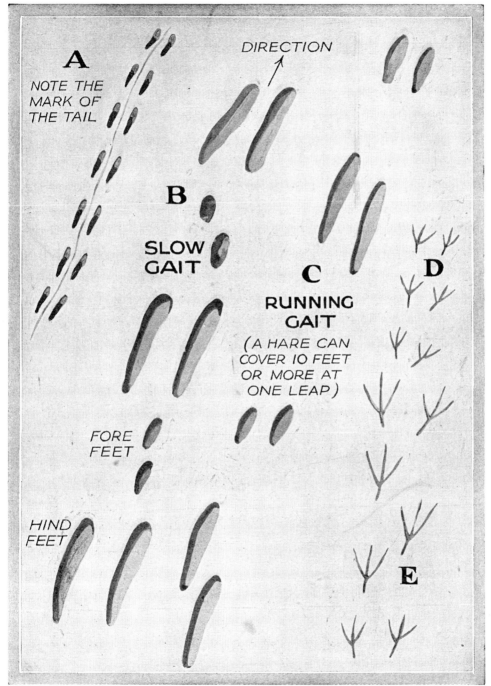

A

NOTE THE MARK OF THE TAIL

DIRECTION

B

SLOW GAIT

C

RUNNING GAIT

(A HARE CAN COVER 10 FEET OR MORE AT ONE LEAP)

D

FORE FEET

HIND FEET

E

The strange marks beside the letter A. above are the footprints made by the dainty little field mouse, and the most curious part of this spoor is that the animal leaves a tiny trail with his long tail. B. gives you a splendid idea of the track of a hare when he is not in any hurry and is just ambling along at slow speed. In C. you observe the spoor of the same creature when he is running and leaping at an amazing speed to get away from some sudden danger. D. and E. are tracks of birds—the former hopping and the latter walking.

PACK OF WEASELS HUNTING

Weasels hunt in packs, running nose to tail as you see in this picture. A pack running in this way through thick grass bears a curious likeness to a great snake. The weasel is smaller than the stoat and has a much shorter tail. Otherwise the two animals are very much alike. The stoat lives largely on rabbits, but the weasel hunts rats, mice and moles, and you will often see a weasel pop his head up out of a mole run.

suddenly swims beneath it, strikes upwards and the fish is caught; then the big otter returns to her little ones and gives it to them to eat.

"Now *you* try to catch a fish," she says. "You have seen me catch one, and you know how to do it. As soon as you can dart this way and that, and learn never to take your eye off your prey, then you will find that it is easy to get as much food as you want."

Off went the little otters, and were soon chasing any fish that came by. But they were not as clever as their mother, and at first could not catch any. Suddenly the smallest cub of all saw a fine trout darting by. He dashed at it, and to his great surprise found that he had caught it. How proud he was!

"Very good, very good!" cried the big otter in delight. "Take it to the bank and share it with the others."

Otters live in many parts of our country. Fishermen do not like them, for they say that they spoil the fishing.

"Yes, I know I rob the river of fish," the otter says, "but as I eat many eels and frogs, which feed on the spawn of fish, I save hundreds of fish too, for the spawn grow into trout and salmon, instead of being devoured."

With that he slid into the water, and presently his flute-like whistle could be heard far away in the distance.

WHEN STOAT AND WEASEL HUNT

THE Stoat and Weasel met in the ditch by the side of the field.

"I have already killed and eaten a rabbit this evening," said the stoat.

"And I have eaten a mouse, and killed a fat rat," said the weasel. "But the farmer in whose ricks I killed the rat came after me, so I had to leave it uneaten. I do wish the farmer wouldn't think I am his enemy. I know I do kill a chicken sometimes, but if only he knew how many mice and rats I kill he would be delighted! "

"I do a lot of good, too," said the stoat. "But I like a fat game-bird at times, which makes the keepers very angry."

The two animals were rather alike to look at. The stoat was about two inches longer, with a tail of $4\frac{1}{2}$ inches. The weasel's tail was only 2 inches, and had no black tip like the stoat's. They were both reddish-brown in colour, but the weasel's coat was the brighter of the two. He was pure white under-

neath, while the stoat was a yellowish colour.

"My legs are a little shorter than yours, and my head is narrower, but we are really very much alike," said the weasel, looking closely at his cousin. "And don't we love hunting! "

"We *do!* " said the stoat. "We hunt by day or by night, and all the creatures we hunt are terrified of us, for they know that we shall get them in the end. We don't mind swimming or climbing if there is a kill at the end of it. We are as fit as can be, very sharp and alert, and our motto is ' Never say die! ' "

"Do you change your coat in the winter? " asked the weasel. "I very rarely do in this country."

"I do when I live in northern parts," said the stoat. "I change to a lovely pure white then, except for the tip of my tail, which remains black. When I am all white my victims cannot see me against the snow. I am called the Ermine then."

"See, here is my wife with her little ones," said the weasel suddenly. "She has brought them out to learn to hunt. Aren't they a fine lot? "

"My wife is teaching her little ones, too," said the stoat. "She likes a nursery like yours—a hole in the bank,

A GREAT LITTLE DIGGER

Eric Hosking.

About 6 inches in length and covered with velvety greyish-black fur, the mole spends practically all its life underground, burrowing for the worms and grubs on which it feeds. The short but powerful front legs with their strong claws act as shovels as it bores its way through the soil.

WILD LIFE IN BRITAIN

In every country in the world where agriculture is an important industry, the problem of what animals are harmful and which are beneficial to man's interests has been debated for many years. Generally the point of view taken depends mainly on sentiment or on a lack of real knowledge. Just as a weed may be a pretty flower in the woodland or by the wayside but becomes a nuisance in the well-kept garden, so a wild animal, however charming to the student of Natural History, may be a pest to the tiller of the soil. In Britain the Ministry of Agriculture set out to find the true facts about the wild creatures of the British countryside. As a result some animals have been given a good conduct badge, and others have been labelled as enemies, while a certain number are in the doubtful or borderline class, with something in their favour but with faults that mar their records. In the pictures on these two pages the artist and the expert have worked together to show the different verdicts reached by the careful investigations into the habits of some of the well-known creatures that find their homes and their food supplies in the countryside.

HARMFUL AND BENEFICIAL MAMMALS

GREY SQUIRREL

RABBIT

BROWN HARE

BROWN RAT

FOX

DORMOUSE

LONG TAILED FIELDMOUSE

HARVEST MOUSE

ANIMALS and the LAND
Beneficial.....
Borderline.....
Harmful.....

HOUSE VOLE

BANK VOLE

I.L.N.

One of the small animals that has come out of the enquiry with a very bad record is the shrew, but, despite all attempts to blacken its character, the hedgehog's innocence has been established. The mole living in marshland is beneficial, but when, as all too frequently, he digs his underground tunnels on cultivated land the verdict is wholly against him. Fishermen condemn the otter, but in its favour is the fact that it eats eels that damage fishing prospects, and some authorities assert that the otter takes mainly the sick and ailing fish. With farmers the fox has for long had a very black record, but it now seems probable that it prefers rabbits, rats and mice to the poultry it sometimes takes. On investigation the fox's character is not as black as it has often been painted. The little harvest mouse is becoming a rarity, but on balance it is now shown to be far more beneficial than harmful. The small amount of corn it may eat during a few weeks of the year is more than compensated by the number of harmful insects it consumes during the rest of the year.

or in a hollow tree. Well, well, I must go hunting again, for I begin to feel hungry once more. Good-bye, cousin."

Off went the stoat, a little snake-like creature, and the weasel ran off too, eager to help his wife.

THE STORY OF A LITTLE MINER

HAVE you ever seen the little miner of the countryside—the Mole? If you have not seen the mole himself you are sure to have seen the hills he makes as he tunnels here and there after the worms and grubs he loves to eat.

Sometimes he tunnels across a tennis lawn or across a wheat field, and then we are angry with him, for he leaves long ridges, showing where he has tunnelled, and throws up unsightly hillocks of earth, uprooting plants as he does so. But as he eats scores of harmful grubs on his way, we ought not to scold him too much.

How does he make his tunnels? Let us have a look at him. We can see he is built for life underground. His body is cylinder-shaped with a pointed snout. His fore-paws are spade-like, and the palms face outwards. They are strong and powerful, and with them he can dig out the earth very swiftly indeed, throwing it up into hillocks as he goes along underground. His hind legs are not spade-like, nor are they so powerful.

Fur that Grows Straight Upwards

Stroke his fur. It has no " set," but grows straight upwards, so that we can brush it forwards or backwards equally well. He prefers his fur to be like this, for when he wants to go forwards his coat lies backwards, and when he wishes to go backwards it lies forwards, and so he gets along without hindrance.

We cannot see his eyes, but they are there, deep-set in his fur. We cannot see his ears either, but he has two and

THE COSY HOME OF THE MOLE   *W. S. Berridge.*

This picture shows the mole's underground home, the nest where the young are born and where they remain until big enough to hunt for themselves. The mole is not only a glutton for food, but must also have water, and the animal is said to dig wells so that it may never be far from drinking water. The nest above is shown in section, of course.

HEDGEHOG

His prickly coat is useful to the hedgehog, saving him from the fox or the dog, and he is perhaps the only British animal that has no fear of the viper. When he meets a viper he allows it to strike at his prickles; then, when its venom is exhausted, attacks, kills and eats his poisonous foe.

Mondiale.

under a bramble bush somewhere.

This hill is about a foot high and 3 feet broad. The room in the middle of it has a passage from it leading to the high road he uses, and also a bolt run in case he needs one in a hurry.

The mother mole brings her babies up in a home rather like the " fortress " of her husband, but smaller and simpler. She lines it with grass and leaves, and makes it very cosy for her litter of blind, pink babies.

Their fur soon begins to grow, and when they are old enough she teaches them to earn their own living. In a short time they become grey, velvet-coated miners like herself.

PRICKLES THE HEDGEHOG

PRICKLES the Hedgehog makes a fine pet for our gardens, for he belongs to the insect-eaters, and loves to feed on caterpillars and grubs of all kinds. He eats snails and slugs too, and will not say " no " to worms, mice, lizards or snakes.

He is a queer-looking creature, with his covering of brown-banded spines. They usually lie flat, but when he wants to he can make them all stand up straight. If he is in danger he rolls himself into a ball, and then few

very sharp of hearing they are, for they tell him at once if any grub or worm is near him in the ground. His nose helps him in his hunting as well, and he eats hundreds of insects every day.

He is always hungry, for the food he eats is not very nourishing. He tunnels continually, and when he wants a rest he goes to his " fortress." This is a stupid name for his home, for it is not in the least like a fortress, but is simply a chamber in a big hill he has made

TUFTED EARS AND BUSHY TAIL   *F. W. Bond.*

This photograph of a red squirrel gives a good idea of the
tufted ears, the immensely bushy tail used as a rudder when
climbing, and the wonderful thickness of the fur which, red in
summer, changes in winter to a duller hue.

animals care to make a mouthful of
him, for he is so prickly.

Foxes and badgers sometimes kill
him, and so do gipsies, who like to
bake him in a covering of clay and feast
on his plump little body. He is an
intelligent-looking animal, for his eyes
are bright and black, and his snout is
sharp. His legs are very short, and
hardly raise him from the ground.

He does his hunting mostly at night,
but you may sometimes see him in the
daytime after a shower of rain, when
he comes out to look for snails or slugs.
But usually he spends the day at the
bottom of a ditch or under a bush, fast
asleep, and sometimes snoring!

When the cold weather comes he
finds a nice cosy hole in a bank, and
lines it carefully with leaves and moss,
which he carries in his mouth. Then
he squeezes himself in, shuts his eyes
and goes to sleep. If warm weather
comes, as it sometimes does in winter
time, he wakens, and goes out on a
little hunting expedition; but he can
last quite well without food until the
spring arrives. He soon makes up for
his long fast then, and grows fat very
quickly.

Prickles chooses his
wife for life. He does
not have a new one
every year as many
animals do. His chil-
dren are strange little
things, quite helpless
and blind. Their spines
are pale and few, and
very short. After a
time they turn to a
dull grey and become
stiffer. Not until the
babies are fully grown
can they roll themselves
into a ball.

Then they wander
off to hunt for them-
selves, and maybe one
will come into your
garden. Keep him
there if you can, for he
will certainly be a good friend.

BUSHY THE SQUIRREL

BUSHY was a little red Squirrel.
He lived in the tree-tops, and had
a fine time leaping from tree to
tree, looking for the nuts he loved.
Sometimes he sprang down to the
ground to nibble at a toadstool.

One day he met another squirrel, and
Bushy stared in surprise, for this
squirrel was not a lovely red-brown like
himself, but a pretty grey.

"What are you doing here?" he
asked the grey squirrel. "These woods
belong to me."

"Then you must leave them, or I
will fight you," said the grey squirrel.
"I want them for myself and my friends
who are grey like me. We are American
squirrels, and were brought to the
London Zoo. Some of us were set free,
and now we have increased in numbers
so much that we are spreading swiftly
and they say we are a pest."

"It is a shame," said the bright-eyed,
red squirrel fiercely. "These woods are
mine, and have been for hundreds of
years. I and my father and grand-

THE GREY SQUIRREL AS HE CLIMBS!

Captain C. W. R. Knight.

Captain Knight has snapped a grey squirrel in the very act of climbing the trunk of a stout tree, and the photograph gives a good idea of the way in which the clever little creature clings to the rough bark. The red squirrel, once common in almost every part of England except the extreme north, is rapidly disappearing before the invasion of this American grey squirrel, which was first introduced into the London Zoo at the end of the last century and has multiplied at an amazing rate. In the Buckinghamshire beech woods the red squirrel is almost extinct.

father all lived in these trees. We built our cup-shaped nests here, of twigs, bark, moss and leaves. Our wives brought up their babies in big, cosy, ball-shaped nests, and cared for them well. I don't see why we should leave the woods we love just because you want us to."

"You will have to," said the grey squirrel, picking the seeds out of a pine cone with his little hand-paw, and eating them greedily. "You may be the native squirrel, but we American squirrels are stronger than you."

"Why can't we live together in peace?" said the red squirrel. "We are cousins, and very much alike. We both have chisel-like teeth in front, which shows we belong to the rodents, or gnawing animals. We both have fine tails, and we both like nuts, wild fruit, beech-mast and pine-seeds. Let us live together in peace."

"No," said the grey squirrel. "If we ate different food we might, but since we

A. H. Willford.

PROTECTIVE COLOURING

Here is a really wonderful example of " protective colouring." The animal is a leveret, a young hare, no more than a fortnight old; yet, young as it is, it has sense to know that by lying perfectly still in its " form " (lair) it is likely to remain unseen by its enemies.

eat the same things there will not be enough for both—so you must go."

"Let me wait until the spring, " said the red squirrel. "I have stored up many nuts, and I will share them with you. I like to go to sleep in the cold weather, and only wake up on a warm day to have a scamper and a feed."

"I do the same," said the grey squirrel. "I am sorry, red cousin, but you must go far away from here and take your family with you. If you don't, my grey friends and I will attack you, and since we are stronger than you we shall defeat you."

Then sadly the little red squirrel left his beloved woods, and went to a far-away copse with his family. Alas! for him! The grey squirrels are pushing further and further into the country-side, and soon our little native squirrel will have but few places in which to live.

C. Reid.

A FAMILY OF YOUNG RABBITS

Six little rabbits with their mother have come out of their burrow on a summer evening to feed and romp, and have made a very pretty picture for this book.

SOME FURRY FRIENDS AT HOME

Frances Pitt.

A. H. Willford.

(1) Here you see the common brown hare of the countryside. He has extremely long hind legs and can travel very fast. He does not live in a burrow like the rabbit.

(2) The nursery of a short-tailed field vole, showing the plump but helpless babies cuddled closely together in their warm nest of grass and litter.

Frances Pitt.

(3) The pine-marten is a sweetly pretty little creature now becoming sadly rare in Great Britain though it may very occasionally be found in fir plantations and deep, wooded glens. It has a yellow breast but is so shy and timid that you may count yourself very fortunate if ever you should see one in a wild state.

10—2

THE BROWN RAT

J. J. Ward.

This brown rat has been snapped just as he was on the point of diving down his hole. The brown rat, though common everywhere, is not a true British species, but came to England from Russia in the eighteenth century and has driven out the old English black rat. Now, in its turn, it is being threatened by the black Alexandrine rat, the true plague rat, which is rapidly increasing.

" Good-bye," he said to the jays and the wood-pigeons. " I hope you won't tell the grey squirrel where I have hidden my nuts! Give my love to the dormouse when you see him, and say he can have all my hidden hoard."

BOBTAIL THE RABBIT

BOBTAIL the Rabbit was making a new burrow when his cousin the Hare came by.

" Good-day," said the hare, pausing. " It always makes me smile when I see you rabbits so hard at work burrowing. Why don't you do as I do, and have your homes in the open fields on the grass ? "

" It is safer underground," said the rabbit, digging with his short front feet, and scuffling out the loose earth with his powerful hind legs. " We have lived in burrows so long that we are quite used to it. Our long ears are rather a nuisance underground though. We have to lay them flat on our backs when we run down the burrows."

" How do you pass each other ? " asked the hare, peering into the hole.

" Quite easily," said Bobtail. " Our runs are about six inches wide, just broad enough to take our bodies com-fortably. But here and there we widen the passages to a foot, and then we can pass one another when we want to. We have a back door as well as a front door in case an enemy calls. We also have many bolt-holes, short passages, running off from our main tunnels."

" What a bother to have to dig such a lot ! " said the hare. " I suppose you bring your children up underground, Bobtail ? "

" Oh, yes," said the rabbit. " They are dear little things, too, though they are quite blind, hairless, and helpless."

" Mine are born with a furry coat and their eyes open," said the hare proudly, twitching his long black-tipped ears. Then off he leapt to the field where he had his " form," or resting-place.

The Warm Coat of the Rabbit

The rabbit went on with his work. There was a cold wind blowing, but he was quite warm, for he had three kinds of fur in his coat—the inner kind was soft and thick, the next was longer, and grey-brown in colour, and the third was longer still, but not so thick.

Soon he felt hungry, so he ran to a

CAUGHT BY THE CAMERA!

Captain C. W. R. Knight.

In this charming photographic study a dear little water vole has been snapped in a wonderfully natural pose, just as you would meet him in his own grassy home. You will note that the animal—often wrongly called a water rat—has a rounded muzzle and not the long, pointed nose of a true rat. He is only a very distant cousin of our enemy the rat, and his coat is a glossy dark brown colour. You should never kill this harmless creature, for his ways are totally different from those of the robber rodents.

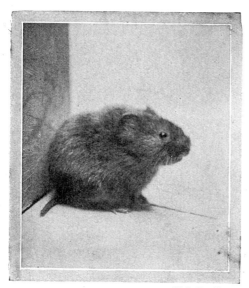

FIELD VOLE   *W. S. Berridge.*

The field vole here pictured is about the size of a house mouse, but has a shorter tail. Its fur is brownish grey. It lives on vegetable food and produces three or four litters a year. Sometimes it increases so quickly as to become a plague and then destroys thousands of acres of grass.

young tree near by and began to gnaw the bark. He showed his four white front teeth as he did so, for his upper lip was split so that it might not get bruised when he gnawed anything. These four teeth never stopped growing, but he used them so often that he wore them down continually and was glad to know they would always go on growing.

Soon other rabbits came to join him. Then, far away in the distance there came the barking of a dog. At once Bobtail stopped his gnawing and ran to his burrow. As he ran his white scut bobbed up and down, and when the other rabbits saw it in the twilight they knew it was a danger signal and ran off too.

Soon the hillside was empty, and not a rabbit was to be seen. The pretty little creatures were all safely below ground.

The Australian farmers might not call them pretty, for in that country the rabbits, which were originally taken from Britain, have become a pest which is now being controlled. But they are not entirely valueless; rabbit is a cheap and popular item on the Australian menu, and the export value of Australian rabbit skins is a useful asset.

OUR ENEMIES—THE RAT AND THE MOUSE

NEVER a ship sails away but a rat goes with it, and when the vessel comes to shore again the rat runs along the mooring ropes and lands as easily as do the sailors.

The Mouse, a cousin of the Rat, is a destructive little creature, and if it and the rat were allowed to multiply without hindrance they would soon make us very uncomfortable.

Not only do these animals feed on our stores of food, but they carry disease, particularly the rat. It can spread a dreadful illness called the bubonic plague, which destroys men and women in hundreds.

The rat does not mind what it eats.

W. S. Berridge.

WATER VOLE

Here is another picture of the pretty little water vole. By comparing his head with that of the brown rat shown on page 148 you will readily notice the marked difference in the appearance of the two animals. The water vole measures about 8 inches in length and has soft dark brown fur.

It will feast on the finest food we have one day, and the next will eat garbage. Goods to the value of millions of pounds are each year destroyed by rats and mice, so it is not to be wondered at that we regard these animals as our enemies.

The Brown Rat is 9 inches long, and has a thick, scaly-ringed tail of 5 inches. The Mouse is only 3 inches or 4 inches long, with a tail of the same length. They live anywhere and everywhere, and eat anything and everything.

Rats and mice have so many large families every year, and these families grow up so quickly and have families of their own so fast that it is almost impossible to keep their numbers down. Indeed, if nine-tenths of the rats now living were suddenly destroyed, there would be just as many again before a year had gone by, for the tenth that was left would multiply so quickly that the living rats would more than equal in numbers the ones that had been killed.

You must not muddle the little Water Vole with the brown rat. His other name—a foolish one—is Water Rat, and because of this and his likeness to a rat he is often killed.

But he is a pretty, harmless creature, with a rounded, not pointed, muzzle, and long thick fur of glossy dark brown. He loves to eat juicy shoots and grasses, and although he is a distant cousin of the savage rat, he is really not in the least like him.

FLITTERMOUSE THE BAT

"SUMMER days are coming," said Prickles the hedgehog, "for there goes Flittermouse the Bat. He only comes out in warm weather. The rest of the time he hangs himself upside down in Farmer Giles's old barn, and covers himself warmly with his curious wings."

"Are you talking about me?" asked Flittermouse, flying down to the ground beside the hedgehog. "I thought I heard my name."

"You did," said Prickles, · putting his paw over a fat

James's Press.

ROBBERS IN THE WHEATFIELD

Here is a pretty picture of the smallest of British animals, called the Harvest Mouse. The creature is so tiny that a penny will more than balance one in the scales. It builds a neat globular nest in tall grass or growing corn where the young are born. At first they are hairless and helpless, but grow up rapidly, and there may be four families in one season. Small as they are, these tiny harvest mice do a deal of harm to wheat.

earwig so that Flitter-mouse shouldn't see it; for bats live on insects, and so do hedgehogs, though they do not belong to the same family.

"Although you call me Flittermouse, and I look rather like one, I am not really a mouse at all," said the bat, trying to walk along. "I belong to the wing-handed animals, as you can see if you look at my hand-wings."

"You don't seem able to walk very well," said Prickles.

"Neither would *you* if your knees were turned backwards like mine!" an swered Flittermouse. "I am not made for walking, but for flying. Look at my lovely wings."

He spread them out, and the hedge-hog looked at them in surprise.

"They are not a bit like a bird's," he said. "They have no feathers, and

THE WHISKERED BAT   *Frances Pitt.*

Perched on one finger of a man's hand, this little whiskered bat is one of the smallest of its kind. Notice the hooks on its leathery wings by means of which it hangs itself up to rest during the hours of daylight, for all bats are night-flying animals.

you have hairs growing on them here and there!"

"Of course they're not like a bird's wings," said Flittermouse impatiently. "I'm not a bird, I'm a bat. Shall I tell you what makes my wings? Well, listen. My finger bones have grown very long indeed, and growing between them is a broad web of skin, which is joined to the sides of my body, and to my legs as far as the ankle. Look, and you can see it plainly."

You will see it, too, if you look at the pictures. It is no wonder that the bat can fly beautifully when he has such wonderfully-made wings.

"My thumb is free," said Flittermouse, "and is a useful little hook. And do you see the skin between my legs? I use that as a pocket, and pop the beetles

LONG-EARED BAT   *J. J. Ward.*

It is easy to see why this creature is called the long-eared bat. All bats have keen sight and hearing to enable them to find their food in the dark hours. This little creature is about to enter a hole, where it will remain until night falls again.

into it as I catch them in mid-air."

"As Blind as a Bat"

"There is a saying 'as blind as a bat,'" said Prickles. "Are you blind, Flittermouse?"

"Of course not," said the bat. "I can see quite well, and my hearing is so good that I use it to find out when I am flying dangerously near to things in the dark. You see, when I am flying I keep squeaking, and my squeaks are so sharp that everything around me gives a tiny echo, which I can hear and use as a guide."

"What wonderful ears you must have!" exclaimed Prickles.

"They are, rather," smirked the bat, "and you will see that I have little covers for them to protect them from harm. They are called 'earlets.'"

"So you have!" said Prickles. "But *I* shall call them 'earlids'—you know, like 'eyelids'! And I dare say they help to keep your ears warm, too."

"I am glad the warm weather is coming," said the bat. "It was dull hanging upside down all the winter, getting thinner and thinner. It's a good thing I was fat when the cold weather came, else I should be in a very bad way. Now, good-bye, Prickles, I must go hunting in the air."

The bat flew up with a thin, needle-like squeak, so high a sound that no one but Prickles heard it. Soon he was chasing insects, and pouching them in his little pocket.

He was a Pipistrelle, or Common Bat, our smallest and commonest bat. We have twelve different kinds in Britain, some with large ears, some with small, some with queer nose adornments and some without. Next time a bat flies into your bedroom look at it carefully, and you will see what a quaint little creature the "Flittermouse" is. You may find him quite friendly, too!

C. Reid.

NOCTULE

The noctule here pictured is a British bat, with a wing expanse of about 15 inches and soft yellowish, silky fur. Yet its body is only 3 inches in length. Like other bats, the noctule carries her young with her while she hunts. Noctules live in colonies in hollow trees and in winter hibernate in similar places.

SNAKES AND LIZARDS

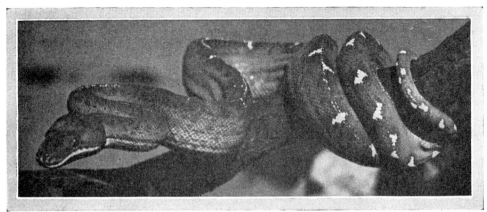

F. W. Bond.

THE GREEN TREE BOA

This snake is green in colour, may grow to be 10 feet or more in length, and is to be found at home in South America. It lays wait for its prey in a tree, and anything it catches is squeezed to death and then eaten. Baby boas are born alive and not hatched from eggs.

SOME BIG SNAKES

THE Anaconda, the Boa constrictor and the Python found themselves together and began talking.

"I come from South America," said the boa, "and, as you see, I grow to quite ten feet long."

"That's nothing!" said the anaconda and the python together. "*We* grow to twenty or thirty feet long!"

"You are certainly very big" said the boa, looking at the other two snakes. "Where do you come from?"

"I come from the East Indies," said the python, coiling himself round a tree trunk, and looking down on the boa.

"And I come from tropical America," said the anaconda. "I am very much feared there, for if I coil myself round any animal—a horse, a goat, or even a man—it is impossible for them to get free. I squee-ee-eeze them to death!"

The horrid snake coiled himself very tightly round a great branch, and showed the others how fast he could hold.

"I coil myself round a tree trunk, too," said the boa, "but I eat smaller animals than you, for I am not so big. I wait until one passes by, and then I grip it quickly in my teeth. After that I coil my strong body closer and closer round it until it is squeezed to death. Then I eat it."

"Our mouths can stretch very, very wide," said the anaconda. "Our teeth are curved backwards so that our prey goes slowly down our throats, and cannot get free, even if it had strength to do so."

"I lay eggs," said the python. "They are soft-skinned, and I hatch them by curling my great body around them and keeping them warm. Then one day the eggs split, and out come baby pythons!"

"Fancy laying eggs!" said the anaconda scornfully. "*I* don't! My babies are born alive, and can wriggle off at once. I wouldn't have the bother of eggs for anything."

"Nor would I," said the boa constrictor; "it's so old-fashioned. Baby boas are born alive too."

The python was cross. He shot his forked tongue in and out and hissed very angrily. But the other snakes laughed at him.

"You can't frighten us!" they said. "You are not any more poisonous than we are! We have no poison fangs like

154

BOA AND GOANNA

Paul Popper.

This fine picture shows a Boa Constrictor, a large snake sometimes 12 feet long, from South America. It is not poisonous, but kills small animals and birds by coiling round them and then crushing them after which it swallows them whole. Like other snakes, it cannot chew its food, but its lower jaw separates into two halves and this enables it to swallow surprisingly large creatures.

Here is an Australian Goanna lizard in the Sir Colin Mackenzie Sanctuary, Victoria. Lizards, like snakes, are reptiles, but one way in which they differ is in having eyelids which enable them to close their eyes. Snakes cannot shut their eyes and sleep with them open. Most lizards have legs, but there is a small family of legless lizards.

the cobra or the adder. We are only dangerous because of our habit of coiling ourselves round our prey and squeezing it tightly! "

The python hissed more loudly, and glided away. He went so silently that neither the anaconda nor the boa constrictor heard him. They were hungry and began looking out for a meal.

When they had caught and eaten their prey they went to sleep, although they did not close their staring eyes, for they had no eyelids. Then it was that they were caught; for two men came along, and, seeing the snakes heavy and stupid with their meal, they captured them.

And now, if you wish, you can see them in the London Zoo!

HOW DOES A SNAKE GET ALONG ?

YOU must often have wondered how a snake gets along the ground. It moves so easily and so silently, and slips over the grass so swiftly, yet it has no feet and no hands. How does it manage it ?

It is very simple really. All the bones in its body are joined together by ball and socket joints, which enable it to move swiftly in any direction it likes.

Your legs and arms are joined to your body by the same kind of joints. Move your arms, and see in how many directions you can swing them—upwards, downwards, forwards, backwards, sideways. The ball and socket joints give you easy movement in any direction.

A snake's ball and socket joints make its body very pliable and sinuous, so that it can glide whichever way it likes at a moment's notice. All its ribs—and it may have 200 or 300 pairs—are jointed to its spine in this way.

The bottom of the ribs are joined to the scales on the under part of the snake's body, and are really the creature's feet. This is what happens when a snake goes along: the scales take a firm hold of the ground, then the ribs move, making

Keystone.

EIGHT MEN VERSUS ONE PYTHON

It took eight men to hold this 23-feet long African python when it arrived in Italy bound for the Rome Zoo. The muscular power of a large python or constrictor is so great that it can crush the body of a buck or pig into pulp, breaking all its bones. Its mouth and throat are so elastic that it can swallow a creature much thicker than itself.

F. W. Bond.

BOA CONSTRICTOR

Here is another big snake, the South American boa constrictor. Some well-known explorers record meeting with a boa more than 50 feet in length which crushed a young buffalo to death, but the average length is from 10 feet to 15 feet. It is brown in colour with black and yellowish markings.

the scales move too, and so the snake moves a little way forward ; then the scales take fresh hold of the ground, the ribs move again, and the snake goes a little further still. Imagine this done very, very quickly and often, and you will easily understand how the reptile manages to slip over the ground at such a rate without hands or feet to help it!

POISONOUS SNAKES

DO you know what makes the bite of some snakes so poisonous? Perhaps you have seen their fangs and wondered how the poison got into them.

Of course, you know that snakes never "sting." Many people still think that they do, but they do not, for they cannot. They bite, and often this is very dangerous indeed, and may be fatal.

A snake's fangs, such as those of the Adder, usually lie back against the mouth roof, but as soon as the reptile opens its mouth to strike, the fangs spring erect. At the top end of each fang is a small bag of deadly poison. A hole runs down to the bottom end of the fang, and as soon as the snake bites, the fangs are pressed against the poison bags, the poison is squeezed out, and runs straight down the hole into the little wound that the snake has made in its victim.

As soon as the poison enters the wound it begins to do its deadly work, for it is usually very powerful. Some remedy must be given immediately or the animal or man bitten may die.

A snake will bite if it is disturbed or trodden on. It is a lazy creature, loving the hot sun, and dislikes to move out of the way if anything comes upon it. It darts its black forked tongue out of its mouth, and lets it quiver to and fro. It knows that its body may not be seen against the background but its moving black tongue catches the eye at once, and horse or man immediately jump aside when seeing it, leaving the snake in peace. It also uses its forked tongue to find out how big its victim is—whether it is small enough to swallow or not, and what shape it is.

The Viper

We have only one poisonous snake in our country, and that is the Viper or Adder. It is usually about 2 feet long, and has zigzag markings down its back. Generally it will not bite unless disturbed.

F. W. Bond.

COBRA—BACK VIEW

The cobra is one of the most poisonous of snakes and its bite is death unless medical help is near. When roused this snake expands a hood of which this top photograph gives the back view, showing the spectacle-like marking.

F. W. Bond.

COBRA—FRONT VIEW

Here is a front view of the same snake ready to strike. The principal enemy of the cobra is the mongoose, a ferret-like animal which lives largely on snakes and is so amazingly quick that it is able to escape the flashing strike of the cobra.

The American Rattlesnake is a very dangerous, poisonous snake. It gets its curious name from the horny hollow rings at the end of its tail. When it is angry it shakes these and makes a noise like dry oats rustling in the wind. Like the anaconda and the boa, the rattlesnake has its young ones born alive, and does not lay eggs.

The Indian Cobra is another poisonous snake. It swells out its neck or hood when it is going to strike, which it does for the slightest reason.

The Mamba comes from Africa. It is bright green and very poisonous indeed.

I expect you have sometimes wondered what would happen if two snakes began eating the same prey. Would one swallow the other? Yes, that is just what happens!

Once two snakes at the London Zoo

began to eat the same dead animal. At last the mouths of the snakes met. Each had half the food down its throat. The bigger snake of the two opened its mouth just a little wider, and the second snake began slowly to disappear down its throat.

Soon a keeper came along. When he saw what was happening, he went into the cage, pulled hard at the disappearing snake, and got it back just in time! Neither of the two creatures was any the worse for the adventure.

THE HARMLESS GRASS SNAKE

THE Grass Snake glided out with his wife by his side, and stopped when he saw two children staring at him.

"Please, please, don't kill us," begged the grass snake, seeing a stick in the boy's hand. "We are quite harmless, really we are. We can't give you a poisonous bite, for we have no poison fangs."

"I thought you were adders," said the boy, lowering his stick. "I was afraid you would bite my sister."

"Oh, no," said the grass snake. "Neither I nor my cousin the Smooth Snake, who is rather like us, but shorter, is harmful. And, as a matter of fact, even the adder himself will not readily bite, unless he is chased or trodden upon, or disturbed in some way."

"Won't you look at us very carefully?" begged the female snake. "Then you won't muddle us with the poisonous adder again. You have no idea how often we are killed because we are mistaken for him."

"I have seen an adder," said the

Paul Popper.

AN AUSTRALIAN PYTHON

This is one of the largest snakes in the world. It reaches a length of 20 feet, and is exceeded only by the pythons of Malaya and Africa, and by the anaconda of Brazil (which is sometimes more than 30 feet long). Like the boa, the python crushes its prey to death and swallows the body—which may be the size of a small deer!

F. W. Bond.

RATTLESNAKE: SHOWING TAIL

The rattlesnake is the commonest poison snake of the New World and is found from the United States to Mexico. A diamond-back rattler killed in Florida was 7 feet 10 inches long. The loosely fitting horny shells at the end of the tail produce a shrill noise when shaken. This sound, which can be heard at a distance of 20 yards, acts as a useful warning.

boy. " It was about two feet long, and had a wavy line all down its body. On its head I saw a little black patch, that looked rather like the letter A or X. I saw too, that the scales on its head were small, and there were many of them."

" I am glad you noticed all that," said the grass snake. " Just look at my head, please. Do you see that the scales there are large and few ? And please look at my length. I am three feet long, and my wife is even more, for she measures quite four feet."

J. Kearton.

SLOW-WORM, VIPER AND GRASS SNAKE

Here are three British reptiles. The first is a lizard and the other two are snakes. The viper, or adder, lives in a hole in dry ground, and its young are born alive instead of being hatched out of eggs. Though they can swim, adders dislike water.

F. W. Bond.

(1) In this illustration you may study the head and tongue of the red rattlesnake, a particularly deadly serpent. It has horny, hollow rings at the end of its tail and shakes them vigorously when roused.

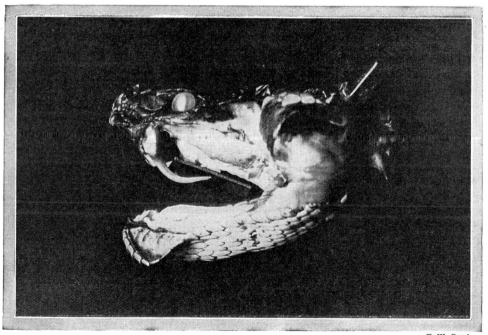

F. W. Bond.

(2) This is a section of the rattlesnake's horrid head. The creature's fangs lie in the roof of its mouth, and when it parts its lips to strike the fangs spring erect. At the top of each fang is a small bag of deadly poison, and this fluid runs down the fang directly the bag is pressed by the striking movement and enters the wound of the victim.

AN INOFFENSIVE CREATURE

The grass snake is longer and more slender than the adder and readily distinguished from it by
the pale band at the back of the neck. It is common everywhere in England, especially in moist
places. It is a fine swimmer, as much at home in the water as on land. It is quite harmless,
and should never be molested, for its food consists mainly of mice and frogs.

The Grass Snake's Collar

" And see how graceful and tapering
our long bodies are," said his wife.
" The adder has a short, thick body,
not tapering like ours. And do you
see the two patches of orange-yellow
behind my head, making a bright
collar? My husband has patches of
white. Whenever you see a snake
wearing a collar like ours you may
know it is harmless. Sometimes the
bright patches are missing, so do not
kill us if we haven't them."

" Do you see what a pretty grey-
green colour runs all along my back ? "
asked the male grass snake. " I am
not so pretty underneath."

He raised himself up, and the children saw that he was dirty white
beneath.

" You have two rows of blackish
spots along your back," said the little
girl, " and a few black patches down
your sides as well. I think I should
know you again if I saw you."

" I do hope you will," said the grass
snake, making ready to move off. " I
feel hungry, so I think I will go and
find my dinner."

" Oh, wait a little longer," said the
boy. " Tell us what you eat."

" Well, we like to swallow a frog or
two, or a few newts are very tasty,"
said the snake. " I must say that I
enjoy fish too."

" *Fish !* " cried the girl. " But how
do you catch them ? Can you swim ? "

" Of course," said the snake, in
surprise. " I swim very well indeed,
and so does my wife. You will often
find us by ditches or ponds, or anywhere marshy."

" We like commons and sandy heaths
too," said the female. " We sometimes
catch mice there, or small birds."

" Do you lay eggs ? " asked the little
girl.

" Yes," said the snake. " I laid
some yesterday. You will find them
in the big rubbish heap in the field
behind your home, if you care to look.
But don't hurt them, will you ? I put

them there because the heap is warm, and they will hatch out nicely."

"But have you left them all alone?" asked the boy. "Aren't you going to look after them?"

"No," said the snake, "there is no need to. As soon as the little things hatch out they can look after themselves. They need no help or teaching. I lay the eggs in a string. They are the size of a pigeon's egg, and have a tough, parchment-like skin. I put about fifty in that rubbish heap."

"When will they hatch?" asked the boy, making up his mind to go and see them.

"In about eight weeks," said the snake. "Each tiny snake has an egg-tooth sticking out from its jaws before it is hatched, and it uses this to break the shell. Once it has used it, and is out of the shell, the funny little tooth drops off and is never grown again.

"Well, I'm afraid I must go, but I do love these hot summer days."

"What do you do in the winter?"

called the girl, as the snake glided off through the grass.

"I and many other snakes all coil together for warmth," said the snake, pausing. "We find a hollow tree, or a cosy place under tree roots, and there we sleep the cold weather away."

"Good-bye!" said the children, and watched her slip into the water near-by. Then they both turned to run to the rubbish heap in which the snake had laid her eggs.

"We'll wait till the little snakes hatch out," said the boy, "and then we'll keep one for a pet."

THE SLOW-WORM AND THE LIZARD

ONE very warm day the Slow-worm happened to meet the Common Lizard on a sandy bank.

"Good morning," said the slow-worm. "Have you come to bask in the sun?"

"I have," said the lizard. "I suppose you are quite safe if I come near you? You look rather like a

J. J. Ward.

SLOW-WORM

This photograph gives a view of the slow-worm hunting. Unlike the grass snake, the slow-worm prefers high ground in which to live and hunt. Its food consists mainly of small white slugs. It does not eat frogs. It can be kept as a pet and soon becomes tame, when it will drink milk. Country folk call it the blind-worm, but this is a slander, for the creature has eyes. It is quite small—rarely, if ever, exceeding 15 inches in length.

COMMON OR VIVIPAROUS LIZARD

Lizards, very common in all hot countries, are rather rare in England. This is a photograph of the common English lizard which lives under stones and is found principally in dry, sandy places. It is harmless and feeds on insects.

snake, and my brother was eaten by one last week, so I don't want to share the same fate."

" Of *course* I'm not a snake! " said the slow-worm indignantly. " I don't belong to the snake family, as you ought to know. I belong to the same family as you, the lizard family."

" Do you really ? " said the lizard, surprised. " You don't look like me, I must say. Still, I see that you can shut your eyes as I can."

" Quite right," said the slow-worm. " I am really a sort of legless lizard. If you looked underneath my scaly skin, you would find the remains of legs, which, long, long ago, we slow-worms used to have. But we do without now, for we have found out how to glide along without them."

" Why are you called a slow-worm ? " asked the lizard. " You seemed to come along the ground quickly enough when we met."

" I don't know why people gave me such a stupid name," said the slow-worm crossly. " I'm not slow, and I'm not a worm. Another name of mine is

Deaf Adder! I'm not an adder, and I can't even bite! Then I have a third stupid name—Blind-worm! Look at my bright eyes, Lizard! And my food is the same as yours—spiders, insects and creatures like that."

" I am about five or six inches long," said the lizard, " and I suppose you are about a foot, aren't you ? Just tell me this—if you break off your tail, can you grow a new one ? Because *I* can! "

" So can I," said the slow-worm. " But I prefer to keep my first tail, if I can, for the second or third one I grow never really looks as if it fitted me."

" Still, it's very useful to be able to break our tails off, if some one catches hold of us," said the lizard. " Heaps of people have caught me by the tail, but I have always broken it off and run away.

" I see that your tongue is notched, not forked like a snake's," the lizard added.

" Didn't I tell you that I am *not* a snake! " said the slow-worm angrily.

" Don't be cross," said the lizard. " My tongue is notched too. I use it to

Gilbert C. Klingel.

THE IGUANA POSES FOR HIS PICTURE

The strange creature seen above in his native haunts is the iguana, a species of lizard that is quite harmless normally. If, however, you were to molest it you would find it could bite savagely and that it possesses a very powerful weapon in its tail. Iguanas live in Central and South America and feed upon foliage and fruits.

touch things with, to see if they are good to eat. I do like a nice, fat caterpillar, don't you?"

"I think I prefer a fat worm," said the slow-worm. "But I don't really mind. By the way, Lizard, I saw some funny little black things about two inches long yesterday. Were they your children?"

"Yes, they were," said the lizard. "My wife laid some eggs yesterday, and the young lizards hatched out of them immediately they were laid. We didn't bother to look after them, for they can do that for themselves. What are your children like?"

"Oh, they are dear little things,"

said the slow-worm. " They are like little silver needles, and they wriggle about everywhere. You will know them if you meet them by the thin, black line they have down their backs. They really are beautiful creatures."

The Queer Chameleon

" Look, there is a Sand Lizard," suddenly said the common lizard. " He is rather like me, but bigger, so he thinks he is very grand. Do you see how like the sand he is in colouring? He is difficult to see when he stays still. I think I shall go away, Slow-worm, for I don't want to hear the boasting of that old sand lizard."

" He has nothing to boast about," said the slow-worm. " He is a very ordinary lizard. You should just see one of our cousins, the Chameleon! "

" The what? " asked the lizard in surprise.

" The chameleon," repeated the slow-worm. " He is a most extraordinary fellow."

" What colour is he? " asked the lizard.

" He is the colour of his surroundings," said the slow-worm. " If he is near something red he turns red. If he is surrounded by green he is green, and so on."

" What a marvellous thing! " cried the lizard. " That must be very useful to him when he doesn't want to be seen! "

" It is," said the slow-worm. " Then you should see his strange eyes. They stick out from his head, and he can move them in opposite directions if he wants to, so that he can see all around him, without moving his head or body at all."

" Dear me," said the lizard. " He *must* be a queer creature. What does he eat? "

" Insects, as we do," said the slow-worm. " But you ought to watch him catching them! He keeps quite still on a branch until a fly lands near by. Then he shoots out a very long tongue—as long as the chameleon himself!—and catches the fly on its sticky, club-shaped end as quick as lightning. It is marvellous to watch."

" It must be," said the lizard. " But pray excuse me now. I think I see a smooth snake coming, and I must go. I don't want to be his dinner to-day."

Then in a trice off slipped the nimble lizard, the silent slow-worm, and the nearby sand lizard. When the smooth snake came up, there was nobody there at all.

Chas. Barrett.

BEARDED DRAGON LIZARD

Fearsome as are the looks of this bearded dragon lizard, it is really harmless. Its open mouth and throat are vivid scarlet, and with its spiked frill give it a terrifying appearance. The mouth is opened wide in moments of great excitement.

A TONGUE LIKE A TELESCOPE

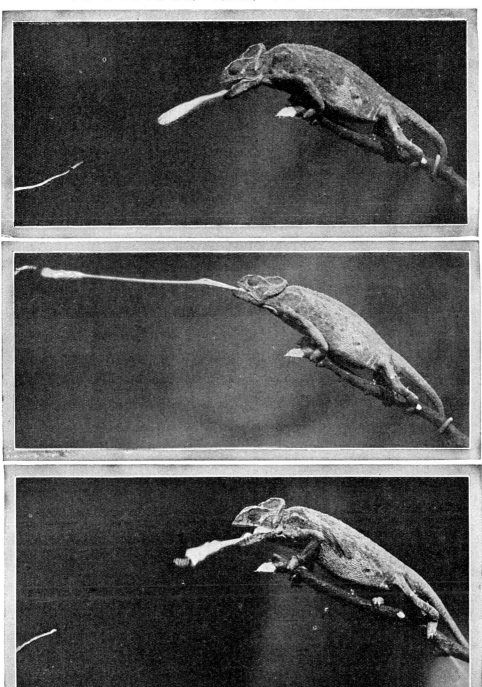

F W. Bond.

The chameleon, a kind of lizard, feeds like a toad. He sits very still until a fly settles near, then out goes his tongue as quick as a flash (top picture). In No. 2 the tongue is at its full length; in No. 3 the tongue is being drawn back with the insect stuck fast to its tip.

THE FROG AND HIS COUSINS

F. W. Bond.

THE AMERICAN BULL-FROG

This particular member of the frog family is noted for the loud croaking noise he makes. In the breeding period these creatures herd together in considerable numbers, and you can hear their croaking even when they are a long distance away.

IT was early spring-time, and the Frogs, who had been sleeping head downwards in the mud at the bottom of the pond, awoke and stretched themselves. They felt the warm sun striking down through the water, and they joyfully swam up to the surface.

"It is egg-laying time," they said to one another, and soon the pond was spread with clusters of white jelly in which were embedded many thousands of tiny, black specks—the eggs. After a time the jelly swelled, and rose to the surface so that the sun might warm the eggs inside.

Then the black specks changed their shape, and became long instead of round. When three weeks had gone by they had grown big enough to leave the jelly, and one day numbers of tiny tadpoles made their way out of it. Each little black tadpole had a pair of suckers underneath its head, and with these it managed to hold on to the water-weed near by.

Then mouths appeared, and all the tadpoles began to feed on the soft leaves of the water-weed. They were strange-looking little creatures, all head and tail, very wriggly and black.

Soon little plume-like gills burst out from the sides of their heads, and they breathed the air in the water by means of these. After a while a flap grew over the gills, and then they could no longer be seen.

Presently came the hind legs, tiny little things, but useful to the tadpole when it wanted to cling to anything. The front legs were growing too, but they were hidden by the gill flap. Other changes took place inside the creature's body, and soon it had changed from a water-breathing animal to an air-breathing one, for lungs took the place of gills, and next it came up to the surface to breathe.

Then the front legs appeared, and the tadpole really began to look like a

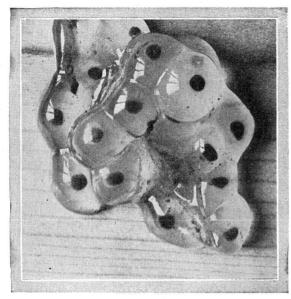

THE STORY OF THE FROG (1) *M. H. Crawford.*

We would like to give you three guesses at the subject of this photograph, but must tell you that it is frog-spawn taken from a pond, each egg enclosed in its jelly-like envelope. The yolks, you see, are at first quite circular, but—

were gone and spring-time came again.

You must often have seen a frog, and wondered at his bold, bright eyes and long hind legs that can give such sudden, startling leaps, taking him away from you in a trice. His skin is smooth and moist, and he breathes through it as well as through his lungs.

His head is very broad, and his mouth wonderfully wide. If you saw it open you would notice that his tongue is fixed to the *front* of his mouth, and not to the back as ours is, which means that he can fling it out a good way to capture flies or other insects. Like the lizard and the slow-worm, the frog has eyelids, and has also a third eyelid such as birds have, which he can flash across his eyes when he wants to.

On each of his two front legs are four fingers, and on his two hind legs are five toes, webbed to help him in his

little frog at last. Its long tail grew shorter and shorter, and soon was gone altogether. It was now a tiny frog.

The Young Frog's First Journey

It played happily in the pond until a wet day came. Then, with its brothers and sisters, it left the water and started out on a journey over the soaked fields to find another home for itself. So many frogs set forth all together that it really looked as if it had been raining frogs!

Some of them made their homes in ditches, some in meadows, and some in gardens. People were glad to welcome them to their gardens, for they ate many caterpillars and flies.

When the cold weather came they all went to the pond to bury themselves in the mud, or found a stone by the river side, and hid under it. There they stayed fast asleep until the winter days

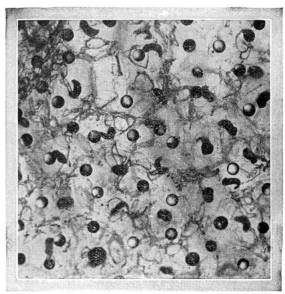

THE STORY OF THE FROG (2) *M. H. Crawford.*

After a few days the hatching process begins and the yolks break up, while the jelly surrounding them begins to be absorbed. This photograph shows them as you would see them when looking down into the pond from above. (*Continued on page* 170.)

swimming. He swims very gracefully indeed, using his long hind legs to send him swiftly along.

A Cousin of the Frog

Do you know the difference between the frog and the toad? They are alike in some things, but very different in others.

The toad's hind legs are not nearly as long as the frog's, which means he cannot leap so well. He crawls instead, occasionally giving a short jump. His hind legs are not so webbed as his cousin's, but he can swim excellently.

Many people think he is hideous, but that is not quite true. He has bright, coppery-red eyes that look most intelligent, and his body is compact and well-proportioned. His skin is different from the frog's, for it is not smooth or moist. It is dry and grey-brown, sprinkled all over with little

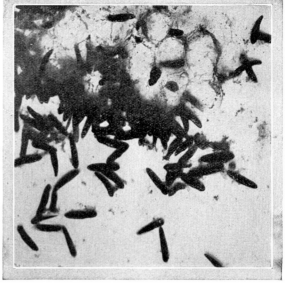

THE STORY OF THE FROG (3) *M. H. Crawford.*
For a day or two the tadpoles look like this. They are hardly alive as yet, and since they have no lungs, no mouth and no eyes, they are still unable to breathe or eat or see. This stage does not last long, and under the influence of the warm spring sun—

warts. From these he can ooze out an evil-smelling substance, very poisonous, which is a protection against his enemies.

He changes his skin very often, and when he has slipped out of it he rolls it up neatly into a ball and swallows it. He does not believe in wasting anything! He likes the same food as the frog, and will eat as many flies, caterpillars, slugs and other insects as he can get. Sometimes he uses his front paws as hands, and tucks his food into his mouth with them.

He likes to come out at night, and then his grey-brown colouring makes him very difficult to see, especially when he squats close to the earth and keeps very still, as he will do for a long time if he thinks that enemies are near.

When winter comes he hides in a hole somewhere, or buries himself in loose earth, or crawls

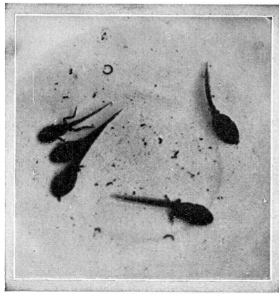

THE STORY OF THE FROG (4) *M. H. Crawford.*
They turn into true tadpoles, fishlike creatures with long tails and large heads, able to swim rapidly and feed on tiny animalcules. The hind legs appear and grow quickly, and the creatures continue to live as fish until the time comes for their change to true frogs.

THE STORY OF THE FROG (5) *M. H. Crawford.*
The tadpole's tail slowly disappears. The little
creature has absorbed it—indeed may be said to have
lived upon it; then gradually the legs appear; and
here is a picture of the young frog just before it leaves
the pond and becomes an amphibian.

times he is called Golden Back,
because of the yellow line along
his back. You will not find him
often if you live in Scotland,
for he is rare in that country, but
he is very common in the south-
west of Ireland.

He is smaller than the Common Toad, and has much shorter
legs. His eyes are bright yellow,
and stick out from his head. He
is not often more than $2\frac{1}{2}$ inches
in length. He does not crawl
like the Common Toad, but
makes little mouse-like runs,
with short stops in between.

His skin is warty, and on the
upper part of his back are spots
of green or brown. Under-
neath he is yellowish-white
with spots of black. He croaks
loudly and harshly, especially
in April, May and June, when
he is seeking a wife.

The eggs are laid in strings
like those of the Common Toad, but the
strings are less than half the length.

under a stone. In the spring-time he
goes to the pond and finds a wife. She
puts her eggs in the water, but
does not lay them in big masses
as the frog does. She lays them
in a long string instead.

The tadpoles hatch out in
about a fortnight, and follow
much the same life as the frog-
tadpoles. There is one difference
you will notice, if you keep both
kinds of tadpoles, and that is
that the front legs of the toad
appear before the hind legs,
whereas the frog babies grow
their *back* legs first.

Toads make very good pets,
and will take up their quarters
in your garden for years if you
will let them.

The Little Natterjack

You may sometimes find a
small, greenish-yellow toad, with
a pretty golden line down his
back. This is the little Natterjack, or Running Toad. Some-

THE STORY OF THE FROG (6) *M. H. Crawford.*
The last of our frog pictures shows the fully grown
animal bright in his summer suit. His powerful hind
legs enable him to hop at a great rate. When winter
comes he will return to his pond, bury himself in the
mud and sleep until the spring.

Mirror Features.

ONE OF THE GARDENER'S FRIENDS

Apart from its eyes, jewel-like in their beauty, the toad is rather an ugly amphibian. Its colour is brownish grey, its skin warty, its head flat. Yet the garden has no more useful inmate, for each toad destroys thousands of harmful insects and grubs in the course of a summer. This photograph shows a young common toad; but we have also the Natterjack, which may be distinguished from the others by the bright yellow line running down its back.

They hatch out into tadpoles, which six weeks later are small four-limbed toads.

Like its bigger cousin, the Natterjack likes to come out at night, but it can sometimes be seen in the daytime. When it is frightened, it often stretches itself out flat on the ground, feigning to be dead. It may quite easily be tamed, and if kept in a vivarium, makes an interesting pet.

When Newts Swim

The frogs and toads have a distant relation called the Newt. Many people mix them up with lizards, and cannot tell the difference between the two, but really they have little in common except general shape.

Newts keep their tails throughout their life, which is one way in which they differ from frogs who, as you have read, soon lose their tadpole tails.

If a newt gets his tail bitten off he grows it again.

His skin is clammy and moist. He has two pairs of legs, all about the same length. The front pair have four " fingers," and the back pair have five toes. They are too small and weak to help very much in swimming, so the newt uses his long strong tail as both rudder and propeller.

The Crested Newt

Our largest newt is the Great Crested, or Warty Newt. It is six inches long, counting its tail, which is usually about $2\frac{1}{2}$ inches. Its name of Warty Newt is due to its warty skin. It is dark brown on its back, and a beautiful bright orange underneath, marked with bold black spots. A sprinkling of white dots can be seen down the sides.

It is in the spring-time that the Great

WHY THE TOAD CAN'T HOP!

F. W. Bond.

The toad's hind legs are not as long as those of the frog, so he has to crawl along instead of hopping. The common toad of Britain is about 3½ inches long and, in colour, is brownish above and whitish below. Toads are found in most parts of the world; one of the most interesting is the Giant Surinam Toad of South America. In this picture a Common Toad is perched on the back of a Giant Toad.

L. Hugh Newman.

The Great Crested, or Warty Newt, is olive-brown and its back exhibits many dark spots. Underneath it is a lovely orange or yellow hue, with dark dots. The male newt in the picture has a long crest running from his head to his tail. There are two other species in Britain, the Common Newt and the Palmated Newt.

Newt is at his best, for then he grows his marvellous crest. This starts from his head in a low frill, and rises high along his back, where it is also deeply notched. Just before his tail there is a gap in his crest, but it rises again above and below as a tailfin. Along the sides of his tail is a bluish silvery stripe. As he swims, his great crest waves to and fro in the water. He is truly a beautiful sight in the spring months.

His wife has the same pretty colouring, but she does not grow the crest. She is a little bigger than he is. Her eggs are laid one at a time and carefully attached to the leaves of water plants. Sometimes she bends a leaf over the egg to hide it. Her eggs stay where they are put because they are sticky.

J. J. Ward.

THE STORY OF THE NEWT (1)

The three little, black-centred globes attached to the leaf of this water-weed are spawn or eggs of the smooth newt, common in the British Isles. This lizard-like animal swims powerfully, but on land can only crawl at a comparatively slow pace.

They are encased in jelly, like the eggs of frog and toad.

In two weeks' time the eggs hatch and tadpoles appear. They are not as sturdy-looking as those of the frogs, but are slimmer and more delicately made. They are far more fish-like, too. In colour they are yellowish-green, and grow three tiny pairs of gills. From their upper jaws appear two pairs of little threads which they use when they want to cling to water-weeds.

They grow slowly, and by the end of the summer they are proper newts. Then they climb out of the pond and go to find a nice damp spot in which to pass the winter. Many of them hibernate together, curled up in a large ball. If by chance the newt tadpoles are not fully grown, and are more tadpole than newt by the time the cold weather comes, they go to the bottom of the pond as the frogs do. Even if they are

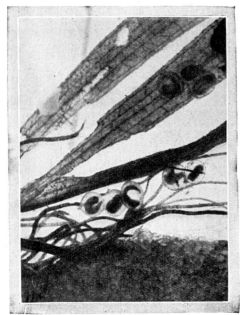

J. J. Ward.

THE STORY OF THE NEWT (2)

Here are the same eggs developing into tadpoles. It takes about fourteen days for the eggs to hatch, and the tadpoles which emerge are quite transparent and fish-like in form. It is not for another three weeks that the gills turn into lungs.

J. J. Ward.

THE STORY OF THE NEWT (3)

We see the mother newt in the act of fixing her eggs to the leaf of a water-weed. The egg itself is sticky and clings to the leaf, but to make all safe the newt uses her hind legs to fold the leaf over the egg.

frozen into the ice, they do not mind—they thaw out alive and kicking in the warm spring-time!

The tadpoles feed on vegetable matter and on tiny living things in the pond, and as they grow they take any fly or grub they can find. When they are on land they eat much the same meals as the frog and toad—flies, insects, grubs and worms.

The newt sometimes changes its skin, and just before this happens it feels rather uncomfortable. The skin splits first around the mouth. The newt uses its hands to try to loosen it, and at last manages to wriggle right out. It wears a fine new coat, and sometimes

eats up its old one. If it does not you may see the empty skin floating about the pond.

When the young newt leaves the water at the end of his first summer, he does not return there for three years. Then, when he is fully mature, he goes back to the pond again in the spring-time. He grows his marvellous crest, dons brilliant colours and seeks a wife. He kisses her, butts her with his head, and fondles her with his tail. He stays in the pond until eggs are laid, and then once more returns to land. Only about a quarter of each year is spent in the water.

The Smooth Newt

This is our best-known newt, for it is commoner than the others, especially in the eastern counties. It has other names—the Spotted Newt, the Common Newt, the Eft. The name Smooth Newt is given to it because of its

J. J. Ward.

THE STORY OF THE NEWT (4)

This photograph gives a good idea of a young newt at the age of about three weeks. The hind legs have not yet sprouted, its gills are still large, and it is only just beginning to breathe through its lungs. It still feeds on vegetable matter. (*Continued on page 176.*)

smooth skin, quite different from the warty one of the Great Newt. It is smaller than its cousin, too, for it is only 3 inches or 4 inches long. It is olive-brown, and on its back are dark spots. It is a lovely orange or yellow underneath, with dark spots.

The colours are at their brightest in the spring-time. The male newt then grows a long crest that runs without a gap from his head to his tail. It is not deeply notched like that of the Great Newt, but is dented regularly all the way along. On each side of the tail is a bright blue stripe with dark dots.

He has a pale throat of white or yellow with black spots, and very pretty golden eyes. His wife is not so bright underneath, and often has no spots. She lays her eggs in the spring-time, four or five in a cluster. They are laid in a stringy film, and stuck to water-weeds. The tadpoles soon hatch out, and are spotted with yellow down the sides.

When egg-laying time is over the newts lose their bright colours. They go to land, and when winter comes curl up into a ball and fall fast asleep.

The Palmate Newt

This newt has its hind feet webbed when in the water, forming a kind of hand or palm, to which it owes its name. It is a small, smooth-skinned creature, seldom growing more than 3 inches long, and found more often in the west than the east.

It grows a smooth-edged crest in the spring, and a fold of skin appears down each side of its back, giving it a four-sided appearance. It is olive-brown, and orange or yellow underneath. The end of its tail is thread-like, and this makes it easy to identify when found.

On Land and Water

Frogs, toads and newts are all called by the long name of *Amphibian*. This means double (*amphi*) life (*bios*) creatures, and when you remember that they pass part of their life in the water and part on land you will see that the name is a good one.

L. *Hugh Newman.*

THE STORY OF THE NEWT (5)

Here is a fully-grown male smooth newt, beautifully spotted and with a frill along his back. The female has no frill, and is spotted only on her long tail. Grown newts live on insects, worms, etc.

WILD LIFE IN AUSTRALIA

Australian Geographical Society

Forms of animal and vegetable life exist in Australia and New Zealand which have become extinct, or possibly never existed, elsewhere. Only in Australia can the Koala bears be found and because of the danger of their extinction they are protected by law. About 2 ft. tall, with grey-brown woolly fur, big bushy ears, no tail and a snub nose, the Koala is gentle, eats only certain kinds of eucalyptus leaves, and drinks nothing. The name, given them by the aborigines, means "nothing to drink."

Australia's best-known animal is the Kangaroo. About the size of a peanut when born, it lives for a time in its mother's pouch. When fully grown it is 6 ft. tall and weighs about 200 lb. It can travel at 40 miles an hour at top speed, leap 20 ft, and jump obstacles 9 ft high. In the picture above the young kangaroo peeps out from its mother's pouch to nibble the herbage.

Photos: Australian News and Information Bureau

One of the world's largest birds, the Australian Emu, is about 5 ft. high and has brownish-black feathers. It cannot fly but runs very fast, and feeds on grass, grain, leaves and berries.

A near relation to the Emu is the Cassowary, a bird found only in Australia, New Guinea and adjacent islands. The skin of the neck is brightly coloured while the plumage is coarse fibrous hair.

SONG BIRDS AND MIMICS

Australia's finest song bird and mimic is the Lyre Bird, which takes its name from its curiously-shaped tail. The male bird is the showman and will spend hours in practising a new noise.

Belonging to the Kingfisher family, the Kookaburra or Laughing Jackass has a call which is just like the human laugh. It is grey in front, with brown feathers and pale blue specks on its wings.

Photos: Australian News and Information Bureau

The bush Budgerigar, sometimes called the Australian love-bird, is bright green with black markings on the wings. It grows to a length of about 7½ ins. of which 4 ins. are taken up by the tail.

Lamington National Park is Australia's "Lost World," a 48,000-acre reserve in Queensland, and here live thousands of these White Cockatoos. The black variety is also found here.

A LIZARD AND TWO SAVAGES

The Goanna is the largest of Australia's 200 types of lizards. A tree-climbing reptile, it grows to a length of 6 ft. or more and is valuable for destroying rabbits, snakes, rats and mice.

Although handsome, the Dingo, the wild dog of Australia, is extremely savage. It is generally regarded as a pest as it raids the sheep flocks at night and does a great deal of damage.

Photos: Australian News and Information Bureau

Found only in the island from which it takes its name, the Tasmanian Devil is a fierce marsupial animal, absolutely untamable and very formidable. Its length is about 28 ins. to which the tail adds another 12 ins. Like the badger which it resembles to some extent, the Tasmanian Devil lives in a burrow and does its hunting at night.

THE WALLABY, OPOSSUM AND PLATYPUS

In this picture is seen a Wallaby, the name originally given by the natives to some of the smaller kinds of kangaroo. They are usually brighter in colour than their bigger relatives.

The Australian Opossums, usually called "possums," are mainly vegetarian and live in hollows or nests in the trees. The Ring-tail Opossum, seen above, has a tail as long as its body, about 14 ins.

Australian News and Information Bureau

The world's strangest creature, and probably the most ancient type of animal surviving today, is the Australian Platypus. It has a bill similar to that of a duck, webbed feet with claws, a tail like a beaver's, and a furred body. It lays eggs but provides milk for its young, and it lives in a burrow but is equally at home in the water where it finds its food.

IN THE GREAT BARRIER REEF

Australian News and Information Bureau

Captain Cook was the first sailor to cross the Great Barrier Reef, the coral reef 1,200 miles long off the North-east coast of Australia. Between the reef and the picturesque Queensland coast are countless palm-shaded islets, and in the warm, pleasant waters, tropical fish abound. Our photograph shows the Red-banded Coral fish at home in the Great Barrier Reef waters.

FLOWER EMBLEMS AND THE SATIN BOWER BIRD

Belonging to the Acacia family, the Wattle flower is Australia's national emblem. Wattles range from dwarf plants to forest giants and are lavish in golden bloom, typical of their sunny homeland.

Next to the Wattle the most spectacular of Australia's many flowers is the Waratah. It has large crimson flowers and vivid green leaves. It is the emblem of New South Wales.

Photos: Australian News and Information Bureau

Found in the eastern coastal districts, the Australian Satin Bower Bird builds a bower or playground away from its nest. All kinds of brightly coloured objects, such as shells, flowers and feathers, are collected to decorate the bower, and here the bird dances and plays. When young the bird is greyish-green, with brown wings and tail, but later the male changes to blue-black plumage.

STRIKING FLOWERS AND WHISTLING LEAVES

There are 13,000 varieties of flowering plants in Australia. They flourish particularly in the South-west and many of them can be found nowhere else in the world. The flower heads of *Banksia coccinea*, seen above, show striking contrasts of scarlet and silver grey. The flower grows on the rocky hillsides around Albany and is particularly rich in honey.

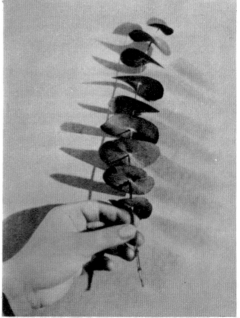

Photos: Australian News and Information Bureau

Growing on the high sandy plains of Western Australia is the Mottlecah (*Eucalyptus Macrocarpa Hook*), 10-15 ft. high. Its blossoms, seen here, are 3-4 ins. in diameter, and its fruit 2-2½ ins.

Eucalyptus Perriniana, 15-20 ft. high, is found in Australia's Alpine regions, and is known as the whistling or spinning gum. The leaves work loose and spin in high wind, producing a whistling noise.

WILD LIFE IN AUSTRALASIA

Australian News and Information Bureau.

KANGAROOS CAN TRAVEL AT 40 MILES PER HOUR

To cover 25 or 30 feet at one leap, the kangaroo has developed hind limbs of great power. These, with the long, thick tail, keep the bulk of his weight at the stern, for his head and front limbs are small and light. All this helps him to keep his balance.

THERE are in Australasia creatures, trees and plants found nowhere else in the world. Australasia consists of Australia, New Zealand, New Guinea, and all the other islands southeast of the " Wallace Line." This is an imaginary line dividing the islands which have animals and plants of the Australian kinds from those which belong to Asia, and it was first marked on a map by the naturalist, A. R. Wallace. Chief of the Australasian countries is, of course, the island continent of Australia, and here live many odd creatures whose forms and habits have puzzled scientists ever since their discovery.

Cut off by the Sea

One thing they do know. In the remote past Australia was joined to India on the north and to the regions round the South Pole (Antarctica), and changes in the earth's crust caused the sea to flow in and turn what is now Australia into a vast island. That meant that all forms of life, except the birds with strong flying wings, were completely cut off, and families of creatures and species of plants that have died out or changed in other parts of the world are still living on the huge island pretty much as they were living thousands of years ago. You could almost call them living fossils.

The Strangest Living Creature

Look at the platypus. It has an animal's body, yet has a bird's bill and webbed feet. It swims like a duck, yet burrows tunnels like a rabbit. It lays eggs like a bird, yet suckles its young like a mammal. But she has not got teats like other mammals. The babies suck the milk from glands in her skin.

Platypus builds a nest, but its cousin, the spiny ant-eater, grows a temporary pouch in which to hatch its eggs and nurse the baby, for the ant-eater is another queer mixture of mammal and bird. It is covered with sharp quills like a porcupine, and has a long, thin nose to get at the ants it loves to eat. Once this has been pushed into an ant's nest, its long stringy tongue shoots out and hundreds of the insects are caught on its sticky saliva.

Kangaroo's Long Jump

The most famous of the pouched animals (called marsupials) is the kangaroo, but Australia has 150 pouched creatures, while the rest of the world has only one—the American opossum. The kangaroo has short front legs, but the great powerful muscles of his long hind legs and thick tail enable him to make 30-foot leaps when he is bouncing along at thirty to forty miles an hour, and he can clear a 9-foot fence.

STRANGE AND SHY

Paul Popper.

This is one of the eight kinds of spiny ant-eaters found in Australasia, and is confined to New Guinea. It is known as the three-toed echidna, or the black-spined porcupine ant-eater, and it lives upon termites and ants. It catches these by means of its long, thin, sticky tongue. The spiny ant-eater is related to the duck-billed platypus and these two differ from all other mammals in that they are egg-layers, like the majority of birds and reptiles.

E. N. A.

The wombat is a heavy burrowing animal often 3 feet long, but it can seldom be spotted. It is shy, and leaves its long tunnel only at night to feed on grass and roots. It is considered a great pest by farmers and its nightly forages cause great damage on cultivated land such as vegetable gardens. It is found only in the Australian and Tasmanian bush.

FIERCE AND FRIENDLY

You would not think these innocent-looking puppies could grow into savage brutes, but they will! The dingo is the only direct descendant of the wolf found in Australasia, and though it has always been hunted down as a pest for its attacks on flocks, it still thrives. Apart from sheep and rabbits, dingoes prey upon bandicoots, wallabies, ground-dwelling birds and other small native creatures.

Photos: E.N.A.

A large bandicoot looks rather like a giant rat, but is an attractive and friendly creature, and amazingly active, whether digging for insects or just playing around. Bandicoots are mainly insect-eaters and they also like roots, and are busy diggers and scratchers, persecuted by farmers as pests. This picture shows a short-nosed bandicoot from South Australia, but there are many other species.

Joey—the Pea-nut Baby

The female has one baby (a " joey ") once a year, and when born it is no bigger than a pea-nut. It is suckled in the pouch, where it stays for nine or ten months.

There are many other members of the kangaroo family, the best known being the wallabies. The bettong—a tiny rat-kangaroo—carries grass to its nest by winding its tail round the heap like a spiral funnel, with the tip as the bottom of the " basket " !

The Cuddly Koala

The koala is a nursery teddy-bear come to life. His cuddly fur, comical face and charming ways have made him popular the world over. The koala really *is* unique—the only member of his family still in existence. The baby, less than an inch at birth, is suckled in its mother's pouch for four or five months. Then it is carried about pick-a-back (sometimes pick-a-chest!) by its mother till it can climb for itself.

The Possums

If the tail-less koala is a clinger, the opossum is a swinger, using his long, whippy tail as an extra limb in climbing among branches. One of the possums is famous as the flying squirrel, though he is not a squirrel and cannot fly. But he can volplane well over 100 feet with the help of a sort of webbing along each flank, joining the fore and hind limbs. The opossums range in size from the cuscus down to the tiny honey-mouse, which sucks nectar from flowers.

A RARE ALBINO ANTEATER   *E. N. A.*

Caught at Dunk Island, North Queensland, Australia, this rare variety of the Australian " porcupine " represents a past age. He is one of the echidnas, which share with the platypus the habit of laying eggs and then suckling their young. Unlike the platypus, however, they carry their young in a pouch.

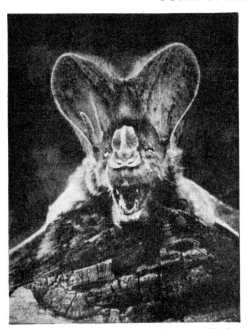

E. N. A.

A GROTESQUE BAT

The false vampire or ghost bat is an Australian cave-bat which feeds on small birds and animals (including other bats), fishes and insects.

Killer Dogs

Australia's only native wild dog is the savage dingo, which preys upon both wild and farm animals. After a century of shooting and trapping, the dingo is still a costly nuisance to farmers. Yet the beasts (about the size of a small wolf) help the farmer in one way: they kill millions of that other pest—the rabbit.

Tasmania has no dingoes, but is bothered by two fierce creatures, 3–4 feet long—the Tasmanian devil and " tiger " —both a menace to farm stock.

Other interesting animals are the bandicoots, of which there are thirty kinds in the continent; the lumbering wombat, and the equally gentle numbat, which has hardly changed for more than a million years.

Of Australasia's 800 kinds of birds, many are, of course, found all over the world, and we must give our space to those that are unique to Australia or New Zealand, and have stories of special interest to tell.

A Bird that Paints

Bower-birds nest in trees, but they also build play-halls on the ground, weaving two parallel walls of twigs and grasses, one on either side of a cleared space. Sometimes the walls are bent at the top in an arch, but always they are decorated with any bright objects they fancy—bits of blue glass or paper, blue feathers, bleached bones.

But the satin bower-bird is world-famous because it mixes coloured juices of berries with saliva and *paints* the play-hall, usually daubing it on with a piece of frayed bark!

The Brolgas' Dancing Parties

Those stately long-legged birds, the brolgas, hold dancing parties. At certain times up to 100 will form a large circle round their leader, and when he begins to jig and twist and turn they all imitate every caper. When they tire of the game, they form up in pairs and stalk off in procession! The few bird-watchers who have been lucky

E. N. A.

THE FLYING FOX

This famous Australian animal is really a large fruit bat, which makes nightly raids on orchards. By day it sleeps hanging upside-down in the trees

enough to see this rare performance say that it is quite uncanny.

The lyre-bird is famous for its tail, for this mass of delicate shimmering feathers is shaped rather like the frame and strings of an ancient instrument called the lyre. Only the male has this strange decoration, and when he lifts and spreads the tail out above his back to please the very plain lady bird it is a wonderful sight. These birds are also very clever mimics, copying any sound they hear, from a dog's bark to the thud of a tree-feller's axe.

Every Australian loves the kookaburra, with his bright eyes, broad grin and loud laugh, which has given him the nickname laughing jackass. He is the largest of the Australian kingfishers. When he laughs,

Copyright.

THE KIWI

This flightless New Zealand bird is a living fossil, for all its near relatives are extinct. Distant relations include the emu and cassowary of Australia, the rhea and the ostrich.

he throws his head back, and the merry uproar can be heard half a mile away.

The emu, which appears with the kangaroo on the coat of arms of the Commonwealth, is the biggest bird in the world after the ostrich. The beautiful black swans of Australia are as familiar a sight as the white swans of Europe. The parrots and cockatoos are the finest in the world. The forty-three kinds between them display every imaginable colour.

Beaks that Light Up

These are but a few of the many interesting birds which are native to Australasia. Others will be found in the pictures. Let us give the last word to the little Gouldian finches of the forests of north Australia. When the parents fly home with food out of the dazzling sun they would find it hard to see the tiny beaks in the jungle gloom, so nature has provided the part round the babies' mouths with luminous spots that light up the open beaks as a guide to mother finch!

Two Oddities

Among the many odd creatures which

Mondiale.

THE KEA

Before sheep were introduced into New Zealand the kea was a harmless and respectable bird. But then it discovered it could dig fat out of the sheeps' backs with its pick-axe bill, and it is now in disgrace.

STRANGE PARTNERS

The tuatera of New Zealand is another living relic of remote ages, for it is the sole remaining member of an otherwise extinct order of reptiles. It is about 20 inches long and olive-brown in colour, with yellow spots. It lives in a burrow which it generally shares with a petrel.

live only in Australasia is the lizard-like Tuatera of New Zealand. This reptile still has, in the top of its skull, the socket in which its remote ancestors possessed a third eye.

New Guinea has a quaint tree-frog, which climbs and leaps about among the branches, holding on by suckers at the ends of its toes. It is by no means unique, however, for there are other kinds of tree frogs in most of the warmer parts of the world.

Famous Trees and Flowers

The plant life of Australasia is wonderfully rich and varied. The first tree and flower we think of as typical of Australia is the acacia, or wattle, though Australians would perhaps put the eucalyptus or gum trees first in importance, because these magnificent trees produce such huge quantities of valuable timber.

Eucalyptus, like the mountain ash of the eastern states, and the jarrah and karri of Western Australia, are such giants in height and thickness that one tree can supply enough excellent timber to build a large country house made entirely of wood. The top of one

A TREE-FROG

This little tree-frog lives in New Guinea, where he climbs and leaps among the branches of the jungle.

A LEAF INSECT

Bright green in colour, this insect looks exactly like a part of the plant on which it rests, its legs resembling partly-nibbled leaves.

mountain ash was only a yard short of the height of the cross on the dome of St. Paul's; and a huge " karri," 342 feet high, was 40 feet round near the base.

The " karri," a gum tree, must not be confused with the magnificent kauri pine, native of New Zealand and Queensland. Both " karri " and kauri are among the many valuable Australasian trees disliked by the " white ant," which eats into other kinds of wood and does great damage.

The World's strongest Timbers

Between them, the gum trees produce not only some of the strongest of the world's timbers, but wood of beautiful markings and unusual colours for decorative work—cream, yellow, gold, pink, red, light and dark browns. But these are all hardwoods, and for many jobs softwoods are better, e.g., for making plywood and wood-pulp for paper. Pine

is the most useful softwood, and great forests are being planted to overcome the shortage of native conifers.

Imagine a tree 60 feet round and only 40 feet high. Those are often the measurements of the queer bottle tree's trunk. All its branches stick out of the bottle neck in a large tuft. In summer it stores up to 80 gallons of water ready for the dry winter.

Another odd-looking specimen is the grass tree. It looks rather like a giant shaving-brush, for out of the top of its short trunk bursts a brush of long, narrow leaves, with a tall spike of whitish flowers soaring up from the centre.

THE TERMITES' TOWER

This is the nest of the termite or " white ant," which is such a pest in Queensland and other parts of Australia. Related to the cockroaches, the termites build underground cities and open-air mounds like those of the true ants.

AUSTRALIAN FLOWERS

H. T. Reeves.

The pink starry flowers seen in these sprays of Snow Myrtle smother the branches of this attractive shrub, which is a favourite in Victoria and South Australia.

New South Wales Govt.

Up to 20 of the brilliant red-and-orange bells may crowd on a single stem of this plant, known as Christmas Bells. There are four varieties found in different parts of Australia.

New South Wales Govt.

These are named Flannel Flowers from the thick covering of hairs on the bracts. In the pink flannel the flowers in the centre are surrounded by reddish-brown hairs.

H. T. Reeves.

The yellow pompoms of the " buttons " of these Golden Billy Buttons make a pretty show on damp flats or in flooded paddocks, their golden heads nodding in the breeze.

Death by Glue

The strange Queensland upas tree oozes from its seed-vessels a gluey substance which is death to birds and insects. Once a wing touches this glue, struggling only spreads the smear and escape is hopeless.

One of the glories of Australia is the Illawarra flame tree. When the groves are in blossom their burning crimson and orange really make one think the hills are aflame. Australia is peculiarly rich in flowers the colour of a glowing fire and the fire-wheel tree is another bearing large red blossoms.

Australian News and Information Bureau.
A USEFUL TREE

In summer time, the bulging trunk of this unique Australian bottle tree may contain as much as eighty gallons of stored waters.

Fantastic Flowers

Most gorgeous of all is the waratah, with its handsome flower-head of deep crimson. The brilliant red and orange of the bottlebrushes are their nearest rival. The crowded stamens stand out from the flower spike like the bristles of a dazzling cylindrical brush. Other glories include the Grevillea, the Banksias, the Christmas bells, Nuytsia, Sturt's desert pea, and the golden wattle pompoms.

It is not surprising that, when Captain Cook saw the wonderful new plants Sir Joseph Banks and the other botanists brought aboard, he changed the name of their landing-place from Stingray Bay to Botany Bay.

Sad P.S.—The early settlers took some pets and other reminders of home with them to Australia. Some escaped and went wild, and now millions of rabbits and starlings are a serious pest. So are the imported Scotch thistles and the St. John's wort, to say nothing of the prickly pear cactus!

Australian News and Information Bureau.
CURIOUS GRASS TREES

Only in Australia will you find these black-boys, or grass trees, which are between 6 and 8 feet high. Their whitish flowers grow on a long stalk or upright spike which increases the height of the trees, sometimes to **as much as 12 or 15 feet.**

From the
Nature=lover's
Notebook

Winged
Creatures
of the Air

C. C. Doncaster.

BRINGING HOME THE DINNER

This young male kestrel returns to the nest with a tasty meal for his family. The kestrel is the most common British falcon and lives mostly on mice and other small rodents. It is sometimes called the "Windhover." Kestrels are very useful to farmers because they prey on small animals, such as the house mouse seen in this picture, which are often the cause of damage to crops.

BIRDS AND THEIR WAYS

ALL ABOUT BIRDS' NESTS

YOU are sure to have seen many birds' nests and wondered at the pretty, cup-shaped cradles in which birds put their precious eggs. How neat they are, and how beautifully made! How did birds learn their art?

They didn't learn it in the same way as you learn to sew, or read, or write, by having someone to show you how and what to do. They know what to do *by instinct*. That is, when a certain time of year comes, a feeling grips the birds to seek for hay, straw, mud, leaves or hair, and place them all together to make a holding-place for eggs.

We think most birds' nests are very beautifully made. The neatness of the nest is partly because the bird tucks in each straw or twig, leaf or hair separately. With its sharp beak it places its material bit by bit together. If *you* collect the same materials as those used by the birds, and weave them together little by little, you will be able to make quite a fine nest yourself!

While a bird is building her nest she frequently gets into it and renders the inside smooth by pressing her breast against the sides. Thus she makes it cup-shaped and it holds the eggs safely.

Birds use all kinds of things for their nests, usually, of course, the material that lies nearest to hand—the Robin uses the dead leaves around her nesting-site, the sea-bird uses the seaweed, and so on; but all birds of the same kind make the same sort of nest, that is, all Thrushes, for instance, make similar nests of twigs and grass lined with mud ; all Kingfishers build theirs in tunnels, and all House Martins make theirs of

187

A. H. Willford.

THE BLACK-HEADED GULL

Right in the centre of a thick tuft of rushes the black-headed gull makes her rough nest, and because she likes such a spot she never builds, as other gulls do, on cliffs or rocks. Here you see this graceful bird in the act of settling on her eggs.

to build near the water, and the Moorhen and Swan put their nests very near to the surface so that their fledglings can tumble straight from the nest into the water and find their swimming-legs at once.

Some birds like to build covered nests. The Long-tailed Tit builds a beautiful ball-shaped nest, and lines it with hundreds and hundreds of feathers. Other birds prefer to put their nests at the end of tunnels. The Kingfisher and the Sand Martin do this. They tunnel 2 feet or 3 feet into banks, and place their nest at the end. Each of them is clever enough to make the tunnel slope upwards so that any water may run out.

Many birds like to put their nests in holes of some kind—a hole in a tree is often used by Tits, a hole in a wall

mud. Of course, one Martin will build better than another, for birds are like human beings—some are clever, some are stupid, some industrious, some lazy.

All kinds of places are chosen for nesting-sites. Trees and bushes are favourite homes, because of the protection they give from enemies and from the weather. Water-birds like

J. Kearton.

A QUAINT NESTING PLACE

Stick an old kettle like this fast between two branches and it is likely that a robin will build in it. Here you see mother robin about to feed her young brood. Robins old and young live entirely on insects.

WAITING FOR THE FLYING LESSON

Capt. C. W. R. Knight.

Two young herons nearly ready to fly are standing in their big, untidy nest, waiting for the fish their parents are catching for them. The nest is near the top of a very tall tree, and in order to photograph it, Captain Knight built a " hide " of sticks and green cloth among the slender branches close to the nest, 60 feet above the ground. Then he hauled up a cinematograph camera by means of a rope and sat there for whole days at a time, taking pictures.

by Starlings, a cliff-hole by Jackdaws. Good holes are used year after year, just as in our world good houses are snapped up and taken possession of.

Bird-babies ready to run at Birth

There are many birds that like to breed on the ground, such as the Lark, the Pheasant and the Partridge. The larger birds do not bother to make much of a nest, which would be too easily seen from above. Their babies hatch out from the egg all ready to run about, and are not blind and helpless as are the young ones of tree-nesting birds.

Terns and Guillemots make no nest at all. The tern puts her eggs among pebbles, or in a sand hollow, knowing that their colouring will make them difficult to see. The guillemot puts hers on a ledge of rock, usually inaccessible, so that it is safe from enemies.

In spring-time the birds are all very busy with their nests. Straw, hay, dead leaves, twigs and grass are easy to find, but lining materials such as hair, feathers or fur are not so widespread. Sparrows will squabble loudly over a feather that has fallen from the breast of a Pigeon, and the Hedge Sparrows will fight for a scrap of rabbit fur. If you have a dog who is brushed on the lawn you will see many little birds waiting near by to pounce on the hairs that fly in the wind.

Posts on which cows or horses like to rub themselves are always visited by the birds, and every hair is taken off and woven into a nest.

Most nests are made, as we said before, of material that lies close at hand. This sometimes leads to funny results. Perhaps you have heard of the little Chaffinch who nested near a church in which weddings had been held. Many-coloured confetti lay on the ground near by, and the chaffinch thought it would be splendid to use it for her nest. She did so, and probably never understood why so many people discovered her nest that year and stared at it so hard!

A Strange Nest

Another curious nest was one made by a Heron. She found a heap of old wire, and built her nest of that. It must have been dreadfully uncomfortable!

Robins, tits and sparrows often put their nests in curious places. Robins build in anything that has belonged to man —old boots, old saucepans, old cans. Once a pair put their nest in a saucepan which had been thrown into a pond, and was floating gaily about! Tits

Oliver G. Pike.

THE FLOATING HOME OF THE GREBE

This nest of the black-necked grebe is really a floating raft made of masses of water-weed, cleverly anchored to the stems of bulrushes. In spite of the damp surroundings the eggs seldom fail to hatch. The young swim as soon as they emerge from the shell.

James's Press Agency.

THE WONDERFUL NEST OF THE WEAVER BIRD

Of nests built by British birds, the most beautiful examples are the bottle-shaped nest of the long-tailed tit and the dainty little hammock in which the golden-crested wren raises her numerous family. But neither of these, wonderful as they are, compare with the marvellous architecture of the weaver birds, of which there are more than two hundred sorts in Asia and Africa. Our picture is better than any words.

sometimes breed in street lamps and letter-boxes.

Next spring-time go into the country and wander along the lanes. There you will learn far more than I can tell you, for you will see the little builders hard at work everywhere, carrying material, choosing sites, and weaving their pretty little nests together in every nook and cranny.

THE MARVELS OF A BIRD'S EGG

WHEN you peep into a bird's nest and see the eggs lying there, do you ever wonder why they are so prettily mottled and marked and are narrower at one end than the other? Why shouldn't all eggs be round and what is the use of the spots?

There is usually a reason for every curious thing in the world of Nature.

The shape and colouring of eggs is most important in birdland, as you will soon see.

Why some Eggs have Pointed Ends

If all birds' eggs were round they would not fit together in the nest so cosily as they do now, for they would take up much more room. If ever you find a Peewit's nest you will see that the mother bird has placed all her eggs so that the narrow ends point towards the centre. Thus they take up little room, and she can brood over all the cluster at once and keep them warm. Turn one or two of her eggs the wrong way round, and she will notice it when she returns, and move them the right way again!

Some birds, such as the Guillemot, have large eggs which are very much

WHEN BIRDS MAKE LOVE

Neville Kingston.

(1.) Did you know there was a bird called the " Peacock Pheasant " ? His plumage is dotted with " eyes " that look to be of metal, and he can spread his tail for the admiration of his lady-love. He comes from India.

Neville Kingston.

(2.) Here is the Great American Egret, which goes in peril of its life on account of the magnificent tail feathers produced during the breeding season. These feathers are known as " ospreys." The bird is a member of the Heron family.

THE GAY PLUMAGE OF MATING=TIME

Neville Kingston.

(3.) Spring is the season when birds mate, and here is a picture of Amherst's Pheasants, from China. Note how the cock-bird is displaying his gaudy plumage to the hen.

Neville Kingston.

(4.) Here is a little-known bird of gorgeous plumage from Manchuria, the Eared-Pheasant or Crossoptilon. There are twenty-two tail-feathers, each nearly two feet long.

RED-THROATED DIVER

Powerful diving birds, with strong straight bills, the Divers are found in Northern lands. Most common of the family is the Red-Throated Diver seen here. It nests in the north of Scotland and in many Scottish islands.

narrower at one end than at the other. The guillemot lays her egg on a rocky ledge, entirely unprotected. If a strong wind comes the egg might blow off, but because of the peculiar shape it simply rolls round and round on the ledge, and does not tumble down to the rocks below. But the bird herself is often careless in rising from the ledge and knocks the egg down!

The Kingfisher has round eggs, but as she places hers safely at the end of a tunnel she does not need to have the usual shape of egg. Birds that lay their eggs in tunnels or on platforms often have round eggs, for there is no fear of them rolling away.

The colouring of eggs is for their protection. In time of war we paint our ships, lorries and tents with spots and splashes, and call it *camouflage*, which means *deception*. The spots break up the outline of the tents and other

things, and so make them difficult to see from a distance.

The Colouring of Eggs

In the same way birds " camouflage " their eggs. A pure white egg in a nest built among green leaves where shadow and sunlight dance together would stand out and be very easily seen. But when it is spotted or streaked with brown or grey it is difficult to see, for it tones in with the spots of shadow and sunlight and is all one with them. Sometimes the eggs are blotched with grey-green like a patch of lichen.

Birds that nest on the ground lay eggs whose colouring matches their surroundings. A bird like the Ringed Plover, which nests on the shore, lays sandy or stone-coloured eggs, speckled just like the shingle on which they are laid. Thus they are almost impossible to see, and if you go to look for them

Photos : Eric Hosking.

SEDGE-WARBLER IN FLIGHT

Another water-loving bird is the Sedge-Warbler. Grasses and sedge, stinging-nettle and bog-loving plants, intertwined in confusion, make its ideal haunt. This Sedge-Warbler was snapped as it returned to its nest in Suffolk marsh lands.

you are likely to tread on them before you see them!

Birds that put their eggs in the darkness of tunnels or holes, or build covered-in nests, do not need to have protective colouring for their eggs, because no enemy can see them. So their eggs are usually white. You will think of the Sand Martin, the Kingfisher and the Barn Owl, all of whom lay white eggs in well-hidden places. Birds that put their nests or eggs in places difficult to reach also have white eggs, and so do birds who are well able to protect them, such as the Heron, who can be very savage when she thinks an enemy is coming to rob her.

Egg-shells

The shells of eggs are not all the same, as I daresay you have found out for yourself. The Kingfisher, for instance,

A. H. Wilford.

THE NEST OF THE CURLEW

All winter through the curlew haunts the salt-water creeks, but in summer comes inland to breed on the moors or mountains, laying four large eggs in a nest flat on the ground. And what a fuss the old birds make if you walk too near their home!

lays eggs with nice, shiny shells, but the Cormorant's eggs are covered with a chalky substance that you can scrape away. If you do, you will see that instead of being a dirty white, as you imagined, it is really a pale green.

The biggest egg laid by our British birds is that belonging to the Wild Goose, which lays a very large egg indeed. Put the smallest by it, and you will smile, for it is the tiny little egg of the Golden-crested Wren.

BIRDS IN THE NURSERY

WHEN the baby birds are in the nest the parents are very busy indeed, for there are many wide-open beaks to feed. Off they go day after day, and make hundreds of journeys to find greenfly, caterpillars and grubs of all sorts for their hungry youngsters. Thousands and thousands of these insect pests are found and

A. H. Wilford.

A TIDY NEST

Down in the osier beds along the south country chalk streams the sedge warbler is common, but with its sober plumage it is not easily seen. Its nest is built in the very thickest of the sedges, and usually holds six eggs. Its song is slight but sweet.

J. D. Rattar.

AN EIDER DUCK'S NEST

Just as a mother rabbit plucks fur from her breast to make a soft resting-place for her babies, so does the eider duck pull the down from her body. In fact, the eggs in the nest are literally packed together in the softest down.

First they must learn to fly. Some parents, such as the House Martin, waste no time in teaching. They simply push their youngsters out of the nest! Then the little ones, fearful of falling, instinctively open their wings and find that they can fly!

Learning to Fly

But others need persuading. The mother bird flutters her wings in front of the nest, and takes a little flight to another branch. Then she comes back again, and tries to persuade the young ones to do the same. One tries, and then another, and soon they all find that it is quite easy to do as mother does, and off they go through the air, following her closely. They know her call, and fly to her when she cries to them to come and be fed or to beware of danger. If any bird is stupid or disobedient it soon perishes. Only the careful, strong and obedient birds grow up to have nests of their own.

Some birds protect their young in a curious way. The Lapwing, for instance, pretends that she has a broken wing, and half-runs, half-flies in front of any one who comes too near her nest, so that they chase her, thinking she is hurt, and can easily be caught. But as soon as she is far from her nest she spreads her wings, which are, of course, not broken at all, and flies triumphantly away.

The Wild Duck plays the same sort of trick. She pretends to be lame, and hobbles in front of you, leading you far away from her ducklings. When she knows they are safe she quacks with delight and flies off to find them.

The Swimming Lesson

Young birds are taught many things besides flying. The Kingfisher teaches his babies to dive into the water and catch fish, the water-birds make their youngsters swim. The Eider Duck does

eaten in nesting-time, and our gardens and orchards are all the better for being rid of them.

When the mother (or father) bird arrives at the nest with a fat caterpillar she sees four or five beaks wide open to receive it. She pops it into the nearest one, and off she goes again. She doesn't know whose turn it is to have the caterpillar, and she doesn't care.

She realises that when a young one has had enough he will sit quietly and keep his beak closed for a while, and then the others will get their chance.

The bright yellow or orange colouring of the nestlings' beaks helps the mother to put the food she brings into the right place quickly. She has no time to waste on a bright spring day, when caterpillars are about in hundreds, and greenfly cluster on all the rose bushes!

Once the chicks have got over the very young stage and have grown feathers and can flutter their wings, their lessons begin. They have to leave the nursery, where they were well fed and protected, and go out into the world to learn how to look after themselves.

A BLACKBIRD'S DAYS IN THE NURSERY

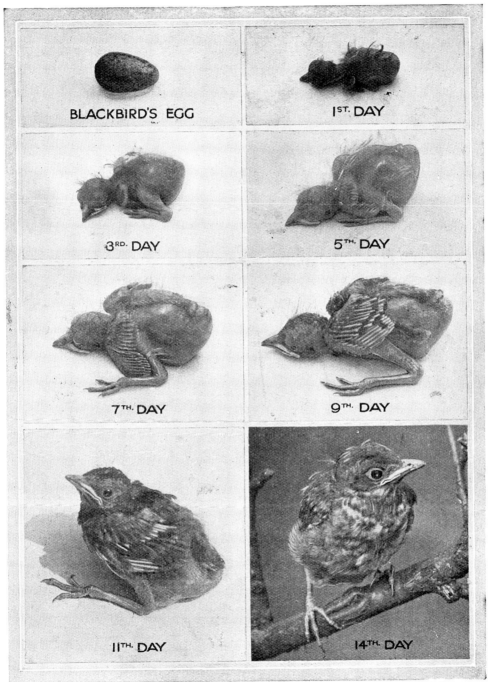

BLACKBIRD'S EGG   1ST. DAY

3RD. DAY   5TH. DAY

7TH. DAY   9TH. DAY

11TH. DAY   14TH. DAY

J. Kearton.

The pale green eggs of the blackbird, speckled with brown, are laid in a nest which is usually made of stout grass stems plastered solidly inside with clay. The young when first hatched have no feathers, and are quite helpless. But they grow quickly, and within a fortnight the young bird is able to leave the nest. Young blackbirds are not black, but brown, and it is only the male birds that acquire a glossy black plumage.

197

this in a curious way. She takes her ducklings for a ride on her back, and swims steadily through the water. Suddenly she dives beneath the surface, and all the little ones find themselves afloat! They *have* to swim then, and off they go, paddling hard with their tiny legs, delighted to do as their mother does!

WHITHER DO THE BIRDS FLY?

WE always listen eagerly for the first Cuckoo to send his pretty double-note on the breeze every spring-time ; then we know he has come back from far lands. We look for the twittering Swallows to come back too, and the little Warblers with their sweet songs.

Why Birds Migrate

Where do they come from, how do they know the way, and why do they leave us again ? These are questions that as yet we can only partly answer. We know that many birds fly off in the late summer and autumn and go to warmer lands, where insects are plentiful. But why do they leave these warm lands with the abundance of food and come back to us in the spring ?

There are many different answers to this. One is that birds like to bring up their young ones in as cold a climate as possible, because they are hardier then; and that is as good a reason as any.

How do they find their way over so many thousands of miles to strange lands ? That we are not sure of yet. We know that birds have a wonderful " homing " instinct, and remember landmarks in a marvellous way, but when we consider that young birds who have never flown to other countries before fly off *by themselves*, without older birds to guide them, we know that memory can have nothing to do with the matter in their case.

Young birds born in the spring start off on their long, long flight quite alone. The old birds follow later. The cuckoos

Eric Hosking.

AS THE TIDE TURNS THE REDSHANKS FEED

Noisy, restless birds, the Redshanks are both residents and winter visitors in all British coastal areas, but particularly on the sandy shores of our Eastern counties. About 12 inches in length, speckled greyish-brown in colour, with black and white barred tails and red legs, they paddle and probe at the water's edge for the small creatures on which they feed

A. H. Wilford.

A NEST FULL OF WAG-TAILS

Wherever there is a pond there are sure to be a couple of pied wagtails, running with quick nimble steps, dainty in their black and white plumage. They are useful as well as pretty, for they live and feed their young entirely on insects and water snails.

are an exception, for the old birds fly off first, and the youngsters some time after.

How the Wind Helps

There is something that greatly helps the migrating birds, both in spring and summer, and that is the wind. In autumn, when a chill comes over the air, the birds become restless and want to fly off. They

rise into the air, and fly with the wind. This blows steadily from the north or north-east, and carries the little migrants southwards, helping them greatly.

In the spring-time, when they feel a longing to go north and nest in the homeland where they themselves were brought up, they once again find that the wind helps them ; for this time a strong south or south-westerly breeze is blowing, which helps them over the hundreds of miles to our land.

Birds fly very fast when migrating. Airmen have told how swallows have raced them, and how very high they have seen birds flying, so high that they are not visible to us down below. Sometimes at night we can hear them calling to one another, keeping in touch. Other birds fly low, so low that

YOUNG SPARROW-HAWKS *J. Kearton.*

These fluffy white chicks are young sparrow-hawks. All hawks build very rough nests, often using the remains of an old nest built by magpie or crow as a foundation. The young are fed on little rabbits, rats, mice, moles and small birds.

they almost skim the waves. They, of course, could not possibly see their way, or be guided by landmarks, but must travel entirely by instinct.

Many, many thousands die on their long journeys to and fro. The weakly ones fall into the sea and perish. Storms destroy many hundreds. Lighthouse keepers tell tales of scores of weary little birds attracted by the light of the lamp, beating their wings against it, only to fall exhausted at last on to the rocks.

But hundreds of thousands of birds in both the northern and southern hemispheres make their long flights over land and sea and arrive safely at their summer or winter homes every season.

This marvel of bird migration has been studied by scientific observers in every continent, and no simple explanation has

MIGRATING BIRDS (2)

The great glare of the lighthouse lantern attracts thousands of migrant birds which in old days beat out their little lives against the hot glass. Nowadays perches are provided by bird lovers, which save the lives of many sweet songsters.

Topical Press.

MIGRATING BIRDS (1)

" Farewell to Summer " is the title of this photograph which shows long lines of swallows perched upon the telegraph wires in late summer. Soon these birds will be off towards Africa.

yet been found. The idea that the birds note special features of the landscape, aided by a keen sense of direction, does not quite work out, though it may play a part in the case of the homing pigeons, which are not really wild birds. Actually, the pigeon is a descendant of the Rock Dove, a bird which is not a migratory creature.

Untrained homing pigeons have very little natural ability to find their way home and it is only by training that they

BRITISH WILD BIRDS — Plate 1

(In order to include as many kinds as possible, the birds shown in these pages have not been drawn in exact proportion to one another.)

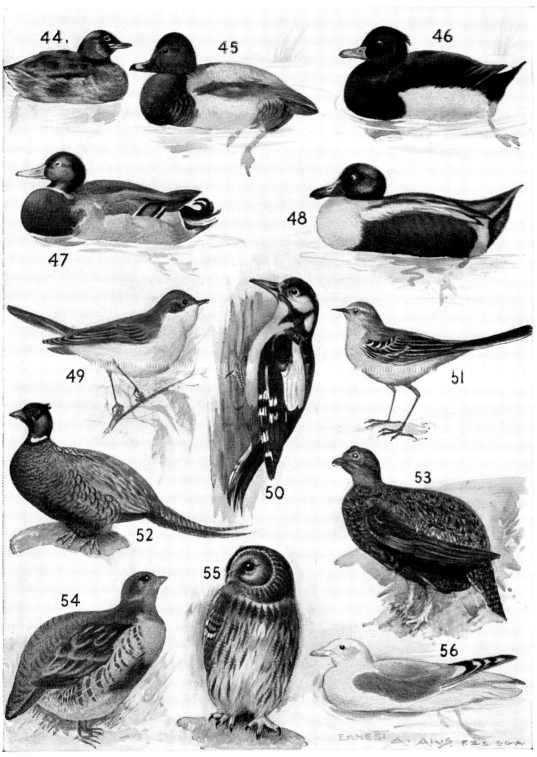

15—Wren. 16—
21—Blue Tit. 22

44—Dabchick. 45—Pochard. 46—Tufted Duck. 47—Wild Duck or Mallard. 48—Shoveller.
49—Whitethroat. 50—Great Spotted Woodpecker. 51—Yellow Wagtail. 52—Pheasant.
53—Grouse. 54—Partridge. 55—Brown Owl. 56—Common Gull.

develop their ability to fly fairly long distances. The migratory birds find their way over much greater distances even when pains have been taken to puzzle and deceive them. Nestling starlings, swallows, storks, terns, petrels and other birds have been removed from their homes and taken great distances by rail and ship, but they have promptly returned home from distances of over a thousand miles.

It is also believed that the routes followed by birds, as well as other migrating creatures, have been the same since pre-historic times. The autumn flight of young birds travelling by themselves, such as the young of the cuckoo who follow their parents after several weeks, is another aspect of this long talked-of puzzle. The mutton-bird of New Zealand which is one of the shearwater family migrates to the southern seas from Siberia. By what instinct, or what methods of navigation, such birds are able to cover such vast spaces, including a wide stretch of open ocean, remains one of the questions to which the scientists are still seeking an answer.

Eric Hosking.

A WHINCHAT ALIGHTS

A summer visitor to Britain, the Whinchat is about 5 inches in length and is common in the hedgerows and gorse-clad districts. This photograph, taken in 1/10,000 of a second by electronic flash, shows the Whinchat in the first stage of alighting. The bird's body is still moving forward, but in another instant its claws will have gripped the perch and the body will be upright.

In recent times much has been learned about the places chosen by certain birds by " ringing." This method, or some variation of it such as " banding," has been used not only for birds but for other animals as well. In the case of birds, a number are caught and round their ankles are put tiny metal rings, with a number on each, and, wherever possible, an address. Whoever finds one of these birds is asked to write to the address and state when and where he found the bird.

Suppose, for instance, that a swallow is ringed in a little Norfolk village. Some one in South Africa finds it a few months afterwards, and writes to say so ; thus it is proved to have flown many thousands of miles! If ever you find a ringed bird, be sure to take its number and address, and then let it go again. You may help to solve some of the many secrets of migration!

Other creatures migrate as well as birds, but their movements are just as mysterious. For instance, many butter-flies fly across the Channel to England every spring, and the eels of our ponds travel over land to their nearest river and swim down to the sea. They then cross the Atlantic Ocean to breed off the Bahamas, where they die. Their young " elvers " then swim all the way back to our ponds again!

BEAKS ARE BIRDS' KNIVES AND FORKS

Neville Kingston.

(1.) This African Marabou Stork has a beak which meets only at the tips. Thus he can hold one catch in the central gap and stab at another with the points.

Neville Kingston.

(2.) Almost as large as a turkey, the South American Curassow's beak is immensely powerful, and the thick upper part is nearly as hard as stone.

Neville Kingston.

(3.) The largest member of the crow family, the Raven was once very common in this country. It has a very powerful beak.

Neville Kingston.

(4.) The Vulture is a flesh-eater, and rends and tears its meat savagely with its sharp strong bill, eating till it is literally gorged.

THE BEAK THAT BECOMES A LARDER

Neville Kingston.

(5.) The lower part of the beak of a Pelican is of soft, pliant skin.　It is like a large elastic bag and forms the larder of its owner.　Thus a pelican which catches more fish than it can gobble at the moment stores them in the portmanteau at the bottom of its bill.

Neville Kingston.

(6.) The Hornbill carries one of the longest and biggest beaks known among our feathered friends, and an interesting feature is that there is a kind of horny appendage which gets bigger and bigger with age until it covers the head and eyes of its wearer.

THE STORY OF THE SPARROW, OUR BEST-KNOWN BIRD

"CHISSIC! Chissic!" call the Sparrows in the garden. "Chissic! Chissic! The Pigeons are being fed. Come and steal their seeds! There is some bread thrown out from the kitchen. Come and get it!"

Then a dozen of the little brown birds come flying down from the wall or trees, and hop jauntily about, pecking at the food.

The Plumage of the Sparrow

If they are country birds they wear bright, clean-looking coats, but if they belong to a town their colours are dull and drab, for their feathers are coated with grime and soot. Look closely at a little cock sparrow. He has chestnut-brown wings, a black bib, pale-grey cheeks and chest, and a slate-grey head. On his wings is a white bar. His wife you will know because she has no black bib under her chin.

Sparrows will eat almost anything. Bread, fat, potato, seeds, insects—they don't mind what it is, and this is partly why they are so common. A bird or animal with a long bill of fare is not so likely to perish in hard times as one with a limited range of food.

Round our houses and farms, and all about our towns, we see the sparrows. They come wherever we are. They like to build their nests about our houses, in our rain-pipes, under the eaves and in the thatch. We cannot help noticing them, for the sparrow always seems to leave straws dangling down from his untidy nest, and he is so noisy when he goes to and fro that we say at once : " Why the sparrows are building there, look ! "

Their nests are made of straw, dry grass, moss and wool, and lined with feathers that they have taken from a hen-run or from a pigeon-cote. So bold are the little creatures that they will even go up to a pigeon basking in the sun, and tug at a nice, soft-looking feather that takes their fancy! The pigeons are very indignant, and peck angrily at the daring birds, but by that time they are not there!

The Babies' First Outing

In the nest are laid the grey-white eggs, spotted with black. When the birds hatch, and grow old enough to fly, they are taken about with their parents and shown where to get food. Mother sparrow takes two

J. Kearton.

THE YOUNG CUCKOO (1)

Barely two days out of the nest, this young cuckoo is already far larger than his foster-mother. He is the hungriest of all young things, and his shrieks for food are so loud and fierce that sometimes other birds will stop to give him a tit-bit.

Sometimes called the " Northern Nightingale," the Blackcap is a member of the Warbler family. In this picture the Blackcap has been suddenly alarmed and gives her warning cry.

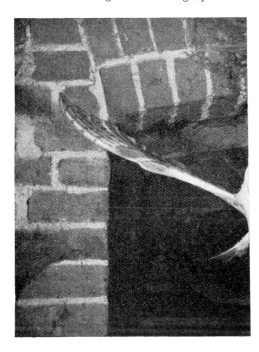

Sweeping through the night on noiseless wings th the smaller creatures on the ground below. Best seen here returning to its nest in an old building, captured on its excursion across the

or three, and father sparrow has his little group too. You must often have seen them flying down to your garden, the youngsters squeaking loudly with open orange beaks, their wings fluttering beseechingly.

The parent finds a crumb and stuffs it right down his young one's throat. It is most amusing to watch. He and mother sparrow have not much time to waste on each family, for they may have three or four families, or even more, every year. So the youngsters are left early on their own, and have to look after themselves. It is easy to make friends with these babies, for although it is said quite truly that sparrows are exceedingly cautious, alert birds, very different from the trustful robin, they soon learn to be daring when there is nothing to be feared, especially when no cats are about. They will even come indoors and explore the floor thoroughly for dropped crumbs, or for seeds thrown down from the canary's cage.

Sparrows do a certain amount of good, for they feed their nestlings on greenfly and caterpillars, but they are also destructive, nipping off the green shoots of new-growing plants, and pulling yellow flowers such as primroses and crocuses to pieces.

Little Robbers

When the corn is ripe the town sparrows take their summer holiday and fly off to the country. There they flock to the cornfields, and do a great deal of damage, for they rob the ears, eating the grain, and shaking it out to the ground. Their strong, cone-shaped beaks are excellent for husking seeds, and even a

THE YOUNG CUCKOO (2)   *Oliver G. Pike.*

Here we see the young monster again with his foster-mother, a meadow pipit, doing her best to satisfy his voracious appetite. Caterpillars he likes best, and he insists upon having them thrust right down his wide throat. One cuckoo eats more food than a nestful of young pipits.

baby sparrow can manage to make a good meal of hard-coated seeds of all kinds.

They are sociable birds, and like to go about in crowds, and do everything together. They fight fiercely, but do little harm to each other. They love a dust-bath, and on a hot day dozens may be seen in the dusty roads scuffling in the dirt to clean their oily feathers. They like a water-bath too, and if you put one in your garden they will splash there all day long.

There is a curious story of a pair of sparrows who were building their nest. They found a pile of old watch-springs, and one by one they took these to their nesting-site. When the nest was finished it looked most peculiar, for it was made

THE O

Most of our owls make their nests ir
Here is a Long-eared Owl, however
quite a sound nest amidst the brar
to their home every few minutes v
which to feed tl

THE NIGHTINGALE——

In appearance the Nightingale is a large, handsome brown bird, as the perky poise and
saucily cocked tail here plainly shows.
It comes to England about the middle of April
and leaves us late in August.

After a while the parents thought it
was time for the young ones to learn
to tear up their own food and prepare
it themselves ; so they began bringing
birds with their feathers on, and hares
with their fur. Then the eaglets tore
them to pieces with their sharp claws
and beak, and feasted hungrily.

Soon they learnt to screen their
food with their wings when they were
devouring it, for that is the habit
of all eagles. By that time they were
nearly eleven weeks old, and their
wings were getting strong enough for
flight.

One day their parents took them on
their first flight. In delight the eaglets
spread out their strong young wings
and launched themselves into the air,
proudly circling up into the sky.

Then they went to seek their fortunes
far away. Fast they flew, and high,
far above all the other birds, for they
knew themselves to belong to the royal
family of great golden eagles.

OUR FRIEND—THE ROBIN

NEARLY every garden owns a
bright-eyed, friendly Robin, or
perhaps it should be the other
way about—every robin owns a garden!
For they certainly regard our gardens
as their own particular kingdoms, and
in the autumn and winter especially are
ready to do battle for their little realms.

Every one likes robins. They trust
us, and are ready to be friends. We, in
turn, welcome the bold little fellow
with his bright red vest, and are glad
to see him eating the caterpillars and
wireworms that destroy our plants.

The robin sings his short, shrill
song nearly all the year round. He is
very emphatic when he sings, and his
song rings out clearly. Only when he
moults in the summertime does he
cease his lovely tune.

In the spring he chooses a mate,
and together they set off to seek for a
nesting-place. They love to make their
nests as near us as they can, and will

Photos : Eric Hosking.

——BEST KNOWN OF SONGSTERS

Famed for its song, the Nightingale sings during
the day but is best heard after nightfall when
most of the other birds are silent. During its song
the bird shivers with energy and its tail quivers.

Topical.

PELICANS IN A LONDON PARK

Two of these pelicans are of the crested type and two are eastern white. Pelicans are found in many countries and are common on the Upper Nile, usually frequenting the seashore and the margins of lakes, as they live almost entirely on fish. They feed early and late in the day, resting during the warmer hours. Their webbed feet have four toes and are used as paddles when the birds swim, which they frequently do with their heads underwater.

even bring up their youngsters inside our houses if we let them. Any outbuilding such as a shed or greenhouse is sure to be chosen if there is a good entry.

Queer Nesting Places

If there is no place indoors where the robins can nest, they seek for something that once belonged to us.

" What about that old watering-can ? " we can imagine them saying to one another. " The gardener used that last year, and I stood on the handle whenever he put the can down. Or, look—here is a broken kettle. The cook used to use that, for I saw her. Let's have that."

Or they may use a hole in a bank, or at the back of an undisturbed garden-bed, or behind a roller. Dead leaves are much used in the making of the

nest, and grass and moss. Hair is woven in for a soft lining, and in this little cradle the pretty cluster of grey-brown, red-spotted eggs is laid.

When the eggs hatch, the parents make hundreds of journeys to and fro, carrying grubs and caterpillars for the young ones. The nestlings have no red breasts at first, but are speckled instead.

The Robins and their Kingdoms

When autumn comes, and the chilly weather draws near, with its scarcity of insects, the robins drive one another away.

" There is not enough food for all of us in one place," the father says to his young ones. " You must go away and find another home for yourselves."

But the robin's wife and children do not want to go away. They wish to

BIRDS HUNTING UNDER WATER (1)

Neville Kingston

(1.) You have often seen a duck in an inverted position on a pond seeking for worms in the mud, but did you know that there are several fish-eating birds which always dive for their food? Here you see a clever picture of a penguin actually swimming under water.

Neville Kingston.

(2.) In this photograph, also snapped under water, a Darter has captured a fish, which is impaled upon its saw-toothed beak. The darter has been called the " snake-bird," because of its long, slender neck. It can swim under water with just its head showing above the surface.

Neville Kingston.

(3.) The Cormorant is a wonderful angler, and is known throughout Europe, many parts of India, and also in North America, as a bird with a most amazing appetite. It swallows quite a large fish whole, head first. Here you see the cormorant under water.

Neville Kingston.

(4.) In this illustration the bird has just caught a fish and it is said that in some parts of the East men train cormorants to fish for them. A string is tied round the bird's throat so that he cannot swallow his catch and on reaching the surface it is easy to remove the fish.

James's Press Agency.

PARROT

One of the largest and handsomest of his family, this is the blue-throated parrot of the Amazon. With his immensely powerful beak he can crack almost any nut. He is easily tamed, but is not so good a talker as his cousin, the grey African parrot.

There are many kinds, most of them gorgeously coloured and quite easily tamed.

Their beaks are curious, for the lower part is much shorter than the upper, which curves down right over the lower. These strong beaks are used like a hand, for the parrot helps itself to climb by means of its beak, holding on to a branch or twig with it, and pulling itself up. It has climbing feet—two toes pointing forward and two backward.

You must have heard parrots screeching, and thought what a dreadful noise it was. They can be taught to speak, and very interesting they are when they have a lot to say. The Grey Parrots from Africa are generally regarded as the best talkers, though the South American Blue-fronted Amazon is a close rival.

Closely-related and equally beautiful with their splendid crests are the Australian cockatoos. Most of them have white plumage but have differently-shaped and coloured crests. Another large branch of the same family, the Parakeets, are brilliantly-coloured and long-tailed birds, and they too have their headquarters in Australia.

New Zealand has the Kakapo, a parrot which does not fly and usually keeps in hiding during the daytime. The Kea is another member of the family which is found only in South Island, New Zealand.

SOME BEAUTIFUL BIRDS

ONE of the loveliest sights in the world is a Peacock spreading his tail. It is like magic, for it is so unexpected and so beautiful.

The peacock spreads it out like a

W. S. Berridge.

COCKATOO

This bird with the fine crest is the sulphur-crested cockatoo. Cockatoos are a sub-family of the parrots, found only in Australia, New Guinea and the Malay Archipelago. Cockatoos include both the largest and the smallest of the parrot family.

THREE MEMBERS OF THE TITMOU

Three kinds of tit are here illustrated, the dainty blue tit, th
mark on the nape of the neck and the more robust great-tit
spend the summer at the edge of woods, finding their food in
months, they are frequent visitors to our gardens, delightin
suet and meat bones. To watch tits feeding upside down and i
wonderful bird acrobats they a

A BEAUTIFUL BIRD   *Sport & General.*

One of the marvels of Nature is the magnificent fan-like tail of the peacock here seen fully
expanded. The peacock is an Indian bird belonging to the same family as the pheasants, and
was brought to Europe at a very early date and spread by way of Italy to Britain. Its voice
is not as beautiful as its plumage, being curiously harsh and loud. The peahen has none of the
gorgeous colouring of her magnificent husband.

great fan, and all the feathered eyes in
it gleam and shine. The bird is very
proud of it, and holds his little bur-
nished head with its quaint crest of
feathers high in the air, as he struts
about before his dowdy-looking mate.

She has no magnificent tail, and is
drab and dull beside her splendid husband. But then she has to look after
the eggs, and would be very noticeable
if she were brightly coloured. She must
be dowdy-looking for safety's sake.

The peacock is a bad-tempered bird,
given to pecking. His voice is very
harsh, so that he is not *all* beautiful.
Perhaps his little wife sometimes wishes
he were plainer and better-tempered.
But when he spreads his wonderful tail
before her she forgets his bad manners,
and is dazzled by his great beauty.

When the peacock's tail is closed it
sweeps the ground, but it is graceful
and lovely even then. Every year he
loses it, for he moults, and the long
tail-feathers fall off, but soon they grow
again, often longer than ever.

Another beautiful bird is the rose-
coloured Flamingo, who loves to stand
with his comrades in the water. His
legs are very long indeed, but are used
for wading, and not for running.

The beaks of these birds are queerly
curved, being bent sharply downwards
in the middle. They use them when
they scoop about in the mud for the
worms or small fish they love to eat.

They are very graceful birds, and are
fond of standing on one leg, with their
long necks curved over their backs,
tucked into the soft feathers. They look

FLAMIN[

These are flamingoes standing in their shallow [
birds which are between the ducks and the hero[
are found in almost all the warmer parts of the w[
make their large nests in the shallow water at th[
is five, and it is an odd thing that, once frighten[
not ret[

very lazy and comfortable then, and are pretty to see.

The Tiny Humming-Bird

The smallest of all birds is among the most beautiful—the tiny Humming-bird. There are over 500 different kinds of these living gems, some not much bigger than a bumble-bee! They are brilliantly coloured, and most fascinating as they fly from flower to flower, hovering in the air on their rapidly vibrating wings.

They fly more like insects than birds, for their wings flutter so quickly that they can hardly be seen, and it is their wings that make the humming noise from which the lovely little creatures get their name. They vibrate at the rate of

THE GOLDEN EAGLE AT HOME

The Golden Eagle is one of the most magnificent of our winged friends, and is the largest bird of prey we can claim. Unfortunately, it is a very rare visitor to England, though seen more frequently in Scotland, especially in the Highlands. This eagle, which is most graceful in flight, proceeds in hops when on the ground; feeds mainly upon the grouse which it captures on mountain and moorland; and is known to live to the age of sixty years, and even more.

Paradise, whose brilliant plumage is worth twenty or thirty times its weight in gold. His wonderful orange-yellow tail sweeps down like a golden water-fall, and the bright-emerald colouring on his throat shines like precious stones. When he displays his gorgeous plumage before his dowdy brown mate he seems too superb to be true. No one could properly describe his beauty, for it must be seen to be believed.

We must not forget the lovely Swan in our list of beautiful birds. Every-one has watched it sailing gracefully on the water, its reflection shining below. Its dazzling whiteness, its slow grace and beautifully-curved neck make it one of the loveliest of our birds.

It is a clever bird, for if the water rises too near the top of its nest it will build it a little higher, and even make a gangway for the cygnets to walk across. It likes to take them for a ride on its back, and will put up its foot as a jumping-up step for them!

SOME SEA-BIRDS

THERE are many, many birds that love the sea and get their living in its waters. Gannets and Cor-morants, Gulls and Shags, Oyster-catchers and Puffins—all these are found by the sea, and some, like the Guillemots, hardly tread on land from one breeding-time to another.

The gannet is sometimes called the Solan Goose, because he is a big white bird, and his feathers are used for stuffing pillows, but he is not really a goose. He has a magnificent wing-spread of more than 6 feet, and to see him in flight is a fine sight.

Sport & General.

A FAMILY OF SWANS ON THE THAMES

A most interesting sight on the Thames is a pair of swans leading a brood of cygnets. The parent birds have plumage of snowy white, but the young are so grey they look like a different sort of creature. Swans on the Thames belong to the Crown, or to the Dyers' or Vintners' Companies of the City of London. Each summer the swans are marked at the ceremony known as " swan-upping." The custom dates from the sixteenth century.

W. S. Berridge.

THE KINGFISHER

Of all English birds none is as brilliant as
the kingfisher which speeds down a winding
stream like a flash of living blue. Its nest
is made deep in the bank of the brook and
the eggs are pure white.

He eats fish, and in order to catch
them he sails high in the air above the
sea. Then, when he sees a fish in the
water below, he shoots down with his
wings half-closed, and plunges right
into the waves.

The cormorant is a handsome, interesting bird. He is dressed in black,
glossed with green and purple. He is
rather ungainly, and looks very queer
sometimes, because he stands in such
funny positions. He likes to sit on a
sunny rock with his wings half-open,
and his beak gaping wide!

But in the water he is far from ungainly. He is a joy to watch then, for
he dives splendidly and swims very
swiftly indeed. He is so good at catching fish that in some countries he is
trained to do this for his master.

The guillemot likes the open sea, and
spends all his time diving, swimming
and flying. Like the cormorant he

is clever at chasing and catching fish
under the water. His dress is a glossy,
brown-black plumage, with a large white
patch on each wing.

The Great Family of Gulls

The sea-birds we know best are the
gulls. There are many different kinds,
but all of them eat practically anything,
and often follow steamers and ships to
snatch up any scraps that are thrown
out on the water. They swim excellently, and can be seen even on the
roughest day, bobbing up and down on
the waves as happy as can be.

The Great Black-backed Gull is the
largest of all. He has pure white
plumage, except for a black back and
wings, and his feet are pink.

Then comes the Herring Gull. He
is very big too, but has pearly-grey
wings tipped with black. His legs are
pink, and the lower part of his beak is
marked with red.

Third in size is the Lesser Black-
backed Gull. You will know him from
the Greater by the colour of his legs,
which are yellow.

The Common Gull is the next smallest, but he is not really our commonest
gull. He is dressed in pearl-grey and
white, and his beak and legs are
greenish-yellow. He has no red mark
on the lower part of his beak, so you
cannot mistake him for the herring gull,
whom he is rather like.

Our commonest gulls are the Black-
headed ones. Their heads are really
dark brown, not black, and their legs
and beaks are blood-red. Londoners
have come to know these black-headed
gulls very well indeed, for in winter-
time they come up the Thames and are
fed on the embankments. Their name
is a stupid one in the cold weather, for
then their dark heads become white,
speckled with brown.

Our Smallest Gull

The smallest gull of all is the little
Kittiwake. He gets his name from his
cry of " kittiake," and is rather like the

SEA BIRDS ON THEIR ROCKY HOME

Sport & General.

Off the wild coast of Northumberland lies a group of seventeen islets known as the Farne Islands. These wild crags are the paradise of sea birds, where they nest, not merely in thousands, but in millions. Our photographer, at great risk to himself, has secured a picture of a part of the rocks high above the tide line, which gives some idea of the way in which the gulls make use of every projecting cornice and crag for the purpose of building their nests and rearing their young. The clapping of wings when these birds are disturbed is like the roar of a storm.

15—1

J. D. Rattar.

THE ICELAND GULL

Of all the many sorts of gull none is more beautiful in shape or plumage than the Iceland Gull, which the photographer has caught in the very act of dropping upon the waves with out-stretched wings.   It is a bird of the far north.

MAKE FRIENDS WITH THE BIRDS

DO you want to make friends with the birds ? Would you like to see them feeding, drinking, bathing and playing near to you? Would you like them to nest in your garden ?

All this can easily be managed. The best way to begin is to put up a bird-table in the cold weather. This is simply pieces of wood about 24 inches by 18 inches, nailed on to the top of a pole out of the way of cats.

common gull in his dress of pearl-grey and white. His legs, however, are different, for they are not greenish-yellow, but black.

The sea-birds are fascinating to watch and to study ; next time you visit the sea, watch them going about their daily business of swimming, diving and flying. You will soon be so interested that you will want to look at them all day !

J. Kearton.

HERRING GULL

The herring gull here pictured is one of the many different varieties which may be seen on the crags of the Farne Islands. It feeds on small fish.

Then you must spread it with food each day for the birds. Any household scraps will do—bread crusts soaked to make them soft, cold potato, soaked dog biscuits, scrapings of rice pudding, bits of fat, lumps of suet—almost anything will do, for if one bird does not like something, another will.

The Sparrows will try anything. The Robin likes soaked bread. The Thrushes will gobble up the potato and rice pudding. The Starlings will fight over the fat. The Tits will come for the suet. Most birds will find something they like on your table, and will visit it day after day to share in the feast.

The Tits and the Coconut

The tits love coconut better than anything. Get one, and knock the two ends off. This is better than cutting it in half, for it keeps good longer. Hang it by a string to the branch of a tree near your window. You will love to see the little acrobats pecking at the coconut, hanging head-downwards as easily as the right way up!

Your bird-table will be full of birds in frosty or snowy weather, when food is hard to find. They will be grateful then for a saucer of water, for when the pools and puddles are frozen it is often difficult for them to find a drink. Fill the saucer every day for them, for it is sure to freeze over-night.

In the springtime you can put nesting boxes about your garden for the birds. Empty coconuts can be tucked away into sheltered corners, and the tits may find these and use them. They will often build, too, in the wooden nest-boxes you buy at the shops ; these are good, because they have a lid which you can lift to see if building has begun.

If you have a great many birds in your garden, you can put a lucky-box somewhere for them. This is a box filled with scraps of rag, straw, hair-combings, feathers, fluff or anything like that. When the birds find it they love it, and poke about in it to find exactly the right kind of lining for their

Humphrey Joel.

NESTING BOXES

These are bird boxes fixed against the trunk of a great oak in Highgate Woods near London. Tits and wrens are specially fond of these artificial nesting places, but they must be made with very small entrances or sparrows will seize them and keep more interesting birds away.

M. H. Crawford.

THE BIRD TABLE

A bird table should be in every garden, especially in winter. The roughest planks will do if fixed so that cats cannot reach them. Suet, soaked bread, cold potato, boiled rice can be laid on it, and do not forget a shallow saucer filled every day with fresh water.

nests! Dog hairs and hen feathers will be greatly welcomed.

A Simple Bird-bath

In the summer-time give the birds a bath for themselves. You can use all kinds of things for this. Sink a shallow dish in the ground, or an old sink. Sow a few seeds round it, and when the hot days come the birds will flock to your little pool and enjoy themselves very much, splashing the water over the plants that are flowering there from the seeds you set.

If you cannot bother to make a proper little pool, you can get a shallow enamel bowl, such as that from which your dog or cat eats. Fill it with water, and put it on the grass. You will find that scores of birds will splash there every day, delighted with the shallow bath. They will come so often that in hot weather you will probably have to fill the bowl two or three times a day!

Save your sunflower heads for the winter-time, and then hang them up somewhere. The Greenfinches will come and feast happily on the seeds. Put your mistletoe out on the bird table when Christmas is over, and see the Missel-thrushes come and feed on the sticky berries. You will love to watch them all, and soon the birds in your garden will learn to love you and trust you—and there are few nicer things than that!

Nor need you be afraid of incurring the wrath of the gardener. Few birds are unpardonable thieves; and even the starlings and blackbirds, who steal the currants, earn their fruit from the number of harmful pests which they devour. Try putting bowls of water in the strawberry bed. Often birds take ripe fruit simply because they are very thirsty.

M. H. Crawford.

A SQUARE MEAL

Tits delight in nuts and in pieces of fat or suet which should be hung by lengths of string from a tree branch or a bird table. See how happy and contented this fine Great Tit looks enjoying a good meal on a chilly winter day.

The Varied
Kinds of
Animal Life

Fishes
of Our
Seas and Rivers

M. H. Crawford.

FIFTEEN-SPINED STICKLEBACK

You might hardly recognise this long, sharp-nosed fish as a member of the stickleback family, yet that is what he is. He is known as the " fifteen-spined stickleback," and his home is in the sea. If his appearance is different from that of the fresh-water fish of the same name his habits are similar, for he builds a nest of seaweed and guards it as faithfully as does his better-known cousin of the brooks.

THE WATER FOLK

THE STORY OF THE STICKLEBACK

MOST boys have gone fishing for " tiddlers " in the ponds, and have caught them with a fishing-rod made of a twig, and a bent pin tied to a piece of thread. The fish they catch are usually the little Sticklebacks, whose name comes from the three spines along their back.

They are tiny pretty fish with a very interesting story. In the spring or summer time the male fish thinks he will build a nest. This seems a strange thing for a fish to do, but there are quite a number of nest-building members of the finny world. The stickleback is very good indeed as a nest-builder.

He looks about for a suitable place in which to put his nest. It is usually on the ground in shallow water. Having decided on the spot, he swims about to seek for nest material. He finds bits of floating straw, and, taking them in his mouth, carries them to his nesting site. He places them in position, and then goes off again. Soon he finds some pieces of water-plant floating loose, and these he takes too. Back he goes to his nest, and by means of a sticky substance from his mouth, cements them to the straw already there.

He works very hard, and presently his efforts begin to look like a nest. He finds all sorts of things of which to make it—hay, grass, root-threads and stuff of that sort—and packs them closely together. He is pleased with his efforts, and often swims round the nest as if he were admiring it.

In Search of a Mate

When the nest is finished it is a dear little place. It is shaped like a muff,

NESTING OF THE STICKLEBACK

The female Stickleback in the nest which the male has built for her. The nest is made of pieces of roots and stems of fresh-water plants, bound together with glutinous threads and fastened to the bottom by sand and pebbles. In the picture the female has laid her eggs and is seen breaking out of the nest on the side opposite to the entrance.

TIGERS OF THE SEA

These huge and hideous monsters are Sharks photographed by a diver as they swam above him. Notice the enormous mouth and wicked teeth, narrow, cruel eyes and huge fins. Sharks are common in all hot seas and some British waters, but these are not dangerous sorts. The largest of all is the huge whale shark, which may weigh five tons or more, but the biggest seen in British seas is the basking shark, which is a slow, lazy creature and quite harmless. Sharks are caught off the Californian and Australian coasts for the sake of their oil, fins and skins.

Fox Photos.

A BRITISH SHARK

Sharks are not infrequently seen off the Atlantic coast of Britain. Here is one caught in Mounts Bay, Cornwall. It is 15 feet long and weighs a ton; it is being hoisted ashore by a crane.

begins to chase her, trying to force her to go in the direction of his nest.

At last he hunts her right up to it, and makes her swim through the open door at one side. When she has laid him a few eggs inside he lets her go out at the other end, and off she swims. The stickleback has a good look at the eggs, and if he thinks there are not enough he goes to look for another little wife to lay him a few more.

A Good Father

When he has a good number he places himself on guard, and will not leave his precious nest night or day. He swims round it, and noses the eggs gently, arranging them exactly to his liking. He even fans them with his fins and his tail, so that they may be nicely aerated. He is very fond of them, and waits anxiously for the time when they will hatch out.

Perhaps another fish swims near the nest, and wonders what it is. At once the little stickleback becomes furiously angry, and rushes at the intruder so fiercely that he is frightened. If he does not go away at once he may be ripped open with the stickleback's sharp spines.

One day the eggs hatch out. The father is delighted. He carefully pulls away the top part of the nest, so that it becomes cradle-shaped. In this quaint cradle the baby fish lie until they can swim off and look after themselves.

Other members of the stickleback family have the same nesting habits. The Ten-spined Stickleback fastens his small egg-shaped nest to reeds near the bank of a stream, but off the bottom, and the Sea, or Fifteen-spined, Stickleback makes his of seaweed, binding the fronds together with a silk-like thread.

with an opening at each end. The stickleback thinks it wants just one thing more to complete it, and make it really beautiful—and that is a nice little cluster of eggs safely in the middle!

So he goes to find a wife who will lay some eggs for him. Off he swims, looking everywhere. Soon he sees a pretty little female fish and swims up to her. He tries to persuade her to go and see his nest. Sometimes she swims off with him willingly, but at other times she refuses. Then the male is very angry, and turns bright scarlet. He

GIANT FISH

ROAMING in the seas are monsters which are so big that they seem too enormous to be true. The Whale, of course, is the biggest sea creature, but it is not a fish. It is a mammal, as you will read in the story of the whale.

Biggest of all the fish is the huge Whale Shark. This may be anything from 30 feet to 75 feet long, and weigh four or five tons! It has about 7,000 teeth, so that you might think it was a truly dreadful monster to meet.

But its food consists mostly of very small creatures, such as shellfish or fry. It rarely attacks anything larger than small cuttle-fish. It likes to swim below the surface of the water with its enormous mouth wide open, letting hosts of tiny fish or swimming shellfish float in. Its hide is so thick that the pellets from a shotgun glance off from it without harming the whale shark at all.

A very different shark is the White Shark. Its other name of Man Eater will tell you its character. It will attack human beings, or any sea animal, such as Sea-lions, and its big conical teeth can soon dispose of its meal.

An Unwelcome Passenger

It may grow to 40 feet or more in length, and is much to be feared. The Chinese enjoy eating the fins of this monster in their soup, and think them a great delicacy. Such a huge creature as this has few enemies, but one of the greatest annoyances it endures is the curious Sucking Fish. These creatures attach themselves to the shark's body and remain there, wishing to be carried some distance away and to share the food of the shark.

The sucking fish is so-called because it has a large " sucker " on the top of its head, which sticks to any smooth surface just like a rubber sucker. It often takes a free ride to new hunting-grounds by attaching itself to the bottom of a ship.

Sometimes a shark attempts to swallow a sucking fish, but then the unwelcome

Central Press.

AN AUSTRALIAN SHARK

This savage White Pointer Shark, weighing more than a ton, is claimed to be the largest fish ever caught by rod and line. It is 16 feet long and was hooked at Streaky Bay, South Australia.

passenger attaches itself to the roof of the shark's mouth. There it lives quite comfortably, taking toll of all the food which the shark swallows.

The sharks become very much irritated by the sucking fish, and often try to get rid of them by leaping high out of the water.

Bats of the Sea

Giant Rays, or Devil Fish, are also large creatures. They measure 15 feet across their "wings" or fins, and may weigh 1,000 pounds or more. These great Skate lie most of the day on the floor of the sea, half-buried in the sand, but at night they shake themselves free, and go flitting through the water like sea bats. Many of them have poisonous spines near the base of the tail, and can give an enemy a terrible wound.

There is a giant fish belonging to the herring family, called the Tarpon. These grow to about 7 feet in length, and weigh perhaps 200 pounds. They give fishermen great sport, and when they are caught are usually taken ashore, measured and weighed, and then returned to the sea again, so that perhaps in the future another battle may be waged with them.

Tarpon fishing is a social sport, not a solitary one. Twenty boats or more all set out together, going about half a mile out to sea. On the hooks are put red mullet for bait. As soon as a tarpon takes the bait the fun begins.

The fish goes round and round the boat, then perhaps it may rush at it and dive underneath. Occasionally it leaps 9 feet or 10 feet in the air, and comes down on the boat!

Other giant fish are the Tunny of the Mediterranean, the Jew Fish of Florida, and the fierce tiger of the sea, the

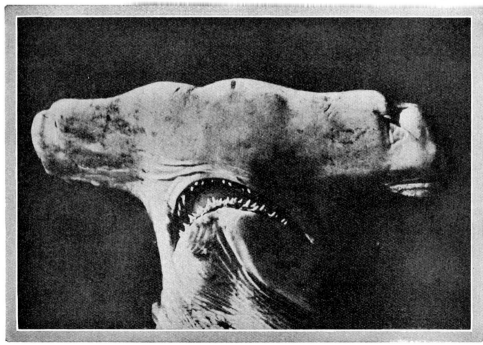

Dr. L. Haden Guest.

THE HAMMER-HEAD SHARK

This is the head of the Hammer-head Shark, a sort which is as ugly in disposition as in appearance. The eyes are at the ends of the "hammer," and the jaws are set with three rows of terrible teeth. It is hard to understand how this shark developed so strangely-shaped a head. The hammer-head always turns on its side before taking its prey, for the mouth is so far back that it cannot feed in any other position.

Barracuda. Some of these monsters can be seen in natural history museums.

FLYING FISH

THERE are some fish that can fly as well as swim. They have no feathered wings, of course, as birds have, but their breast fins take the place of these, and with them they manage to glide a little distance through the air.

Some Flying Fish are only a few inches long, but there are other kinds that grow to a length of 2 feet. The best flyer is the Common Flying Fish, often seen in the Mediterranean, and even occasionally off our own British coasts. They are a foot or more long, and look rather like herrings, except that their breast fins have grown so big that they reach back nearly to their tails !

The tails are not like those of ordinary fish, for the lower half is longer than the upper.

The reason that these little fish have taken to flying above the water is easy to find. They use their wing-fins in order to help them to escape from their enemies, such as the dolphins, the porpoises and the tunnies. But in the air other enemies await them, for gulls are quick to swoop down.

Dr. L. Haden Guest.

TIGER SHARK

This mighty fish is closely related to the man-eating blue shark. Tiger sharks have been known to attain to a length of 25 feet.

How They Fly

The flying fish swim so very fast that when they leap out from the water their velocity carries them through the air for quite a distance ; and this, together with the assistance of their big wing-fins, enables them to travel through the air for about half a minute.

They do not fly very high, usually about 2 feet or 3 feet above the water, though if there is a good wind behind them they sometimes shoot high enough to fall on the decks of ships. They are very clever at suddenly changing their direction while flying, and can turn off at right angles or even reverse their direction completely!

They can fly about 300 yards, and sometimes by dipping down to the water and taking a fresh spurt there, they are able to rise again, and continue their aerial journey for another few hundred yards. They are a pretty sight to see, but too often their flight ends in the open jaws of the pursuing dolphin.

QUEER SPECIMENS!

Central Press.

This rare fish is quite small for a shark, measuring only 16 inches in length. It was caught off Melbourne, Australia. It is called the Elephant Shark and gets this name from its curious trunk-like snout, which it uses for seeking small prey in the mud or under stones on the ocean bed.

Australian News and Information Bureau.

Like the *Coelacanth* illustrated on page 16 the Lungfish is a living fossil, for varieties of it flourished 350 million years ago! It lives in a few rivers in Queensland, and it has relatives in South Africa and South America. It is able to breathe air as well as water. It is a slow-moving fish and lives on water vegetation and small creatures such as shrimps.

A FISH THAT WEIGHED TWO TONS!

Dr. L. Haden Guest.

Our picture makes one think of some huge and hideous idol, but the subject is the Australian Devil Fish. This specimen weighed over two tons and required a substantial truck for its conveyance. It was caught off the north-west coast of Australia. In spite of its enormous size and formidable appearance the devil fish is not dangerous to man, and if you look at its mouth you will see that it has no biting teeth like the shark. Actually it lives upon seaweed and plants.

Sport and General.

GRACEFUL FLYING FISH

Flying fish are common in almost all warm seas. When chased by dolphins or other large fish they rise out of the waves and skim through the air, using their large fins as wings. Sometimes they rise so high as to fall on the deck of a passing ship, and when this happens are eagerly seized by the sailors, for they are excellent pan fish ; as good, indeed, as herrings. They are all small, rarely exceeding a pound in weight.

FISH THAT CLIMB AND FISH THAT WALK

LONG ago stories were told of a strange fish that could climb trees. Modern people smile to think what absurd tales were believed in bygone days; but, to our astonishment, we have now found that this extraordinary story is true.

Away in Burma, Ceylon and India there really does exist a fish that can climb trees. It is called the Climbing Perch, and has been seen actually climbing up a palm tree. However, it uses this habit only when a drought is to be feared, and the level of pools and rivers is gradually getting lower.

The climbing perch knows that it will be left stranded if the pool in which it lives is dried up. So before that happens it leaves the water, and goes to seek for a deeper and better pool. It travels over the land, using its spiny fins to help it along.

Ordinary fish die out of water, because as soon as their gills cease to be wet they cannot breathe. How does the perch manage to survive away from the water that gives it life ?

It Takes Its Own Water

It manages quite well. At each side of its head it has a peculiar organ which can store up water. This water keeps its gills moistened as it journeys over the land, and lasts until it reaches another pool.

Sometimes the travelling fish cannot

YOUNG OTTERS TAKE THEIR FIRST LESSON IN FISHING

Mother otters teach their babies to swim by the very simple process of taking the youngsters into the water on their backs. Mother then dives deeply and the little ones quickly learn their lesson. She also trains them very carefully in the art of catching fish for their food, as you will see in this illustration, which was prepared from real life.

FISH IN THEIR NATURAL ELEMENT

Fish lose much of the brightness of their colouring when taken from the water, but are here reproduced pictorially in their natural hues. The following is a key to the picture, many of the subjects being found only in foreign waters: 1, 3, and 6. Coral Fish of different classes which live round coral reefs. 2. The Conger Eel. 4. A Demoiselle. 5. The Fire Fish. 7. The Angel Fish. 8. Sticklebacks. 9. The Coffer Fish.

FISH CLIMBING UP A WALL!

Illustrations Bureau.

This photograph shows that the term " fish out of water " is by no means so far-fetched as one might imagine. Certain fish can beyond any doubt climb, using their fins much as we should employ our hands and feet. These particular finny creatures are Catfish. They are ascending an almost perpendicular wall as they make their way from the Jumna Canal to the river of the same name which flows at a higher level and empties into the Ganges.

HOW FISH KEEP WARM IN WINTER

Elwin R. Sanborn.

This truly remarkable photograph of living fish was taken under water in the famous New York Aquarium. It shows a colony of Bass, which are akin to our own perch, huddling together in a dense cluster with their heads all turned in precisely the same direction. This strange habit enables the fish, by herding closely like so many sheep in a storm, to keep themselves warm. At the time the snapshot was made the temperature of the water was dropping with the near approach of winter's cold.

find a new pool, or the one it is making for may be dried up too. What is it to do then?

A likely place to find a little pool of water is in a hollow tree or in a depression of a branch. The perch looks for one as a last hope. To do this it must climb up the tree.

It uses its spiny fins to help it to climb, and clings to the bark of the tree with its gill-covers, which are edged with little spines. So it ascends, slowly but surely, and perhaps finds the water it needs so badly.

The Curious Mud Skipper

Another fish that can walk is the little Mud Skipper. It is a curious-looking creature, with enormous eyes bulging from its head. These can be turned in any direction, so that enemies may be seen immediately they approach. The breast fins are changed into a sort of arm with flattened ends that can be used like hands.

When the tide goes out the mud skippers walk about on the mud, using their arm fins to do so. They hold their heads up in the air, their protruding eyes looking round about them, and are most interesting to watch.

If they see an enemy they bend their tails forward, and then suddenly jerk them straight again, and this sends them 2 feet or 3 feet away. Besides using their tails for this, they also use them for breathing purposes. They often sit on a stone and let their tails hang down into a little pool below, drawing in the oxygen they need.

Topical Press.

A GOOD CATCH!

With its enormous mouth and thick body the Jew Fish is not an attractive looking creature, but it gives very fair sport to the angler who hooks it off the coast of Florida. In weight it reaches a couple of hundred pounds, and although somewhat sluggish pulls like a cart horse. Tarpon anglers often hook Jew fish, and one of this size needs careful handling when lifted into a small boat as the result may be a capsize. The creature is common in the Gulf of Mexico.

F. A. Mitchell Hedges, F.L.S., F.R.G.S.., F.Z.S.

A FORMIDABLE CREATURE

The Sawfish gets its name from the huge saw-toothed horn which projects above its mouth and is used to rip up its prey. This one was so heavy and powerful that, when hooked, it dragged a boat for miles before it could be raised to the surface and killed with rifle bullets.

When the dry season comes the mud skippers begin to dig a hole in the mud, and lie several feet below the surface with a little hole for ventilation. Then along come the people with cloths, and pop them over the holes. The fish cannot breathe, and are forced to come up for air. Then they are easily caught.

FISH IN ARMOUR

MOST fish are harmless and easy-going, but there are some that have fearful weapons for attack, and others that wear excellent armour for protection.

If you have ever been fishing in a boat you are sure to have seen the poisonous Weever Fish, with its spiny fins. Inside each spine is a double groove leading to poison glands, and when the poison runs down the spines into the wound inflicted by them the victim suffers very much.

Another armed fish is the Sting Ray, also found off our coasts. It has a long, slender tail, which owns a sharp spine with which it can give painful stabs. When its weapon wears out it grows a new one.

Ferocious Fish

You are sure to have heard of the Sawfish and Swordfish, both of which are most ferocious. They are large fish, and will attack small prey such as men and women swimming in the sea, or large prey such as whales. They will even attack ships !

The sawfish has its snout developed into a long, flat blade, with a saw-like edge on both sides ; the snout of the swordfish is not saw-like, being more like a sword. These awful weapons project far in front of the creatures' heads, and can be used for cutting or stabbing.

Another well-armed fish is the curious Trigger Fish or Crossbow Shooter. It gets its name from the two stout spines that take the place of a back fin.

One spine acts as a sort of safety catch to the other. When the first one is touched the second is shot out with such force that a dangerous wound is inflicted on the enemy, especially when the spine is poisoned, as it generally is in the trigger fish.

The Porcupine Fish are very queer. Their bodies are covered with spines that usually lie flat, but when an enemy approaches the fish blow themselves out with air or water until they are almost round. This makes all the spines stand up straight, and it would be a brave fish indeed that would swallow such a prickly meal!

Sometimes these porcupine fish expand themselves and rise to the top of the water, where they float along upside down like balloons. When the children find them, they take them and use them for footballs!

Escape From a Shark

As well as their spiny armour, these queer fish have curious teeth, which are joined together in such a way that they form sharp cutting-plates, able to cut through anything their owner wishes. When a shark swallows one of these fish it very much regrets it, for the Sea Porcupine at once sets to work to eat its way out of the shark's body.

First it bites through the creature's stomach, and then cuts a path through the body, emerging from the side. The shark dies but the porcupine fish calmly swims off!

One of the most remarkable fish is the Electric Eel, which lives in the rivers of South America. Almost the whole of its length consists of an electric battery, and when it touches a wading or swimming animal with its head and tail at the same time, it gives a powerful electric shock of about 600 volts! It can stun a horse or kill a man, but an animal which is only stunned usually falls over and is drowned. Other electric fish include the Electric Catfish of the river Nile, and the Torpedo Fish, which gives a 40-volt shock.

High Commissioner for New Zealand.

SWORDFISH

The finest sea fishing in the world is obtained off the New Zealand coast, where sportsmen angle for the Swordfish, which runs to 800 pounds in weight. This monster is just breaking the surface after being hooked. It may take hours to land it.

THE STORY OF THE FLATFISH

HAVE you ever wondered why some fish are flattened out, whilst others are the normal shape? What makes Plaice, Turbot, Sole, Halibut and the rest so peculiarly flat?

"Oh," you say, "perhaps they were born like that!"

But the curious thing is that they were not. Baby plaice or turbot are the same shape as herring or trout when they first hatch from the eggs. They change to flatfish as they grow up!

At first the body of a young flatfish is symmetrical, and it has one eye on

Australian News and Information Bureau.

THE STONE FISH

This fish from tropical Australia carries on its back poisonous spines which can inflict a dangerous wound. It lies on the shallow bottom among the coral, and its colour and pattern make it almost invisible.

The upper part of its body is sand-coloured or spotted in such a way that it can hardly be seen when it lies on the sea floor. Sometimes it covers itself with a light layer of sand, and then it is impossible to see, except for its bulging eyes sticking up from the sandy floor. It can move each one independently of the other, and this often gives the fish a very strange appearance.

The under-surface is not coloured, and when the fish swims in the water the pale under-part is difficult to see from below, and is a protection from enemies.

A Difficult Task

The flat fish has the power of changing its colour to match its surroundings. One of the most difficult tasks it was ever set was when one was placed in a tank, the floor of which was patterned like a chess-board!

But in a short while the fish had succeeded in mottling its body so cleverly that from a distance it was difficult to see it lying on the chequered floor.

Occasionally some flatfish are double-sided—that is, coloured both sides. Some kinds are right-sided, some are left-sided, and usually the different species keep to their own habits.

Skates and Rays are also flattened, but they are not true flatfish such as the plaice or turbot. Their bodies are flattened from above downwards instead of from side to side.

Perhaps the queerest of all the true flatfish is a little fish found on the eastern shores of America. It is nearly transparent, and looks like a live piece of glass. It has been given the pretty name of Window-pane Fish.

each side of its head. As it grows older, it feels a great desire to go and lie down on its side in the sand. When it does that only one eye is available, for the other is in the sand.

So the eye that is hidden comes round to be close to the other eye. The bones of the skull twist round, bringing the lower eye with them. Soon the young flatfish has both its eyes on one side, and can use each of them when it is lying on its side in the sand.

The back fin grows all along the fish's body, and ends on the outer side of the eyes, instead of between them. Shortly the fish begins to swim on its side, instead of vertically as ordinary fish do, and is then a proper flatfish.

DANGEROUS CUSTOMERS!

Topical;Press.

The Weever or Sea Viper has sharp poisonous spines on its back, which can inflict a sting like the bite of an adder. The fish buries itself in the sand, with the tips of its poisonous spines protruding. It lives chiefly upon shrimps and is found on the coasts of Europe and Africa.

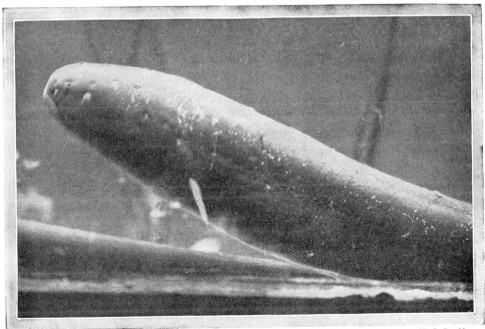

W. S. Berridge.

The tail of this South American river eel consists of a battery of 6,000 electric cells, giving 600 volts. Specimens kept in tanks can be made to light electric lamps. Other fishes which can generate electricity include the Electric Rays or Torpedoes of the warm seas and the Electric Catfish of African lakes and rivers.

THE STORY OF A FLATFISH

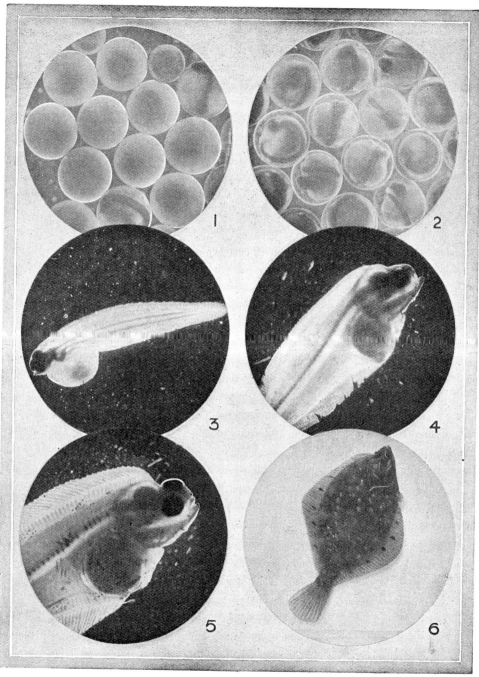

Here is a series of pictures showing the growth of the flatfish from the egg onwards. Nos. 1 and 2 illustrate the spawn. No. 3 is the young just hatched, with the yolk sac on which it feeds for the first part of its life. Nos. 4 and 5. Young flatfish are like other fish, with an eye on each side, and swim in the usual way. No. 6. It is only after they grow up that they flatten out and take to living on the bottom. Then the eyes work round to the top of the head and the top side becomes coloured to match the sea floor, while the underside remains quite white.

THE STORY OF THE GOLDFISH

GOLDFISH are kept as pets in nearly every civilised country. They are pretty, intelligent creatures, and will live a long time if well looked after.

Their real home is China, where they can still be found wild. The Chinese began to breed them hundreds of years ago, but it was not until the seventeenth century that they were introduced into England. They are really brightly-coloured varieties of the wild grey-green carp. By carefully selecting the gayest colours in each generation the Chinese succeeded in producing a fine race of goldfish.

At first the baby fish are furnished with a small yolk-sac, which contains nourishment enough to last them for a few days. Once that is finished they must look about for microscopic life in the water and feed on that. They soon grow, and if they are in a sunny pond with water-weed growing at the bottom they will in a short time be big, bonny fish, ready to lay eggs of their own in the hot weather.

Many Varieties

There are many kinds of goldfish. Some are very beautiful, and some are ugly. The Comet, the Veil-tailed and the Fan-tailed are beautiful. The Comet has an elongated body, with long-flowing fins, and its tail is lengthy and free-flowing, as might be imagined from its name.

The Fan-tailed Goldfish is the commonest of the fancy goldfish. The Veil-tailed has a short, round body, with a beautiful tail hanging down behind it in long graceful folds. Other kinds include the Star-gazer and Lionhead, but these odd fish are grotesque rather than beautiful.

Goldfish are usually intelligent, and can even learn to perform simple tricks. There are some in the Roman baths at Bath that have been taught to ring a bell when they want their dinner!

The bell is supported on a float from which a string hangs down. When the fish want their dinner one of them tugs at the string. The bell rings, and a little cup of ants' eggs tips into the water! Then the fish swim round and snap up the food hungrily.

COMET GOLDFISH *F. W. Bond.*

This is a red " goldfish," but as with other varieties it only acquires its colour as it grows up. The young are grey-green like their wild carp ancestors.

Neville Kingston.

THE BEAUTIFUL ANGEL FISH

Fish take shapes more remarkable than any other living creatures, and here is one which rather reminds us of a bird of Paradise. Its brilliant colours match its bird-like appearance. It is known as the Angel Fish, and is an inhabitant of tropical seas. It is quite small, being only an inch or two long.

QUEER FISH

IN the waters of the world dwell many very curious fish. A clever and entertaining one is the Archer Fish. It owes its name to the strange way in which it catches its prey.

Its chief food is insects which hover over the water, or rest upon water-plants. The archer fish has excellent sight, and as soon as it sees a fly on a leaf it rises to the surface and smartly shoots from its mouth a drop of water. This hits the fly sharply; it tumbles from the leaf and is snapped up quickly by the waiting fish.

The fish's aim is good, and it can hit its mark as far as 3 feet away. Its eyes are curious, for they can be moved in any direction except downwards.

Another strange creature is the Angler Fish. Its body is broad and flattened, its head enormous, and it has a great, gaping mouth with many teeth. It likes to lie still upon the floor of the sea and angle for its victims.

Growing on the top of its snout is a long, flexible tentacle, which has a leaf-like, flattened end. This the angler cunningly waves about in the water. Soon an inquisitive fish swims up and sees the strange object. What can it be? Is it something to eat? It looks good, and is certainly alive.

The fish swims closer to examine the waving tentacle more closely. The watchful angler fish heaves up his enormous head, opens his mouth wider—and that is the end of the inquisitive intruder!

The Four-eyed Fish

In the rivers of tropical America lives another curious fish. It is called the Four-eyed Fish, because each of its pair of eyes is divided into two sections, one to see above water and the other to see below.

It swims at the top of the water, with the upper part of its eyes above the surface, and the lower part beneath. Thus it can see the happenings above and below at one and the same time!

Another quaint fish is the little Sea-Horse, which is common in the seas round Britain. Some Australian Sea-Dragons, which are not unlike it, are illustrated in the coloured plates. Both these and their odd relatives, the Pipe-fishes, have very small mouths at the extreme ends of their " snouts."

Shell=fish
and other
Strange Creatures—

Which Live
Where
Sea Meets Land

F. Martin Duncan.

MUSSELS

Mussels are the commonest of all shellfish in British waters, and this photograph gives a good idea of the vast number that attach themselves to a breakwater between high and low water-mark. Mussel beds will sometimes protect a beach from destruction by the sea. Clean mussels are good to eat, but those taken from the stagnant waters of a harbour may be poisonous.

THE LITTLE WORLD OF THE SEASHORE

ALL ABOUT SHELLFISH

YOU are sure to have seen many different kinds of shellfish when you played on the seashore. Their name is rather stupid, for they are not fish at all. Their proper name is Mollusc, which means *soft-bodied*. Another name for them is "Mantle-wearers," which refers to the loose, leathery envelope that covers their soft bodies, giving them protection, and helping in the making of their shell.

Two Kinds of Shellfish

Shellfish are of two kinds, those with one shell, the uni-valves like the Limpet and the Sea Snail, and those with two shells, the bi-valves, like the Mussel and the Oyster.

You must often have found the dark-blue mussel on the rocks. It clings there by means of many little threads called the byssus. These are very strong, and hold the mussel so firmly to the rock that only very rough seas indeed can tear it away. When the creature wants to move it puts forward a few of its threads and takes hold of a fresh place. Then the other threads are moved too, and these pull the mussel's shell with them. Afterwards the first threads move again, and so on.

The Whelk is a spiral-shaped uni-valve. Its eggs are laid in a cluster in a tough yellowish bag, each cluster containing about 500 eggs. When first laid, each egg is no bigger than a pin's head, but soon the elastic skin around them swells up, and in a short time the cluster is as big as a ball, each egg having swollen as large as a pea. Inside the cluster in the spring-time you will find numbers of tiny little whelks all complete with their shells.

251

The Clinging Limpet

The limpet and the sea snail are both one-shelled creatures. The limpet clings so tightly to the rocks that you will not be able to move it, however hard you pull or push. Only a sharp knock that takes it by surprise will make it lose its grip. The sea snails wander over the rocks, rasping off pieces of seaweed with their curious ribbon-like tongues, which are set with hundred of tiny hooked teeth.

The Scallop is a bivalve. Its shell may be found empty on the sands. It is prettily ridged, and is yellow, pink or mauve. The Cockle is another bivalve.

F. Martin Duncan.

A COCKLE SHELL

The cockle is a bivalve, a double-shelled fish, and there are more than two hundred varieties known to naturalists. They live buried in mud or sand, are able to burrow rapidly and also to *jump* a few inches at a time.

When it is alive it likes to bury itself in the sand, and this it does so quickly that if you try to dig it out, it will always work faster than you!

Periwinkles (Winkles) are often eaten. They are found in thousands on the rocks, brownish-green or black. They are rather like the sea snail. Top-shells are pretty, cone-shaped shells, often streaked and spotted with lovely colours.

One of the most beautiful shells is the little Wentle-trap (which means " winding stair "). It is a slender, graceful shell, with pretty spiral curves.

The Oyster

The oyster, in whose double shells we sometimes find beautiful pearls, likes to rest on a muddy bed, for sand gets into the hinges of the shells, preventing them from being closed. In May the mother oyster squirts out 800,000 or 900,000 eggs, and the tiny baby oysters swim about for some time in the sea. Then one day they sink to the bottom and rest in the mud, never to go voyaging again, and after a time they grow to be just like their mother.

CURIOUS EGG-CASES

WHEN you walk along the seashore you may pick up a curious black thing, about 2 inches wide, and 3 inches long. At each end it has two little horns sticking out. It looks rather like a tiny hand-barrow, with the four horns making the handles.

You might think it was an extra big seaweed pod, but it is not. It is the egg-case of a large, deep-sea fish, the Skate.

At one end of the case is a slit through which the baby fish escaped when it was hatched. You are not likely to find a little fish inside the case you see on the beach, for the babies are hatched in the sea. Then the empty egg-cases drift in to shore, and are flung upon the beach.

You may find another kind of egg-case on the shore, one rather like that of the Skate, but with long curling

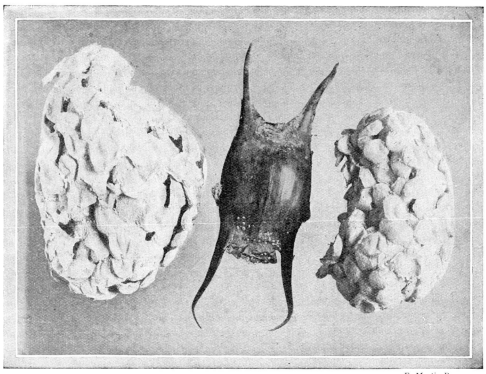

F. Martin Duncan.

EGGS OF THE SKATE AND THE WHELK

Often when walking on the beach you may find something that looks like a little empty purse with a curious horn at each corner. This is the egg of the fish called the skate, or rather the empty egg shell from which the young fish has been hatched. You see one of these in the centre of this photograph. The other two objects are clusters of the eggs of the whelk, a shellfish common in British waters. Shellfish, like other fish, lay eggs.

tendrils at each of the four ends, instead of horns. These are the cases of the Spotted Dog-Fish. They are fastened to fronds of seaweed by the tendrils, but if a storm comes some of them are torn off and tossed ashore. Then we find them and pick them up, wondering what they can be.

SEA ANEMONES

SOME of the prettiest things to be found in the rock pools are the Sea Anemones. They are not really like anemones at all, but are much more like chrysanthemums or dahlias. When they are closed they look like lumps of red or green jelly, but when they are open they are lovely, for they are fringed with waving petal-like tentacles. They cling firmly to the rock with their one sucker foot, and you will find it difficult to move them. They can move themselves if they wish to, but it is not very often that they do. Their tentacles are used to catch any little sea creature that comes near, and once he is caught he is pulled down to the middle of the anemone and digested. Then, some hours afterwards, the anemone opens again, and sends out the empty shell of its victim.

The body of the anemone is filled with water. When it wants to expand its tentacles, it contracts the muscles in the walls of its body, sending the water upwards into the tubes of the tentacles. As the water fills them, they expand, and wave about in the sea, hoping for some unwary little creature to swim against them.

SEA ANEMONES

The most beautiful ornaments of a rock pool are those curious plant-like creatures called Sea Anemones. Lovely as they are, they are hungry creatures, catching their food by throwing out tentacles armed with stinging cells. They are very long-lived.

The Smooth Anemone

The Smooth Anemone is our commonest one, and can be found in hundreds in the rock pools when the tide is out. When their tentacles are open a row of tiny, turquoise-blue " beads " can be seen round the edge of the body, just between the roots of the tentacles. They are very pretty, and because of these the smooth anemone is often called the Beadlet.

The Daisy Anemone is not so common as the smooth one, but you will sometimes find it if you look in the rock pools at low tide, on our western or southern coasts. It is a pale grey-yellow in the centre and its tentacles are ringed with grey and white, spreading out like the petals of a daisy.

It can alter its shape in a curious fashion, sometimes making itself tall and narrow, and sometimes short and fat.

A Beautiful Anemone

Among our prettiest anemones is the one with the strange name of Snake-locked. Its body is long and slender, and at the top it has a cluster of thin, snake-like arms, white and restless. It can be found on the coasts of Cornwall and Devon. When it closes itself up it draws in its little snake arms and makes itself so squat and flat that it is hard to see.

A very handsome anemone is the one called Thick-armed. It may be purple, red, green or white, with its tentacles ringed with white and scarlet. It gets its name from its fat tentacles, as perhaps you will guess.

Sometimes the sea anemones decide to become little boats and go adventuring over the sea. They loose their hold of the rocks, float up to the top of the water, and turn upside down. Then they make their bodies hollow, and so form tiny boats, which go tossing up and down on the water for a long way. At last they settle down again, and take up new quarters in another rock pool.

ABOUT THE JELLYFISH

SOMETIMES a Jellyfish is thrown up on the shore and we find it. If we try to pick it up our fingers sink into the soft jelly-body, and it breaks. It is a curious creature, for its body is nearly all water, and if it lies in the sun for long it dissolves and disappears, leaving a little, ring-shaped mark on the sand to show where it rested.

In the water the jellyfish are lovely creatures. They swim by opening and shutting their umbrella-shaped bodies. Round the edge of their umbrellas is a fringe of fine threads, and hanging down from the centre is a bunch of ribbon-like streamers.

The " Fishing-lines " of the Jellyfish

The threads are the " fishing-lines " of the jellyfish, for it is with these that they catch their prey. As soon as a baby shrimp or prawn swims up against

A MARVEL OF TROPIC SEAS

Fox Photos.

This picture was taken, not on English coasts, but in a warm tropic sea. The photographer went down in a diving-bell. It is a pity that we cannot show the scene in the gorgeous colours of reality. The large dark object in the centre is a sea urchin, the hard shell of which is covered with sharp spikes. Around it are living corals of all shapes and exquisite hues. Corals, although they are firmly attached to the rocks and cannot move, are not plants, but animals. Corals form immense reefs which gradually become islands of dry land.

one of these threads, it becomes para-lysed, and in a short time it is dead. Every thread is set with great numbers of tiny cells, and in these, coiled up like a watch spring, are minute darts, each with a barbed point.

As soon as any little creature touches a thread, out spring numbers of these tiny darts, and bury their barbed points in the victim's body. They are poisonous and soon paralyse it. If *we* happen to swim up against a stinging jellyfish ourselves, and brush against the threads, we shall feel those little darts, too. They sting rather like nettles, sharply and painfully, and may perhaps make us ill.

There are many kinds of jellyfish, and most of them are beautiful when they swim along in the sea. At night they shine like fairy lamps, and are lovely to watch. Some jellyfish are big, some are small, some like to have their umbrellas wide open, and some do not. Some have long fringes of threads around their bodies, whilst others have short ones, or none at all.

Often a whole colony of tiny crea-tures, such as shrimps or baby fish, make their homes under the jellyfish umbrella, keeping well out of the way of the sting-threads, you may be sure. When the jellyfish floats away in the sea they go with it, and feast on the food that the strange creature wafts under its umbrella by means of its many tentacles.

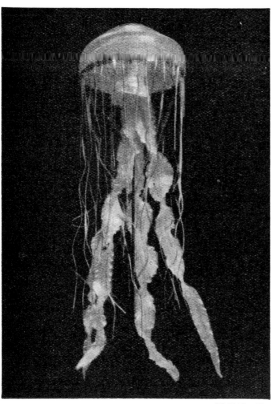

A BEAUTIFUL JELLYFISH

W. S. Berridge.

This beautiful bell-like object is a jellyfish, of which one giant sort has a bell 7½ feet across and streamers 120 feet long. These streamers or tentacles are extremely poisonous, and may actually paralyse a swimmer who is unlucky enough to be stung by them.

THE STARFISH

WHEN you wandered about the shore, look-ing into rock pools and picking up shells, you probably came across a stranded Star-fish. There it lay, with its five arms stretched out, quite still. Perhaps it was dead, but maybe if you put it into a pool it suddenly came alive again and began gliding away.

How a Starfish Walks

Do you know how a starfish walks? You might think it had no legs, but it has hundreds of them! If you put a starfish into a glass tank, and watched it creeping up the sides, you would see its legs clearly. They are little white things that jut out from many tiny pin holes on the under-side of the creature's body.

Each little " leg " has a sucker-like cup at the end, and these suckers take hold of the rock (or glass if it is in a tank) and hold tightly. When the starfish walks it puts forward some of its legs, and then pulls its rays after them. Now the

A MARVEL OF TROPIC SEAS

Fox Photos.

This picture was taken, not on English coasts, but in a warm tropic sea. The photographer went down in a diving-bell. It is a pity that we cannot show the scene in the gorgeous colours of reality. The large dark object in the centre is a sea urchin, the hard shell of which is covered with sharp spikes. Around it are living corals of all shapes and exquisite hues. Corals, although they are firmly attached to the rocks and cannot move, are not plants, but animals. Corals form immense reefs which gradually become islands of dry land.

one of these threads, it becomes para-lysed, and in a short time it is dead. Every thread is set with great numbers of tiny cells, and in these, coiled up like a watch spring, are minute darts, each with a barbed point.

As soon as any little creature touches a thread, out spring numbers of these tiny darts, and bury their barbed points in the victim's body. They are poisonous and soon paralyse it. If *we* happen to swim up against a stinging jellyfish ourselves, and brush against the threads, we shall feel those little darts, too. They sting rather like nettles, sharply and painfully, and may perhaps make us ill.

There are many kinds of jellyfish, and most of them are beautiful when they swim along in the sea. At night they shine like fairy lamps, and are lovely to watch. Some jellyfish are big, some are small, some like to have their umbrellas wide open, and some do not. Some have long fringes of threads around their bodies, whilst others have short ones, or none at all.

Often a whole colony of tiny crea-tures, such as shrimps or baby fish, make their homes under the jellyfish umbrella, keeping well out of the way of the sting-threads, you may be sure. When the jellyfish floats away in the sea they go with it, and feast on the food that the strange creature wafts under its umbrella by means of its many tentacles.

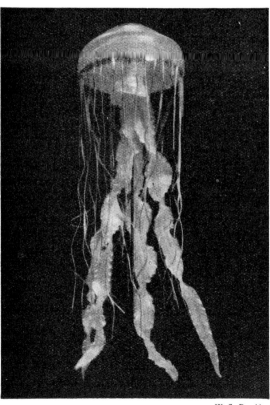

W. S. Berridge.

A BEAUTIFUL JELLYFISH

This beautiful bell-like object is a jellyfish, of which one giant sort has a bell 7½ feet across and streamers 120 feet long. These streamers or tentacles are extremely poisonous, and may actually paralyse a swimmer who is unlucky enough to be stung by them.

THE STARFISH

WHEN you wandered about the shore, look-ing into rock pools and picking up shells, you probably came across a stranded Star-fish. There it lay, with its five arms stretched out, quite still. Perhaps it was dead, but maybe if you put it into a pool it suddenly came alive again and began gliding away.

How a Starfish Walks

Do you know how a starfish walks? You might think it had no legs, but it has hundreds of them! If you put a starfish into a glass tank, and watched it creeping up the sides, you would see its legs clearly. They are little white things that jut out from many tiny pin holes on the under-side of the creature's body.

Each little " leg " has a sucker-like cup at the end, and these suckers take hold of the rock (or glass if it is in a tank) and hold tightly. When the starfish walks it puts forward some of its legs, and then pulls its rays after them. Now the rest of its legs move forward into the place where the first ones were. Next the foremost ones move onward again, drag the rays after, and are followed by the rest of the legs once more. Thus it moves along, and can travel quite a distance in this way.

In the centre of the starfish is its mouth. The creature is really a walking stomach. It crams itself full of shellfish of all kinds, and will even devour the prickly Sea-urchin. The fishermen hate the starfish because it robs their fishing-lines of the bait. It also eats the Oysters from the oyster beds, and does a great deal of damage in that way. It swallows the oysters whole, digests the soft body-part, and

F. Martin Duncan.

THE STARFISH (1)

This is one of the many forms of starfish found in seas in all parts of the world. Owners of oyster beds hate the starfish, which has the power of opening and eating oysters and other shell-fish. It crawls along the bottom by means of little soft " tube-feet " bearing suckers, which are pushed out through holes in the arms.

then ejects the shell from its mouth.

Starfish can easily grow their arms again if they are broken off. Not long after an arm is severed a little new one begins to grow, and in a few weeks' time it is as long as the others.

Sometimes a starfish is cut in half. It does not die, but, instead, each half begins to form new arms, and in a short time there are two starfish where only one was before. This seems very extraordinary, but it is quite true.

The Brittle Starfish

Starfish keep their eyes at the tip of their rays, and some kinds have eyelids which open and shut. They are strange creatures, and perhaps the most curious

F. Martin Duncan.

THE STARFISH (2)

A starfish may be said to be five creatures in one, for each arm is complete in itself, and if broken away from the rest can grow four or five more arms. This photograph shows one complete six-rayed starfish and others in the process of growing fresh arms.

of all is the Brittle Starfish, which has a habit of breaking itself entirely to pieces, so that nothing of it is left whole except the disc in the centre. But very soon new rays grow, and then the brittle starfish is as good as ever it was. Its arms are very long and slender, and are continually wriggling about.

The Five-finger Starfish is the commonest, and the Sun Starfish is perhaps the handsomest. It has twelve rays, and may be as much as 10 inches across, looking like a large, bright-scarlet sunflower. Sometimes you may find a curious-looking starfish, with its five arms all joined together by a membrane, rather in the same way as a duck's toes are joined by webbing. This is the Bird's-foot Starfish, and you can easily guess the reason for its queer name.

THE STORY OF THE PRAWN

THE Prawn in the rock pool is a very different creature from the prawn in the fish shop. In the shop it is red, for it is boiled, but in the pool it has hardly any colour, and is nearly transparent.

It looks rather like a small lobster, and is a cousin of that big-clawed creature. It seems to have a great many legs, but the five pairs at the back are not true legs, but swimmerets. These help the prawn to swim forwards when it wishes to.

When it wants to dart backwards it stretches its body straight out, and then suddenly doubles it up. As it does this it strikes the water with its spread-out tail, and so drives itself sharply backwards.

Neville Kingston.

SPINY-LOBSTERS

The Spiny-Lobster, often miscalled " Crawfish," is red and orange in colour and bears sharp spines on its head-shield, with an extra long spine over each eye. Its feelers are twice as long as its body, and by rubbing their first joints against the rough edge of the head-shield it makes a curious noise like the grunting of a pig. The spiny-lobster has no great claws, but it can nip hard by means of spines on its first pair of legs. The true Crawfish, or Crayfish, is a fresh-water creature much like a lobster.

F Martin Duncan.

THE LOBSTER

Nearly a million lobsters are taken yearly in lobster pots off the coasts of the British Isles. A lobster may grow to the very large size of twelve or fourteen pounds. The colour in life is bluish black, which changes to red in boiling. The lobster lays two thousand to twelve thousand eggs, but fewer than half of these hatch. Lobsters are found in all the cooler seas of the world, in the Southern Hemispheres as well as the Northern. They are the most palatable of shellfish.

Little Scavengers

Prawns and Shrimps are very useful, because they feed upon dead and decaying matter, which might make the water foul and poisonous. But although their food is made up of such horrid stuff the little creatures themselves are very clean.

They spend a great deal of time performing their toilet. On their front legs are many stiff hairs, and these the prawns use as brushes, rubbing them against their legs and body to brush off any tiny speck of dirt. On their second pair of legs are little pincers, and sometimes the prawns use these to pick off particles the brushes have missed.

A shrimp does not turn red when it is boiled, as the prawn does. In the pool it is nearly transparent, and so like the sand, that when it lies down upon it, it can scarcely be seen. It is not so fond of swimming as the prawn is, and likes to bury itself, shovelling sand over its body with the two large scales at the foot of its feelers.

Can you tell the difference between a shrimp and a prawn ? A shrimp, which is smaller than a prawn, has two little " feathers " on its head, between the feelers, and a sharp hook on its front legs, but a prawn's head bears a sharp, jagged " sword," and its legs have no hook.

About the Lobster

The Lobster is not found in the shallow rock pools, but is caught in the deep water in lobster pots. In the sea it is blackish, but when it is boiled it goes bright red, like the prawn. One of its claws is much larger than the other, and this is the one it uses for

F. Martin Duncan.

THE FIDDLER CRAB

They call this big fellow the Velvet Fiddler Crab, but you
would not think there was much velvet about him if he caught
your hand in his hard claws. Yet he is velvety enough when
he moults his shell, and has to skulk in a hole till a new one
grows.

fighting, or for defence. The other claw
is used as an anchor.

Lobsters swim forwards and dart
backwards in the same way as the
prawn. With one stroke of their
powerful tails they can drive themselves 30 feet or 40 feet away.

When they lay eggs they carry them
glued to the hairs on their swimmerets,
and take them about with them until
the time comes for the babies to hatch.

THE CURIOUS CRAB

DID you know that a Crab baby is
not at all like the grown-up crab
we find in the pools ? It is a curious little thing called a Zoea, very tiny,
with a long, curved horn in front of its
body and another one behind. It has a
long tail, and when it swims, what do
you think it does ? It turns head over
heels in the water again and again !

Whales are very fond
of eating these zoeas.
They swim through
great shoals of them
with their enormous
mouths wide open, and
the crab babies float in,
in their thousands.

After a time the little
zoea, if it has escaped
being eaten by its many
enemies, changes its
skin, and becomes a
different-looking crea-
ture altogether! It is
then called a Megalopa,
and has enormous eyes
set on long stalks. It
has lost its curved horns,
its legs are longer, and
its claws are beginning
to appear. It still has
a tail, and swims as
before, turning head
over heels at a great
rate.

Then comes the last
change. Its skin splits
again, and out comes
—a perfect little crab!

How the Crab Changes its Shell

The crab is not a shellfish such as the
mussel or oyster, for its shell is not in
the least like theirs. It never grows
larger, and so the crab has to throw it
off every now and again, and grow a
new one, for its body gets bigger and
becomes cramped.

The crab feels rather queer before
shell-casting time comes along. It
goes to a dark hole somewhere and
waits. Suddenly part of its body inside
the shell turns to water, and the crab
feels more uncomfortable than ever. It
begins to wriggle about, and twists and
turns this way and that. It rubs its
legs against one another, and does all
it can to get its body loose from its
shell.

At last it succeeds, and suddenly the
shell splits in halves across the back.

SECRETS OF THE SHORE

These two naturalists are studying life in a rock pool at low tide. The man is examining something he has taken from the water in a bottle, and the boy is netting for prawns and small fishes. Many of the interesting creatures are too small to be seen without the help of a microscope. Others do not swim about, but are rooted to the rocks and have to be carefully detached.

Crabs are fierce fighters. They seem to quarrel over anything or nothing, but the bone of contention is generally food. Here are two spider crabs engaged in fierce combat at the bottom of their tank in an aquarium. In the course of such a fight a leg or even a claw may be wrenched off, but this is no fatal injury. The damaged crab merely hides away in a corner among the rocks and grows a new one.

CRAB BABIES LOOK LIKE THIS

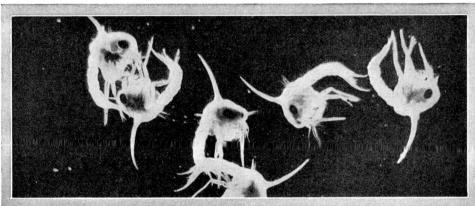

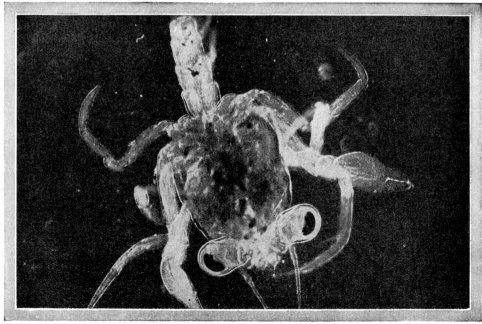

F. Martin Duncan.

The crab baby is very different from the grown-up crab (*see p.* 260).   When hatched from the
egg (*top*) it is very tiny, and as it grows it passes through the other stages shown above.

ANIMAL OR VEGETABLE?

Douglas P. Wilson.

The Bladder Wrack is one of our most common seaweeds, though it is not the only one which has small bladders of air to raise its fronds in the water. In Knotted Wrack the bladders occur singly ; in Bladder Wrack they are in pairs.

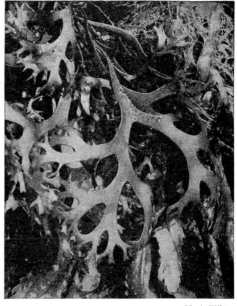

M. A. Wilson.

Irish Moss, or Carrageen, is a pale green or pink seaweed which can be cooked and eaten. In the Far East a similar seaweed, Ceylon Moss, provides agar-agar, a jelly used in soups. Another British seaweed, Laver, is also used for food.

Douglas P. Wilson.

You often find the biscuit-coloured fronds of the Sea Mat on the rocks, but though they look rather like dead plants they are really colonies of minute animals. With a magnifying-glass you can see the tiny holes in which these harmless creatures live.

Douglas P. Wilson.

These little cones on the rocks belong to Acorn Barnacles. When submerged they open their lids and wave tiny purple " feathers " in the water. These are really their legs, and they are fishing with them while standing on their heads inside their shells !

263

M. A. Wilson.

LIFE AT THE BOTTOM OF THE POOL

On the bottom of this pool you can see two Beadlet sea-anemones waving their tentacles, three Top-shells (on the left), a Periwinkle, or Winkle (on the right) and a Limpet (at the foot).

The Crab we find oftenest is the Shore Crab, often called the Green Crab, because of its colour, though it is sometimes brown or bright yellow. The Fiddler Crab has its hinder legs flattened into little paddles, and with these it can swim very fast indeed, unlike most crabs, which can only crawl.

The Crab's Eye

The crab has its eyes on little stalks at each side of its head. If you look closely you will see tiny black specks at the tips of these stalks. These specks are made up of hundreds of minute eyes, each looking in a slightly different direction from the others, so that the crab can see above, below and around it without moving its head.

Out leaps the crab, and then the split in the shell joins up, so that it is hard to tell that it is there. The crab lies quietly for a time, for it is tired out.

Soon it begins to grow, and it *does* grow fast! In a short while it is very much bigger than it was before, and it is difficult to imagine that it could ever have been in the small, empty shell lying nearby. Then a new shell forms upon its skin, and soon the crab has an entirely fresh suit of armour, and dares once again to go out from its hiding-place and face its enemies.

Lobsters change their shells in the same way, and so do shrimps and prawns. As soon as they are fully grown they keep the same armour and do not bother to grow it anew.

In some parts of the world there are land-crabs which make long journeys to lay eggs on the seashore, and there are others which climb trees and tap holes in the " eyes " of coconuts, to get at the milky juice!

Though the Barnacle is not in the least like a crab to look at, it is another member of the same class of creatures. Barnacles attach themselves firmly to the sides and bottoms of ships, or the timbers of break-waters, and a small kind, called the Acorn Barnacle, is very common on the rocks and may be found everywhere at low tide. When the tide begins to turn you may hear a curious rasping noise all around you. It is made by the thousands of acorn barnacles all stirring within their shells as the water covers them!

THE GREAT BARRIER REEF

Australian National Publicity Assoc.

AN ISLAND OF THE GREAT BARRIER REEF

The Great Barrier Reef extends for some 1,250 miles along the Queensland coast. Its islands, reefs and shoals embrace an area of about 80,000 square miles and make it the greatest coral reef in the world. Heron Island, where this picture was taken, lies at the southern end of the Reef. Notice the strangely rooted Pandanus trees.

OFF the coast of Queensland, Australia, from Breaksea Spit in the south almost to the coast of New Guinea in the north, there stretches the most remarkable coral kingdom that Nature has ever devised. It is the Great Barrier Reef, and it is the largest, and the most wonderful, coral reef in the world. Its length is about 1,250 miles.

The Coral Polyp

This fantastic and colourful realm of strange fish and sea creatures owes its existence to a tiny marine animal called the coral polyp. The skeletons of these minute creatures form the substance that we know as coral. For a long time, corals were thought to be plants or flowers, because of their many beautiful hues and petal-like structure. But we now know that the delicate fronds, branches and clusters of the coral garden are the work of a small organism which is a member of the Cœlenterata division of the animal world. This division includes sea anemones and jellyfish.

Although we may be familiar with the bleached dead coral, few of us have seen a living coral polyp, with its soft, almost unreal colourings. The average coral polyp is probably smaller than a pinhead. It consists chiefly of a fleshy tube, divided within into a number of sections by plates that resemble the spokes of a wheel. At the top of the tube is the mouth, fringed by the tentacles with which the coral catches its food. This mouth also serves as an outlet for the waste matter and eggs of the polyp. At the other end of the tube is a cuplike base which rests on some hard object—probably the skeletons of dead corals. The polyp attaches itself to the hard object by sending out a cementing fluid, which forms this base.

Only when they are larvæ do corals move about freely in the water, and even then they are such weak swimmers that they may be propelled hither and thither by tides and currents. When they have attached themselves to a hard surface— and as they approach maturity they must do this or perish—they begin to secrete the lime for their skeleton castle. By day, the coral keeps within the castle, but at night, when the tiny animals which are its food come up to the surface waters, it expands its tentacles to catch them.

How Corals shoot their Food

They do not really " catch " their food; they shoot it. Each tentacle is armed with poisonous darts which wound and immediately paralyse any tiny animal touching the tentacle. The tentacles then envelop the animal and convey it to the mouth of the coral. Most corals food in this way, but some collect their food by the continual movement of tiny hairs (cilia), which convey it to the mouth of the polyp.

Some corals live alone, but most form colonies and it is by these that the coral reefs are built. The reef-building corals are found only in warm tropical waters and usually at depths no greater than 150 feet. The water must be clean and sunlit, and there must be sufficient movement by tide and current to bring food and oxygen within reach of the corals; for, like all animal life, they must breathe.

Once a coral has established itself, the way in which the colony develops varies according to the type of coral. For example, branching (staghorn) coral throws off new corals from the side as it grows upwards. These in turn develop in the same manner, creating the characteristic antler-like formation. Another type of coral splits down the centre to form two corals, which subsequently split to form further corals and so on.

Hundreds of different kinds of corals are found on the Great Barrier Reef, and because there are variations in each kind it is not easy to classify them. The task is made more difficult by the contraction in daytime and expansion at night of the coral. At night the corals unfold their tentacles to the fullest extent to form the " blooms " in the wonderful coral garden; but by day the corals remain within their stone castles and may seem quite different.

Types of Coral

Broadly speaking, there are two main types of corals: the staghorn, which has been mentioned already, and the solid corals. Brain or meandrine corals are examples of the latter kind. The more common is the staghorn, which is found in beautifully soft shades of blue, yellow, purple, red, green and other colours. Some staghorns have vivid green branches tipped with lilac; others, branches of yellow with their tips in rose-pink. The solid corals are usually rounded Their surfaces are either smooth but plited, or ridged and twisted into strange patterns. They are mostly bright green or brown and in the deeper waters may take the form of large boulders.

Another common type of coral is called Porites. These would normally be dome-shaped were it not for the tide, which bares the upper surface so that it dies. Most Porites are therefore flat or saucer-shaped, growth continuing around the sides until the colony is about 20 feet in diameter. Layers of fresh coral grow from the platform made by the tide. The growing corals are the colour of lavender, the tips of the tentacles being a greyish-green.

The mushroom coral is about the size of a soup-plate and was given this name because its patterns resemble the " gills " of a mushroom. Its tentacles, which are green or brown, sometimes extend 2 or 3 inches beyond the coral itself. Yet another group of corals is known as Alcyonaria, or " soft " corals. These can always be recognised by their tentacles. The polyps of Alcyonarian corals always have eight feathery

BEAUTIFUL CORALS OF THE GREAT BARRIER REEF

Some of the many lovely corals to be found in the waters of the Great Barrier Reef are seen in this picture. There are several hundred species of coral and because some do not always take the same form, it is often difficult to identify them. The most common are the staghorn corals. Their beautifully coloured branches resemble antlers.

tentacles. Alcyonaria secrete only very minute spikes of lime. Exceptions to this are the hard Alcyonarians—the organ-pipe and blue corals.

Soft corals are found in many parts of the Great Barrier Reef. The smaller varieties are quite attractive, but the larger are leathery and unpleasant to look upon or touch. Green or brown is the most common colour for these corals. The organ-pipe coral, one of the hard Alcyonarians, is a brilliant red.

There are also the horny corals, which look rather like small bushes that have lost their leaves. The two chief types are the Antipatharians and the Gorgonids. Antipatharians are usually black; the most common Gorgonid is a brilliant red.

The Making of the Reef

From the edges of reefs and atolls the water often descends sharply to great depths, sometimes amounting to many thousands of feet. How, then, do the corals manage to exist? Surely these great depths cannot support coral life, which, as we know, can only survive in shallow waters? The answer to this problem was provided by that great naturalist, Charles Darwin. His theory, which is still largely accepted, was that our present-day reefs and atolls rest upon older reefs which became submerged as the sea bed slowly settled or as the water level rose. The corals themselves fought against such movements, building upwards towards the sunny shallow waters and so creating the great coral ramparts and rings that we know to-day. Let us see how this theory applies to the Great Barrier Reef.

A very long time ago, the area between the Reef and the mainland was a coastal plain, with a few hills and low peaks here and there. But in time, as these coastal lands settled, only the hills and peaks were left above the surface. They are, in fact, the present inshore islands of the Reef. But the sea was shallow and warm. Corals began to grow, and gradually the Reef took shape. Scientists have said that it was built at the rate of about 3 feet in every thousand years. And although the work of the reef-builders was, and for that matter still is, subject to attack by other natural forces—the pounding of the waves, exposure to air by the tide, fresh water from the rivers, typhoons—they were, and are, more than able to hold their own. It is thought that in time whole sections of the Barrier Reef may be knitted into a single mass. Sand may pile up against this mass, forming a beach, and presently seeds conveyed by bird or driftwood, or brought by ocean current, will come to life in the sand. Such is the way in which fresh islands supporting vegetation might be formed from the Reef.

A Real Coral Island

What kinds of trees and plant life might we expect to find on a true coral island ? Coco-nut palms immediately spring to mind, and indeed they do grow on the northern islands of the Reef, where we might also find mangroves—those ugly growths that seem to have more roots than tree and do, in fact, send tendril-like roots down from their branches to their muddy anchorage. The largest of the mangroves of the northern coral islands is the red mangrove, which has been known to reach heights of 50 or 60 feet. Of a similar height, but much more attractive, are the pisonia trees, with their fresh green foliage and grey trunks. But they are treacherous for climbers. Their boughs, that look so stout, may be quite brittle and may snap off the moment that weight is put upon them.

Another interesting tree is the pandanus, or " screw-pine," whose branches and stilt-like roots can weave themselves into an impenetrable jungle. It is called the " screw-pine " because its leaves form spiralled tufts. It is also known as the " breadfruit tree " because its fruit was used by the aborigines to make a doughy " bread." You may remember that Captain Bligh of the *Bounty* had the task of introducing the breadfruit tree into the West Indies, and that the voyage during which the historic mutiny occurred was made for this purpose. The Captain was, in fact, nicknamed " Breadfruit Bligh."

The pandanus has roots like stilts for a very good reason. The tree has to grow in sand, where wind or sea might soon shift ordinary roots. But its strange stilts give the pandanus a firm hold.

The papaw tree is found on many of the islands. This tree is noted for its luscious fruit, which makes a splendid breakfast dish. We may also see the silvery-green tournefortia tree, the banyan, and the casuarina or beach-oak. And it will not be long before we discover that our coral island is the place to delight any bird-watcher or ornithologist. For it has rightly been said that " the most notable tenants of the Barrier Reef isles are birds."

Birds of the Barrier Reef

Let us imagine that it is summer-time and that we are approaching one of the coral islands. From a distance it seems that the island has a large black cloud poised above it, but as we come nearer we realise that the black cloud is a huge flock of soaring, wheeling birds—noddy terns, perhaps, sooty terns, mutton birds or shearwaters. Every season vast numbers of these birds come to the Great Barrier Reef to mate, build their nests and raise their young. How many there are! Some of the islands become nothing more than crowded roosting and nesting grounds. A single island, with a circumference of about three miles, may house as many as two million mutton-birds during the breeding season.

The most active bird is the sooty tern, or wide-awake. It is called the wide-awake because it seems to be

Roy P. Cooper.

A GROUP OF PISONIA TREES

The pisonia tree may grow to a height of some 60 feet and the diameter of its trunk, at the base, may measure several feet. The trunk is a mottled grey, and the leaves are a charming shade of soft green. Pisonias are dangerous trees to climb because their boughs break easily and without warning. Heron Island, in the Capricorn Group, is one part of the Reef where Pisonias may be seen in large numbers.

continually on the wing during the day, when it forages for fish and other water food. By day, when the birds are away foraging, the island may be quiet. But when the sun sets and the foragers return, the noise of feeding, quarrelling, mating, fighting and nest-building begins and seems to continue through the night. The noise made by the terns and other birds is so great and so eerie that the superstitious sailors of old often declared the islands of the Reef to be haunted.

The sooty tern makes its nest by scooping out a shallow depression in the sand. Here the mother tern lays her single egg. The young chick which presently appears will have speckled white and brown plumage; but when

he grows up, his back will be black and his underneath white. Although the mother tern lays only one egg during the breeding season, the total number produced by a colony is so great that they seem to cover the beaches favoured by these birds, such as those of Michaelmas Cay, near Trinity Passage.

The mutton-bird, which is about the same size as a small duck, is also called the shearwater because it almost brushes the surface of the water during flight. Its tail is in the shape of a wedge, its hooked bill is red and its plumage a dark brown. During mating, the male bird wails plaintively and then, when he has been accepted, purrs. Their nests are burrows, which they scratch out of the sand, but they are quite content to clean out and use the burrows that they made the previous year. Their daily search for food starts very early in the morning, long before we should even think about getting out of bed. Leaving their burrows, the birds make their way down to the sloping shore, where they take wing to hunt fish, squid and other food. Dawn breaks to find very few of the mutton-birds upon the island.

Only one egg is laid during the breeding season, and both male and female mutton-bird share the work of looking after it. The young bird at first lives in the burrow with its parents, and if it is wise it will not enter the water until nearly all its down has been replaced by adult plumage. Young birds that enter the water too soon usually drown.

The noddy tern, which is about the same size as a pigeon, builds his nest in one of the many pisonia trees of the Reef, and is helped by his mate in this work. The nest is an untidy structure built from the yellow pisonia leaves, seaweed and grass. These materials are cemented together with the droppings of the birds and with the sticky seed-heads of the pisonia. Sometimes there may be no fewer than a hundred and forty nests in a single tree. But life in these tree-top homes is not entirely secure. Somewhere on the island a pair of sea-eagles may be nesting, and these will prey mercilessly upon both mutton-birds and terns.

The white-capped noddy and the sooty are not the only kinds of tern that we might see upon the Reef. There are black-naped, roseate and crested terns. Each kind usually has its own breeding grounds, the roseate terns favouring one island and visiting it each year, the sooty terns frequenting another.

Nor do the terns and mutton-birds represent the entire feathered life of the Reef. Another regular visitor in large numbers is the Torres Strait, or nutmeg, pigeon, which was once cruelly slaughtered in thousands by aborigines and white men alike, but is now protected. Then there are the silver gulls, the reef herons, the sea-eagles, turnstones, frigate birds and scrub fowls. The latter have unusual nesting habits; they do not sit upon their eggs, but bury them under leaves and other matter, which is piled up in the form of a mound and which does the incubating. The same mound may be used year after year, and in time reach a height of 15 feet and have a circumference of 50 feet. At least one scrub fowl mound was estimated to contain some 200 tons of matter gathered and built up by these birds over the years.

Turtles and Crabs

Among the other interesting inhabitants of the Great Barrier Reef are the turtles and the crabs. In midsummer, when the female turtles come to the beaches to lay their eggs, a popular sport is turtle riding. Visitors to the Reef find it easy enough while the huge turtle is moving across the sand, but once the turtle gets into the water only the skilled or lucky rider can keep his seat.

Several species of turtle are thought to live in the Reef waters from the Capricorns to Torres Strait, but only three kinds are found in numbers. They are the green turtle, the hawksbill turtle and the loggerhead turtle, and of these the green turtle is most common. The largest is the loggerhead, which may weigh as much as 1,500 pounds. Next in size is the green turtle, which is usually more than 4 feet in length and which weighs at least 500 pounds. The weight of the hawksbill is never more than 300 pounds.

If we were to visit one of the beaches by night during early November, we might see a large shape making its way slowly across the sand, almost heaving itself forward a short distance at a time and leaving in its wake tracks rather like those made by a tank. The shape is a female green turtle, and she has come ashore to lay her eggs.

STRANGE TREES OF THE GREAT BARRIER REEF

Among the unusual sights of the islands of the Great Barrier Reef are Pandanus trees. They are also called " walking trees " or " screw-pines "; their fruit is often called " bread fruit " because it was used by the aborigines to make a doughy " bread." The stilt-like roots give the trees a secure hold in the shifting sand where they grow.

When the mother turtle has pulled and heaved herself well up the beach, she finds a spot for her nest and begins to dig, scooping out the sand until she has made a depression large enough to take her whole body. Within this depression she digs an egg-pit about 18 inches deep and 12 inches in diameter. Here she lays her small, hard eggs— perhaps as many as 150 of them. When this is done, the turtle scoops the sand back into place, pats it down and levels it, and then makes once more for the sea. The egg-laying season lasts from late October until about the end of February. The average time taken by a turtle to come ashore and lay its eggs is about two and a half hours. The average clutch consists of some 120 eggs, but clutches may contain only fifty, although clutches of 200 eggs have been found.

The eggs are hatched by the heat of the sun about nine or ten weeks after they have been laid, but only about half of those laid normally hatch out. The baby turtles are each about 3 inches long. They are ready at once to take to the water, but they usually wait until night before leaving the nest. Many of those who make the journey by day fall victims to gulls, terns and other birds. Even at night there is danger from sand crabs or from predatory fish in the sea itself.

Fully-grown turtles are also preyed upon by man. The shell, or carapace, of the hawksbill turtle provides tortoiseshell. The green turtle has succulent, tender flesh that makes good eating and is also the source of a rich soup.

Crabs of all kinds are found on the Reef—giant crabs, small crabs, hermits, soldier crabs, others that disguise themselves by attaching seaweed to their backs, sand crabs, spider crabs and fiddler crabs. At ebb tide an entire army of soldier crabs may be seen marching in formation on the shore. They are cowardly creatures and retreat hastily to dig themselves into the wet sand when anyone approaches. Because they are a pale blue, soldier crabs are sometimes called " bluebottle " crabs.

In the mud where the mangrove trees grow from a fantastic tangle of roots, we might find the fiddler crab. He can easily be seen when he moves across the surface, because his claws are a brilliant red or orange. One claw is much larger than the other; sometimes it is larger than the crab's body. The movements of this large claw are said to be like those of a violinist playing his instrument—which explains the name given to this crab. When the fiddler crab detects danger, it will make for its burrow and remain just within the entrance, with its large and threatening claw protruding.

Unlike many inhabitants of the Reef, the spider crab does not have a protective colouring that blends well with its natural background and conceals the crab from its enemies. The spider crab therefore prepares its own disguise, cutting off pieces of seaweed and other underwater plant life and fixing these to its hairy legs and back. The crab carefully keeps its " roof garden " under control, trimming the weed whenever it threatens to spread beyond the shell.

The crab has several interesting relatives—the beautifully coloured " painted " lobster, the fierce mantis shrimp, the nipper prawn that snaps its " fingers " noisily, and the barnacle. All can be found on the Great Barrier Reef.

Beautiful Shellfish

The Reef has many beautiful and interesting shellfish. Some we know well, because their shells often become ornaments in our homes. Among these are the cowrie, beautifully striped or spotted, and the pink spider-shell.

The Reef is also the home of the largest shellfish in the world—the giant clam. Clams 3 feet in length are quite common, shells weighing several hundredweight and measuring $4\frac{1}{2}$ feet in length have also been found, and divers have declared that even larger clams exist in the deeper water. The giant clam does not attach itself to a rock or similar surface. It merely rests on the sea bed, hinged side down. When the two sections of its shell open, a wide velvety mantle is revealed bordering the inner rim. Be-

Roy P. Cooper.

AN ENEMY OF OTHER BIRDS

Silver gulls are very common on the Great Barrier Reef and are noted for stealing the eggs of other birds. During the season, they are always ready to swoop down and make off with an egg when the parents are away from the nest. They are great scavengers and their diet also includes small fish.

Specially painted for this work by Dennis Adams.

IN BARRIER REEF WATERS

Many unusual fish and other sea creatures live in the waters of the Great Barrier Reef, off the coast of Queensland, Australia. The painting shows us: 1. Beaked Coral Fish. 2. Butterfly Cod or Lionfish (*Pterois volitans*). 3. Boxfish (*Ostracion sebal*). 4. Red-banded Coral Fish. 5. Emperor Angel Fish. 6. Blue Demoiselles. 7. Clam shell showing violet-coloured "mantle." 8. Two forms of Bêche-de-mer. 9. Rhinoceros Sea Star. 10. Linckia Sea Star. 11. Cowrie Shell. 12. Sea Anemone. 13. Soft Coral. 14. Soft Coral. 15. Mushroom Coral. 16. Branch Coral. 17. Brain Coral.

Paul Popper.

AN ELEPHANT SCHOOL IN THE BELGIAN CONGO

The elephant is the largest of living land animals. There are two main species, the African and the Asiatic. This picture shows a school of African elephants in the Belgian Congo making their daily visit to the river for bathing and drinking under the supervision of their keepers. The young elephants are tied by rope to the large monitor beasts and are thus kept well under control. At one time African elephants were thought to be untameable and were only used for the ivory their tusks provided, but to-day, as in India, they are employed in various kinds of heavy work. They are no longer slaughtered in large numbers by hunters in Africa and special licences are necessary for elephant " shoots."

Australian National Publicity Assoc.

SOOTY TERNS AT MICHAELMAS CAY

Many of the islands in the northern part of the Great Barrier Reef are inhabited by sooty terns, or "wide-awakes." Michaelmas Cay, north-east of Cairns, is a nesting ground particularly favoured by these birds. During the breeding season (October to January), so many eggs are lying on the sand or grass that it is difficult to walk about without treading on them. The birds are almost continually on the wing and fill the air with their screeching cries.

tween the mantle on either side are two circular openings. Through one of these water is drawn, the minute sea life which the water contains being the chief food of the clam. When this food has been extracted, the water is ejected through the other opening. The muscle by which the clam closes and opens its shell valves is amazingly powerful. The valves have a vice-like grip and it is quite possible that bare-footed native divers have been caught by accidentally putting a foot into the open shell of a giant clam. But it is generally considered that there have not been nearly so many tragedies of this kind as the story-tellers would sometimes have us believe.

Some very beautiful clams of a different kind are found in the southern parts of the Reef. About 12 inches long, they display their beauty to the greatest advantage when the sun shines down upon the crystal water to light the rich and varied colours of their mantles.

The bailer-shell, which is often 16 inches long, is also known as the melon-shell because it resembles a water-melon in both shape and appearance. Its more common name arose from its use by natives for bailing out their canoes. The blacks also found it a useful carrier, drinking stoup and saucepan. The shell is a creamy yellow and is sometimes crossed by two bars of light brown. The animal that lives in the bailer cannot, in fact, get its entire body into the shell. It possesses a large foot that may be twice as long as the shell itself. By means of this foot it burrows into the sand, where it lives half buried. Extending beyond the shell is a cone-like trunk by which the animal draws in water to bathe its gills. Another large shell found in the northern part of the Reef is the helmet shell, so called because of its likeness to the helmets worn by the warriors of old.

Some of the cone shells found on the Reef are very pretty, but be careful! some are also very poisonous. It is safer, perhaps, to avoid the cone shells and turn to the most popular shells of all —the cowries. There are many kinds of cowries, and all are beautiful. By day they hide themselves away under rocks and in crevices; at night, when they come out in search of food, their wonder-fully coloured mantles are fully extended.

If we want a real prize for our collection of shells we shall try to find a tiger cowrie ; and the chances are that if we find one tiger cowrie we shall find another close by, for they seem to go in pairs. The tiger cowrie is about 4 inches in length. The shell may have a background colour of creamy white, pale brown or pale green, upon which will be circular spots of dark brown or green. The whole shell is richly glazed. Along the lower side of the shell is a jagged opening, through which the live cowrie spreads out its delicately spotted mantles, sometimes so far that they cover the entire shell. Upon the mantle are small stubby tentacles. Other cowries we might find are pure white or tortoise-shell in colour. The money cowries, so called because they were once used as currency by native tribes-men, are cream, brown, blue or green. Another shell esteemed by collectors is the disc-shaped " cat's-eye."

Mutton-Fish and Sea-Hares

The mutton-fish is also known by several other names—ass's ear, aba-lone, ormer and ear-shell. " Ear-shell " is the usual name given to the shell of the animal, on account of its oval shape. The shell is very much smaller than the animal, which cannot fully draw its soft parts within the shell. The exposed part of the animal consists mostly of a large dappled cream and green foot, by which the animal moves about or attaches itself to a hard sur-face. The shell is carried on the back of the animal at the rear and contains a row of small openings through which the animal can extend the tentacles of its mantle. The foot of the mutton-fish makes very good eating after it has been boiled or fried, which perhaps accounts for its name.

The sea-hare is another soft animal with a very small shell. It is about 15 inches long and, in its most common form, a yellowish-brown colour. From its head extend

Roy P. Cooper.

A CRESTED TERN

Terns of many species are found on the Reef. In the southern parts, the white-capped noddy tern is the most common. In the north, other species are more numerous. Large colonies of crested terns may be found on Masthead Island, in the Capricorn Group, in the south. They do not build nests, but lay their eggs on the grass or sand.

MANGROVES THRIVE IN MANY PARTS OF THE REEF

Mangrove trees like salty, swampy ground and thrive in the leeward parts of the Barrier Reef, where they grow in the muddy swamp waters. Their spreading roots enable mud and debris to collect and, in time, soil is formed in which other vegetation will grow. This picture of typical mangroves shows us the breathing shoots of the tree.

two pairs of tentacles, one pair being more prominent than the other and giving the animal the likeness of a crouching hare. The sea-hare defends itself by " putting up a smoke screen." If it is attacked, the sea-hare sends out a large stream of violet fluid which clouds the water.

The Beautiful Sea-Slug

Whoever named the sea-slug could not have seen those living on the Great Barrier Reef, for they are among the most beautiful of its inhabitants. They are flat and oval and may be as much as 10 inches in length. Some are dappled brown and yellow, others yellow and black. They are sometimes seen resting upside-down on the surface of the water, to which they can attach themselves by sending out a sticky fluid.

A more fearsome denizen of the Reef is the octopus. This repulsive creature, which is, however, a popular food in some parts of the world, has a flabby bag of a body and eight whip-like tentacles whose inner surfaces are covered with powerful suction discs. The tentacles extend from the head, below which is the horny curved beak used by the octopus to bite and paralyse its prey. The lair of the octopus is a convenient ledge or coral crevice; or perhaps a nest, made of broken pieces of coral or oysters, which the octopus builds for itself. Within this lair, the octopus waits and watches, always ready to shoot out a tentacle to seize a passing crab or fish. The octopus normally moves over the sea bed, but it can swim backwards by powerfully and repeatedly opening and closing the web between head and tentacles while spurting out a jet of water from just below its head. If it is attacked it can quickly cloud the water by squirting fluid from its " ink-bag " and escape under cover of the darkness it has itself created.

No one has yet found the giant octopus that sometimes appears in sea stories. But giant squids more than 50 feet long are known to exist. They inhabit the deep waters. Their brethren of the shallow seas are usually only a few feet in length. Both the squid and the octopus can vary their colour to suit their surroundings.

Anemones and Starfish

Much of the beauty of the underwater gardens of the Barrier Reef comes from " flowers " that are really animals. Even though their beautiful " blooms," which may resemble chrysanthemums or other garden flowers, sway gracefully in the water like petals caught in a gentle summer breeze, these are not flowers but sea-anemones—animals that have certain points in common with the corals.

Sea-anemones are found in many parts of the world, but only in tropic waters, such as those of the Reef, do

they reach a great size. On the Reef, anemones with a diameter of 12 inches are quite common, and some have been found which measure 2 feet across. Most anemones can be handled safely, because the stinging cells with which they paralyse their food cannot harm human beings. But there are some that can bring up a sore rash on one's hands that can last several days. Certain small fish and crustaceans enjoy immunity from the stinging cells and live within the tentacles of the anemone, which give them protection from their enemies and provide a convenient feeding ground.

Starfish of all sizes and many colours are found on the Reef, from small specimens no more than an inch in diameter to those measuring 12 inches across. The most common is the blue starfish. Relatives of the starfish—brittle-stars and sea-urchins—also abound.

A strange creature which we should almost certainly see during our visit to the Barrier Reef is the bêche-de-mer, or trepang, sea-cucumber, or sea-sausage. These names give us a clue to its shape. The French form, bêche-de-mer, comes from the Portuguese *bicho-do-mar* (sea-slug) which was given to the animal by early Portuguese seafarers in Far Eastern waters. Smaller specimens, upwards of a few inches long, will be found in the shallows; larger varieties, up to 24 inches in length, live in the deeper waters. Some are creamy-white; others yellow or orange, brown or black. Bêche-de-mer are much esteemed by the Chinese, who make soup from them. One of the first industries to be established in Reef waters was the catching of bêche-de-mer for shipping to China by way of Hong Kong.

E.N.A.

A BRISTLE WORM
Along the side of the worm are clusters of needle-sharp spines which can easily pierce a leather glove. The bristle worm seen in this picture is probably about a foot in length.

THE CURIOUS MUD-SKIPPER

Paul Popper.

The mud-skipper, or " walking fish," is about 10 inches long and is dark green or brown in colour.
It lives in the mud flats and mangrove swamps and can move about by lever-like motions of its side
fins. The eyes are set close together on top of the head and can be turned in every direction.

One of the ugliest, most unpleasant and dangerous fishes in the world lurks among the coral. It is the slimy, wart-covered stonefish. The interior of its cavernous mouth is a ghastly green.

A Dangerous Fish

On its back are thirteen needle-sharp spines, each loaded with nerve poison which can cause extreme pain for many months—or even death—to humans. These spines normally lie flat along the back of the fish; but as soon as they are touched they spring up ready to pierce whoever is molesting their owner. This hideous fish moves sluggishly. Much of its life is spent just waiting for its prey, which approaches unsuspectingly, for the stonefish merges perfectly with its background.

By contrast, the Reef can offer us the amusing mud-skipper or " walking fish." About 10 inches long, and dark green or brown, it spends most of its life out of the water. Indeed, if it stays too long under the surface, it may drown! Its natural home is the mud-flats, and when these are uncovered by the tide any number of mud-skippers may be seen, either on the surface of the mud or clinging, above it, to the roots of the mangroves. They move about by thrusting themselves forward with lever-like motions of their side fins. When they are alarmed they will literally skip across the surface of the mud and into the water. They can also jump from root to root.

Other unusual fish include the sucker-fish, which attaches itself to a shark or turtle, whose food provides sufficient scraps for this lazy lodger; the angler fish, which catches its food with its own rod, line and bait; and the archer fish (a denizen of the estuaries of eastern Queensland), which shoots down the insects upon which it feeds by spitting at them as they rest on overhanging branches or hover above the surface. We might also see " skippers," fish which can rise erect on the surface of the water and skip along for about a hundred yards; the giant devil ray, which, unlike the venomous sting ray, is quite harmless; fish called " jumping blennies," that can actually hop; striped catfish, box-fish, cow-fish, toad-fish and porcupine-fish; the " dugong " or sea-cow, which may have led seafarers of old to believe in the existence of mermaids; the large and savage giant pike; the sharks and the gropers.

A Fisherman's Paradise

The Reef is a wonderful place for the true fisherman. The rewards are not the small everyday fish that would be prized trophies in our home waters, but the big fellows of the deep—pink and silver king-snappers, weighing perhaps 15 pounds each; blue-spotted groper, coral cod, emperors and hussars. We might also seek the Spanish mackerel, the chief game fish of the Reef; a single specimen may weigh

well over a hundred pounds.

Spanish mackerel are found along the outer barrier throughout the year, but the great shoals fished by the professionals occur only in winter.

Trochus and Pearl-shell

Many a pearl button is not made from pearl-shell, but from the cone-shaped trochus shell, which is found in the shallower waters of the reef and is brought up by divers. Pearl-shell itself has been described as the " Reef's richest treasure," for it can be made into buttons, cufflinks, brooches and many other things. Notice that it is the pearl-shell that is the fishermen's reward. The valuable pearl is found but rarely.

Do you believe in sea-serpents? No one can say that they do not exist, but a genuine specimen has still to be captured. You may not see a serpent in the Reef waters, but you may well find sea-snakes lying on the surface and enjoying the sun. Beware ! They are poisonous.

Paul Popper.

This holiday-maker at Heron Island enjoys an unusual ride down the beach. A rope tied round the turtle's flippers helps her to keep her balance.

Queensland Railways.

The waters of the Great Barrier Reef are a happy hunting ground for anglers. Among the best game fish are the barred Spanish mackerel and the queenfish.

What the
Naturalist
Can Tell Us

About the
Smaller Forms
of Animal Life

J. J. Ward.

THE HOUSE-FLY AND HER EGGS

This is the common house-fly magnified considerably, and the eggs which she has just laid. The eggs will hatch within forty-eight hours into small white grubs which live on any kind of refuse. These grubs rapidly become flies, so that one fly may be the parent of millions within a single summer.

THE MARVELS OF INSECT LIFE

EVERYBODY knows the little House-fly, and has heard it buzzing round the room, and seen it crawling slowly up the window pane. It is found in almost every country where man has established himself, and it does such a lot of harm that we are trying as much as we can to prevent it from breeding.

It begins life as a dirty-white egg among 100 or 200 others. It is laid in filth of some kind, usually horse manure, for that is the sort of thing on which the grub feeds. In less than forty-eight hours it hatches out, and is a white, footless creature, very small. It has a hook at the front end, and with the help of this and some pads under its body it can move about.

It feeds on the filth for about a week, and then changes into a pupa, when it eats nothing, and simply lies still. It is then a little barrel-shaped thing. Inside the hardened skin a great change is going on, for a fly is forming there, complete with wings and legs. When it is ready it forces its way out of the pupa by breaking off a little cap at the front end.

At first it does not look like a fly, for its wings are a grey, crumpled mass, but they soon straighten out, and are ready for flight. Besides the two wings are a curious pair of knobs called the "balancers," which you will see when you examine a fly closely.

How Flies are able to Walk Upside Down

Soon the fly spreads its wings and goes off on its first flight, buzzing loudly. Perhaps it flies into your room, and walks upside down on the ceiling. How does it perform a marvellous feat like that?

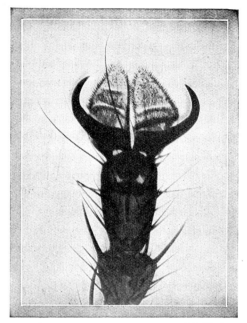

J. J. Ward.

FOOT OF THE HOUSE-FLY

The pair of claws enable the insect to climb on rough surfaces, while the two soft pads are for walking on smooth surfaces such as glass. These pads are covered with a sticky substance which enables the fly to walk upside down.

If we could see the underneath of the fly's feet through a magnifying glass we should soon find out the secret. Each of its six feet has two soft, rather sticky pads, and with these it manages to cling to any surface quite easily, and can run along upside down if it wishes.

Perhaps it flies down to our sugar bowl. See it put out its proboscis—the long mouth tube—and suck up the sugar. First it sends saliva down on to the lump and melts a little, then sucks it up. Then off it flies out of doors, and goes to the dustbin. It spends a long time walking over the rubbish there, and after a while comes back to the house again.

It smells our meat on the table and flies down, for it loves meat juice. Unless we are quick it will run all over it, pausing now and again to send saliva down its mouth tube before sucking up the

moisture. On its hairy legs and sticky footpads are particles of dirt and filth from the dustbin. These it leaves on the meat, and we swallow them when we eat our dinner. If dangerous disease germs are anywhere about the fly's feet pick them up too, and pass them on to us, making us very ill indeed. So it is no wonder that we say "Kill that fly!" for it is far more dangerous to us than a wasp. If only we can get rid of our rubbish quickly, cover up all our food, and prevent the fly from laying eggs anywhere near us, we shall be safe, for no eggs mean no flies.

A very dangerous cousin of the house-fly is the big, buzzing Bluebottle. It loves to feed on garbage of all kinds and lays its eggs in meat, making it go putrid very soon. We must kill every bluebottle we see, for it and the house-fly are our bitter enemies.

THE CLEVER GARDEN SPIDER

THE Spider is a clever creature. It does not belong to the insects, although it lives among them, and has many ways like them; for insects, as you know, have six legs, one or two pairs of wings, and their bodies in three parts, whereas the spider has eight legs, no wings, and its body in two parts only.

Another great difference is that from the eggs of insects come caterpillars or grubs, which change into chrysalids and then into perfect insects, while the spider simply hatches from its egg as a spider and nothing else. No caterpillar comes from a spider egg; a tiny spider emerges instead, and grows until it becomes the garden or the house spider we know so well.

Its eight legs are hairy, and the feet have claws. Some spiders have eight eyes, and some have six. Just above the mouth is a pair of claws or fangs, which seize the spider's victim and poison it.

Where does the spider get the silk for her wonderful web? We have seen caterpillars sending out silken thread from their upper lips ; does the spider

HOW THE SPIDER BUILDS HER WEB

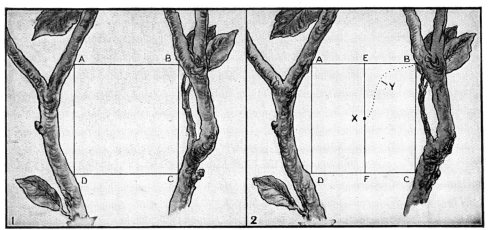

How a garden spider makes her web. Here are shown the four foundation lines.

The line E to F is the one next spun. Follows then a thread from B to X, lettered Y.

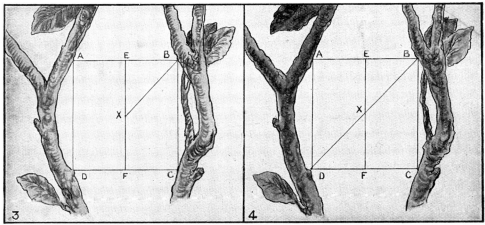

In this diagram the thread B to X has been tightened and made perfectly secure—

Whilst here it is joined by a second ray running from D to X.

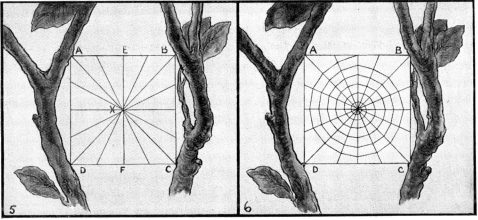

The next stage is the spinning of further rays, first one section and then the other, so that there is no unequal strain upon either.

Finally come the scaffold thread and the sticky trap-thread, the scaffold thread being eaten by the spider as the trap-thread is laid.

do that too? No; she takes her silk from quite a different place.

If we turn a spider upside down we shall see underneath her body some little wart-like knobs, the spinnerets. From tiny tubes in each of these a sticky fluid oozes out, which hardens when it reaches the open air and becomes a silken thread, fine but strong.

How the Spider makes her Web

Watch the spider as she makes her lovely web in the garden. She chooses a sheltered spot where flies are likely to come. Then she first of all builds the outer threads of her web, like a square. She drops a thread down from the middle of the top one to the middle of the bottom one, and then begins to fix the radiating spokes of the web, drawing them tight at the centre

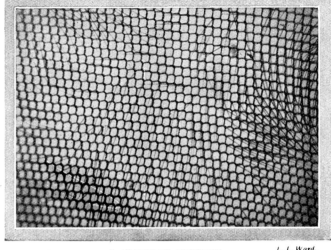

A CURIOUS PICTURE   *J. J. Ward.*
The eye of a fly seen under a powerful magnifying glass looks like this. Each circle is a separate little lens, and in all there are no fewer than 4,000 of these lenses, making up what is called a compound eye. Many insects have these curious eyes.

where their odd ends form a " hub-knot." She next spins the spiral " scaffold " thread, starting in the centre and winding outwards to the edge of the web.

None of these threads is sticky, but all is now ready for hanging the sticky elastic " trap-thread " which will catch the flies. This is really a fine porous tube which oozes a sticky liquid when it is stretched. The spider now works inwards along the scaffold thread, attaching the trap-thread to the spokes between the lines of the scaffold thread, which she removes and eats as she goes along. The centre of the scaffold spiral is left for a " hunting-platform," but she cuts out and eats the hub-knot.

The spider now rests on the hunting-platform, head downwards, each

THE HOUSE-FLY'S " FEELERS "   *J. J. Ward.*
Another fly photograph showing the antennæ or " feelers " greatly enlarged. Watch a fly sitting on a lump of sugar, and you see it feel the surface with its antennæ, then lower its proboscis or trunk and begin to feed through this organ.

THE HUNTING SPIDER MOTHERS HER BROOD

J. J. Ward.

(1) In this picture we are shown the Hunting Spider busily engaged in making a kind of silken tent with which to cover the delicate cocoon containing her eggs.

J. J. Ward.

(2) This particular spider is an adept at climbing over the twigs of trees, but it can carry its egg cocoon and still climb in comfort, as is depicted above.

J. J. Ward.

(3) In this remarkable picture the mother spider has broken the silken tent which she constructed with such loving care, and you see her babies in the very act of escaping from their nest. After nursing her large family till the young ones are safely started in life, the mother generally dies.

THE SPIDER'S FROZEN HOME

J. J. Ward.

In this picture the spider's web is covered with thick white hoar frost and its unlucky owner
is frozen at her post. But the frost brings out a pretty picture of the web showing it to be
slightly different in shape from that on page 281. Yet all spiders' webs are built in the same
way. First, the outer guide ropes are secured in position, next the cross lines, and lastly the mesh
is spun in ever lessening circles. Spider's web is actually stronger, bulk for bulk, than steel.

J. J. Ward.

This common garden spider, for reasons best known to herself, has decided to descend the silken cord which she has so skilfully spun. If you look closely you will see that the line immediately above the creature is slightly bent or kinked, and that one pair of feet is held firmly against the cord. It is by this method that the spider prevents herself from dropping too rapidly. In other words, this is how she puts on the brake!

J. J. Ward.

THE LURKING SPIDER

A spider is seen resting in the centre of her web awaiting prey. The fine silk lines composing the web are slightly sticky, so that an insect striking it is caught at once. The spider seated in the centre feels the vibration, and hurrying to the spot kills her prey, and after sucking the body dry gets rid of the remains. If the victim is large or dangerous, such, for instance, as a wasp, she binds it with fresh web or else cuts away the web and frees her foe.

leg upon a spoke-thread, waiting for a fly to blunder into the sticky spiral. As soon as a fly is caught and begins to struggle she feels a spoke vibrating, and knows that she has a victim. Out she runs, and in a trice wraps the fly round and round in a mesh of web so that it cannot struggle. It is curious to see her turning it round in her front feet. Then she pierces the body with her poison fangs, and sucks the victim's blood.

Sometimes a bee gets caught in the web, and the spider fears it. She runs near, and begins to cut the web here and there until at last the bee tumbles to the ground, freed. She will not repair her web, but make a new one.

When the spider is tired of her husband she eats him. He is smaller than she is, so he cannot put up a fight to save himself.

She lays many hundreds of orange-gold eggs in the autumn under a stone or bush. First of all she spins a beautiful little saucer of yellow silk to hold them, and puts them carefully into it. Then she spins another saucer of silk to fit over the top.

In the spring-time the eggs hatch out, and from them come hundreds of tiny spiders. They hang themselves all together in a little ball, but if you touch it the tiny creatures spread out like a mist. After a while they all scramble back again into a ball, and cling together tightly.

You will know the garden spider by the white or cream cross on her body. Look for her in the summer-time.

A SPIDER THAT EATS BIRDS!

In hot countries are to be found spiders of great size and distinctly terrifying appearance. They live for the most part in underground burrows, though by no means averse to hollow trees. The specimen shown above is one of the Mygale spiders. These creatures may be 7 inches across, including their legs. Though they do actually devour small birds, insects are the chief prey of these monsters.

Specially drawn for this work.

HUMMING BIRD HAWK MOTH

One of the most interesting of the many moths found in Britain is seen in the drawing above. This was sketched by the artist in his garden as the Humming Bird Hawk Moth hovered in the air near the bindweed and sipped the nectar from the flower with its long proboscis.

BUTTERFLIES AND MOTHS

A BUTTERFLY or a Moth begins as a tiny egg placed, with many others, on the top of a leaf or underneath. These eggs are often very beautiful if we look at them under a microscope. Some are like little acorns, some are tiny melons, and each of them is covered with a lovely raised pattern.

One day the eggs hatch, and out come many tiny caterpillars. They may be all shapes, and all colours, some with hairs and some without; it depends on the kind of butterfly or moth that laid the eggs.

Caterpillars and their Coats

Caterpillars have a tremendous appetite, and all day long they eat. They feed on the leaves of the plant upon which they were hatched, and grow very fast. Soon their coat becomes too tight for them, and suddenly it splits down the back. The caterpillars wriggle about, and rub themselves against the leaves of the plant, trying to get rid of the torn coat. At last they manage to do so, and lo and behold! they have a brand new coat underneath perfect and complete!

Now they feel quite comfortable and begin to eat ravenously once more. They grow larger, and soon their new coat is much too tight again. A second time they cast it, and creep out of it with a new one underneath. They do this many times, eating without pause in between the skin-casting.

Then one day they have no appetite. The leaves no longer taste nice. They feel queer and uncomfortable, and once again they cast their skins. Then a curious change comes over them. Each turns into a Chrysalis, a tough case with neither legs nor mouth.

Sometimes the chrysalis is barrel-shaped, sometimes it has tapering ends or horns. It may be brown or yellow, green or black. Often a moth caterpillar spins a silken case for itself called

THE TALLEST OF ANIMALS

This giraffe does not seem at all perturbed by the presence of a cameraman. The picture was taken in a National Park of Southern Rhodesia, and in all such parks and game reserves care is taken to safeguard the many wild animals against damaging human interference. This tends to give them confidence. The long legs of the giraffe enable it to run very fast, although its queer, yet graceful strides render this rather a comical sight. The giraffe is the tallest of animals and can grow to a height of over 20 feet. The ancient Egyptians and Greeks knew it as the " camelopard " because it was thought to be a mixture of the camel and the leopard.

The Bee Eater is a bird of Southern Europe. Its nest is a circular chamber at the end of a tunnel burrowed into sandy banks or flat ground. It lives on insects caught on the wing, such as bees and butterflies.

The Turnstone breeds on small islands from West Greenland to Russia and as far south as islands in the Baltic. In autumn and winter the birds lose much of their colouring and come south to British shores.

Photos : C. C. Doncaster.

EUROPEAN BIRDS AND THEIR NESTS

Found in many parts of Europe, but commonest in South Spain, the White Stork (left) builds its nest on buildings and telegraph poles, adding to its home year after year. It feeds mostly on frogs and tadpoles, but also on snakes, lizards, fish, worms and insects. The nest of the Black-necked Grebe (right) is built on remote lakes or meres and is a floating mound of vegetation moored to reeds.

a cocoon, and then the chrysalis is found inside it.

An ordinary chrysalis is hung up against a wall or fence, or on plant stems or leaves. Often it has a silken belt round its body to hold it up, or a silken rope at its tail. It cannot move, see or eat; all it can do is to wriggle its tail if it is touched.

There it stays for weeks or months. Meanwhile a marvellous change is taking place inside, for the caterpillar that turned into the chrysalis is now turning into a butterfly! How this change happens we do not quite know. It is like magic.

When the right time comes the chrysalis splits open, and out creeps a perfect moth or butterfly. Its wings look crumpled, but it is not very long before the sun dries them and they expand. Then the lovely little creature spreads them out and flies away to sip honey from the flowers.

Have you seen the " trunk " with which the butterfly or moth sucks up honey? When it is not feeding it coils it up underneath its head like a watch spring, but when it wants to suck the nectar it unrolls it and puts it right down into the flower to where the honey is hidden.

The Magic of the Butterfly's Wing

A butterfly's wings get their lovely colours from the hundreds of minute scales with which they are covered. When you touch a butterfly you notice that your finger is powdered with something that looks rather like pollen dust from a flower, so fine it is and soft.

Put it under a microscope and you will see that the powder on your finger is really made up of very tiny scales, all most beautifully shaped and coloured, with a tiny stalk at one end. These scales are arranged on the butterfly's wings in rows, and each row overlaps the next one, like the tiles on a house. It is these tiny scales that give the wings their lovely colour. If they were all rubbed off a butterfly's wing

J. J. Ward.

RED ADMIRAL

The Red Admiral is one of the handsomest of British butterflies and a very strong flier. Yet even the finest of our butterflies are small and pale compared with the great splendid insects of the tropics. There is, for instance, an Indian Swallowtail, 6 inches or more across the wings, which are jet black with scarlet or golden eyes.

J. J. Ward.

These caterpillars of the Swallowtail butterfly are shown life size. The swallowtails are the most gorgeous of the whole butterfly family, and there are more than 500 different sorts. They are distinguished by the swallow-like tails on their hind wings. The caterpillars of this European variety are green with black stripes, spotted with orange on the sides. They feed upon what are called umbelliferous plants of which the common carrot is an example. The butterfly itself is sulphur yellow with black markings and black borders round its wings.

A PAIR OF SWALLOWTAILS

J. J. Ward.

Here we see portraits of a pair of Swallowtail butterflies. They are rare in England, and the only part of the country in which they are at all frequently seen is the Fen district of Cambridge-shire; yet across the North Sea they are common enough, in gardens, clover fields and woods. The swallowtail has great powers of flight and is most difficult to capture, or even to approach near enough to secure a photograph. In many of the tropical species of swallowtails the male only has the pointed wings, while the females are tailless and much less brilliant in colour.

THE GOAT MOTH (1) *J. J. Ward.*

The Goat moth, a sort common in England, is a heavy-looking insect with a thick body, and measures 3 inches across the wings. Here we see a female on a tree trunk, searching the crannies of the bark for a suitable spot in which to deposit her eggs.

you would see that it was quite transparent, just like that of a bee or fly.

Do you know how to tell the difference between a moth and a butterfly? It is quite easy, if you look carefully. There are two chief points to notice.

First, look at the insect's feelers or antennæ. If they are feathery or quite plain they belong to a moth. If they have little knobs at the end they belong to a butterfly.

Second, look at the wings. A butterfly always places its wings back to back when it is at rest, so that they stand upright, but a moth usually spreads them out, or wraps them round its body.

Most moths fly by night, though many fly by day; but no butterflies ever fly by night. Most moths—but not all —have fat furry bodies, whereas butterflies usually have slender bodies and may even show a waist.

The Death's Head Hawk Moth

There are many different kinds of butterflies and moths, most of them lovely little things. They vary in size

from tiny insects hardly to be seen, to great big creatures such as the Death's Head Hawk Moth, which may measure as much as 5 inches across the wings. In foreign countries the moths and butterflies grow to great sizes, and are magnificent creatures with their wings beautifully shaped and coloured.

Some moths, such as the Tiger Moth, are as gay-looking as butterflies, and you have probably seen a great many in the summer evenings flying round the lamp indoors. There will be the pretty Orange Underwings and Red Underwings, whose names tell you what they are like. Then you will see the Silver Y, on whose grey-brown wings is the silvery letter after which they are named, and perhaps the pretty Swallowtail moth, whose yellow wings are pointed at the ends like those of a swallow.

The little Clothes-moth is a great pest for it lays its eggs in our clothes, and when the caterpillars come out they bite holes and ruin our garments.

THE GOAT MOTH (2) *J. J. Ward.*

These are the eggs of the Goat moth much magnified. Poplars and willows are the trees which the mother moth chooses in which to plant her eggs, for it is on the leaves of these trees that the caterpillars, when hatched, find their food.

Our commonest butterfly is the Cabbage, which, as its name tells you, is fond of laying its eggs on cabbage plants. It is a white butterfly with black spots, and you are sure to have seen it. Perhaps you have seen the Orange-tip too, with its white wings tipped with bright orange.

The bright-yellow Brimstone butterfly is often seen very early in the year. When we see it then we may know that it is a last year's butterfly which has slept the winter through in a warm corner somewhere, waking up on a sunshiny spring day to go for a flutter.

In the summer time we see the lovely Tortoise-shell, the pretty Peacock, and the handsome Red Admiral. They hover over the flowering brambles, and suck the honey from every flower to which they come. Soon they lay their eggs, and when winter arrives and some of them die, we know that the eggs will provide another generation of butterflies for the following year.

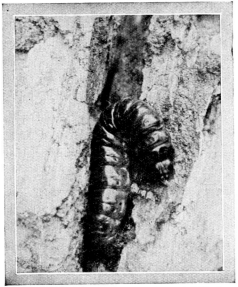

J. J. Ward.

THE GOAT MOTH (3)

The Goat moth caterpillar takes a long time to grow up and become a perfect insect—no less indeed than three years. We see here one of these caterpillars twisting its body round, showing annoyance because an inquisitive finger has touched it.

J. J. Ward.

THE GOAT MOTH (4)

In the last picture of the series giving the life history of the Goat moth, we see the moth which has just emerged from its chrysalis, hanging itself up to dry in the sun. It cannot fly until its wings have fully dried.

WHY THE GARDENER LIKES LADYBIRDS

DID you know that the gardener is very glad to have Ladybirds in his garden?

" Why is that ? " you will say.

Let us have a look at one. Its red wing-covers are spotted with black. Perhaps there are two spots, perhaps there are seven. The bright red colour says " Danger! " to any bird that might think of eating it, for the ladybird has the power of giving out a yellow, evil-smelling fluid that possesses a most unpleasant taste.

When the ladybird is ready to lay her eggs she chooses a place where her grubs, when they hatch, will find food all ready waiting for them. Generally she puts them on the rose-shoots in our garden, or if she is out in the country she may choose the leaves of a hop plant.

When the eggs hatch, out come curious little dark grubs called " niggers." They

J. J. Ward.
PEACOCK BUTTERFLY

This handsome peacock butter-fly is resting for a moment before again taking wing. It is a common English sort and gains its name from the pea-cock-like eyes which it displays on each of its four wings. It is a near relation of the Tortoise-shell.

grown, there came an insect blight which ruined the crops. The growers were helpless, for the little scale insect that did the mischief multiplied so rapidly that plantation after plantation was destroyed. How could the pest be stamped out?

Can you guess how it was cured? A number of orange Australian ladybirds were sent at once to California and there set free in the plantations. They bred freely, and since the scale insects were their favourite food, the planta-tions were soon clear of the blight that had ruined the crops.

have six legs, and are very hungry creatures. As soon as they hatch they look for their food, and when I tell you what it is you will know why the gardener likes ladybirds. The food of the "niggers" is made up of the horrid greenfly or blight on the roses! They eat scores and scores of these, and help to clear our rose trees of the nasty little pests.

How a Pest was stamped out

Once, in California, where oranges and lemons are

J. J. Ward.
THE CAMBERWELL BEAUTY
The butterfly, called the Camberwell Beauty, well deserves its name. Its large wings are of chocolate colour with a yellow border. This butterfly is abundant in America and parts of Europe, but rare in England.

A FRIEND OF THE GARDENER

J. J. Ward.

Here is a ladybird just emerged from its pupa. You notice several pupæ clinging to the grass
blades. This pretty little beetle is a most valuable insect to man, for it eats up scale insects and
other blights which prey on fruit trees. Ladybirds saved the Californian orange growers from the
deadly cottony-cushion scale insect. They are bred in large quantities and sent to all parts of the
world where citrus fruits are grown.

So if you find a ladybird, put it on to
one of your rose bushes.

A GOOD PARENT—THE EARWIG

IT seems curious to think of the Earwig as a good parent, but it certainly
is. When the mother lays her eggs
she looks after them carefully, and
does not go away and leave them as
most insects do.

If she thinks they are too cold, or too
damp, she moves them to a better
place. She gathers them beneath her,
and broods over them as birds brood
over their young ones; some people
say that she looks after them when
they hatch out, but she usually dies long
before this happens.

Although earwigs are insects, they
do not pass through a grub and
chrysalis stage. When the eggs hatch,
tiny earwigs come out, exactly like
their parents, but smaller and with no
wings.

Perhaps you did know that some earwigs have wings? They carry them
under the horny wing-cases on their
backs, but do not often use them. The
wings are beautifully folded, like a fan.
When they are unfolded they are
shaped rather like an ear, and that is
why the earwig has its curious name.

It does not creep into people's ears.
Why should it? There is no food there.
It likes tiny grubs or small slugs and
snails, though sometimes it eats flowers
and fruit. Gardeners often try to trap
it, but really it does more good than
harm, for it prevents hundreds of
harmful slugs and caterpillars from
growing big enough to lay eggs.

Don't be afraid of the nippers at the

J. J. Ward.

(1) Here is a photograph taken under water showing nymphs of the Short-bodied Dragon Fly. The larva on the right is just about to burrow beneath the surface mud. Dragon flies commence life as water nymphs ; and, during this stage of their existence, cast their coats several times.

J. J. Ward.

(2) After a period that may last for a couple of years the nymph leaves the water for the first time, and is depicted above making its earliest appearance in the air, awaiting events.

J. J. Ward.

(3) Now, after the manner of a transformation scene, a great change takes place. Resting in this position for about twenty minutes the nymph undergoes rapid development.

J. J. Ward.

(4) Here you can see clearly that considerable alterations have already taken place, chief among which is the fact that wings are beginning to unfold.

J. J. Ward.

(5) Barely five minutes later than the time the last snapshot was taken the wonderful wings can be still more plainly seen, in this phase just about half-way extended.

J. J. Ward.

(6) In this stage the dragon fly has won free from its nymph-skin, upon which it is actually resting, and is ready to spread its newly-acquired wings, which are still limp, into their normal position.

J. J. Ward.

(7) Now the dragon fly has completely emerged and is proudly displaying its wings. Though it feeds in the air, it always returns to deposit its eggs in water to produce new generation of nymphs.

LIFE IN STAGNANT WATER

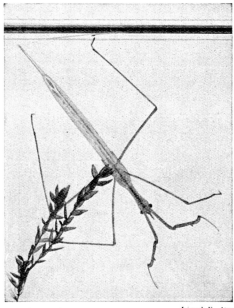

Lionel E. Day.

Sometimes called the Water Stick-insect, this slender creature is a relative of the Water-Scorpion shown on the opposite page. It catches small insects with its fore-legs, using its other legs for walking and swimming, and its long tail for breathing.

Harold Bastin.

Here is a Water-Spider putting a bubble of air into her silken diving-bell. She keeps this underwater globe filled with air so that she can live in it, for she is an air-breathing creature. She also rears her baby spiders in it until they make bells of their own.

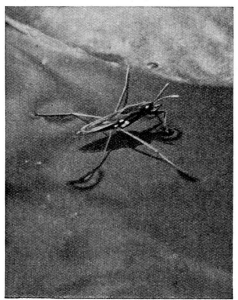

Walter J. C. Murray.

This is the Pond-Skater, and it is able to stand and run about on the surface of the water without getting wet. It is not to be confused with the much more slender Water-Measurer or Water-Gnat, which also lives on the surfaces of ponds.

Ray Palmer.

The Water-Boatman rows himself along on his back, just beneath the surface of the water. His long legs are feathered to serve as oars, and his back is keel-shaped. Another kind of " Boatman " has a flat back and swims right-way up.

MONSTERS OF THE POOL

Ray Palmer.

Here is the ferocious Great Diver, recognised by the narrow, yellowish border to his black plates of armour. He is one of our largest beetles, and preys on small water-insects. Though he lives in ponds he breathes air and occasionally flies during the night.

Harold Bastin.

This is the Great Water-Beetle, the largest insect in our ponds and the second largest beetle in Britain (the largest being the Stag-Beetle). The Great Water-Beetle is a vegetarian and a useful scavenger, feeding upon decaying water-weeds. It is wholly black in colour.

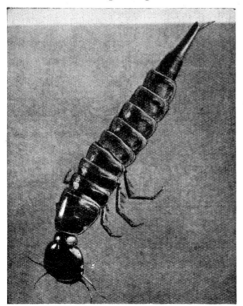

Harold Bastin.

This dangerous-looking creature is the larva of the Great Diver, shown above, and it can give a painful bite if carelessly handled. A tube on its tail projects above the surface of the water so that it can draw in air for breathing.

Lionel E. Day.

This is the Water-Scorpion, which crawls about on the bottom of the pond seeking small insects to seize in its fore-legs. It gives a painful stab with its beak, but the long spine on its tail is not a sting but an air-tube.

THE EARWIG   *J. J. Ward.*

Most of us dislike the ugly earwig, yet it is more of a friend than a foe to the gardener, for it eats up eggs of injurious moths that do great harm to plants. Much of the damage attributed to the poor earwig is really done by night-feeding caterpillars.

end of its body. They can only give you a feeble nip. We do not really know their purpose, unless they are used in folding the wings, for they are not effective weapons. Perhaps if you use your eyes well you will be able to find out more about them!

THE GARDENER'S ENEMY— DADDY-LONG-LEGS

EVERYONE knows the Crane-fly, or Daddy-long-legs. It comes drifting into our rooms, a great long-legged creature, sometimes with a pointed end to its body, sometimes with a blunt one.

The daddy-long-legs with the pointed end is the female, and she uses the point to pierce the soil; then she lays a few hundred small black eggs there and leaves them.

Two weeks later the eggs hatch. Tiny grubs come from them, and burrow into the ground. We call them Leather-jackets then, and the gardener hates them, for they feed on the roots of grass, corn, and other plants, doing a great deal of damage. You can guess why they have the name of leather-jacket. It is because their coats are hard and leathery. The grubs are brownish-grey or black.

After a while they change into pupæ, and no longer eat. When the time comes for them to emerge from the pupa-cases they struggle up to the surface, using the bristles on the cases to help them. Then the cases split, and out come fully-developed daddy-long-legs.

The brown empty cases are left sticking up in the ground, and perhaps you will find them and wonder what they are. Their occupants are now flying about aimlessly, and soon the time will come when the females once more seek the ground to lay their shiny black eggs and the whole process is gone through all over again.

We ought to kill the daddy-long-legs, because of the great damage they do, but even if we killed all we saw we could not get rid of very many. However, we have great and willing helpers in the wild birds.

Rooks catch hundreds of them, and so do swallows. Blackbirds, starlings and thrushes dig them up from the ground when they are leather-jackets and eat them hungrily and greedily.

What would happen if the birds did not destroy them in this way is hard to say; there would be such millions of daddy-long-legs as to form a plague and we should hardly be able to see in front of us!

THE WONDERFUL HONEY-BEE

ONE of the most interesting members of the insect world is the little Honey-bee. Most of us have seen the hives in which bees are kept, and certainly every one must have seen the insects visiting the flowers to get the nectar that they need for food.

Three different kinds of bees are found in the hive; a small kind with slender bodies, the worker bees; stout bees with rounded bodies and large eyes, the males or drones; and a big bee with a long body, the queen.

The workers are the busy bees we see every day in the garden. They have many tasks to do, and sometimes toil so hard that they kill themselves with overwork. They collect the nectar from the flowers, fill their leg pockets with pollen to make " bee bread," make wax to build the cells in the hive, look after the eggs, feed and bath the baby bees, and clean the hive.

The drones do not collect nectar, but feed on honey which is given to them by the workers. When winter comes,

J. J. Ward.
GRUB OF THE CRANE FLY
The " leather-jacket " is the grub of the crane fly, or " Daddy-long-legs," and is the pest of the man whose duty it is to attend to golf-course greens. It lives upon the roots of grasses, and will destroy the most carefully-kept turf in a short time.

and the bees know that there is only a limited amount of food, they set upon the lazy drones, turn them mercilessly out of the hive, and kill them.

The queen bee lays the eggs, and this she does all her life long.

Life in the Hive

The workers build the cells in which the queen lays the eggs. They are beautifully made from wax, and are six-sided. These cells make up the *comb* of the hive. They are used for storing honey and for nurseries. Most of the cells are small, and in these the queen places eggs which will grow into worker bees. In larger cells she places drone eggs, and in other big cells she puts eggs which will develop into young queen bees.

As soon as an egg is laid in a cell the worker bees care for it. They mix honey with pollen, and put a little of the

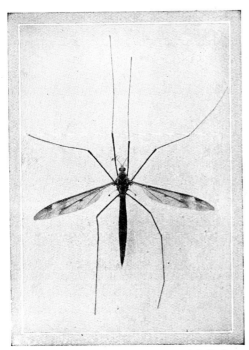

J. J. Ward.
CRANE FLY
Here is " Daddy " himself, harmless-looking enough, yet one of the most troublesome of British insects. With her long " ovipositor " the female daddy buries her eggs in the ground; and the grubs that hatch out work ruin to pastures and crops, bowling greens and tennis courts.

THE TONGUE OF THE BEE

The curious-looking object is just a part
of the tongue of a bee very highly magnified.
It is shaped rather like an elephant's trunk,
but furnished with short, stiff hairs used in
the process of collecting honey from the
flowers visited by the insect.

resulting jelly into the cell. The grub
that hatches from the egg feeds on this,
and after that on bee-bread. In a week
the grub is fully grown, and then the
workers put a lid on the cell and shut it up.

The grub spins itself a silken cocoon,
and becomes a pupa. In ten days the
pupa skin breaks, and out comes a
little brown worker bee. At first it
helps the other bees about the hive, and
then flies off to collect nectar and pollen.

Eggs that will become queen bees are
given larger cells, and are fed on special
food, the " royal jelly." When they
hatch out they are queens. If the queen
of a hive dies, the workers enlarge the
cell of a three days' old grub, and feed
it on the " royal " food, when it becomes,
not a worker, but a queen bee.

Swarming Time

If there are too many bees in a hive
the queen flies off with some of them to
find a fresh home. This is called
swarming. The bees become very much
excited then, and make a loud humming
sound on a higher note than usual. The
queen perhaps flies to a branch of a tree
or an overhanging eave. All the bees
fly after her, and cling on to each other,
forming a great cluster. Then the bee-
keeper comes up and takes the swarm.

When the old queen has left the hive,
one of the young queens that has
developed from the royal eggs becomes
ruler in the old hive. If young queens
are developing in a hive that is not over-
crowded, and which therefore needs only
the one queen, the old queen goes to the
queen cells and stings the grubs to death.

It is interesting to look closely at a
worker bee. It has two pairs of wings,
and each pair is hooked together in
flight by means of little hooks along the
edge of the hind wing. The humming
sound is made by the wings, and also
by the walls of the chest.

The pollen baskets are hollow places
on the hind legs, and are enclosed by
stiff hairs. Pollen is collected on the
hairs called the pollen brush, stuffed
into the broad first joint of the hind leg,
and then the lower part of the leg is
moved upwards ; this crushes the pollen
up into the baskets. You will often see
a bee's baskets full if you look at one
collecting nectar from the flowers.

How a Bee's Sting Works

The sting is at the hinder end of the
body. It is connected with two little
poison bags. When we are stung this
is what happens : the bee sticks its
sting into our flesh, and in doing so
presses upon the poison bags. A drop
runs down the hollow sting and enters
the little wound. As the sting is barbed
at the end the bee cannot withdraw it,
and it is left in our flesh.

Bees draw up the nectar of flowers by
means of their tongues. Some kinds of
bees have short tongues, and some have
long ones. You will see a bee using its
tongue if you watch it delving down in
a flower.

WONDERFUL WAYS OF THE BUSY BEES

J. J. Ward.

In this photograph an ordinary beehive has been turned upside down so that you may peep into the interior and see the way in which the combs are arranged.

M. H. Crawford.

When a colony of bees becomes too large the queen will fly away, closely escorted by a swarm of attendants. Here is such a swarm on a garden gate ready to be hived.

Harold Bastin.

The Humble Bee constructs an underground homestead, often in a field-mouse's hole, in which she collects a larderful of food and rears her young family. Above is her entrance.

THE COMB OF THE HONEY BEE

Ellison Hawks.

You are here looking down at the surface of a brood comb of honey bees. In some of the " uncapped " cells you will see the young grubs which will shortly develop into bees. As it gains strength the grub is able to rear up in its cell and take food supplied by the workers. The queen grubs are fed on " royal jelly."

THE

HONEY BEE

continued on page 4.

1

MRS. BUMBLE BEE MAKES HER NEST

(1) Here is a nest of the humble, or bumble, bee, new nests being made each spring to found fresh colonies.

Photos: H. Bastin.

(2) This is the same nest, but with the side removed so that you may observe the cocoons. It is one of Nature's mysterious edicts that all the humble bee families except the queens should die at the end of every summer, so that the queen has to build the first nest every season.

Ellison Hawks.

BEES: THE DRONE, THE QUEEN AND THE WORKER

These are the three sorts of bees found in every hive. To the right is the worker who gathers the honey and wax, feeds the grubs, and as a rule works herself to death in about six weeks. In the centre is the queen, who sits in solitary state laying eggs sometimes at the rate of 100 an hour. The bee on the left is the drone, the queen's lazy husband, who loafs through life, but pays in the end by being turned out to freeze or starve at the end of summer.

We could not do without bees, for not only do we eat their honey, but also depend upon them for pollinating our flowers. Bees carry pollen from flower to flower, and this helps in the making of seeds. The flowers have developed their nectar glands to entice the bees to them. "You bring us pollen from other flowers, and we will give you honey in return," is the bargain between the flower world and the insect world.

This exchange is a splendid one. The bees obtain the honey they need, and the plant-world is able to form good strong seeds ; as for ourselves, we eat the fruit that is the result of the bargain and enjoy the honey too!

THE STORY OF THE WASP

THE story of the Wasp is nearly as interesting as that of the bee. Both insects belong to the same family, but you can tell a wasp by its thread-like waist and naked body.

The sting of a wasp is different, for it has no barbed end, and can therefore be withdrawn from our skin and used again and again.

There are Solitary and Social wasps, just as there are Solitary and Social bees. It is the story of the Social Wasps that is told here.

The Quest of the Queen Wasp

On a morning of May, when the sun is shining warmly, a queen wasp stirs in her hiding-place beneath the ivy leaves. It is time for her to go forth and seek a place in which to build her nest. For a few days she flies about sipping nectar, and then she begins to hunt for a nesting hole.

She examines many holes, and at last chooses one. It may be a mouse-hole in a sunny bank, with a nice root sticking down from the roof. The wasp thinks that this root will do splendidly on which to start building her nest.

She flies off to rotting fences or posts, and strips off little splinters of wood, chewing them powerfully until they have become a grey paper-pulp. Then

A BEE AMONG THE SUGAR

Arthur E. Smith.

This photograph shows an ordinary bee feeding from a piece of loaf sugar surrounded by other lumps. The crystal cubes when depicted in this manner make one think of great masses broken by giant hands from a glacier or iceberg, and the bee appears as a strangely furry creature with wonderfully jointed legs and possessing the most amazing tongue.

20—2

she flies back to the hole, and carefully sticks the pellet of pulp on to the root there. To and fro she goes, bringing back more chewed-up wood until a short stalk is hanging from the root. At the end of this she makes a curved, umbrella-shaped plate, on the under side of which she puts four cells, laying an egg in each. Soon she builds yet more cells, and the umbrella covering is made bigger to shelter them.

Then the first eggs hatch, and the queen feeds the grubs. These little creatures hang head downwards, but they cannot fall out, for they are attached to the cell. Soon they grow fat, and become tightly wedged. Then they make themselves silken coverings and form cocoons.

After a while the wasp babies bite their way through the cocoons and look around the busy world in the nest. For a short time they stay there with the queen and help her, but soon they crawl up to the entrance of the hole, and, spreading their wings, go off to find wasp paper to increase the size of the nest, and to hunt for caterpillars and flies with which to feed the young grubs.

J. J. Ward.

THE QUEEN WASP

The queen wasp, having slept through the winter in some sheltered spot, comes out in spring and starts making a new nest. She begins work by chewing up dry wood into a sort of paper. The first batch of grubs are soon hatched and the young workers increase the size of the nest.

A WASPS' NEST   *J. J. Ward.*

The nest may be made in a tree or in a hole in a bank as this one was. The outer coating of paper keeps it warm and dry, and the combs inside are built up in tiers. In the picture part of the outer shell has been broken away to show the interior.

80,000 in One Family

In a short time the second batch of eggs has hatched and more young wasps are developing. The queen ceases her labours of building the nest and feeding the grubs, and lays eggs all the time. At the end of the season there may be 20,000 to 80,000 wasps from her eggs! The worker wasps take on the tasks of building and feeding, and make many journeys a day to find food. They catch flies on the window pane, cut off their legs, wings and head, and carry off

A WASP COMB

M. H. Crawford.

Here is a part of a wasp comb showing the empty cells from which the young wasps have been hatched. And there is inserted a separate photograph (enlarged) of a cell with a grub or larva in it. It is an interesting point that these larvæ lie in their cradles head downward. Wasps live not on honey, but on juices of plants and fruit ; also on other insects, grubs and caterpillars. Though they do much harm to fruit, they make up to some extent by the number of injurious insects they destroy.

the body. They take bits from any joint of meat they see, extract juice from ripe fruit, find caterpillars, and so on. They also enlarge the nest as needed, for now five, six, seven or even eight combs are wanted. The umbrella-like covering has been taken right down the sides to cover warmly the new combs that are built, and the nest is now in the shape of a large ball.

Each wasp cell is used three times for a grub nursery. The little wasps always leave their pupa-skins behind, and when the queen sees three of these in a cell she knows that it must not be used again. It is then cut down.

A wasp nest in the height of the season is a very busy place. Hundreds of wasps make their way in and out. Those that go in are carrying wasp paper or food, those that come out carry a pellet of earth, for in order to enlarge the nest the hole itself must be excavated farther, and every wasp is bidden to take a little soil away.

When Winter Comes

Summer ends and autumn begins. Cold winds come, and the wasps, who are warm-weather creatures only, know that their end is near. All the remaining eggs and grubs are taken away and destroyed. For every dozen workers that go out to hunt, only one or two return. The queen then lays drone eggs and queen eggs and these hatch out, the last of the season.

The day comes when there are no workers left. The great nest is empty now save for the queens. They creep

M. H. Crawford.

HEAD OF A WASP

The great compound eyes, similar to those of a house-fly, are the most striking features of this magnified head of the common English wasp. The antennæ, or feelers, have no fewer than twelve joints, and the jaws work sideways instead of up and down like ours.

out and go to find a sheltered spot. Some choose the ivy, for that blossoms late and provides nectar as a last feast. Some enter our houses and hide there.

The old nest is invaded by mice, who use the paper for their own nests. Earwigs come creeping in, and eat up any dead wasps remaining. The great wasp city is silent and empty.

But in the warm, spring days the queens bestir themselves again. They set out to find new nesting holes, and once more the paper cities grow, and hum with busy life as the thousands of new wasps fly happily in and out.

THE BUSY LITTLE ANT

JUST as wonderful as bees, and perhaps even more wonderful, are the busy little ants. They belong to the same family as bees and wasps, and, like them, live in communities together. There are over 5,000 different species of ants and they are found all over the world. In Britain there are some thirty-six species.

Perhaps you have wandered in a wood, and seen little hillocks here and there. They are probably ants' nests, and if you could see inside one you would find it a marvellous place.

Outside the hillock are many ants, all hurrying here and there. Some are carrying bits of wood or straw, pine needles or grains of earth to add to the hillock; some are carrying food; some may be helping along an ant that has been hurt, for these little creatures are good to one another.

In an Ant-hill

Let us go down into the ant-hill and see what it is like. In the top part of the hill are many passages, but lower down there are rooms. The ants' nest may go quite a foot down into the ground, and everywhere there are passages and rooms. In the latter are bundles of eggs, which the busy ants lick all over each day, and carry about to the warmer parts of their "town."

In other rooms are the grubs, little legless things, white and helpless. The ants look after these carefully, washing them and feeding them daily. After a time the grubs spin little cocoons, and when they are ready to come forth from these as perfect ants the workers gently tear the cocoon apart and help them out, caring for them until they are strong enough to join in the daily work of the nest.

The ant *cocoons* are what we give to our goldfish as "ants' *eggs*," so that really we are wrong to call them eggs.

The queen ant wanders about at the bottom of the nest, dropping tiny eggs which are seized by the workers and taken away to be packed in a little room. Like the bees and the wasps, ants are of three kinds, queens, males

A PEEP AT A WASPS' NEST

J. J. Ward.

In this photograph we are looking right into a wasps' nest and watching the insects at work. The combs are only one cell deep and built, like the rest of the nest, of wood fibre worked into a paste by the jaws of the wasps. The combs are connected by scaffoldings which hold them together, and the nest has usually two doors. Not all wasps build nests, for there are solitary wasps, small in size and dark in colour, which burrow holes in the ground.

and workers. The queens go out for one flight on their gauzy wings, then return to the nest, tear off their wings, and settle down to the task of egg-laying. None of the workers has wings, as you know.

Stinging Ants

You must often have seen ants hurrying about the garden. Some kinds bite, some sting. The ants that bite squirt formic acid into the wound from the end of their body. They use this poison when attacking stranger ants. They always recognise their own comrades, and often " talk " to them with their feelers.

Some ants are very fond of the aphides or green flies that infest many bushes in the springtime. They find these insects and stroke them gently with their feelers, causing them to exude a drop of sweet-tasting liquid. This the ants take greedily. The little field ant is so fond of this juice that it collects the eggs of the green flies in the autumn, and carefully keeps them till the spring, so that it may be sure of having some of the sweet liquid it loves. These aphides are often called the ants' cows, for they certainly milk them, in their own fashion.

Many foreign ants are very interesting. There are some called the Harvesting Ants, which gather and store grain, and others which cultivate underground " fields " where they grow a fungus for food. Other ants again capture ant-slaves and make them do all their work for them.

A WATER-BABY—THE GNAT

THE little yellow-brown gnat is a water-baby, and spends all its childhood in a pond. It began as one of many eggs all stuck together in a raft on the surface of the water. Each cigar-shaped egg has a lid at the

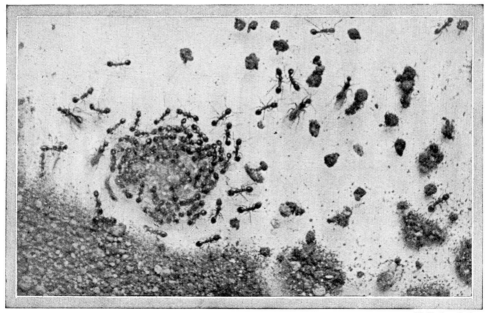

M. H. Crawford.

ANTS AT WORK

Just as is the case with bees and wasps, an ants' nest contains three sorts of insects, queens, workers and drones. You can distinguish the males in this photograph by the fact that they have wings. The queens also fly, and on a still day in late summer they and the males leave the nest on their honeymoon. There may be several queens in one nest, and they are treated with the greatest respect and affection by their subjects.

ANTS KEEP THEIR OWN COWS

J. J. Ward.

Most aphides give forth a sweet honey-dew, and ants keep these creatures as " milch cows." In this picture you see ants shepherding their aphides on a stem of ivy.

J. J. Ward.

Here you will observe an ant sipping sweet nectar from the leaf-scales of the bushy vetch. While the ant is so engaged, bees are busy extracting nectar from the flowers.

J. J. Ward.

This photograph shows you how the queen or winged ants emerge from the pupa skins. The queens possess wings only for a time.

E. J. Bedford.

This heap of pine needles and small sticks is the well-arranged nest of the wood ant. It is about a yard in height.

J. J. Ward.

THE GNAT (1)

This is not a bit of honeycomb but merely the egg raft of the common gnat. This insect lays her eggs on the surface of stagnant water in a mass shaped something like a shallow spoon. The number of eggs laid is usually about 300.

bottom, and one day this flies open and out comes the gnat grub.

It is a large-headed creature about ½ inch long. It is legless, but very active. It has bristles on its head, and with these it gets its food. When it

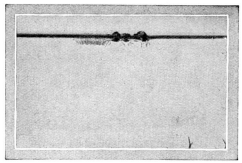

appear at the hinder end of its body. The grub is now a pupa.

It eats nothing, but it is very active. When it wants to breathe it goes to the surface of the water as before, though this time it does not take in the air by means of an air-tube at the end of its body, but breathes through two tubes on its head, so that it does not need to hang itself upside down.

Its two small tubes cannot be flooded

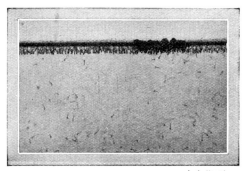

THE GNAT (2)   *J. J. Ward.*

Here are three of these watertight little egg rafts floating close together. The eggs are just beginning to hatch and already you can see the slender larvæ or grubs pushing their way downwards into the water which will be their home for some time to come.

with water, for a little fringe of hairs prevents that. When it had one tube on its tail it was provided with a tiny cap that fitted over the tube and protected it from being flooded.

J. J. Ward.

THE GNAT (3)

Six hours later and the hatching is in full swing. The water beneath the rafts is full of larvæ which swim in a queer jerky fashion by doubling themselves up, then shooting forward at considerable speed. On a warm day in spring you will see them in thousands.

wants to breathe the air it rises to the top of the water and hangs upside down with its tail at the surface. It has a little air-tube on its tail.

For a few weeks it jerks itself about the pond, casting its skin now and again as it grows bigger; and then comes the next change. Its head grows very big, almost helmet-like, and fins

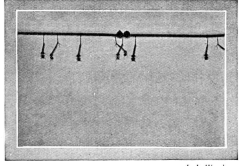

THE GNAT (4)   *J. J. Ward.*

In this fourth photograph the larvæ are seen at the age of six days. They are suspending themselves head downwards from the surface of the water for the purpose of breathing, which they do through an air tube provided near the tail.

Now comes the last change of all, and the most dangerous, for the water-baby may lose its life. It rises to the surface and lies there a little while. The skin dries, and then suddenly it cracks down the middle, making a little boat that rocks up and down.

Inside is the perfect gnat, all complete with legs and wings. It begins to climb out, drawing its legs up one after another, clinging on to its fragile boat.

THE GNAT (5)   *J. J. Ward.*

The odd little creatures are easily frightened, and at the approach of any danger at once plunge below, driving themselves downwards at a quick pace. They are able to stay under water without breathing for a considerable space of time.

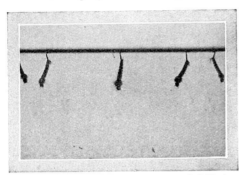

J. J. Ward.

THE GNAT (6)

The first stage of the young gnat's life lasts about ten days. Then the little wrigglers are ready to develop into pupæ. In this photograph they are lying just below the surface, getting ready for the change that is coming.

If it is a calm day the gnat creeps out successfully, dries its wings, and flies away. But if there is a wind that ruffles the water the little boat upsets and the gnat is drowned. Numbers of

gnats lose their lives in this way, but there still seem far too many!

Beware of the Female Gnat

It is the female gnat that bites us

THE GNAT (7)   *J. J. Ward.*

Those two dark objects floating just below the surface are cast-off skins of the gnat larvæ. In the centre is a young gnat that has not yet got rid of his skin, but is just about to do so.

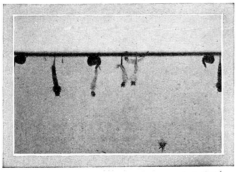

J. J. Ward.

THE GNAT (8)

Our photographer has succeeded in catching one of the little fellows in the very act of casting off its larval skin. The skin is still sticking to its tail, but in another couple of minutes the creature will be free. (*See page* 316.)

and makes those horrid bumps swell up on our arms and legs. She has a wonderful set of mouth-parts that can both pierce the skin and suck up the blood. She needs strong food of this sort before she can lay her eggs.

You will know the female when you see her, for her feelers are thread-like, whilst those of the male gnat are feathery. There are many different kinds of gnat, but there is no special

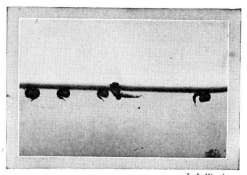

J. J. Ward.

THE GNAT (9)

The pupa stage is very short. It lasts only three days, and then the gnat complete with wings is ready to emerge. Its first task is to straighten out its body. In the fourth figure from the left you see this happening.

kind called a " mosquito." This word is only a Spanish name for the gnats, though people often use it without knowing this.

The common biting gnat is often confused with an equally common gnat

J. J. Ward.

THE GNAT (11)

The surface of still water is covered by a sort of elastic skin. The gnat, as it slowly clears itself of its encumbrance, delicately steps upon this skin or film, which is strong enough to bear its weight.

which cannot bite, but you can tell the difference by seeing how they stand. They both rest on four legs only, but the biting gnat raises its hind legs over its back while the other one raises its forelegs.

Another biting mosquito, found in warm countries, is a terrible spreader of disease. When it bites it passes disease germs into the victim's blood

and makes him ill. Then when another mosquito comes along and bites that same person it takes up some of the germs again, and off it goes to give them to yet another victim.

Millions of these disease-spreading mosquitoes have been killed by pouring oil on to the pools in which they breed. This means that the grubs cannot breathe, and so they perish before becoming adult mosquitoes.

J. J. Ward.

THE GNAT (10)

Then through the burst casing the head and body of the complete insect slowly emerge and it raises itself above the surface. So light is it that the whole process does not cause the shell to sink or even make a ripple.

This is how the spread of diseases like malaria and sleeping-sickness is checked, and how Panama was freed from yellow fever so that workmen could safely dig the Panama Canal.

J. J. Ward.

THE GNAT (12)

Twisting round, the gnat gradually frees itself, but its wings are still crinkled and moist, and it must remain on the surface until they are dry. Until that happens it is the prey of any fish that may rise at it, and may perish before it ever flies.

Keystone.

THE FLOWERS THAT BLOOM IN THE SPRING

In the botanical sense the word " plant " covers trees, shrubs, herbs, flowers, ferns, mosses and other forms of vegetable growth. Though plants lack the brain and nervous system possessed by the higher order of animals, they live and breathe, are sensitive to light and touch. In this section is told the story of their growth and development through the seasons of the year.

HOW PLANTS LIVE AND BREATHE

ALL ABOUT ROOTS

HAVE you ever watched men setting up a tall flagstaff or a wireless mast? First, they dig a deep hole in the ground to hold the base of the pole. When the mast is set in this hole the hole is usually filled with concrete, which sets hard and so holds the mast. But this is not enough. The men affix strong wires to a point some way up the mast and fasten these to posts driven into the ground in a wide circle around the base. Then, whichever way the wind blows, there is something to take the strain and prevent the mast from being blown down.

How Trees are Anchored

In doing this the men are following the example set by trees. If you dug down beneath a Scots fir or any tree with a tall, straight trunk, you would find a *tap root* running deeply into the earth, a sort of underground trunk. Spreading from the top of this tap root you would see a large number of branch-like roots running out just beneath the surface of the soil in a wide circle, each of these in turn dividing into smaller roots until, at the ends, there are mere hair-like fibres, thinner than the smallest twigs on the branches above. In all, a large tree has thousands of feet of rope-like roots anchoring it firmly into the soil.

Roots as Mighty Engines

A prospector sinking a shaft for gold in the desert of Western Australia

A. W. Dennis.

HOW TREES ANCHOR THEMSELVES

We know that all trees fling out surface roots both in order to obtain food and for the purpose of anchoring themselves firmly in the ground, but it is rare to get so good a proof as this photograph affords. These oaks are growing on a sandy hillside from which rain has washed away the soil, exposing the roots to view and showing plainly how far they extend.

only once in seven years, so the ground is dry far down, and the only chance a tree has of life is to push its roots very deeply until it finds a little moisture, which it pumps up to its parent trunk ever so far above.

" Pump "—yes, that is the right, the only, word; for root pressure, as botanists call it, is simply enormous, especially in the spring of the year, when the tree or plant is growing most rapidly. Professor Curtis, of Columbia College, has measured it and found that it amounts to *thirty pounds to the square inch.* It is so great that you can actually make a fountain by cutting off the stem of a growing shrub and capping it with a glass tube having a small nozzle. The joint, which must be air-tight, is made with a small piece of rubber tubing bound with wire.

Roots Feed the Tree

Plant an acorn in moist soil and see what happens. The acorn swells and splits, and out of its lower end pushes forth a tiny rootlet. Not until this has got a good grip of the soil does the

found living roots at a depth of *eighty feet* below ground. They belonged to a mulga tree which grew near the head of the shaft, a scrubby-looking, half dead bush no more than twenty feet high. **In this desert it rains on an average**

stem begin to push upwards. It is the same with all other seeds, and the reason is that the seedling must have food and water before it can begin to grow.

The plant feeds by means of the

little hairs which grow near the end of each rootlet. These pick up water, not merely pure water, but water charged with the chemical salts which make the substance of the plant. The plant turns the water into sap, which rises through its trunk and branches, and is used to build it up and increase its growth.

Roots Useful to Man

We have seen that the two main uses of roots are to anchor a plant or tree in the ground and to feed it. But there are some roots which do more than this, and these are the ones which you know best. We are talking of potatoes, carrots, turnips, beetroot and similar plants. In these the plant has turned its roots into storehouses; and man, by cultivating these roots, has increased their size and improved their flavour so that they provide a great part of his daily food.

Curious Roots

You all know that many plants and trees are propagated or increased by cuttings. Cut a little branch from a geranium and stick it into moist soil; it soon throws out roots and becomes a separate plant. Roses, carnations, pentstemons, geraniums, lavender, and various other plants can be grown from cuttings.

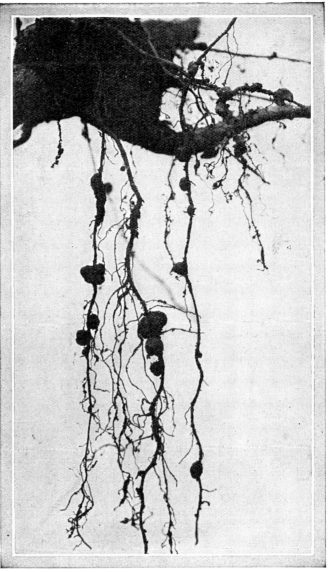

J. J. Ward.

SCARLET RUNNER ROOTS

This photograph shows us the roots of a scarlet runner bean lifted from the earth. Those odd rounded lumps are nodules caused by useful microbes which collect from the air in the soil the nitrogen on which the plant feeds. The good gardener never pulls up the roots of peas or beans, but digs them in so that, in the following season, they may act as fertiliser and supply nitrogen to whatever crop is next sown or planted.

Now there are a good many plants which—so to speak—make their own cuttings. The rhododendron is an example. It spreads out trailing branches which when they touch the

J. J. Ward.

(1) The way in which the lily of the valley spreads is well illustrated by this photograph of the root stock of the plant. To the right you see two long underground stalks with buds at the end, which in the coming summer will push up and form new plants.

A. W. Dennis.

(2) The dahlia grows rather like the potato, forming a quantity of underground tubers, from which strong new shoots appear.

A. W. Dennis.

(3) These are bulbs of the common garlic photographed to show how new bulbs form. All the bulbous plants have a similar habit.

AN ORCHID THAT ·LIVES ON AIR

J. J. Ward.

Several thousand different sorts of orchids are known, and these grow in all parts of the world. In temperate climates they spring from the ground, but in tropical forests are mostly " epiphytes " —that is, they live like air plants on trees or rocks, and have no direct connection with the soil. Some seem to live entirely on water and air, and our illustration shows one of these growing in a pot in a hothouse and flinging roots out over the edge of the pot.

ground, form roots, so that one rhododendron bush will, in course of time, make a regular plantation. The common bramble (blackberry) does the same thing, but this is described in another part of our plant section.

Strangest of all is the banyan, a large tree common in India and other tropical countries. Every branch from the main stem throws out roots first in small, tender fibres, which thicken as they near the ground, where they strike into the soil, rapidly increase and grow into new trees. In this manner one tree may become a small forest.

On the banks of the River Nerbudda in India is a banyan so huge that formerly 7,000 men could shelter under it, and though part of it has been

destroyed by storm and floods, it still possesses no fewer than 3,000 trunks.

BUDS TO LEAVES

AFTER the leaves of the horse-chestnut have fallen off in the autumn you will find at the tip of each twig a bud. Pull one of these and examine it. The first thing you notice is that the outer sheath is sticky. It is in fact covered with a resinous oil which renders it waterproof.

Little Cabbages

Peel off that outer waterproof coat and you find another sheath, and under that still another, all folded over one another like the leaves of a cabbage; until, in the very centre, you come to the real bud which in spring will turn

J. J. Ward.

THE STORY OF A WATER PLANT

(1) We know that hedgehogs and badgers hibernate—that is, go into a sort of trance state in cold weather—but that a plant should have such a habit is rather strange. Yet that is exactly what the frogbit does. The frogbit is quite common in English ponds, and if you watch a plant you will see that in the autumn it produces buds on long stalks under water. One of these can be seen in this photograph.

(Continued on the next page.)

THE STORY OF A WATER PLANT

(2) These buds fall off from the ends of the stalks on which they grow, and lie quietly on the bottom all through the winter.

(3) When warm weather comes and the temperature of the water rises to a little above 40° the bud floats upwards.

(4) Having reached the surface, the bud remains there basking in the sun until it opens out (as seen in the next photograph).

Photos : J. J. Ward.

(5) Our last photograph shows two buds of the frogbit, one just swelling, the other bursting out into leaves and making a root.

21—2

A. W. Dennis.

A PLANE TWIG

The plane is a favourite tree in London, because it does not mind smoke or fog. Here is a twig of the plane in early spring, which shows how the bud is protected from frost by the base of the leaf stalk.

leaves and flowers. In the flower bud the growing point has become, as it were, paralysed. It is a stunted branch end, and instead of continuing to grow, it gradually forms a blossom.

As all gardeners know, anything that stops the growth of a plant is apt to force it into flower. Often an old pear tree on a wall will look well and grow very rapidly, but for years on end produce no fruit. The gardener then tunnels down beneath and root-prunes it, with the result that next spring it bursts into bloom and produces quantities of fruit.

Again, you will sometimes see a cone-bearing tree such as a cedar of Lebanon suddenly produce cones all over. This usually means that the roots have got down into sour soil, and that the tree is going to die.

Plants are " All Bud "

It is the bud that year by year

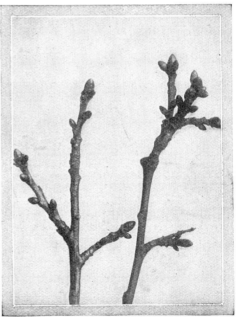

A. W. Dennis.

OAK BUDS

You will easily recognise these as the tips of an oak branch with the buds just beginning to swell. The oak is one of those wise trees that never puts forth green leaves until all danger of frost is over. It rivals the ash in this respect.

into a shoot bearing the familiar seven lobed leaves of this tree. These coverings, known as " bud-scales," are really little blankets provided by kindly Mother Nature to keep the bud warm and prevent it from being destroyed by the bitter frosts of winter.

Not all tree buds are as large as those of the horse-chestnut; some, indeed, are extremely tiny and almost hidden by a coating of bark. The common garden shrub called Philadelphus gives a good example of a bark-clad bud.

In the case of the beech, the bud scales are thrown off like dead leaves at the beginning of spring, and you may see them covering the ground with a dark brown carpet, but in a few cases they expand and form the first leaves of early summer.

Two Kinds of Buds

Buds are of two kinds. One sort produces leaves and branches, the other

THE HORSE-CHESTNUT AND ITS BUDS

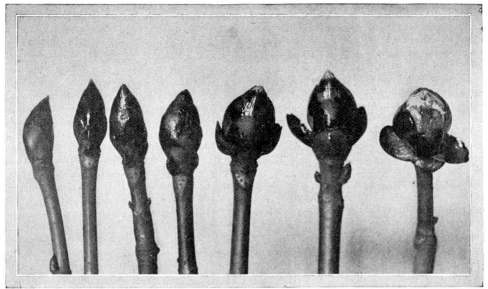

(1) Few trees protect their young buds more carefully than the horse-chestnut. The winter frost cannot strike through the many sheaths around the bud, which is covered by a sort of waterproof coat of sticky gum.

(2) The speed at which tree buds open depends a good deal on the weather. A late frost keeps them back, but warm sun brings them out with great speed. Here we see the same horse-chestnut buds photographed seven days after the first picture was taken. (*See next page.*)

I. I. Ward.

(3) Another two days have passed and the scale leaves are pushed completely back, while the delicate pale green buds have swollen still further. It is already possible to see the veining of the leaves.

J. J. Ward.

(4) On the eleventh day after the bursting of the scale leaves the true leaves begin to appear. Soon the scale leaves, which have served their useful purpose, will wither and fall to the ground, while the big palm-shaped leaves will develop and the great spikes of creamy flowers show up.

WHAT A BUD IS LIKE INSIDE

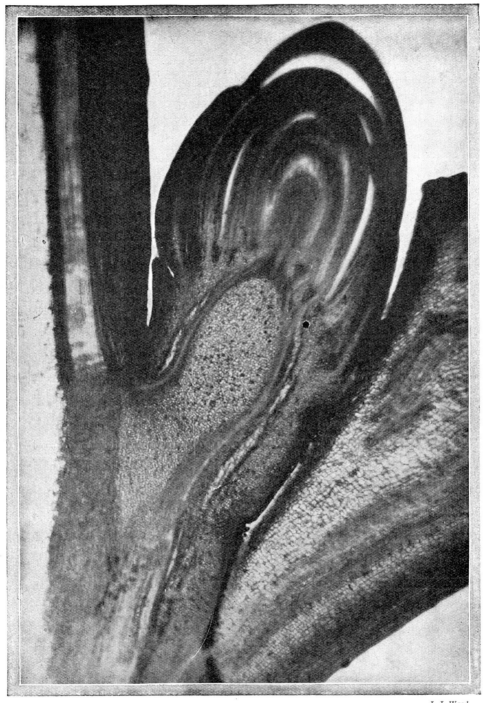

J. J. Ward.

(5) With a very sharp knife this horse-chestnut bud has been sliced right through, and the photograph shows the section greatly magnified. It gives an excellent idea of the way in which the young shoot at the core is surrounded by leaves just beginning to grow, and of the bud scales still protecting them. The scales are lined with a sort of down. (*See next page.*)

J. J. Ward.

(6) On emerging from the bud the leaves are seen to be covered with a delicate down, but this is soon thrown off. This photograph was taken only three days after the bursting of the bud.

J. J. Ward.

(7) When the leaves of the horse-chestnut appear they are seen to be broken up, finger fashion, into seven toothed leaflets of different sizes. They start, as you see here, as ovals, but crowding forces the part nearest the stalk to take a wedge-like shape.

increases the growth of a plant, supplies the flowers and replaces branches
that have disappeared. It may be said
with truth that a plant is all bud, for
there is no part of the plant that cannot
or does not at times produce buds.
Not only the branches, but the roots,
the trunk, the leaves and even the
flowers may produce buds.

Cut down a willow to a mere stump and
dozens of buds are produced around the
cut crown, each making a fresh branch
and forming what we call a pollard. An
accidental cut or bruise on the bark of a
tree will often cause the formation of a
bud and the growth of a new branch.

One of the most pathetic sights to a
tree-lover is that of an elm trunk lying
in the timber merchant's yard and producing buds and fresh green shoots from
the sap remaining in its mutilated body.

What " Budding " Means

A bud is so much a separate growth

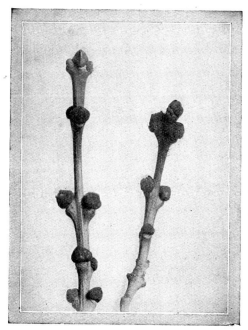

A. W. Dennis.
BUDS OF THE ASH
The ash, like the oak, takes no chances
about frost and its leaves do not usually
break until the " ice-days " of May are past
and gone. The ash is very sensitive to
frost, and with the first sharp cold of
autumn the majority of its leaves fall.

A. W. Dennis.
FLOWER BUDS
If you look closely at this picture you will
see that there are two quite different
sorts of buds growing from these twigs.
The plain ones are leaf buds, but those
shaped like tiny fir cones are the male
flower buds. The tree itself is the walnut.

that it may be cut away from its
parent plant and placed upon—one
should say in, another plant; and if
this work is properly and carefully
done it will live and grow upon its
foster-parent as well as on its own root.
Gardeners profit by this to raise upon
wild stocks their finest fruits. All our
best roses, for instance, are grown upon
wild briar stocks, all our best apples on
crab or similar stocks, all oranges on
sour orange stocks.

The process of " budding " is simple.
You cut a T-shaped incision in the
soft bark of the stock, slip in the bud,
which has been carefully removed from
its parent tree, bind it in with soft
string so that no rain can get into the
slit, and within a very short time the
bud joins its new nurse and throws out
a strong shoot. Then you cut away
that part of the foster-parent *above*
the bud, and the bud produces the
same flowers and fruit as its parent.

TREE BUDS AND TREE FLOWERS

A. W. Dennis.

(1) In the wych elm as in the walnut the buds are of two different sizes and shapes. The larger, rounder ones are flower buds.

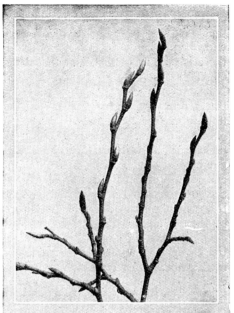

A. W. Dennis.

(2) The hornbeam belongs to the beech family, but has a smaller leaf and does not grow so large. It produces long, narrow buds, with light brown sheaths.

M. H. Crawford.

(3) If only ash blooms had colour equal to their delicate shape they would be prized as table decoration. In this first photograph the flower buds of the ash are shown just breaking into bloom.

M. H. Crawford.

(4) Here are the buds, seen in the last photograph, fully opened. Ash is one of the most English of trees, and its wood is greatly valued because of its toughness and straight grain. The ash roots firmly.

LEAVES ARE OF MANY SHAPES

A. W. Dennis.

(1) Leaves are all kinds of shapes—circular, oval, elliptical or spear-shaped ; and here we show examples of a number of different leaves. The first is that of the poplar.

A. W. Dennis.

(2) This leaf looks somewhat lop-sided, yet if you pluck a number of leaves from a wych elm you will find that they all have just the same peculiarity.

A. W. Dennis.

(3) The Service Berry has what botanists call a " pedate " leaf. It is of very graceful shape. The Service tree is small, and is sometimes called the " sorb."

M. H. Crawford.

(4) We have seen several pictures of the bud of the horse-chestnut. Here is a photograph of the leaf fully expanded. It is what is termed a " compound " leaf.

A. W. Dennis.

THE TREE OF HEAVEN

Leaves shown in this photograph are, to the left those of the
ailanthus, to the right a leaf of the black walnut. The ailanthus is
sometimes known as the Tree of Heaven.

Without the puri-
fying influence of
leaves we could not
live. The oxygen
of the air is being
constantly con-
sumed by our lungs,
by the fires we light
or by the decay of
animal matter, and
carbonic acid va-
pour given out in-
stead. But myriads
of leaves are con-
stantly absorbing
the suffocating car-
bonic gas, turning
it into wood, and
giving out in ex-
change the purify-
ing oxygen. Leaves
are indeed life, both
to the plant and the
animal.

The Nature of a Leaf

A leaf, when fully
formed, consists of
two parts, a foot-
stalk and a blade.
It may be looked
upon as an expan-
sion of the bark and fibre of the shoot
from which it grows. It is therefore a
contrivance by means of which the *ab-
sorbent* surface of the plant or tree is
increased. In the leaves the sap is
aerated, the superfluous water evapo-
rated by the sun's rays, while—as has
been said—carbonic acid gas is absorbed
and oxygen given out.

THE LIFE-GIVING LEAVES

A PLANT could no more live without leaves than you or I could
live without lungs. And—here
is a wonderful thing—leaves are just as
necessary to us human beings as they
are to the plants.

Leaves are Life

The roots, by absorbing food from the
soil, contribute their part to the growth
of a plant, but the leaves are the
real architects. Each leaf seen under
the microscope shows hundreds or
thousands of tiny " stomata " or
mouths which absorb from the air the
carbonic acid gas necessary for the
plant's growth and give out oxygen
which is essential to the life of warm-
blooded animals like ourselves.

Leaves of Many Shapes

Nothing in Nature is more varied
than the shapes assumed by leaves.
The nasturtium has circular leaves;
the gladiolus leaf is the shape of a
sword; in the juniper or the gorse the
leaf has the form of a needle; in the
water plant called arrowhead there are
two sorts of leaves, blade-like under
water, while those above the surface

are shaped like the head of an arrow.

The fly-catching plants have leaves modified into the shape of traps covered with sticky hairs, by means of which they snare the insects on which they feed, but the strangest of all leaves is that of a tropical plant called Nepenthes. Each leaf of the Nepenthes has at the end a stiff, curly thread terminating in a curious little cup or vase provided with a cover. This cup is always full of cool, clear water which has been known to save the lives of travellers lost in the jungle.

THE FALSE ACACIA   *A. W. Dennis.*

Any one looking at these leaves would be ready to declare they were those of the acacia, but the tree to which they belong is really the " robinia," called " pseudacacia," or false acacia. The tree grows fast and the wood is very hard, but, unfortunately, also brittle.

Plants whose home is desert country often use their leaves or branches as reservoirs. Of these the cactus is an example. The ground in which the plant grows may be as dry as powder, but the fleshy plant-body holds a quantity of moisture.

Valuable Leaves

Blades of grass are leaves. Without grass we could have no sheep or horses or cattle. Leaves, too, form a large part of the food of man. We eat the leaves of lettuce raw, and those of cabbage cooked.

Even after they are dead, leaves are of the greatest value to mankind. They decay and make leaf mould, which, in course of time, enriches the soil. No land makes a finer garden than a beech or oak wood after the trees have been cleared away, and no manure is more valuable to the gardener than well-rotted leaves.

THE PARTS OF A FLOWER

BEFORE we can understand very much about flowers, we must learn the names given to their different parts. We will take a flower you are sure to know, to look at it carefully. Let us choose the buttercup.

The Calyx or Sepals

Do you see the outermost leaves of the flower, the small green ones under the yellow cup ? Those are the sepals, and they form the *calyx*. Most flowers have a calyx, and its use is to protect the bud. You must often have noticed how tightly the green calyx covers the bud, before it opens. Sometimes the green covering falls off when the flower opens, for it is not needed any more. You will see this in the poppy.

When the calyx is in many pieces, as it is in the buttercup, these separate pieces are called *sepals*. Usually sepals are green, but sometimes they are coloured.

The Corolla, or Petals

You are certain to know which are the petals of the buttercup. They are the yellow leaves forming the brightly polished cup. Each one is called a petal, and together they make up the *corolla*. Petals are nearly always the showiest part of a flower, for their purpose is to attract insects.

Petals are of all colours, shapes and sizes. In one flower, as in the buttercup, each petal may be exactly the same as the others. In another flower, such as the violet, one of the petals may be quite different from the others. The violet, you will remember, has a spurred petal, and in this it keeps its honey.

Other flowers adapt their petals to insect needs. Have you ever seen a bee visit a snapdragon, or an insect call upon a dead-nettle ? If you have, you will have noticed that each of these flowers has provided a convenient platform upon which the insect may land. The callers use the lower lips of the flowers as a landing-stage whenever they visit them.

Sometimes the sepals and the petals are so alike that we cannot tell one from the other. Think of the snowdrop or the bluebell—the sepals and petals of the snowdrop are all white,

Reginald A. Malby.

THE LARCH

Though the larch is now one of the commonest trees in Great Britain, it was treated as a curiosity less than 300 years ago, and was not planted out of doors until the middle of the eighteenth century, when large plantations were made in Scotland. It is a pretty sight in spring, and though a cone-bearing tree it sheds its leaves in winter. It grows rapidly to a height of 60 feet to 100 feet and lasts for two centuries. Its trunk is beautifully straight ; the wood remains sound almost as well as oak and at one time was much used in shipbuilding.

THE PARTS OF A FLOWER

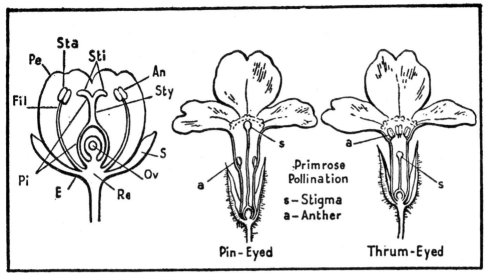

Primrose
Pollination

s — Stigma
a — Anther

Pin-Eyed   Thrum-Eyed

Sti. Stigma ; An. Anther ; Sty. Style ; S. and E. Sepals (forming Calyx) ; Ov. Ovary ; Re. Receptacle ; Pi. Pistil ; Fil. Filament ; Pe. Petals ; Sta. Stamen (of which the Anther is a part). Centre and Right : Sections through the Pin-eyed and Thrum-eyed Primrose.

Some of the best-known types of flowers : 1. Regular (Dog Rose) ; 2. Salver-shaped (Primrose) ; 3. Masked (Snapdragon) ; 4. Wheel-shaped (Periwinkle) ; 5. Trumpet (Daffodil) ; 6. Funnel (Bindweed) ; 7. Butterfly (Sweet Pea) ; 8. Bell (Harebell).

H. Bastin.

POPPIES

The variety of poppies is very great, both in shape and colour, but almost all are alike in that the blossoms have only four petals. A few—a very few—have six. The large showy flowers readily become double by cultivation. Some poppies are annual (die in the first year), some biennial (last for two years), some are perennial, coming up year after year. One variety of poppy is grown in the East to produce opium.

while those of the bluebell are all blue and are joined together. When we cannot tell calyx from corolla, we give the name perianth to the two sets of flower leaves. Perhaps you can think of another flower which has its sepals and petals exactly alike.

The calyx and the corolla are not the most important parts of a flower, although you might think that, at any rate, the corolla was. The plant's chief purpose in life is to make seed, so that the race may go on. Neither sepals nor petals make seed, though they help towards it by taking care of the young flower (in the case of the sepals) and by attracting insects (in the case of the petals).

Look for the Stamens

There are two parts of the flower which are necessary for seed-making—the stamens and the carpels. Sometimes plants do without sepals and petals, and exist simply with stamens and carpels. But most flowers have all four parts, and we are glad they have, because it is the petals of a flower that give it its loveliness.

Look into the middle of the buttercup, and you will see a group of yellow-headed green stalks. These are the stamens. They are slender threads, each with a fat little head called an anther. In the anthers is kept the pollen that is necessary for seed-making. Usually the pollen-dust is yellow, and is taken from flower to flower by the wind or by insects, who, of course, do it all unknowingly in their search for honey.

Stamens are usually free, not joined to one another. They make a beautiful centre to a flower. When the pollen

WILD ROSE

A hover fly strongly resembling a wasp is seen here feeding on the pollen of a wild or single rose. The wild rose has no nectar, but a sticky substance is mingled with the pollen which attracts insects and causes them to fertilise the blooms.

is ripe the anthers split open, and out flies the yellow dust as soon as the wind blows, or an insect pushes by.

The Carpels or Pistil

Right in the very centre of the butter-cup you will see the green carpels, which make up the pistil, or, as you may have heard it called, the seed-box. That name will tell you what the carpels are for. They bear the seeds for the plant, and therefore they are very important indeed, for without carpels no plant can produce seeds.

Look inside as many flowers as you can, and see what their carpels are like. There are many different kinds, but all of them do the same thing—grow the seed safely inside them.

Some carpels are sticky, and some are hairy. Do you know why this is ? Before they can grow their seeds the carpels need a tiny grain of pollen. No seed can grow unless it is touched

with the magic pollen. So some carpels produce hairs in order to make sure of catching hold of a little grain, and others make themselves sticky, so that if some of the yellow dust is blown on to them it stays there, and can be used by the carpels for making their seeds grow.

Once they have got the pollen from the stamens, the seeds begin to grow at a great rate. Now the carpels are indeed the most important part of the flower! The sepals are no longer of any use, and very often they fall off. The petals have done their work, and they fade away too. The stamens drop to the ground, only the seed-box being left with its precious hoard of seeds.

Once these are scattered, the work of the carpels is also done. But where one flower was before, a hundred flowers may be next year, for the seeds take root, and once again the mar-vellous circle of life begins.

SNAPDRAGON

Bumble bees delight in the blossoms of the snapdragon, and it is most amusing to watch one of these big insects push his way in through the closed lips of the blossom, to come out presently with his velvet coat liberally powdered with golden pollen.

And what a wonderful thing it is to think that with all the myriads of varieties of plant-life no two types of seeds are identically the same. In a florist's shop you will undoubtedly have noticed a large rack containing a collection of flower and vegetable seeds in brightly-illustrated packets. Were you to open each one of these packets and carefully examine the contents— more especially if you could use a magnifying glass—you would find no two varieties of seeds precisely alike.

Varying Sorts of Seeds

The form which seeds take depends very largely upon the seed-case in which they grew, and to some degree upon Mother Nature's method of scattering her products over the face of the earth to raise fresh generations of plants. Some seeds remain only on the surface, to be lightly covered and put to bed merely by the fluttering, falling leaves; whilst others must sink more deeply into the soil. Some may drop quite close to the parent plant, whilst others are required to travel a considerable distance, so that the new plant does not rise up too near its parent.

Nuts are really seeds provided with a hard outer-casing to protect them through the winter so that only with the sun and warm rains of spring do they open and liberate the baby shoot and root system inside.

J. J. Ward.

NOT FUNGI

These are not fungi, but stamens of different flowers considerably magnified. The first is that of the garden fuchsia, the second that of the African lily, and the third that of the Tiger lily. Then comes nasturtium, and last of all snapdragon. Stamens are the male part of a flower, and are inside the flower leaves, petals and sepals, but outside the carpels or fruit leaves. The anther, which contains the fertilising pollen, is a part of every stamen, and the pollen is set free by the splitting of the anther.

FLOWERS OF THE WAYSIDE

Mondiale.

" A PRIMROSE BY A RIVER'S BRIM "

One of the most familiar as well as one of the most delightful of the many wild flowers to be found in Britain's countryside is the primrose. The name itself means " first rose," the word rose being used in bygone days for many different flowers. The yellow flowers herald the Spring in April and poets have sung the charms of this sweet woodland bloom. Hold up a leaf to the light and examine its veining so that you can see why it is crinkled. Primroses are found not only in the woodlands but on sunny banks and, as Wordsworth has sung, by the river's brim.

NO one could possibly state with any degree of certainty how many distinct sorts of wild flowers there are to be found during a walk through the countryside or along the seashore. It is known that many hundreds of varieties exist and each possesses a name, just as you do, a name that may go back to the times before history began and one that has usually a meaning of the utmost interest.

It is useful that we should understand as much as possible about our wild plants of the hedgerow, common, woods and waterside, because such knowledge enables us to appreciate the wonders of Nature, and we must bear in mind that most of the wildlings were growing just as they do to-day many hundreds of years ago. Probably the Roman and Norsemen invaders saw primroses, foxgloves and buttercups flourishing in this fair land precisely as we see and welcome them every spring.

We cannot say this, however, of all the lovely flowering plants we cultivate in our gardens because many of them are of comparatively recent origin. Apart from those first introduced to us from overseas, the plants we so esteem have been evolved from common wayside ancestors and it is very seldom

22—2

Reginald A. Malby.

WILD WHITE CONVOLVULUS

This plant is known as bindweed and the
creeping stems twine corkscrew-like round
other plants. One variety of bindweed
grows in cornfields or even among long
grasses.

little trouble we still call stitch, wort
being merely the old-time name for
any plant.

In the Middle Ages the monks were
our chief men of learning and it was
they who began carefully to cultivate
wild plants. Often they named newly-
found subjects after the saints, such as
St. John's Wort ; or after Satan, like
Devil's Fingers for bird's-foot trefoil.
These, too, were the fanciful times
of witches and sorcerers, so the
curious weed shepherd's purse came to
be called witches' pouch ; and of fairies,
hence fairies' or folks' glove for foxglove.

As far back as the Greeks and the
Romans there was a Language of
Flowers, and the use of flowers was
studied in the East so that every degree
of warmth and affection could be conveyed by flowers. The study was revived
in Europe in the Middle Ages when
flowers became particularly appropriate
in an age of chivalry.

that a cultured plant escapes and
returns to a wild state. As merely one
passing thought for consideration, do
you realise that the ordinary moon
daisy of the fields was the forebear of
chrysanthemums ?

To go back to the beginning, the
Greeks loved all beautiful things and
were so attracted to wild flowers that
they named some of them after their
gods and goddesses. Most of these
names we use still, such as Iris, who was
messenger of the gods. The Romans,
when they held sway, continued to use
Greek names and added others of their
own creation. The Anglo-Saxons discovered wild plants, the leaves, flowers
seeds or roots of which they could
use as remedies for their bodily ills,
and it was with actual complaints
that the plant names were linked.
Thus, stitchwort was helpful in the

Charles A. Hall.

RAGGED ROBIN

You will not be searching for wild flowers
very long before you come across ragged
robin. It is usually found in damp fields
and along the sides of brooks and is related
to the campions.

Later, in the middle years of the nineteenth century, little volumes were published in which the language of flowers was set out. Gorse, for instance, indicated enduring affection, while eglantine, which was the old English name for the sweet-briar rose, conveyed the message " I wound to heal." The violet is the emblem of modesty, the daisy of innocence, and the pansy of thought.

By getting to know the wild plants, finding out when they flower and where they grow ; being able correctly to identify unusual examples and group them into families, one forms a delightful hobby and the interest of a stay in the country is broadened. There are, indeed, few studies more fascinating.

Flowers of the Field

Of what flowers growing in meadow-land do you think first ? Almost certainly of buttercups and daisies, because

Reginald A. Malby.

LESSER CELANDINE

This charming wayside plant belongs to the buttercup (crowfoot) family while the greater celandine is one of the poppy family. Lesser celandine, seen above, has heart-shaped leaves, and its flowers seven to twelve petals.

they are so abundant. Daisy means day's eye, or eye of the day, because the flowers open at sunrise and close at sunset and the plant is most persistent through the habit of its leaf clusters coming flat on the ground, preventing anything else (even grass) from growing too closely. If you step on the leaves not the slightest harm is done to them. Further, though the daisy blossoms produce countless seeds, the plant also marches on by means of runners from which new baby rosettes form until there is soon a considerable expanse. You have only to think how daisies in a lawn will very quickly gain the mastery of other herbage if left unchecked.

Of the buttercups, there are five distinct varieties, but in a field we are most likely to find the true meadow

Charles A. Hall.

THE BUSH VETCH

There are several kinds of vetch but they are all related to the pea family. Note how the flowers are crowded on the stalks and study the tendrils closely as well as the narrow, pointed leaflets.

buttercup and the creeping buttercup. Both have cup-shaped golden flowers, but the latter puts forth strong runners to reach outwards in every direction and gain a foothold so that from a single plant many are soon produced, covering a large area. The family name for buttercups is crowfoot.

The dandelion (*dent de lion* is French for lion's tooth, from the manner in which the leaves are toothed) we all know and how the seeds are distributed by the wind, for it is another denizen of the field, but perhaps thistles are not so familiar. In a meadow we are most likely to discover plume thistles which have a tenacious underground root system so that they spread at a great rate. At the same time, if there is a damp corner we may find the marsh thistle, whose leaves are deeply cut and which bears a large purple plume towards summer's end.

Coltsfoot we may locate round the edges of the field. It belongs to the daisy family and puts up a striking yellow flower stalk in March. Heart-shaped leaves appear after the flower head, which is really a cluster of tiny flowers that is followed by downy growth. Coltsfoot was once regarded as a remedy for coughs.

In the hedge banks round the edge of our field the primrose may be revealed. Its name means prime or first rose, the word rose in olden times being used for many flowers, of which this is one of the earliest to open. Hold up a leaf to the light and note its veining. Then, among the herbage of the meadow, we are almost certain to find cowslips, with leaves not unlike those of their primrose cousin, but having many flowers suspended on a stalk. They are said to be like a bunch of keys—hence the name Peter's Keys.

Clover is sure to be in evidence and its blossoms yield a great wealth of honey to the bees. The flower heads are themselves made up of tiny florets and you will know that the leaves unfold in threes like those of shamrock. Ox-eye or moon daisies you are likely to find, especially if the field has been put up for hay. Common sorrel you will identify by its spear-shaped leaves and reddish flowers, and you ought to look out for vetches, which belong to the pea family and have tendrils with which they can cling to anything near them. Then there is eyebright, which belongs to the foxglove group and bears white or purple flowers. It is a lowly plant, seldom exceeding 8 inches in height.

The grasses in the meadow are themselves well worth studying because there are so many varieties. You will soon know the common foxtail grass with its bushy top and the meadow grass that puts up such dainty seed heads which canaries and

John Markham.

WILD PANSY

Growing in pastures and the odd corners of fields, the wild pansy, or heartsease, flowers from May to September. The colour of the flowers varies from white to yellow or purple, and sometimes a mixture of tints.

other cage birds enjoy. Going farther, we may well find the field scabious, with its tall flowers painted like lilac and growing to the cornflower pattern. In some fields, especially if the land has been neglected, there may be bindweed or convolvulus, for when once it obtains a start its underground roots creep along with tremendous vigour, a fresh plant springing from every joint. Shepherd's purse is so called from the little seed-cases shaped like old-fashioned pouches or purses, and we may well light upon yellow rattle, which has lance-shaped leaves with its flowers topping a sturdy spike.

Possibly, if the field we are exploring is damp, we may seek out the tall plant meadowsweet, with its sweet-smelling, cream-coloured blossoms, or the marsh marigold which bears large yellow buttercup-like flowers in spring. It has heart-shaped leaves which are very glossy and may make its home in the

THE SNAKE'S HEAD PLANT

Known as fritillary or fritillaria meleagris, this wildling has drooping flowers, usually spotted. Thus, the reason for the name snake's head becomes quite plain. The leaves are long and narrow.

ditch on one side of the meadow. It is sometimes known as kingcup. Near by we might well discover Ragged Robin with its gay pink flowers and leaves growing in pairs, or possibly one of the meadow crane's-bills, with pretty purple flowers, really like a wild geranium. If we would see an example of the field gentian we must search for its large lilac tubular flowers in a dry situation at the end of the summer.

Flowers of the Wood

In the woodlands our attention will be directed to flowers quite different in habit from those of the meadow. Except very early in the year, before the trees are fully in leaf, most of the treasures will come to view in clearings that the woodmen have left, and the galaxy of plant life that does appear as soon as timber has been cut shows how impatient Nature is to avail herself of every opportunity that presents itself.

Photos: Reginald A. Malby.

WITCHES' THIMBLES

This is the sea campion, most of the leaves and stems being covered with fine hairs. The plant blossoms all through the summer. It is a member of the silene family, sometimes known as witches' thimbles.

Have you ever noticed, to give but one example, how rapidly a sunny, open space in the woodland is covered with wild strawberries? They should rightly be called stray-berries because of the straying habit of their runners. The blossoms are white and five-petalled, the small specks in the fruits being seeds. We may be attracted by foxgloves in among them with their large hanging purple (or occasionally white) spotted flowers, so very much like the fingers of a glove. On the other hand, the scented wood violet (white or mauve) and the primrose are certain to be in evidence in the spring, or we may happen across that old favourite goldilocks, a species of buttercup that favours such a position. Very likely, too, we shall see the dog violet, so called because it is inferior to the sweet violet, the word dog being often used in this way, i.e., dog rose. Look for the heart-shaped leaves

and the purple or almost blue scentless flowers.

In the woods, however, as spring approaches, we may see the green points of bulbs spearing through the carpet of old dead leaves. If we are specially fortunate we may find the wild daffodil with its trumpet whose invitation to enter is accepted by so many insects. More likely though we shall observe the common bluebell, sometimes known as the wild hyacinth, for the flower spikes of the two plants are not unlike.

One should search, too, for the bell-flower with its nettle-like leaves and, of course, for the wood anemones. Their name means really wind-flower and they bear white (sometimes slightly pink) star-like blossoms on slender stalks, forming in their profusion a richly-patterned carpet.

Do you know dog's mercury? It reminds one in its appearance rather of the stinging nettle and may reach a height of 15 inches or more. It belongs to the spurge family and delights in shade. The plant bears both male and female flowers and is poisonous. Then there is the yellow pimpernel, a creeping plant that flourishes where the earth is damp, and bears star-like, cup-shaped blossoms that are followed by interesting seed vessels.

Another plant you may find in a clearing or most likely at the edge of the wood where the soil is moist is the bugle, so named from the shape of the blue or white flowers which offer perfect accommodation for their insect visitors. Wood sorrel we can regard as one of the gems in the crown of spring, for its flowers are pure white with dainty lines of violet. Look for the leaves on strangely slender stalks. They are greenish-yellow in colour, broken

John Markham.

BUGLE

The mauvish-blue flowers of bugle grow on erect stems and may reach a foot in height. They are in bloom from early May to the end of July. White flowers are sometimes produced.

TWO CHESTNU

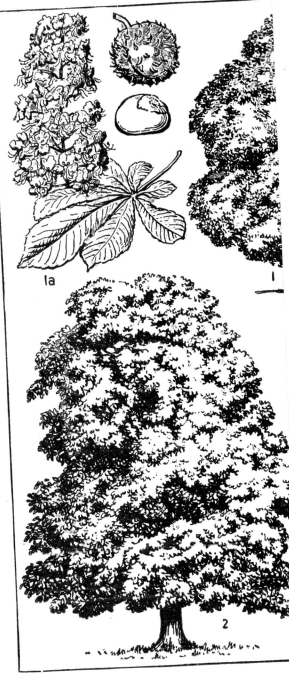

1a

2

Except for the fact that their nuts bear some outward
Chestnut (1) is not related to the Sweet Chestnut (2). Th
up of seven large leaflets and the tree bears big snowy s
in the spiky ball with a single nut inside. The leaf of th
The tree bears long catkin spikes with male (2c) and fem
The bristly green ball contains two

357

tr
w
a
st
tr
th

ho
tr
T
ba

BRITISH WILD FLOWERS—Plate 1

1—Buttercup (Meadow). 2—Field Scabious. 3—Bluebell (or Wild Scilla).
4—Marsh Marigold (or King-cup). 5—Lesser Celandine. 6—Honeysuckle. 7—Lady's Smock.
8—Gorse (or Furze). 9—Forget-me-not. 10—Daisy. 11—Cinquefoil.

THE ALDER—A V

Usually the Alder is found growing along the
best where there is plenty of moisture. It gr
stems. Even in winter, it is not bare-looking
empty seed cones. Above, on the left, is show
male catkins, purplish in colour,

Early in spring the Rowan buds
appear and then, as the end of June
comes, the creamy flowers fade and
presently a cluster of bright red berries
hangs in a bunch from the main stem.
It is among the wild glens and hills of
Scotland that the Rowan is seen at its
best. Its name means the whispering
tree because it whispers secrets to those
who care to listen, and no evil spirit
dare cross the threshold above which a
Rowan branch hangs, nor have the
witches any power where a Rowan
tree grows.

At least, these were the stories they
told of the Rowan long ago, and they
are still pleasing to recall even though
we no longer believe in witches. The
Rowan is a pleasant, happy tree and
both thrush and blackbird love its
bright berries in the autumn.

Common and Wych Elms

Elms are probably the most numer-

by a long thin stalk. The result is that
the foliage is almost continually in
motion and even the faintest breeze is
sufficient to set the leaves quivering.
" Trembling like an aspen-leaf " is a
popular saying, and Scott referred to its
peculiar characteristics when he wrote
" Variable as the shade, By the light,
quivering aspen made."

Its bark is grey and its branches
spreading, while it grows to a height of
40 or 50 feet. The flowers are borne in

THE LIME OR LINDEN

The Lime, like the Plane tree, thrives in the smoky streets
of our large cities, but it flourishes best in fairly open spaces
where there is plenty of air and sunlight. Its flowers appear
in May, and the small fruits appear later in clusters, but
these fruits very rarely ripen in England.

catkins not unlike the other Poplars,
but both the stamen and the seed catkins are very similar in appearance and
grow on the same tree.

The Willow trees are a large family,
but the differences between many of
them are not very great. The White
Willow and the Goat or Sallow Willow
are two of the best known. Most
Willows like a moist soil and are
usually found along river banks or in
water meadows. The stamen and seed
flowers grow on separate
trees. The White Willow
leaves are narrow and
covered on both sides with
grey down. This gives the
tree a glistening grey look
when seen from some little
distance.

Occasionally the Goat or
Sallow Willow becomes a
tall tree, but like so many
other willows it is more
usually found in bush form
with short, tough stem sending up many tall, slender
branches with smooth,
purplish-brown peel. Early
in spring the flowers appear
before the leaves and the
velvety buds have given it
the name of " pussy willow "
or " palm," and branches
are used for decorative
purposes at a time when
flowers are not so plentiful.
The leaves of the Goat or
Sallow Willow are not the
long and narrow type of
most willows but are
broader, rather oval-shaped
with toothed margins, and
tapering to a short, curling
point.

Useful to Sportsmen

Nearly all willow
branches are tough and
flexible and so are often
used for basket-making.
From the trunk of the

THE HARDY EVE

One of the best-known of our trees and shrubs, th
species have been brought in from other count
prickly, though there are some varieties with va
much less prickly. The leaves remain on the tr
formed at the same time so that tl

THE MUCH-PRIZED WALNUT TREE

A tall, spreading tree, with distinctive grey bark, the Walnut is not merely one of our most handsome trees but is valuable in several other ways. Fine furniture is made of its wood, and juices
extracted from the tree are the basis of a useful stain, while the nut it produces is excellent in its
raw state or in pickle. The oil from the nuts is highly regarded by artists as a medium for
mixing their paints.

flowers, bunches of yellow grains from which a tuft of green spears rises, are in dense spikes at the end of last year's twig, but the seed flowers, tiny pale pink cones, come at the end of this year's new twig.

At the end of the first summer the pink cone becomes green but is still soft. During the next year the cone grows harder and bigger, gradually

Willow cricket bats are made and "Willow the King" has been praised in song and prose by cricket-lovers.

While thinking of the trees that are not among the stately or noble orna- ments of field, forest and parklands but are more in the " common or garden " class, the Hawthorn must take a front place. There is nothing very imposing even about a full-grown Hawthorn, but it is a friendly, happy tree doing a lot of useful work besides having an ornamental side at certain times of the year.

It is often called May, and sometimes referred to as Whitethorn, because of the flowers with which it clothes itself in May. It has had its place in history, too. Homer tells how the father of Ulysses was preparing to plant a haw- thorn hedge when his son came home from his wanderings, and there is a story concerning the wonderful haw- thorn staff of Joseph of Arimathea. In England when May time came they

used to dance round the Maypole, which was decorated with Hawthorn blossom.

As these blossoms fade the berries form. They are green at first but gradually change to red. These are the haws and birds eat them gladly. The leaves are pale green at first, cut into blunt fingers, but they become darker and more glossy as the summer comes, then turn yellow, red or brown before the frosts come to strip them from the branches.

Well Known to Londoners

The Plane tree is not a native of Britain. One kind, the oriental, came from southern Europe and the Levant some four centuries ago, while the western variety came to us about a century later from America. Then there is a cross between these two known as the Maple-leafed Plane, and sometimes called the London Plane, since it is this variety of the tree which

common in these days as it or
in this country. When its va
timber was appreciated a centu
a half ago people began to cu
Walnut trees ruthlessly and tl
mendous reduction in their num
never been made up. It is a fi
both in appearance and in its
ness, producing nuts, oil and
The smooth trunk of its earlie
becomes marked and rugged
grows older. Its branches are
though the tips invariably tu
wards.

The leaves are made up of
pairs of leaflets opposite each ot
the same stem with a single le
the end. They are smooth and s
become a pale olive green whe
out. The stamen flowers take a
year to develop into the slender
ing catkins which, when the time
drop from the tree and scatte
pollen dust on the tiny seed-
growing on the same tree.
seed-vessels become smooth gree
about the size of a plum.

This green fruit contains the n
after it has been gathered and th
casing grows hard and dry we h
well-known walnut which is so
esteemed as a dessert fruit.

Before History was Written

The Holly tree is too well-knov
distinctive to need description.
scarcely among the forest trees,
it is often found sheltering unde
trees in our woodlands. In this
try the Holly tree has been kno
long as the Oak, and its begin
lost in the mists before histor
written. Its prickly leaves gro
down on the tree, while those
top are smooth and have only the
prickly point right at the tip
leaf.

May is the month when the
flowers appear in small crowded
ters. Sometimes the same flow
both stamen and seed-vessel and
times the two will be separate

FAIR BLOOMS THE HAWTHORN

Though not one of our great forest trees, the Hawthorn will sometimes reach a height of 30 feet. It is regarded by most of us as a friendly, lowly tree, growing our hedgerows, and making the world gayer at Maytime with its blossoms, while later in the year its red berries (haws) provide food for the birds.

In appearance the Silver Fir is very similar but the leaves have two silver streaks on the underside.

A conifer that is readily known is the Cedar of Lebanon, a massive and handsome tree which is generally seen in this country as an ornament in a large lawn or parkland. Its lower branches almost invariably droop right down to rest on the ground.

If the Larch looks grim when it has lost its leaves in winter it has compensations in spring and summer when its fine new delicate foliage and wide-spread branches give it a most graceful appearance. It was originally introduced into this country as an ornamental tree but is now one of the most widely-spread of all the conifers in Britain and is easily identified by its broad-based pyramid appearance, its bareness in winter and its delicate foliage when spring renews its growth.

The Yew is among the trees that have helped to make history. At one time the yeoman and fighting men of England carried bows of yew wood from which they shot their arrows. Harold, William Rufus, and Richard Cœur de Lion were slain with arrows shot from yew bows. Nowadays it is apt to be associated more with churchyards than battles, and in Gray's Elegy there is a reference to " that yew tree's shade."

As a tree the Yew grows very slowly and rivals the Oak in longevity. Some specimens are said to be nearly 2,000 years old, yet the tree never reaches any great height, though its trunk attains a huge girth and becomes a curious shape as though several trunks had decided to grow together and the whole tree becomes a dense bush. Yew tree leaves are poisonous to both human beings and animals.

Some of the conifers are grown specially for their timber—the Larch, Douglas Fir, and the Pines are well-known, while other substances such as pitch, resin, and turpentine are obtained from them. The timber of the Firs and Pines is generally known as deal.

UNUSUAL AND INTERESTING PLANTS

DOG VIOLET

A. W. Dennis.

The violet is one of the most widespread of wild flowers and is said always to follow the white man round the world. It actually grows in East Africa and in part of South America. The violets and all the beautiful pansies of our gardens belong to the viola family.

SOMETIMES a tree, a plant, an animal, or a bird is taken from its native country and introduced into another. It may be destroyed at once; or, if its natural enemies are entirely absent, may run absolutely wild. The most terrible example of such a happening was the release of the English rabbit in Australia, and its increase into such numbers as have cost the continent untold sums of money; but a second, and almost equally dreadful, blunder was the importing into Australia of the American cactus called the prickly pear.

This plant was introduced into Queensland about a century ago, and in the next twenty years or so cuttings were distributed to land owners to grow hedges around their homesteads. At first it spread slowly, but birds and aborigines, who liked the fruit, distributed the seeds far and wide. In the beginning the fruit also proved of value as fodder for the cattle.

All the time it was spreading and by the beginning of the present century it was already regarded by some of the graziers as a pest. Some of them endeavoured to eradicate it from their land, but without success. During the next twenty years an average of nearly 7,000 acres a day was being invaded! Hundreds of square miles of pasture land became a solid barrier of prickly pear, and the hinterland lost the best of its grazing country.

A Valuable Caterpillar

The Queensland Government offered rewards for some means of destroying prickly pear, and a Royal Commission was appointed. Then a scientist member of a travelling Commission investigating the problem discovered that in the Royal Botanic Gardens at La Plata, Argentina,

24—2

to help them. Poison sprays were used, but it was like trying to put out a volcano with a garden syringe. At last a kind of mould or fungus was found which would attack and kill the hyacinth, and the plague was stayed.

Waterways in Danger

It was just before Queen Victoria came to the throne that here in England we were threatened with a danger very similar to that from which Florida has suffered. About the year 1836 a Canadian water weed, the water thyme (*Elodea canadensis*), appeared in an English river. No one knew how it came, and no one paid much attention to it for quite a long time, when it was noticed that the plant was spreading rapidly.

Within five years the water thyme

SCOTLAND'S BADGE

M. H. Crawford.

"*Nemo me impune lacessit*" is the Latin motto which appears under the Scottish thistle. "No one provokes me with impunity" is what it means, and truly the big Scots thistle is the thorniest plant imaginable. It is one of the finest of British thistles.

was blocking ponds, rivers and even canals all over the country. It took to its new home with amazing enthusiasm, and grew as it had never grown in Canada. Dredges were set to work, but did very little good, and in those days people knew nothing of the insects and fungi which are now used to destroy unwanted plants. For twenty years the weed spread and spread, and then oddly enough the great spurt of growth ceased, and though you will still see it in most English waters, it is no longer the peril it once was.

Garden Flowers run Wild

Very often a cultivated flower will escape from a garden and run wild. On the St. Vincent's Rocks at Clifton wallflowers grow in masses, and so does Valerian on the chalk cliffs near Broadstairs; the blue periwinkle is often met with along our roadsides, and the mimulus grows beside many a Devonshire river. (The mimulus, by-the-by, is really musk or the "Monkey Flower.") Snapdragon frequently blooms on quarry edges far away from gardens, and the ivy-leaved toad-flax or "Kenilworth Ivy" bespangles many a wall with its myriads of tiny flowers.

In similar fashion many English wild flowers have followed British colonists to all parts of the world. The Indians of North America call the common plantain "The White Man's Footstep," because it seems to appear wherever white men have settled.

The hawthorn, in a bush of which the crown of Richard III. was hidden, has pushed its way to Australia, South Africa, and many other parts of the Empire. The sweetbrier has grown into huge thickets in Tasmania, and become such a nuisance that farmers grub it up wherever it is seen. The wild rose, too—the dog-rose as we call it—has colonised the same island, and grows larger and finer there than in English hedgerows.

White clover has naturalised itself in South Africa, while English dog-violets bloom along the railway embankments in Kenya Colony, East Africa. Mallow, chamomile and milk thistle cover huge tracts of land in the Argentine, and the artichoke has made itself a great plague there, for it grows to a huge size and is difficult to destroy.

Following the Flag

Two plants which seem to follow the flag all over the world are the raspberry and the blackberry. The former is now spreading across North America.

In parts of Brazil can be found borage, wild geranium and fennel, which fight for life against the native plants. Near St. Theresia on the Rio Negro, in Patagonia, and close to the Andes, an astonished traveller found whole colonies of violets growing wild.

Even in the Arctic regions plants act as colonists, for the former abodes of the Greenland settlers can be traced by the vetch or tare which grows on the long-abandoned sites.

M. H. Crawford.

BUCK'S-HORN PLANTAIN

The plantain is known to the Indians as "The White Man's Footstep," because it seems to follow him all over America. The Buck's-horn Plantain here pictured grows in poor, sandy soils, usually near the coast. It blooms from June to August.

FLESH-EATING PLANTS

SEEING that we ourselves live largely upon plants and that the animals, such as oxen and sheep, the flesh of which we eat, are also *graminivorous* (that is, grass eaters), it seems surprising to hear of plants that live on flesh. Yet there are such plants—quite a number of them; and you can find some even in our own country.

Scattered over the moors of Scotland, Wales and Devonshire, and also on the sandy dunes close to the sea, numbers of tiny plants can be seen nestling among the grasses just above the soil. They are rosettes of eight to twelve small leaves, of which the outer ones touch the ground while the inner are pointed upwards. These are called Butterworts, and are so small that they often escape notice, though some of them have violet-coloured, bell-shaped flowers.

Pull up one of these little plants and look at its leaves under a magnifying glass. You will be surprised to see that they are covered with small, knob-like glands, from which there oozes a thick greasy fluid which is so sticky that it can be drawn out in long threads like treacle. You will also notice that some of the leaves have small insects adhering to them. The leaves act, in fact, like

A PLANT THAT LIVES ON INSECTS

M. H. Crawford.

(1) Although small, the sundew is one of the most interesting of British plants. It lives in bogs and marshes.

H. Bastin.

(2) Here we see one of the leaves of a sundew attracted by a piece of raw meat at the end of a thread.

H. Bastin.

(3) The glands secrete a clear, sticky fluid which catches insects which settle on the leaf. The leaf then curls up.

H. Bastin.

(4) The insect is caught in the hollow and digested exactly as it would be in the stomach of an animal.

THE CURIOUS VENUS'S FLY=TRAP

S. Leonard Bastin.

(1) The Venus's Fly-Trap, a North American plant, has developed a wonderful mechanism for catching flies.

S. Leonard Bastin.

(2) When an insect touches the sensitive hairs in the centre of each lobe of the leaf, the teeth interlock.

Harold Bastin.

(3) " A terrible plant from the standpoint of flies " is what our photographer says of Venus's Fly-Trap, and when you see how big it grows and how many separate traps each plant sets for the insects you realise the truth of this remark.

R. A. Malby.

THE PITCHER PLANT (1)

Here is one of the Nepenthes, or pitcher plants, common in many tropical countries. The "pitcher" is formed on a stalk at the end of the leaf and is filled with sweetish water which attracts insects. These die, their bodies decay, and the plant makes use of their remains as food.

glutinous fly-paper, and the insects, when they are caught, are rolled up in the leaf and digested.

A Living Fly-paper

The Sundew, which is even smaller than the butterwort, is equally good as a fly-trap, and there are few things more interesting to watch than one of these leaves at work. Place on the leaf a morsel of raw meat as big as a pin's head, and notice what happens by means of a strong magnifying glass. The leaf hairs which are really glands, bend over towards the meat and cover it with some sort of digestive fluid. More and more tentacles fasten upon the food, and if it is a large piece the whole leaf curls over upon it. When all the nourishment has been extracted from the food the leaf opens again and drops the useless remains.

A sundew, if dug up and kept in a saucer in wet moss, will live for a long time, and its methods of feeding can be studied. If a bit of stone or glass is put on the leaf instead of food the leaf curls, but very soon finds out how it has been cheated and drops the useless prey. It is just as well to warn readers that a little goes a long way with a sundew. One minute particle of meat or white of egg will last the tiny plant for a week, and if too much is given the plant dies of over-feeding.

Trapping Real Insects

Butterworts and sundews are found all over Europe, and the people of Lapland use the juice from the leaves of the butterwort for the purpose of making a kind of rennet which curdles milk and turns it into junket. Other countries have other sorts of insect-eating plants of which one of the most

R. A. Malby.

THE PITCHER PLANT (2)

This is the cup of another of the Nepenthes, which has been cut open in order to show the inside. There are at least forty sorts of pitcher plants. The length of the pitcher varies from 2 inches to a foot, and it is often delicately coloured.

interesting is Venus's Fly-trap, found in many parts of North America. This plant is so sensitive that the merest touch of an insect on one half of its divided leaf causes the leaf to snap together like a spring trap, capturing its prey with wonderful certainty.

Farther South live the Pitcher Plants, in which a part of the plant forms a perfect little cup or pitcher which is partly filled with a liquid which seems to attract insects just as honey and beer in a bottle attract wasps.

The insects fall into this fluid and the plant digests their juices. There are many kinds of pitcher plants and bladderworts, some of which actually devour their catches; while others live on the products of the dead and drowned bodies of the victims. Some of the pitcher plants are so large that birds, mice and even rats have been found in their " larders."

M. H. Crawford.
DEADLY NIGHTSHADE
A big, strong plant, growing 3 feet or 4 feet high, the deadly nightshade likes chalky soil. The whole plant has an unpleasant smell and is all poisonous, but the glossy berries, each as big as a cherry, are deadly. Another name for the plant is " Belladonna."

The bladderworts are floating pond-plants which catch small creatures like water-fleas in an underwater trap like a little bladder.

A Moth Catcher

Araugia Albens is the name which scientists have given to a plant growing in Central Africa, which has a peculiar appetite for moths. The plant has large, white, very sweet-smelling flowers which are a great attraction to moths. But the whole thing is a heartless fraud, for when the moth dives down into the calyx (cup) of the flower, and pushes its proboscis in after the honey which it expects to find, it is suddenly nipped between two strong, hard, black pincers and devoured. The araugia has been imported into Australia in the hope that it will catch some of the moths, the caterpillars of which destroy fruit.

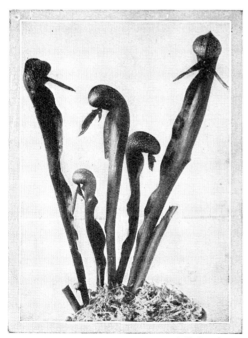

A. W. Dennis.
ANOTHER LIVING TRAP
On the western side of the North-American continent we find a different type of insect-eating plant, the Darlingtonia, of which this is a Californian specimen. It is very similar to the pitcher plant, for each of these stalks is hollow and acts as a trap for flies.

BEWARE OF THESE BERRIES

(1) There are two sorts of buckthorn in Great Britain. This is the thorny one that bears berries, from which is made syrup of buckthorn, a medicine for ailing dogs.

(2) Broad, hairy leaves and large, rounded heads of white flowers make the Viburnum, or wayfaring tree, a favourite. Later the flowers are succeeded by berries of glowing coral.

(3) The spindle tree may be 20 feet high, but usually grows only to 12 feet. The shiny leaves have toothed edges. The scarlet berries in their orange cups are poisonous.

(4) It is the leaves and seeds of the yew tree that are poisonous, not the fleshy part of the pink berry, yet this cannot be recommended as food except for birds.

BRITISH WILD FLOWERS — Plate 1

1—Buttercup (Meadow).   2—Field Scabious.   3—Bluebell (or Wild Scilla).
4—Marsh Marigold (or King-cup).   5—Lesser Celandine.   6—Honeysuckle.   7—Lady's Smock.
8—Gorse (or Furze).   9—Forget-me-not.   10—Daisy.   11—Cinquefoil.

12—Ragwort.   13—Willow Herb.   14—Cowslip.   15—Corn Cockle.
16—Wild Chamomile.   17—Cuckoo-Pint (or Lords and Ladies); also known as Wild Arum.
18—Red Centaury.   19—Cornflower.   20—Sow-Thistle.

21—Heath.	22—Goat's Beard.	23—Wood Sorrel.	24—Agrimony.
25—Primrose.	26—Field Poppy.	27—Dog Rose.	28—Flax.	29—Rock Rose.
30—Violet.	31—Scarlet Pimpernel.	32—Coltsfoot.

BRITISH WILD FLOWERS — Plate 4

33—Bird's-foot Trefoil.   34—Wood Anemone (or Windflower).   35—Germander Speedwell.
36—Red Clover.   37—Bladder Campion.   38—Field Thistle.   39—Yellow Flag.
40—Dandelion.   41—Red Campion.   42—Yellow Toadflax.   43—Harebell.

with trios of leaflets which close together as evening comes on.

You will know, I am sure, how honeysuckle loves to appear where sufficient light falls between the trees, clinging on gamely to any available undergrowth, whilst red campion, with downy leaves and pinkish or purple flowers, is a wood-loving member of the chickweed family. It, too, will scramble over undergrowth and people call it the Robin Flower. Other plants for which to seek more or less beneath the shade of trees are centaury, with its flattened flower head of rosy hue and smooth long-shaped leaves ; the yellow deadnettle ; ivy ; perhaps periwinkle and St. John's Wort, and very likely the trailing wood rose with willowherbs a-plenty.

Flowers of Hedgerow and Common

Those of us who have been privileged to visit other lands, or who go to those

John Markham.

FIELD SCABIOUS

In dry fields and downs the pale lilac flowers of field scabious are very plentiful from June to September. The flower-heads are borne on long, stout stalks.

parts of the British Isles where the fields are parted one from another by cold stone walls, miss there most of all the hedges. We can, indeed, think of our hedgerows as a natural characteristic. Not only do they separate the fields, but they also form homes for countless birds and other small creatures and provide us with such an abundance of wild plant life that there will almost always be something interesting if not unusual to find.

Can you think of some very common hedgerow plants ? One beloved of children is the wild arum lily or cuckoo pint, when its brilliant red berries are in evidence. Nor must we forget, as is told elsewhere in this book, what a deadly poison these berries are. Almost certainly we shall find stinging nettles in the hedge, and country people often cook them like spinach when the leaves are young to form a wholesome vegetable.

In this hedgerow along which we are

John Markham.

YELLOW PIMPERNEL

Sometimes known as woodland loosestrife, the small flowers of the yellow pimpernel are seen from May to July and are about two-thirds of an inch across.

John Markham.

FOXGLOVE

This is one of the best-known flowers of the countryside and its masses of purple blooms are found on woodland slopes and dry waste land in many parts of Britain.

walking in imagination one of the first thoughts will be of the infinite variety of plant life. There may be one or two upstanding trees, but most of the main growth will be shrubby and composed of hazels (nut bushes) ; hawthorn (or quick) ; elder ; privet ; wild cherry ; spindle ; elm suckers and so forth to constitute the hedge itself as originally planted and since kept dense and neat by regular cutting and laying flatways of the long growths. It is this woody material of the hedge that affords support for so many self-set wildlings, the majority of them rooting in the moist earth of the ditch below.

When we sow scarlet runner beans in our kitchen garden we provide rods or netting over which the quickly-growing strands may climb. Wild plants thrive in a hedgerow because there they find support to which to cling. Can you think of some plants that are ever eager to reach upwards to the light as though they were trying to get as high as

possible away from other things into a little world of their very own ?

We are sure to come upon the white bryony, which clings on by means of spiral spring-like tendrils, and there will almost certainly be honeysuckle, its stems encircling any woody growth, especially that of the hazel, as it stretches towards the sunshine. Blackberry briars or brambles we shall see hanging on as they climb by means of stout hooks that form all along the branches ; and there is likely to be ivy, which sends forth hungry, clinging rootlets from the underside of each green shoot.

Do you know a hedgerow plant called goosegrass ? Some people call it cleavers, and those who live in the west of England say cliver or clider, whilst " sweethearts " is a title sometimes bestowed because the plant cleaves or clings to our clothes. Goosegrass is good food for ducklings and it is so persistent, though by no means

John Markham.

TRAVELLER'S JOY

Also known as old man's beard, traveller's joy is a climbing shrub, found mainly in chalky soils. After flowering they show masses of feathery awns, as seen here.

PURPLE LOOSESTRIFE

Growing to a height of 3 to 5 feet, purple loose-strife is in flower from July to September. The reddish-purple flowers grow in long, leafy, attractive spikes.

John Markham.

suckle, its tubular flowers so rich in honey, also produces its fruits and there is thus no shortage of bird food.

Named after St. Robert

On the hedge bank we shall probably note herb Robert, one of the wild geraniums. It may have been called after St. Robert, a godly abbot of long ago, and the plant is often in bloom on his day of dedication, April 29th. This is a true annual, coming up afresh from seed every year, and the small pink flowers always form in pairs. Growing along this bank, we may find, too, wild strawberries, primroses and violets, as well as speedwell or bird's-eye.

Foxgloves there are likely to be, growing just where they can find a foothold ; and, if the ditch is broad and damp, you may see cow parsnip, bearing flattened flower heads like a parasol at the top of thick hollow stems from lengths of which country boys some-

John Markham.

WILD MIGNONETTE

This wild flower is similar to the sweet mignon-ette grown in our gardens. Wild mignonette is more erect and almost scentless. It grows in dry waste places, preferably in chalky soil.

strong, that it forces its way up the hedge whether there is a crowd of competing plants or not. Further, the little fruits (containing seeds, of course) are armed with hooks so that they can be attached to and carried far away by any creature that chances to pass, human beings included.

Old man's beard you will know, for it is a particularly rapid climber of the clematis group, sometimes known as travellers' joy. One of its beauties is the grey feathery masses that form in early autumn and remain for many weeks. Within these growths, which are called awns, are the precious seeds. The dog rose we shall, of course, look for. Apart from its lovely flowers, its hips (fruit) contribute to the hedge harvest of late summer, coming with the haws (fruit of the hawthorn), hazel nuts, blackberries, the sable berries of privet and the crimson berry clusters of the viburnum or wayfaring tree that prospers on chalky soil. The honey-

times make popguns. Dead nettles (which do not sting) will attract attention ; and docks, which send their parsnip-like roots far into the ground. We may see the yellow flower groups of tansy and one or two of the nightshades.

Let us look, too, for the greater celandine. Its daintily veined leaves have their edges cut in curves, each yellow flower possessing four petals, to be followed by a curious seed-pod. The plant has a yellow-tinged sap which people used to apply to cure warts, hence another name, wartwort. Lesser celandine belongs to the crowfoot family. It has roundish, heart-shaped leaves and bright yellow flowers, which make their appearance in April. Celandine in Greek means swallow, and these plants are often in flower when the swallows first arrive.

Leaving the hedgerow now, let us stroll across some, breezy common or stretch of downland and we shall discover there wild flowers totally different from those we have already discussed.

Maybe we shall see the hawthorn again, not headed back as it was in the hedge, but possibly with its thorny branches somewhat stunted and growing away from the prevailing breezes. The sloe or blackthorn will very likely be there too, a form of wild plum whose blossoms open early before the unfolding of the leaves and give us the so-called " blackthorn winter." Furze or gorse we shall surely find on this common covered with spines and bearing flowers of buttercup yellow. You have merely to examine some of the seed pods to understand that gorse belongs broadly to the same great family as do beans and peas.

Among the more lowly plants let us look for yarrow, sometimes called milfoil. It has an underground root-stock and its stems are covered with grey woolly hair like felt. The flowers, resembling miniature daisies, carried in groups, are usually white.

Another plant for which to seek is bird's foot trefoil. As the name suggests, the leaves grow in threes like those of clover or shamrock, and the flowers vary from yellow to deep orange.

There are, too, many wild plants which grow beside ponds, or streamsides, and at the fringe of the seashore.

Photos: Reginald A. Malby.

SOME GRASSES OF THE MEADOW

Grasses are always full of interest and each has its own type of flower. The first picture shows briza, which is popularly known as quaking or totter grass. The other two are common meadow grasses and when freshly gathered with long stems they go admirably with bunches of cut flowers. The tiny purple flowers of meadow-grass are very beautiful when seen through a small magnifying-glass.

How to Identify the Oak, Ash, Elm, Beech—

And Other Trees That Grow in Britain

IN AN ESSEX WOODLAND

E. W. Tattersall.

Centuries ago, Great Britain was largely covered by great forests, but as man discovered the value of timber, as well as the need for more corn and pasture land, the trees began to vanish rapidly before the axe. To-day, with fuller knowledge both of the charm as well as the practical advantages to the countryside of our woodlands, a happier balance is preserved, and both government and private societies do good work in planting new trees to replace those cut down.

TREES OF OUR COUNTRYSIDE

A GREAT deal of the charm of our English countryside is due to the number and variety of trees which adorn it. Even the person who cannot tell an oak from an elm or a sycamore from a chestnut tree can still feel with the poet who wrote " No tree in all the grove but has its charm, though each its hue peculiar."

There is very much greater interest, however, if one knows the different trees and something about their habits. The trees are much more than just a background and their ever-changing aspects are a continual source of pleasure and wonder. There is romance, too, in some of our trees. An oak tree sheltered a king in desperate peril of his life, and it was under the oak that the ancient Druids held their courts of justice and performed their religious rites.

Massive Girth and Branches

The Oak can be regarded as the most essentially British tree of them all. There are a good many different species in the world, but the true British Oak

THE OAK—KING OF BRITISH TREES

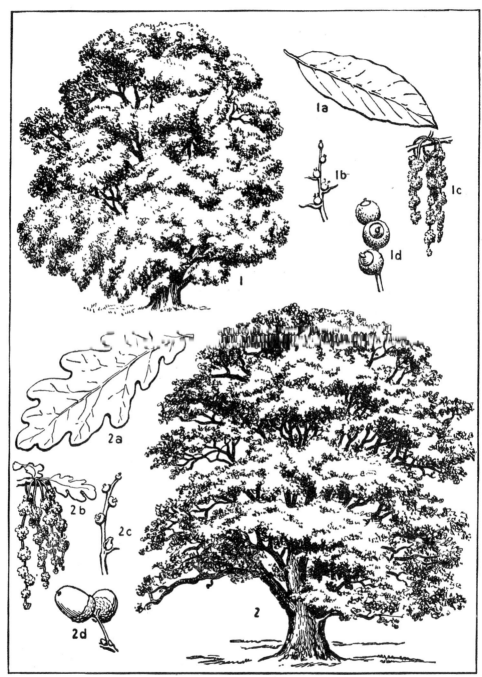

No tree is better known in this country than the Oak, with its massive trunk, wide-spreading branches, and deep-seated roots. Two kinds are found everywhere in our countryside: the smaller of the two, the Holm Oak (1) has a thick, leathery leaf (1a) with dark green upper sur-face and grey-green to whitish under-surface. The female (1b) and male flowers (1c) grow on the same tree and the small acorns (1d) develop slowly, reaching maturity in their second year. The Common or British Oak (2) is rather a larger tree with thick, rough bark, and its leaf (2a) has deep rounded lobes. The male (2b) and female flowers (2c) grow on the same tree producing the familiar acorns (2d).

(*Quercus robur*, as the botanists label it) is a magnificent tree, not so tall perhaps as some of our other trees, its average height being around 60 to 70 feet, though it may reach as high as 120 feet. Its girth is usually from 50 to 60 feet when fully grown and its bark is marked with deep furrows. Its branches, too, are massive and spread widely.

The long leaves are oval-shaped and lobed while its fruits are the well-known acorns, usually on long slender stalks. Before the acorns, however, and just about the same time as the leaves, come the flowers: long slender hanging catkins and on the same branch a stouter upright catkin with the tiny cups, in the centre of which is the seed-vessel. These gradually develop into the acorn, the seed of a new tree or food for the squirrels in the woods.

This British Oak is a long-lived tree, the age of some of them being estimated from 700 to 1,500 years, and they are still flourishing. Acorns do not grow on an oak tree until it is between sixty and seventy years old and when used for timber the tree should be well over a hundred years old.

There is another species of Oak, the Holm Oak (*Quercus ilex*), which is not really a native of this country though it is often seen in parks and large gardens. In the countryside generally it is not very common. The Holm Oak is rather smaller than the ordinary Oak and is an evergreen with dark leathery leaves varying in form from oblong to lance-shape and without the lobes which distinguish the leaf of the better-known tree. The underside of the leaf is whitish.

Cousin of the Oak

Another truly British tree which has grown in this country as far back as any records exist is the Beech, a cousin

THE SHADY BEECH TREE

Like the Common Oak, the Beech tree has grown in this country ever since trees have been known. Our illustration shows the Beech with, below, a leaf spray bearing the small triangular nuts, the seeds of new trees or food for the squirrels and other creatures of the woods.

THE ROWAN AND THE ASH

The Ash tree (2) has been called the Queen of the Woods and many legends are connected with it. The Mountain Ash, or Rowan tree (1), is not really an Ash at all though the leaves have some resemblance to those of the Ash (2a). The Rowan bears clusters of rich yellow-red berries (1a) while the Ash, a much larger tree, bears green seed-vessels (2b) which gradually become " keys " or " spinners " (2c) carrying the seed. In time, the wind carries these keys away and they fall to the ground

THE COMMON AND WYCH ELMS

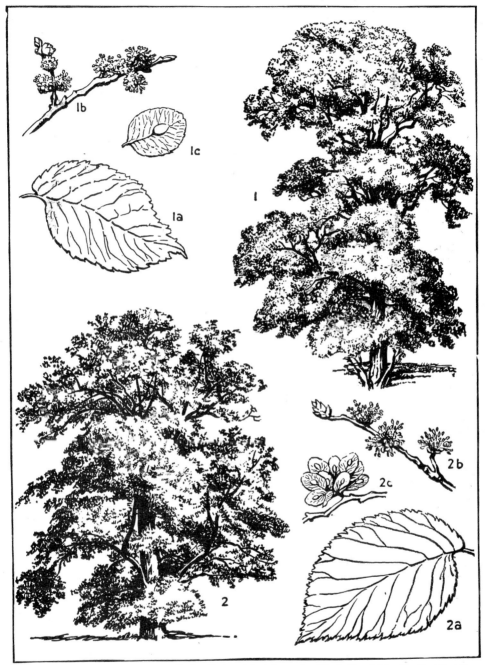

The Common Elm (1) can generally be distinguished from the Wych Elm (2) by the fact that its trunk is clothed to the ground with a mass of brushwood and suckers from the roots. The Wych Elm's leaf (2a) is rather longer and broader than that of the Common Elm (1a) but both bear similar flowers (1b and 2b). The little seed in the flat green wing which develops after the flower has fallen is rather smaller in the Common Elm (1c) than in the Wych Elm (2c) while the wing itself has a slightly deeper notch at the end.

THE HORNBEAM

Superficially, the Hornbeam resembles the Beech, but its leaf differs in having strongly toothed edges, the spaces between the larger teeth being occupied by smaller ones. The trunk is usually oval in section instead of round. The green and yellow catkins open early in April; the female flowers are smaller and develop bracts between which come the seeds, as shown in the bottom left-hand corner.

of the Oak. It grows rather taller than the Oak and is a large, handsome tree with a straight trunk, smooth olive-grey bark, and densely covered with leaves in summer. No other tree in all our woods gives such shade as the Beech and no retreat is so cool in hot weather as one beneath its widespread branches.

Its leaves, bright green in the spring, become much darker as the summer passes. They are pointed oval in shape with plain edges. As autumn comes the leaves change colour to many shades of gold, red and orange.

The young flowers come about the same time as the leaves; the stamen flowers, on long drooping stalks, appear as hanging clusters of purplish brown with yellow heads. Not far away on the same twig is the seed flower growing upright on a short stalk with bristly oval ball at the end. From these come the shining three-cornered nuts which as they ripen and become brown are blown from the tree to become food for the squirrels and other creatures of the woods. There was a time when beech nuts, like acorns, were regarded as excellent food for pigs, but no one takes the pigs to the woods in search of food in these days.

The Copper Beech is a well-known variety, though its history goes back for little more than a century. It is usually seen as a park tree and its ornamental shape together with its leaves, light copper which slowly turns through the summer to a deep purple red, make the Copper Beech one of the most easily recognised of all our trees.

Romance and the Ash

One of our well-known native trees, the Ash, is sometimes associated with the Oak in an old saying, " If the Ash before the Oak, then you're sure to have a soak; if the Oak before the Ash, then there'll only be a splash," but the weather experts have little faith in this ancient lore. Like the Oak, however, the Ash has romantic touches in its long history. Achilles had a great ashen spear and the Greek gods met under the boughs of the Ash. In

England it was at one time believed that sick babies would be cured by being passed through a cleft in the trunk of the tree. Under certain conditions the Ash would bring about other wonderful cures both for men and for animals.

There are several points which make the Ash fairly easy to distinguish. Its trunk is very straight and when young the bark is grey and smooth, but older trees develop a network of upright irregular cracks. Then, unlike other trees, the branches do not fade out into delicate branching little twigs; each branch ends abruptly as though someone had pinched the end and flattened it. At the tip and along the sides of the twigs are black buds.

In the spring the Ash is one of the late trees in putting on its coat of new leaves. Not until most of the other trees are fully clad do the black buds of the Ash begin to open and then the flowers come before the leaves. These leaves are divided into narrow leaflets which grow in pairs on opposite sides of the stalk. The fruits are hanging bunches of "keys," twisted in shape so that when they fall they are blown round and round to be carried clear of the tree before touching the ground.

Often these seed envelopes or "keys" will hang on the tree through the winter. When fully grown the Ash reaches a height of 70 or 80 feet and its wood is valuable, being used for many purposes from furniture and tool-handles to shipbuilding.

The Tree of Whispering

Another tree, which is sometimes called the Mountain Ash, though Rowan is a better name for it, is no relation at all of the real Ash tree. The leaves are rather similar in the fact that pairs of small leaflets grow opposite each other on a centre stalk and with one odd leaflet right at the end. The Rowan is a much smaller tree than the true Ash and 20 feet is somewhere about its average height.

SILVER BIRCH

Graceful and dainty the Silver Birch is also one of our hardiest trees and most easily recognised by its distinctive bark. The slim trunk, small leaves, and its delicate branches and twigs also distinguish it from any other tree. The green slender female catkins grow on the same tree as the male catkins which in the spring look like hanging caterpillars swaying in the breeze.

THE ALDER—A WATER-LOVING TREE

Usually the Alder is found growing along the banks of streams or in marshy ground as it thrives best where there is plenty of moisture. It grows both as a tree and as a shrub with spreading stems. Even in winter, it is not bare-looking, as it is covered with immature catkins and old empty seed cones. Above, on the left, is shown a leaf spray with female catkins and below are the male catkins, purplish in colour, and hanging loosely from their twig.

Early in spring the Rowan buds appear and then, as the end of June comes, the creamy flowers fade and presently a cluster of bright red berries hangs in a bunch from the main stem. It is among the wild glens and hills of Scotland that the Rowan is seen at its best. Its name means the whispering tree because it whispers secrets to those who care to listen, and no evil spirit dare cross the threshold above which a Rowan branch hangs, nor have the witches any power where a Rowan tree grows.

At least, these were the stories they told of the Rowan long ago, and they are still pleasing to recall even though we no longer believe in witches. The Rowan is a pleasant, happy tree and both thrush and blackbird love its bright berries in the autumn.

Common and Wych Elms

Elms are probably the most numer-ous among all our trees. The Common Elm is a tall, upright tree and usually it has just the one main trunk, thick and rough with large gnarled bosses or knobs on the rugged, furrowed bark, while its branches are twisted and knotted as though they were never quite sure which way they meant to grow

At the foot of the tree there is a forest of small shoots and twigs which would become Elm trees if planted separately. It is this brushwood growth at the base which quite definitely distinguishes the Common Elm from its relative, the Wych Elm. There are no growths at the base of the Wych Elm and its branches are more graceful, being longer and not so twisted. Often, too, its main trunk divides into several great branches. The leaves are much the same shape, rough and slightly notched, but the Wych Elm leaf is rather larger and

TWO CHESTNUT TREES

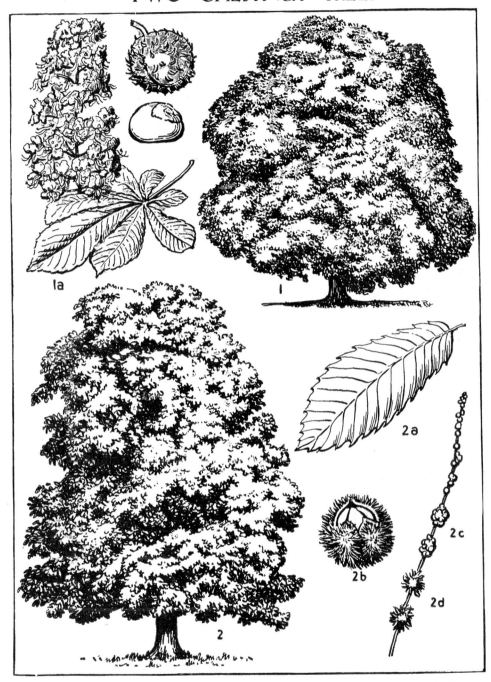

Except for the fact that their nuts bear some outward resemblance to each other, the Horse Chestnut (1) is not related to the Sweet Chestnut (2). The leaf of the Horse Chestnut (1a) is made up of seven large leaflets and the tree bears big snowy spikes of flower. The fruit is contained in the spiky ball with a single nut inside. The leaf of the Sweet Chestnut (2a) is oval in shape. The tree bears long catkin spikes with male (2c) and female flowers (2d), the latter near the base. The bristly green ball contains two or more nuts (2b).

rougher. The leaves of both the Common and the Wych Elm are unsymmetrical in shape, one side of the leaf being definitely lower at the base than the other.

In early spring the flowers appear, reddish stamens with purple heads, while the oval seed-vessels grow close to these stamens in the one flower. When the stamens fall off, bunches of flat green wings with a seed knob in the centre of each make their appearance. When the seed is ripe the wind blows these wings away.

Elm is rather valuable as timber, but the tree, which grows between 60 and 80 feet high, is not among the long-lived ones. The Common Elm in particular is liable to a form of rotting, for which reason it is not wise to choose this tree for shelter in a storm. It is not uncommon for a big branch to break and crash to the ground without any real warning.

Where the Hornbeam Differs

The leaf of the Hornbeam tree is not unlike the Elm leaf and it also has some similarity to the Beech. The Hornbeam is a fairly common tree and often mistaken for the Elm because of its leaves. There is this small point of difference, however: with the Hornbeam leaf the two sides meet exactly opposite each other and not, as in the case of the Elm, one side farther down than the other. Nor is the Hornbeam leaf quite so rough as the Elm's, though it is not as smooth as the Beech leaf.

The bark of the Hornbeam is rather like that of the Beech, smooth and grey. But the trunk is often more of an oval shape than round. Its flowers appear in catkins, the stamen coming with the young leaves early in April. They are made up of green scales and at the foot of these is a thick bunch of yellow-headed stamens. When these yellow heads are ripe they burst and scatter their pollen dust over the seed flowers and so produce the fruit, small hard nuts about the size of a pea, attached to three-finger bracts.

In autumn the leaves are brown and, as with the Oak and Beech, the dead leaves often remain on the trees through the winter until the new growth in the spring pushes them off. There have been arguments about the way in which the Hornbeam came to get its name, and one explanation is that from this tree the yoke worn by oxen in days gone by was always made. The oxen were used for ploughing and each pair was kept together by means of a wooden collar or yoke which was fitted over the horns.

With Bark of Silver

Perhaps the daintiest of all our woodland trees is the Birch. There is no mistaking the Silver Birch with its distinctive bark, and the tree itself, tall, slender and graceful, gives the impression that it is not very hardy. Yet it grows in exposed positions on heaths and mountains as well as in the woods, and flourishes equally well wherever it grows.

The bark peels off easily enough but is remarkably tough and lasting. In some countries it has even been used for roofing houses. When April comes the young and very small leaves cover the tree like a green mist. These leaves never grow very large and are roughly oval in shape, but with a sharp tapering point making the leaf almost triangular, while the edges are cut into irregular teeth, first a large and then a small one. The leaf-stalk is fine but tough and the twig from which it grows is not much thicker. The gentlest breeze is sufficient to make the Birch tree leaves flutter and dance. In autumn the leaves turn to yellow and gold and fall quite early.

The flowers of the tree are not always seen very easily and it takes a full year for the stamen catkins to grow. During autumn these catkins are purple but in the following spring they unclose and grow longer till they look like a

There are four or five species of the Poplar family found in Britain, the best-known being the White Poplar, or Abele Tree (1), with greyish-green bark and dark green leaves (1a) having almost white undersides. The Black Poplar (2) is probably named because its leaves (2a) lack the white coating. They are also different in shape. Most distinctive of all is the Lombardy Poplar (3) the leaves of which (3a) are similar to the Black Poplar but distinctly smaller. The catkins (3b) always appear before the leaves.

pair of reddy-brown caterpillars. The seed catkins are small and green and when the seeds are ripe they become tiny nuts with little wings to support them as they flutter to the ground.

It is not among the long-lived trees and from eighty to a hundred years is its limit. Despite its delicate appearance the Birch will flourish in poor or sandy soil and is often found in company with the pines and fir trees.

Alder and Hazel

A cousin to the Birch and to the Hazel is the Alder tree, and it bears catkins just as they do. It is a water-loving tree, usually found near streams or in swampy ground. In rather drier ground the Alder is apt to develop into a large bushy shrub and is probably found in this form more frequently than as a full-grown tree of 30 or 40 feet. Rough, brownish-black bark covers the trunk, and the leaves,

from 2 to 4 inches long, taper from a point at the stem to a broad rounded head, with edges waved and toothed. When the leaves are newly opened the underside is covered with tufts of soft down and is slightly sticky.

The stamen catkins are small and green, eventually opening out into hanging red tassels, while the tiny seed catkins, hard and oval, slowly open and from these the seeds are released, while the empty cones dry and shrivel on the twigs right through the winter.

Another tree which is apt to lose its proper form and develop into a big straggling bush is the Hazel, though it does at times grow into a tree 50 or 60 feet high. It is a tree with a long history and the Romans knew it well, using its supple twigs for tying up the shoots of the vine.

At any time in the early part of the year the Hazel catkins appear, the " lambs' tails " as children have called

ONE OF THE WILLOW FAMILY

The Willows are a numerous family and there are many different kinds in this country, but most of them possess certain common characteristics: rapid growth, smooth bark when young but furrowed as they grow older; long, thin, pliant branches. The White Willow shown above is, perhaps, the best known, with its narrow silky leaves covered on both sides with grey down.

them for centuries past. These are the stamens and when the tightly-folded scales begin to open the yellow heads within ripen and burst. The bright red threads of the tiny seed flowers, which look like buds, catch the fine powder as it is blown from the cat-kins. The seed flowers produce ripe Hazel nuts in the autumn.

The leaves of the Hazel are roundish, fairly large and broad, and taper to a point with teeth cut round the edges. They are rather rough leaves, covered with a network of veins which seem to give a puckered effect to the leaf. Yet these leaves hang on longer than most others and only the chill winds of the winter strip them from the branches.

Hazel shoots are used for basket-making and the branches make fishing-rods and walking-sticks. It is with the aid of a Hazel rod that many water-diviners work. A diviner grasps a springy, forked rod in such a manner that it dips sud-denly when he passes over underground water.

THE NUT-BEARING HAZEL

In common with several other trees the Hazel often decides not to develop into a tall tree, but instead grows into a large straggling shrub. Early in the year the " lamb's tails " or catkins appear. Later come the nuts, different varieties of which are known as filberts, cob-nuts and Spanish nuts.

Chestnuts and Conkers

We have two trees bearing the name of Chestnut in this country: the Sweet or Spanish Chestnut and the Horse Chestnut. Actually, they are not related to each other and the only resemblance that does exist is in the outward appearance of their fruits, the well-known chestnuts which can be eaten and the horse-chestnut, com-monly known as the " conker." The Sweet Chestnut is the true chestnut tree, large and bushy with beautiful thick, glossy leaves, 8 or 9 inches long,

sharply oval in shape and with strongly-toothed edges.

The trunk of the Sweet Chestnut is massive, and while the bark is at first smooth and brown it becomes grey and strongly marked with deep ridges which twist in a slightly spiral direction as the tree grows older. In May and June come the flowers, the stamens in long catkin spikes, while near the foot of the same spike are the seed flowers. The dust from the stamens falls on the green upright points of the seed flowers and in due course, after the stamen flowers have withered and fallen, the fruit appears—a round green ball covered with prickles. When this green covering splits in October the seeds, or nuts, fall to the ground. In this country these chestnuts do not usually ripen properly nor grow so large as in the sunnier climes of Southern France and Italy.

THE PLANE TREE

There are two or three kinds of Plane trees growing in Britain: the Oriental from the South and the Occidental first introduced from America, while the Plane which flourishes in London's streets and squares is the Maple-leafed Plane. An outstanding characteristic of Planes is that the bark strips off in patches.

The Horse Chestnut has a very different leaf from the real Chestnut, its large leaves being formed of seven long leaflets, each pear-shaped with narrow end joining the leaf stalk. These leaves are not all the same size and run two small, two medium and three large leaves or leaflets, all toothed round the edges, to form the one big leaf.

In May the flowers come, big white or pink pyramids standing stiffly erect and giving the tree a wonderfully ornamental appearance. The upper flowers on these pyramids or spikes have no seed-vessel and fall off when their stamen dust has been blown about. It is the lower flowers which produce the rough green balls, similar in a way to the Sweet Chestnut fruit, but not prickly all over. Instead there are a few thick prickly spikes, some distance apart.

When this green ball is fully ripe it splits and inside is the nut. In the sweet chestnut there are two or three dull-looking nuts; in the horse chestnut there is one nut only and that gives the appearance of having been highly polished. The horse chestnut is the schoolboys' " conker," and is a very different fruit from the sweet chestnut, as a small nibble will prove. Nor will horses eat it, though cattle and sheep appear to like it.

Tall Poplars of Lombardy

There are several kinds of Poplar tree grown in Britain and all like open spaces best, preferably where there is plenty of moisture. Probably the most distinctive of the Poplars is the one that was first introduced into this country less than 200 years ago, the Lombardy Poplar. Here is another tree which is very easy to identify. Tall and slender, its branches grow upwards so that the whole tree has the shape of a flaming torch, or is not unlike a church spire. The stamen flowers, drooping red catkins, grow on one tree while the seed flowers, little green capsules on hanging stems grow on another. When ripe ·these capsules burst open to reveal a tiny white fluffy cotton ball with small seeds among the cotton.

It is highly unlikely, however, that you will see these seed flowers on any tree in this country as practically all the Lombardy Poplars in Britain are male trees and are propagated by cuttings and suckers. When fully grown these trees may reach a height of 150 feet.

The White Poplar, sometimes known as the Abele tree, takes its name from the light colour of its bark and the white underside of its dark green leaves which are roughly heart-shaped. The trunk is straight, but, unlike the Lombardy Poplar, the branches grow out in a horizontal direction instead of turning upwards and trying to keep parallel with the trunk. It is a much broader tree than its Lombardy brother, though not nearly so tall, 60 or 80 feet being an average height.

A very close relation of the White Poplar is the grey variety, with leaves having undersides of grey instead of white. Then another kind is the Black Poplar, and here again the name comes from the colour of the leaves, which, though not really black, are dark green on both sides. There are other little

SYCAMORE OR GREAT MAPLE TREE

The Sycamore was originally given this name in error and it really belongs to the Maple family. It is also sometimes known as the Mock Plane, owing to its habit of shedding patches of its bark as the Plane trees do. Winds have little effect upon it and it is invariably a tree of symmetrical growth.

differences between these Poplars, but they are not very important ones, white, grey and black all making graceful trees, with the black variety usually the smallest of the three.

A Trembling, Quivering Tree

The Aspen is also a member of the Poplar family and has many resemblances to its cousin. The leaves, dark green above and a paler green on the underside, are attached to the branch by a long thin stalk. The result is that the foliage is almost continually in motion and even the faintest breeze is sufficient to set the leaves quivering. " Trembling like an aspen-leaf " is a popular saying, and Scott referred to its peculiar characteristics when he wrote " Variable as the shade, By the light, quivering aspen made."

Its bark is grey and its branches spreading, while it grows to a height of 40 or 50 feet. The flowers are borne in catkins not unlike the other Poplars, but both the stamen and the seed catkins are very similar in appearance and grow on the same tree.

The Willow trees are a large family, but the differences between many of them are not very great. The White Willow and the Goat or Sallow Willow are two of the best known. Most Willows like a moist soil and are usually found along river banks or in water meadows. The stamen and seed flowers grow on separate trees. The White Willow leaves are narrow and covered on both sides with grey down. This gives the tree a glistening grey look when seen from some little distance.

Occasionally the Goat or Sallow Willow becomes a tall tree, but like so many other willows it is more usually found in bush form with short, tough stem sending up many tall, slender branches with smooth, purplish-brown peel. Early in spring the flowers appear before the leaves and the velvety buds have given it the name of " pussy willow " or " palm," and branches are used for decorative purposes at a time when flowers are not so plentiful. The leaves of the Goat or Sallow Willow are not the long and narrow type of most willows but are broader, rather oval-shaped with toothed margins, and tapering to a short, curling point.

THE LIME OR LINDEN

The Lime, like the Plane tree, thrives in the smoky streets of our large cities, but it flourishes best in fairly open spaces where there is plenty of air and sunlight. Its flowers appear in May, and the small fruits appear later in clusters, but these fruits very rarely ripen in England.

Useful to Sportsmen

Nearly all willow branches are tough and flexible and so are often used for basket-making. From the trunk of the

THE MUCH-PRIZED WALNUT TREE

A tall, spreading tree, with distinctive grey bark, the Walnut is not merely one of our most handsome trees but is valuable in several other ways. Fine furniture is made of its wood, and juices extracted from the tree are the basis of a useful stain, while the nut it produces is excellent in its raw state or in pickle. The oil from the nuts is highly regarded by artists as a medium for mixing their paints.

Willow cricket bats are made and "Willow the King" has been praised in song and prose by cricket-lovers.

While thinking of the trees that are not among the stately or noble ornaments of field, forest and parklands but are more in the "common or garden" class, the Hawthorn must take a front place. There is nothing very imposing even about a full-grown Hawthorn, but it is a friendly, happy tree doing a lot of useful work besides having an ornamental side at certain times of the year.

It is often called May, and sometimes referred to as Whitethorn, because of the flowers with which it clothes itself in May. It has had its place in history, too. Homer tells how the father of Ulysses was preparing to plant a hawthorn hedge when his son came home from his wanderings, and there is a story concerning the wonderful hawthorn staff of Joseph of Arimathea. In England when May time came they used to dance round the Maypole, which was decorated with Hawthorn blossom.

As these blossoms fade the berries form. They are green at first but gradually change to red. These are the haws and birds eat them gladly. The leaves are pale green at first, cut into blunt fingers, but they become darker and more glossy as the summer comes, then turn yellow, red or brown before the frosts come to strip them from the branches.

Well Known to Londoners

The Plane tree is not a native of Britain. One kind, the oriental, came from southern Europe and the Levant some four centuries ago, while the western variety came to us about a century later from America. Then there is a cross between these two known as the Maple-leafed Plane, and sometimes called the London Plane, since it is this variety of the tree which thrives so well in the streets and squares of our great city.

There are not many differences between these three Planes and all grow to a height of 70 to 90 feet. The trunk is smooth and massive, ash-grey in colour, and a peculiarity of the bark is that it peels off in places, leaving patches of greenish yellow. This curious characteristic helps to identify the tree quite easily. The leaves are broad, smooth and quite thin, lying flat when laid down. They are divided into broad fingers, sharply pointed, and cut all round with pointed teeth.

The base of the leaf stalk fits like a cap over the resting-bud of next year's growth. Early in spring the seed balls appear, dangling in little green chains. One ball is the stamen and when these are ripe their pollen dust is blown away. The seed balls, similar in appearance, have small green seeds, and, after the stamen dust has fallen on them, they develop into small hard nuts which remain on the tree through the winter but are carried away by the breezes in spring when the seeds are scattered.

A tree that is sometimes called the Mock Plane, though it is really no relation to the Plane, is the Sycamore or Great Maple. The Sycamore is actually one of the Maple family but was misnamed Sycamore (meaning fig or mulberry) when it was first introduced here five hundred years ago. The name has stuck and this large tree with wide-spreading branches is covered with masses of thick foliage. The bark is light grey, which often peels off and leaves patches of different shades, a habit that sometimes misleads people to think it is a Plane tree. It is a well-shaped tree and unlike most trees its development is not affected by the prevalent winds; it grows symmetrically wherever it may be placed.

The leaf is shaped rather like a large hand with five thick fingers having toothed edges. They grow on long stalks in clumps of different-sized leaves. Often these leaves are disfigured with small black spots caused by a fungus growth which frequently attacks the Sycamore. The flowers appear before the leaves are fully out and grow in drooping spikes or pendants of yellowish-green. When they wither the seed develops wings with two seeds at the joint where the wings are attached to the stalk. When these seeds are ripe the pink-tinged wings are blown off by the wind and carried some distance before falling to the ground. There they lie till the hard covering slowly decays and the seeds are ready to send up the first small shoots of a new tree.

A Tall and Stately Tree

A tree that shares with the Plane a taste for town life is the Lime or Linden. It thrives quite happily in the smoke and grime of our great cities, but it grows even better in the wider spaces of the countryside. There are three kinds of Lime: small-leaved, broad-leaved, and the Common Lime. A tall, stately tree, with smooth, grey-green bark which becomes slightly furrowed in older trees, the Lime lives to a fairly good age, four or five centuries being not uncommon.

In the spring the Lime twigs seem to be coloured a delicate green touched with crimson until the buds open and the pale emerald green leaves break forth. These leaves are heart-shaped, pointed at the end, and finely-toothed round the edges. The flowers hang in clusters of yellow-coloured heads which attract bees to gather the sweet juice from which they make their honey. The bees also help to fertilise the seed-vessels. Lime tree honey is highly prized for its flavour.

A little above the flowers is a small leaf or bract and when the flowers have set and the fruits are ripe this bract serves as a wing to carry the seed away from the tree.

The Walnut tree is not nearly so

TREES THAT BEAR CONES

One of the largest and oldest woodland families is the Conifer or cone-bearing species of tree and shrub. In the drawing above five of the best-known Conifers are seen, each with its cone or berry: 1. The Pine, whose soft timber, known as deal, is largely used by builders; 2. Cypress, which ranges in height from 4 feet to 80 feet; it is chiefly used for ornamental purposes; 3. The Yew, one of the slow-growing, long-lived trees; it does not bear a true cone but has a red berry; 4. Larch, which, unlike other conifers, is not an evergreen and sheds its leaves in winter; 5. Fir, of which there are many varieties though the Silver species is generally accepted as the true fir.

common in these days as it once was in this country. When its value for timber was appreciated a century and a half ago people began to cut down Walnut trees ruthlessly and that tremendous reduction in their number has never been made up. It is a fine tree both in appearance and in its usefulness, producing nuts, oil and timber. The smooth trunk of its earlier years becomes marked and rugged as it grows older. Its branches are twisted though the tips invariably turn upwards.

The leaves are made up of several pairs of leaflets opposite each other on the same stem with a single leaflet at the end. They are smooth and soft and become a pale olive green when fully out. The stamen flowers take a whole year to develop into the slender drooping catkins which, when the time comes, drop from the tree and scatter their pollen dust on the tiny seed-vessels growing on the same tree. These seed-vessels become smooth green fruits about the size of a plum.

This green fruit contains the nut and after it has been gathered and the outer casing grows hard and dry we have the well-known walnut which is so much esteemed as a dessert fruit.

Before History was Written

The Holly tree is too well-known and distinctive to need description. It is scarcely among the forest trees, though it is often found sheltering under large trees in our woodlands. In this country the Holly tree has been known as long as the Oak, and its beginning is lost in the mists before history was written. Its prickly leaves grow low down on the tree, while those at the top are smooth and have only the single prickly point right at the tip of the leaf.

May is the month when the Holly flowers appear in small crowded clusters. Sometimes the same flower has both stamen and seed-vessel and sometimes the two will be separate, or a whole tree will have the tiny white flowers but no seed-vessels. When that happens the Holly will bear no berries when winter comes. It usually happens, too, that if a Holly tree has a good crop of berries one winter there will be a poor show the following winter.

The red berries are poisonous to human beings but harmless to birds. There are some Hollies with variegated leaves and these are cultivated as ornamental shrubs for the garden. The leaves remain on the tree for several years and with new leaves being formed over the same period the Holly is always clothed in its evergreen coat.

Among the Firs and Pines

The Conifers or cone-bearing trees are a large family of great antiquity and include the Firs, such as the Douglas, Silver, Spruce and Larch; the Pines (Scotch, Austrian, Cluster, Weymouth), as well as the Juniper, Cedar, Cypress, and Yew. It may be noted that the Yew does not bear a true cone but grows a red berry instead. In all other ways it remains true to the family habit. The Larch, too, has its peculiarity in the fact that unlike other conifers it sheds its leaves each year and looks rather a gaunt, drab figure in winter.

The Scotch Pine, sometimes though not quite correctly called the Scotch Fir, is a tall, rugged tree, and like many other conifers will be found growing in sandy or poor soil, even though it flourishes still better in deep soil. The lower branches are inclined to drop off, while its bushy rounded top sways and bows before the wind, giving the impression of being a grim, picturesque, weather-beaten old fighter.

Its leaves are rather like green needles with blunt points and the edges are rolled back so that they appear round above and boat-shaped below. The underside is lighter than the upper dark green. Its catkins are of two kinds and grow on the same tree and sometimes on the same branch. The stamen

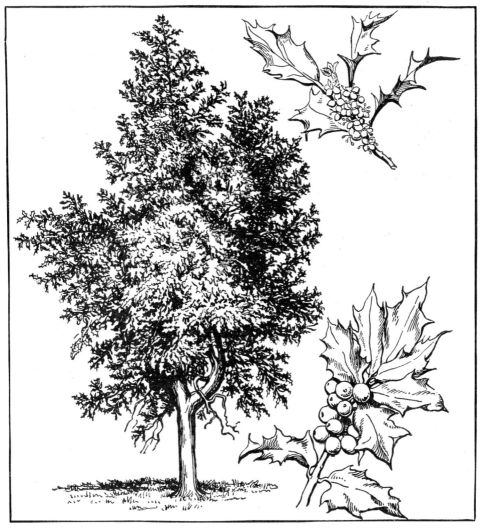

THE HARDY EVERGREEN HOLLY
One of the best-known of our trees and shrubs, the Holly is a native of Britain, though different species have been brought in from other countries. Its leaves are usually dark green and prickly, though there are some varieties with variegated leaves, while others are smooth and much less prickly. The leaves remain on the tree for some years, but new leaves are being formed at the same time so that the holly remains an evergreen.

flowers, bunches of yellow grains from which a tuft of green spears rises, are in dense spikes at the end of last year's twig, but the seed flowers, tiny pale pink cones, come at the end of this year's new twig.

At the end of the first summer the pink cone becomes green but is still soft. During the next year the cone grows harder and bigger, gradually turning ash-grey and becoming woody. Then the tightly-pressed scales curl back, revealing two white seeds at the base of each. When these fall from the cone they are carried away on the breeze to fall on the ground some distance away.

The Spruce Fir is the Christmas tree in its very early years and still maintains that shape as it grows taller.

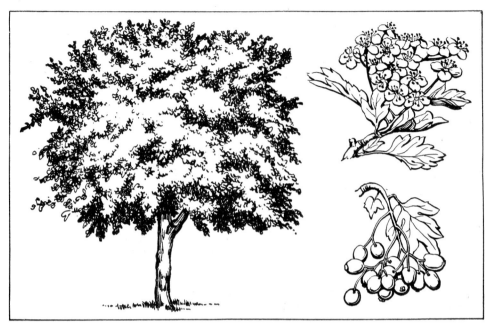

FAIR BLOOMS THE HAWTHORN

Though not one of our great forest trees, the Hawthorn will sometimes reach a height of 30 feet. It is regarded by most of us as a friendly, bushy tree, growing everywhere, and making the world gayer at Maytime with its blossoms, while later in the year its red berries (haws) provide food for the birds.

In appearance the Silver Fir is very similar but the leaves have two silver streaks on the underside.

A conifer that is readily known is the Cedar of Lebanon, a massive and handsome tree which is generally seen in this country as an ornament in a large lawn or parkland. Its lower branches almost invariably droop right down to rest on the ground.

If the Larch looks grim when it has lost its leaves in winter it has compensations in spring and summer when its fine new delicate foliage and wide-spread branches give it a most graceful appearance. It was originally introduced into this country as an ornamental tree but is now one of the most widely-spread of all the conifers in Britain and is easily identified by its broad-based pyramid appearance, its bareness in winter and its delicate foliage when spring renews its growth.

The Yew is among the trees that have helped to make history. At one time the yeoman and fighting men of England carried bows of yew wood from which they shot their arrows. Harold, William Rufus, and Richard Cœur de Lion were slain with arrows shot from yew bows. Nowadays it is apt to be associated more with churchyards than battles, and in Gray's Elegy there is a reference to " that yew tree's shade."

As a tree the Yew grows very slowly and rivals the Oak in longevity. Some specimens are said to be nearly 2,000 years old, yet the tree never reaches any great height, though its trunk attains a huge girth and becomes a curious shape as though several trunks had decided to grow together and the whole tree becomes a dense bush. Yew tree leaves are poisonous to both human beings and animals.

Some of the conifers are grown specially for their timber—the Larch, Douglas Fir, and the Pines are well-known, while other substances such as pitch, resin, and turpentine are obtained from them. The timber of the Firs and Pines is generally known as deal.

UNUSUAL AND INTERESTING PLANTS

DOG VIOLET

A. W. Dennis.

The violet is one of the most widespread of wild flowers and is said always to follow the white man round the world. It actually grows in East Africa and in part of South America. The violets and all the beautiful pansies of our gardens belong to the viola family.

SOMETIMES a tree, a plant, an animal, or a bird is taken from its native country and introduced into another. It may be destroyed at once; or, if its natural enemies are entirely absent, may run absolutely wild. The most terrible example of such a happening was the release of the English rabbit in Australia, and its increase into such numbers as have cost the continent untold sums of money; but a second, and almost equally dreadful, blunder was the importing into Australia of the American cactus called the prickly pear.

This plant was introduced into Queensland about a century ago, and in the next twenty years or so cuttings were distributed to land owners to grow hedges around their homesteads. At first it spread slowly, but birds and aborigines, who liked the fruit, distributed the seeds far and wide. In the

beginning the fruit also proved of value as fodder for the cattle.

All the time it was spreading and by the beginning of the present century it was already regarded by some of the graziers as a pest. Some of them endeavoured to eradicate it from their land, but without success. During the next twenty years an average of nearly 7,000 acres a day was being invaded! Hundreds of square miles of pasture land became a solid barrier of prickly pear, and the hinterland lost the best of its grazing country.

A Valuable Caterpillar

The Queensland Government offered rewards for some means of destroying prickly pear, and a Royal Commission was appointed. Then a scientist member of a travelling Commission investigating the problem discovered that in the Royal Botanic Gardens at La Plata, Argentina,

24—2

PRICKLY PEAR

A native of Mexico and well-known in South America, Prickly Pear was introduced into Australia over a century ago and became popular for hedging, but it flourished too well and by 1883 had become a pest. By 1925 Prickly Pear had 60 million acres in its grip and its control became an urgent Government concern. Eventually a moth (*Cactoblastis cactorum*) was introduced to conquer the pest.

prickly pear was being attacked by the caterpillars of the *Cactoblastis cactorum* moth which seemed to be destroying it.

Many experiments were made before an intensified campaign was carried out between 1927 and 1931. Big stocks of the insect's eggs were imported and distributed in Queensland and New South Wales. The caterpillars bored into the pulpy segments and down to the very roots of the plants.

The effect was dramatic once the campaign was well under way. Mile after mile of prickly pear collapsed and died. From 1930 onwards the insect's operations made tremendous sweeps as the moths flourished and their larvæ multiplied. By 1934 the victory of *Cactoblastis cactorum* was certain. The moth itself flourished or died away according to the amount of prickly pear it found. It is apparently the only plant food on which the larvæ can live.

The conquest of prickly pear and the reclamation of the " pear country " so that it has become excellent sheep pasture land has been a triumph for the tireless investigations undertaken by the small team of scientists who were given the task of solving the prickly pear problem.

A similar kind of problem faced the New Zealand Government some years ago. Settlers imported gorse to cheer them with its golden bloom. The New Zealand soil and fine climate suited the gorse admirably and it increased rapidly. Thousands of acres of rich grazing were ruined, and the peril became so serious that the New Zealand Government applied to the authorities at home to help find something · to check the invader. After much trouble an insect was discovered that feeds on the very young gorse plants while they are spineless and tender, and some were sent out to New Zealand with excellent results.

War on the Blackberry

What at home in England is a friendly sort of fruit, has changed for the worse by emigration, and the blackberry, which in England confines itself to the hedgerows, is marching like an army across the country in New Zealand, and growing to such a huge size that even cattle cannot force their way through its thorny thickets. Thousands of pounds have been spent in vain efforts to defeat it, and in 1926 the Empire Marketing Board granted £2,000 a year for five years to help in the fight with this and other invaders. The storm troops in the campaign are insects collected in various parts of the world, which feed upon the blackberry shoots.

Watercress reached New Zealand from England about the year 1850, and liked the climate so much that it grew 15 feet high with stems as thick as a man's wrist. It blocked almost every river in the country, causing disastrous floods. Fortunately it has now returned to its usual English size, but is still a most troublesome weed.

Even worse was the Scotch thistle, which grew into perfect trees 14 feet to 16 feet in height and with prickles fit to pierce a good thick boot. This plague was stopped by importing the hedge sparrow, which eagerly devours the seeds.

Some other misguided person brought heather from Scotland and planted it in New Zealand. Now it has simply swamped the Tongariro National Park in the North Island, and the Government is having it all grubbed up.

One more pest that must be mentioned is *couch* or *twitch* grass. Bad enough in England, twitch has played havoc in New Zealand ; and, under the name of *Quack*, is now the most troublesome weed in North America.

A Lovely Peril

About forty years ago a young orange grower settled in Florida had sent him a specimen of the South American water hyacinth. This is a most beautiful plant which floats on the surface of the water and throws up long stalks of exquisite blue flowers. The soft warm water of the clear Florida lakes suited it to perfection and it grew most amazingly. It filled the lakes, it filled the creeks, it filled the great St. John's River (which is in many places four miles wide) so completely that no steamers could get up or down.

The State Government in despair called on the experts from Washington

J. J. Ward.

FLOWERS AND FRUIT TOGETHER

The blackberry is a queer plant, for you will often see flowers and ripe fruit on the same branch at the same time. The blackberry is classed as a deciduous shrub, that is, one which loses its leaves in winter, yet it seems to be turning itself into an evergreen.

to help them.   Poison sprays were used, but it was like trying to put out a volcano with a garden syringe.   At last a kind of mould or fungus was found which would attack and kill the hyacinth, and the plague was stayed.

Waterways in Danger

It was just before Queen Victoria came to the throne that here in England we were threatened with a danger very similar to that from which Florida has suffered.   About the year 1836 a Canadian water weed, the water thyme (*Elodea canadensis*), appeared in an English river. No one knew how it came, and no one paid much attention to it for quite a long time, when it was noticed that the plant was spreading rapidly.

Within five years the water thyme

M. H. Crawford.

SCOTLAND'S BADGE

"*Nemo me impune lacessit*" is the Latin motto which appears under the Scottish thistle.   "No one provokes me with impunity" is what it means, and truly the big Scots thistle is the thorniest plant imaginable. It is one of the finest of British thistles.

was blocking ponds, rivers and even canals all over the country.   It took to its new home with amazing enthusiasm, and grew as it had never grown in Canada.   Dredges were set to work, but did very little good, and in those days people knew nothing of the insects and fungi which are now used to destroy unwanted plants.   For twenty years the weed spread and spread, and then oddly enough the great spurt of growth ceased, and though you will still see it in most English waters, it is no longer the peril it once was.

Garden Flowers run Wild

Very often a cultivated flower will escape from a garden and run wild. On the St. Vincent's Rocks at Clifton wallflowers grow in masses, and so does Valerian on the chalk cliffs near Broadstairs; the blue periwinkle is often met with along our roadsides, and the mimulus grows beside many a Devonshire river. (The mimulus, by-the-by, is really musk or the "Monkey Flower.") Snapdragon frequently blooms on quarry edges far away from gardens, and the ivy-leaved toad-flax or "Kenilworth Ivy" bespangles many a wall with its myriads of tiny flowers.

In similar fashion many English wild flowers have followed British colonists to all parts of the world.   The Indians of North America call the common plantain "The White Man's Footstep," because it seems to appear wherever white men have settled.

The hawthorn, in a bush of which the crown of Richard III. was hidden, has pushed its way to Australia, South Africa, and many other parts of the Empire. The sweetbrier has grown into huge thickets in Tasmania, and become such a nuisance that farmers grub it up wherever it is seen. The wild rose, too—the dog-rose as we call it—has colonised the same island, and grows larger and finer there than in English hedgerows.

White clover has naturalised itself in South Africa, while English dog-violets bloom along the railway embankments in Kenya Colony, East Africa. Mallow, chamomile and milk thistle cover huge tracts of land in the Argentine, and the artichoke has made itself a great plague there, for it grows to a huge size and is difficult to destroy.

Following the Flag

Two plants which seem to follow the flag all over the world are the raspberry and the blackberry. The former is now spreading across North America.

In parts of Brazil can be found borage, wild geranium and fennel, which fight for life against the native plants. Near St. Theresia on the Rio Negro, in Patagonia, and close to the Andes, an astonished traveller found whole colonies of violets growing wild.

Even in the Arctic regions plants act as colonists, for the former abodes of the Greenland settlers can be traced by the vetch or tare which grows on the long-abandoned sites.

M. H. Crawford.

BUCK'S-HORN PLANTAIN

The plantain is known to the Indians as " The White Man's Footstep," because it seems to follow him all over America. The Buck's-horn Plantain here pictured grows in poor, sandy soils, usually near the coast. It blooms from June to August.

FLESH-EATING PLANTS

SEEING that we ourselves live largely upon plants and that the animals, such as oxen and sheep, the flesh of which we eat, are also *graminivorous* (that is, grass eaters), it seems surprising to hear of plants that live on flesh. Yet there are such plants—quite a number of them; and you can find some even in our own country.

Scattered over the moors of Scotland, Wales and Devonshire, and also on the sandy dunes close to the sea, numbers of tiny plants can be seen nestling among the grasses just above the soil. They are rosettes of eight to twelve small leaves, of which the outer ones touch the ground while the inner are pointed upwards. These are called Butterworts, and are so small that they often escape notice, though some of them have violet-coloured, bell-shaped flowers.

Pull up one of these little plants and look at its leaves under a magnifying glass. You will be surprised to see that they are covered with small, knob-like glands, from which there oozes a thick greasy fluid which is so sticky that it can be drawn out in long threads like treacle. You will also notice that some of the leaves have small insects adhering to them. The leaves act, in fact, like

M. H. Crawford.

(1) Although small, the sundew is one of the most interesting of British plants. It lives in bogs and marshes.

H. Bastin.

(2) Here we see one of the leaves of a sundew attracted by a piece of raw meat at the end of a thread.

H. Bastin.

(3) The glands secrete a clear, sticky fluid which catches insects which settle on the leaf. The leaf then curls up.

H. Bastin.

(4) The insect is caught in the hollow and digested exactly as it would be in the stomach of an animal.

THE CURIOUS VENUS'S FLY=TRAP

S. Leonard Bastin.

(1) The Venus's Fly-Trap, a North American plant, has developed a wonderful mechanism for catching flies.

S. Leonard Bastin.

(2) When an insect touches the sensitive hairs in the centre of each lobe of the leaf, the teeth interlock.

Harold Bastin.

(3) " A terrible plant from the standpoint of flies " is what our photographer says of Venus's Fly-Trap, and when you see how big it grows and how many separate traps each plant sets for the insects you realise the truth of this remark.

R. A. Malby.

THE PITCHER PLANT (1)

Here is one of the Nepenthes, or pitcher plants, common in many tropical countries. The " pitcher " is formed on a stalk at the end of the leaf and is filled with sweetish water which attracts insects. These die, their bodies decay, and the plant makes use of their remains as food.

glutinous fly-paper, and the insects, when they are caught, are rolled up in the leaf and digested.

A Living Fly-paper

The Sundew, which is even smaller than the butterwort, is equally good as a fly-trap, and there are few things more interesting to watch than one of these leaves at work. Place on the leaf a morsel of raw meat as big as a pin's head, and notice what happens by means of a strong magnifying glass. The leaf hairs which are really glands, bend over towards the meat and cover it with some sort of digestive fluid. More and more tentacles fasten upon the food, and if it is a large piece the whole leaf curls over upon it. When all the nourishment has been extracted from the food the leaf opens again and drops the useless remains.

A sundew, if dug up and kept in a saucer in wet moss, will live for a long time, and its methods of feeding can be studied. If a bit of stone or glass is put on the leaf instead of food the leaf curls, but very soon finds out how it has been cheated and drops the useless prey. It is just as well to warn readers that a little goes a long way with a sundew. One minute particle of meat or white of egg will last the tiny plant for a week, and if too much is given the plant dies of over-feeding.

Trapping Real Insects

Butterworts and sundews are found all over Europe, and the people of Lapland use the juice from the leaves of the butterwort for the purpose of making a kind of rennet which curdles milk and turns it into junket. Other countries have other sorts of insect-eating plants of which one of the most

R. A. Malby.

THE PITCHER PLANT (2)

This is the cup of another of the Nepenthes, which has been cut open in order to show the inside. There are at least forty sorts of pitcher plants. The length of the pitcher varies from 2 inches to a foot, and it is often delicately coloured.

interesting is Venus's Fly-trap, found in many parts of North America. This plant is so sensitive that the merest touch of an insect on one half of its divided leaf causes the leaf to snap together like a spring trap, capturing its prey with wonderful certainty.

Farther South live the Pitcher Plants, in which a part of the plant forms a perfect little cup or pitcher which is partly filled with a liquid which seems to attract insects just as honey and beer in a bottle attract wasps.

The insects fall into this fluid and the plant digests their juices. There are many kinds of pitcher plants and bladderworts, some of which actually devour their catches; while others live on the products of the dead and drowned bodies of the victims. Some of the pitcher plants are so large that birds, mice and even rats have been found in their " larders."

M. H. Crawford.

DEADLY NIGHTSHADE

A big, strong plant, growing 3 feet or 4 feet high, the deadly nightshade likes chalky soil. The whole plant has an unpleasant smell and is all poisonous, but the glossy berries, each as big as a cherry, are deadly. Another name for the plant is " Belladonna."

The bladderworts are floating pond-plants which catch small creatures like water-fleas in an underwater trap like a little bladder.

A Moth Catcher

Araugia Albens is the name which scientists have given to a plant growing in Central Africa, which has a peculiar appetite for moths. The plant has large, white, very sweet-smelling flowers which are a great attraction to moths. But the whole thing is a heartless fraud, for when the moth dives down into the calyx (cup) of the flower, and pushes its proboscis in after the honey which it expects to find, it is suddenly nipped between two strong, hard, black pincers and devoured. The araugia has been imported into Australia in the hope that it will catch some of the moths, the caterpillars of which destroy fruit.

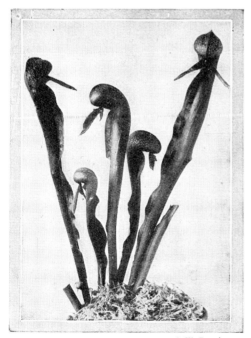

A. W. Dennis.

ANOTHER LIVING TRAP

On the western side of the North-American continent we find a different type of insect-eating plant, the Darlingtonia, of which this is a Californian specimen. It is very similar to the pitcher plant, for each of these stalks is hollow and acts as a trap for flies.

BEWARE OF THESE BERRIES

(1) There are two sorts of buckthorn in Great Britain. This is the alpine one that bears berries, from which is made syrup of buckthorn, a medicine for ailing dogs.

(2) Broad, hairy leaves and large rounded heads of white flowers make the Viburnum, or wayfaring tree, a favourite. Later the flowers are succeeded by berries of glowing coral.

(3) The spindle tree may be 20 feet high, but usually grows only to 12 feet. The shiny leaves have toothed edges. The scarlet berries in their orange cups are poisonous.

(4) It is the leaves and seeds of the yew tree that are poisonous, not the fleshy part of the pink berry, yet this cannot be recommended as food except for birds.

BERRIES THAT ARE HARMLESS

M. H. Crawford.

(1) Shiny black, the berries of the elder have long been a favourite with country folk for making elderberry wine, which is a drink with a pleasant taste.

A. W. Dennis.

(2) We have noted elsewhere the way in which the blackberry is changing from a deciduous to an evergreen bush. The fruit becomes more popular every year.

M. H. Crawford.

(3) The sloe is the fruit of the blackthorn, which flings out its snowy bloom early in spring before there is a leaf on the tree. Sloes are too sharp to be considered eatable.

A. W. Dennis.

(4) Commonest of all hedge shrubs is the hawthorn or May tree whose lovely white or pink blossom is succeeded by bright red berries called "haws."

A. W. Dennis.

MISTLETOE

A betwixt and between plant, mistletoe is not a tree or a shrub or a flower. It is a parasite which grows on a variety of trees, the apple more often than any other, but is frequently seen on the poplar. Many varieties of mistletoe are found in different parts of the world. Portugal has one with pretty pink berries, and America a species which frequently grows upon oaks, although the English mistletoe has no special liking for oak.

The Curious Cordyceps

Years ago an early settler in New Zealand wrote home that he had met a creature that was half caterpillar, half plant, but the story was laughed at as a traveller's tale. Yet it is quite true.

There is a whole family of plants— vegetable parasites known as *Cordyceps* —which actually grow on living insects and spiders. One variety belonging to the West Indies makes itself the guest of a kind of wasp, and the insect may be seen flying about with a plant growing from it as great as the length of its own body.

Others of the cordyceps sow themselves on the bodies of caterpillars or grubs, as is the case with the New Zealand sort already mentioned, and a caterpillar three inches long may have **six inches of plant sprouting from its**

body. The Chinese call a similar variety " the summer grass of the winter worm." In the long run, of course, the plant destroys its unfortunate host.

POISON PLANTS

IN the autumn the hedgerows hang thick with wild fruits and berries, some of which, like the blackberry, are pleasant and wholesome, while others are so poisonous that eating them is almost certain death.

The worst of the lot, the deadly nightshade, resembles a ripe black cherry. Holly berries are mildly poisonous, but they are also very bitter. The best rule is never to eat any berry you don't *know* to be good.

Plants that Poison the Skin

Of these the one we all know best is

THE STORY OF THE MISTLETOE

(1) We usually cut mistletoe for the sake of its berries, but here is mistletoe in bloom.

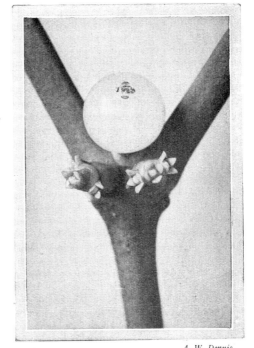

(2) Here you see the female bloom of the mistletoe and one berry (*magnified*).

(3) This is a section of an apple branch showing the way in which mistletoe roots.

(4) This bunch is twenty years old for each branch forks twenty times.

the nettle. Each hair of the nettle is a separate little hollow needle provided with a poison gland at its base. When you touch a nettle leaf the needle not only pricks you, but also injects a tiny dose of poison. The sting of a nettle is painful, yet not dangerous, but in other countries there are nettles which are as much worse than ours as a hornet's sting is worse than that of a wasp. One of the most terrible of these plants is the " Ongaonga," or New Zealand nettle. It is rather a pretty shrub growing 8 feet or 10 feet high. The under side of each leaf is set with hair-like spikes which are terribly poisonous. The spines will pierce the skin of a horse as easily as that of a man, and a dog who chased a rabbit through a

clump of these nettles and was pricked on the tongue died the same night.

Another dangerous plant is the " Devil's Club," which grows in the coastal forests of British Columbia, and a third is the poison ivy (*Rhus toxicodendron*). This is a creeper which strongly resembles the common Virginian Creeper, but is most hideously poisonous. It may cause dreadful inflammation from which it takes months to recover. It is a plant that ought to be destroyed on sight—rooted up and burned—for it is a treacherous thing, trading as it does on its likeness to the harmless *Ampelopsis*.

Daffodil pickers suffer badly from a rash caused by the poisonous juice of this beautiful flower, but the most dangerous of garden flowers is the *Primula obconica*, the one with pretty heads of pink flowers, which is so often grown in a conservatory. Round the edges of the leaves are tiny hairs, very sharp, which enter the skin and cause the most dreadful irritation. If these hairs get into the eyes they may cause serious trouble.

We read that the great Greek Socrates was killed by drinking hemlock whilst in prison, and the poisonous properties of this family of plants have been known for thousands of years. The curious point about hemlocks is that several plants of this order are wholesome vegetables. These are the carrot, celery, parsnip and parsley ; and the seeds, even of the poisonous varieties, are harmless.

Beware of Hemlock

The common hemlock is a plant from 3 feet to 5 feet high and its hollow stem is blotched with purplish-red spots. Its heads of white flowers expand in June and July. The water hemlock is equally virulent. It grows in wet places to a height

A. W. Dennis.

CUCKOO-PINT

No hedge plant has more names than this one. " Lords and Ladies," " Priest's Pintle," " Calves' Foot," " Ramp," and " Wake-Robin " are only some of them. The handsome arrow-shaped leaves are spotted black or purple, and the flower-stalk shows a purple " poker."

of about 4 feet. The roots are full of a yellow juice which will actually blister the skin. Farmers call it cow bane, for it is a fatal poison to cows, yet curiously enough it does not kill horses.

The pretty corn cockle belies its appearance, for stalk, leaves, seeds and roots are all poisonous. The Greater Celandine is another treacherous plant containing an alkaloid poison. Soapwort, commoner in the South of England than in the North, a stout, leafy perennial plant, contains a poison called "saponine." In old days the leaves and flowers of soapwort were used for washing purposes. The common laburnum, with its lovely yellow flowers, is poisonous in every part, and children are sometimes made very ill by chewing the seeds. All poppies are poisonous, and it is from these plants that the sleep-giving drugs laudanum, opium and morphine are obtained.

Life and Death Plants

The Indians of South America live largely on the root of the cassava, which is the same plant from which we ourselves make our tapioca puddings. Life and death are blended in this plant in the strangest fashions. Cattle eat the leaves and stalks, the roots are ground into pulp, which, when pressed and baked, forms a kind of bread. Yet the juice found in large quantities in the roots is a deadly poison, and a teaspoonful will kill a strong man in half an hour. The strange thing is that *heat* drives off this poison, so that the root, after being thoroughly crushed and baked, is perfectly wholesome.

HOW PLANTS PROTECT THEMSELVES

A HOLLY tree has prickly leaves. Every leaf is edged with spines, making it difficult and painful to handle. But get a ladder and examine

A. W. Dennis.

CUCKOO-PINT FRUIT

Late in the summer the green stem-casing or hood withers and there appear the scarlet berries. There are two sorts of cuckoo-pint in England. This is the common *Arum maculatum*, a relative of the arum lily. Even the leaves are poisonous, though the roots were once used for starching clothes.

the top of a holly bush, and you will find that at 8 feet or so above the ground the leaves become less spiny, and at the edges most of them are quite smooth. The explanation is that the lower part of the tree is forced to guard itself against the attacks of grazing animals, but the top, being beyond their reach, needs no prickles.

Gorse protects itself in similar fashion, and so does the thistle. So do many other plants of which we shall have more to say later. Why, you may be tempted to ask, does not grass protect itself in similar fashion ? The answer is that grass grows so fast it does not need such protection. Even if grazed level with the ground, the roots are still

THE CHRISTMAS HOLLY

Holly likes a good soil, but it will grow almost anywhere. The leaves at the top of a holly bush often have no prickles. There are many varieties, and one American sort makes a tree 60 feet high. There is another giant holly in the Himalayas with immense leaves.

there, and fresh shoots are thrown up rapidly.

Vegetable Fish-hooks

The thorns flung out by some tropical plants in an effort to protect themselves are of a really dreadful nature. All the cacti are masses of thin, hard, sharp spines, and in some cases these spines are barbed, so that once they get into the flesh it is almost impossible to remove them. Even the fruits are covered with thorns. Such protection is very necessary to plants that live in a desert and which contain a great deal of moisture, for if they were not guarded they would soon be eaten up by various thirsty animals.

Aloes and agaves, which are also desert-dwelling plants, invariably grow most fearful spines. A hedge of aloes planted round a field is better than any barbed-wire fence. A leaf of one of the agaves forms a weapon which might easily kill a large animal if gripped properly and used as a bayonet.

South Africa has some terrible specimens of thorny plants. There is, for instance, the " wait-a-bit " thorn, so hooked that any one who tried to force his way through a thicket of it would have every stitch of clothes, to say nothing of his skin, torn from his body.

The worst of them all is the South African grapple plant, the seed vessels of which are provided with curved hooks almost as hard as iron. Animals which get these hooks into their flesh suffer absolute torture, and there are cases on record of lions being killed by these thorns. They have tried to *bite* them out of their flesh and have been choked. A similar device is used by the Central American " Martynia," which

ALWAYS IN BLOOM

The curious thing about gorse is that although it blooms all through the year it is not really hardy. The great frosts of 1895, 1917 and 1940 killed thousands of acres of gorse down to the very roots. Yet it flourishes on the poorest land, and is a joy in every month of the year.

R. A. Malby.

LIKE A LIVING BAYONET

So sharp and stiff are the leaves of the Agave that horses have been killed by running against their points. The Agaves are natives of Mexico and the adjoining countries, and the leaves, when the fleshy part is soaked away, leave a fibre so strong it can be spun into ropes. The plant is slow-growing, and when fully developed flings up a huge spike of flowers which may be 20 feet high. It is also called the American aloe.

has hooks several inches long and possesses the power of destroying animals in similar fashion.

The nettle is well protected against its enemies by its hair-like poison prickles. Another plant, the dead nettle, has no poison about it, but its defence is to make itself look almost exactly like the quite unrelated stinging nettle. Just as some harmless flies have much the appearance of wasps, so are there many non-injurious plants which mimic poisonous ones, and are therefore left alone.

The wild arum looks succulent, but no animal that has once tried to chew a portion of the leaf of one of these plants will ever repeat the experiment ; for the most terrible inflammation results. The trouble is caused *not by*

poison, but by quantities of small, sharp crystals which pierce the soft skin of the mouth. A plant found in the West Indies, called the " Dumb Cane," has a similar, but even more terrible, effect upon any creature which attempts to chew it. The mouth swells so badly that the unfortunate animal may die of suffocation.

Insect Defenders

Perhaps the strangest of all methods of defence is that used by the " Bull's Horn Acacia," a peculiar tree which grows in Central America to a height of 15 feet or 20 feet. On its trunk and branches appear great curved thorns set in pairs, just like horns. These thorns are hollow, and form homes for a kind of ant, small in size, but able to bite

A FOREST OF WEIRD PLANTS

Fox Photos.

This avenue of giant cacti may be seen in the Exotic Gardens at Monte Carlo, and forms the finest collection of outdoor cacti in Europe. Here you can see clearly that the green parts of all cacti, no matter what their shape, are really modified stems, and not thickened leaves. The leaves, when present, are represented by the sharp spines. The grotesque shapes of these strange plants suggest some bewitched corner of Fairyland, yet they are common enough in many semi-desert countries.

A CACTUS AS TALL AS A HOUSE

Will F. Taylor.

Cacti are among the plants that store water. Many sorts and sizes grow in a garden at Riverside, in California. Cacti are found in all the desert places of the New World, from British Columbia southwards, but most of them belong to the hot deserts of Arizona, California and New Mexico. Some, such as the Candlestick cactus, grow into real trees with hard, woody stems; others are so tiny they may be grown in a bottle. Many have showy flowers, white, yellow and scarlet.

HALF-AND-HALF PLANTS
The humble lichen which spreads itself on
stones is a combination of an alga and a
fungus. Each patch is a colony, consisting
of thousands of individuals, the master
being the fungus, the slaves the green algæ.
Truly the strangest of all plants.

good supply of food. At the base of the
leaves the plant produces a little open
gland which it fills with a sweet, sticky
liquid, of which the ants are very fond
indeed. More than this, it grows a vast
number of little fruit-like bodies which,
under a microscope, look like yellow
pears. There is one of these tiny fruits
at the base of each leaf, and as the
leaves do not all unfold at once, here is
a constant supply of capital provender
for the ants, who break them off one
by one and carry them away into the
hollow thorns which are their homes.

And if you ask how the acacia
came to do all this, and whether the
acacia invited the ants or the ants
persuaded the acacia, we can only
answer that we do not know, but that
the whole strange business is only
one of those scores of interesting
puzzles which Mother Nature offers to
those who watch her mysterious ways.

STRANGE LITTLE PLANTS

THERE is no need to visit Patagonia or Kamchatka to find them.
The most extraordinary plants in
the world are to be found all around

most viciously. You may see
these ants moving all over the
tree, and if a branch is shaken
they fall in showers on the intruder, and bite so severely that he
is glad to make his escape as
quickly as possible. These ants
protect the tree not only from
grazing animals, but from a much
more dangerous enemy, the cele-
brated leaf-cutting or parasol
ant, a creature which will cut up
every leaf on a tree in a few days
and take them away to make
leaf mould on which it raises the
fungus which is its food.

Payment for Ants

In return for these services
the acacia provides its own ant
armies not only with a sound
weather-tight home, but with a

H. Bastin.
LICHEN-COVERED STONES
Here are stones with patches of lichen upon them.
The root-like filaments absorb water and salts from
the porous stone. Lichens propagate by spores.
They are incredibly slow in growth and will last for an
amazing space of time. A patch of lichen on a rock
may be as old as the greatest of trees.

LICHENS FIND A HOME ON TWIGS

H. Bastin.

(1) Lichens are found in every part of the world, even in the Arctic regions and above the snowline on high mountains. Neither baking sun nor intense frost have any power to destroy them. They do much work in breaking down and weakening rocks, but their action is extremely slow. Lichens are pure air plants and are seldom found in large towns.

H. Bastin.

(2) Not all lichens grow on rocks, for some find a home on the twigs of trees or on their trunks. There are no fewer than 6,000 different species of these strange plants known to science and others are constantly being discovered. Some, such as Iceland Moss, can be cooked to form food for man : others, such as the so-called Reindeer Moss, are immensely important, because they are the principal food of caribou and reindeer. From one a kind of brandy is made, and others yield various coloured dyes.

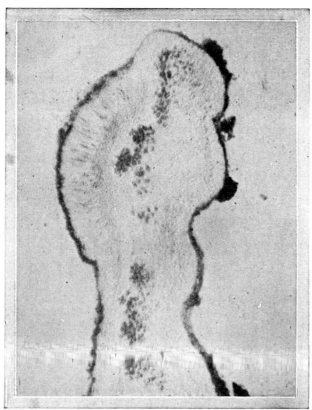

H. Bastin.

THROUGH A MAGNIFYING GLASS

Look at the little dots in the centre of this photograph. They are groups of the algæ which are a part of this strange composite plant, the lichen. The picture represents a section of a lichen, and is, of course, enormously magnified. The algæ cannot be seen with the naked eye.

see them in circular patches of various colours clinging to the rock much more tightly than sealing wax.

Let us look at an old wall well-clothed with lichens. The surface of the stones is nearly covered by thick crusts of these odd plants. The colours are really wonderful. There are many yellows, ranging from pale ochre to citron and orange. There are patches of cream, others of lead, brown, rusty red, and here and there blue-black. The fruit they bear resembles a tiny saucer only one-sixteenth of an inch in diameter, but some of these fruits are of a brilliant scarlet hue, others lake, others again, a dazzling yellow

Food from Stones

How intensely sturdy these little plants must be! On a real summer day the stones grow almost too hot for the hand to touch; in winter they may be covered for weeks at a time with snow or ice. And as for food, well it is difficult to imagine how the plant can get any nourishment at all. Yet the lichen goes on stolidly and grows. Not much of a growth, for even the larger forms do not expand their circles at the rate of more than half an inch a year. The plant gets its food out of the rock itself, and by degrees breaks up and roughens its surface to the point when the stone becomes fit to grow moss, which, in the end, smothers the lichens with its heavier, tougher growth.

The secret of the lichen's ability to " stick it out " under all conditions is that it is a double plant. Each patch is made up of an alga (a simple plant related to seaweed) and a fungus closely combined. The master is the fungus,

you, on every old wall, on granite rocks, sea cliffs, tree trunks, high on the hills and low in the valleys. They are the Lichens (pronounced " lie-kens "), scaly growths so small that few notice them, yet under the microscope or even an ordinary magnifying glass showing wonders you never dreamed.

The Long-lived Lichens

Another queer point about the lichens is the slowness of their growth. Some of them do not begin to seed until they are nearly fifty years old. How long they live no one can say, but certainly for centuries. It is perhaps on cliffs near the sea or above lakes and rivers that lichens are most numerous. You

the slaves are green algæ. The fungus cells develop an acid which dissolves the rock on which the lichen grows, the alga cells get their food from the rock and in return give the fungus the food which is necessary to its existence.

TOADSTOOLS

ONE of the things we should like to know is the name of the man who was brave enough to eat the first oyster ; another is, who had the pluck first to fry a mushroom and make a breakfast off it ?

Mushrooms are only one variety of the enormous family of fungi which vary from giant toadstools larger than a man's head down to spores invisible to the naked eye, such as those which cause the potato disease, and which (as yeast) make our bread rise.

Are Mushrooms Plants ?

Plants you say, but surely mushrooms are not plants ? Well, the ancients did not think so, for they could not conceive of a plant that was not green and had no leaves or blossoms. But we know better, and from the time of Linnæus in the eighteenth century, the fungi have been put in their proper place as a natural order of the plant kingdom.

Some, like the mushroom, grow above ground. Others, like the truffle, spend all their lives below the surface. Their variety is enormous, and even in the small space of the British Isles we have several thousand species of the larger fungi as well as countless sorts of smaller kinds—some good, some bad, some very bad. Not only the potato disease, but many other diseases of

R. A. Malby.

JUST MUSHROOMS
Early botanists were much puzzled about the fungi family, which they did not class as plants at all. They regarded their sudden appearance and rapid growth as an argument for spontaneous generation. It was not until the time of Linnæus, the great Swedish botanist who lived in the eighteenth century, that fungi, including the moulds and mushrooms, were recognized as true plants. The mushroom is only one of many edible fungi. The chanterelle, morel and truffle are all good for food.

plants and animals are caused by fungi. As a matter of fact, there are certain forms of fungi which grow upon the human skin.

But we will not deal with such horrors. It will be more interesting to talk about fungi that are good for food, and—about those that are not.

Foods we Neglect

Let us begin by saying that there are quite a large number of British fungi which are good to eat and only about eight which are definitely poisonous, while a few others are so indigestible that they cause distress. There are several mushrooms better than the one we usually eat.

One is the Fairy Champignon, a mushroom which grows in rings in the open fields. Another is called the St. George's mushroom, and you may find it

often on the chalk downs. Yet another is the white "*helvella*," a queer-looking toadstool with wide, irregularly shaped stalks and small caps stuck on at all sorts of angles. It is found in the strips of coppice or waste land that fringe country lanes, and it is in similar places that you find the "morel." The giant-puff-ball (*Lycoperdon*), cut in slices and fried in egg and breadcrumb, is excellent. It is *white all through*. Large fungi with coloured or viscid flesh should be avoided.

There are red and yellow varieties which grow on trees in the same way as this fungus, but these are unwholesome, if not actually poisonous. "Agaricus deliciosus" deserves its name, and when cooked resembles lamb's kidneys. It grows in fir woods. The "Heterophylla" or Blue Cap has a crayfish flavour.

H. Bastin.

PUFF-BALLS

There are several sorts of globe-like fungus of the Lycoperdon family to which we give the name of puff-ball. All are very quick growers and some reach an enormous size. Puff-balls as big as a man's head are sometimes seen. All puff-balls dry up when old, and when kicked, burst, releasing a yellow dust which flies with the wind, and is, of course, composed of spores or seeds. The common puff-ball is good to eat, but like the "beefsteak" fungus, it should be picked young, cut into slices and fried in butter.

THE POISONOUS SCARLET FLY CAP

M. H. Crawford.

A brightly coloured fungus is never to be trusted. It is a pity we cannot show this particular specimen in colour, for the top is a brilliant scarlet dotted with snow-white warts. It is a poisonous fungus, yet is curiously attractive to flies. It grows in woods of fir and beech. It is often called the Fly Agaric, and can be used as a poison for flies.

J. I. Newman.

JACK IN THE BOX

This is a rare fungus, the Earth Star or Jack in the Box. During the summer the cone lies buried in the earth, but in the autumn the centre rises up into this curious shape. The cap at the top contains the spores which will form new plants.

Some of the cookery books give what they call rules for distinguishing between good and bad fungi, wholesome ones and poisonous. Some say that the poisonous one will discolour a silver spoon ; others that poisonous mushrooms grow under trees or in woods; others again explain that only mushrooms that have pink gills are wholesome. All such rules are pure nonsense. There is only one way to tell a good fungus from a bad one, that is to get someone who knows how to identify the different kinds to teach you.

Giant Fungi

Fungi differ from other plants in that they grow with such immense speed. The great puff-ball will reach the size of a pumpkin in a

single night. A specimen of our largest fungus, *Polyporus squamosus*, 7 feet 5 inches round, was once found and weighed no less than 34 lb. It took four weeks to reach that size, growing at the rate of 19 ozs. a day.

The power exerted by growing fungi is simply terrific. At Basingstoke some of the pavements were found to be uneven and this greatly puzzled the people who had laid them. Then one day a great slab of stone weighing 80 lbs. was found to have been lifted out of place by a huge fungus which had sprouted beneath it. In another case a large kitchen hearth-stone was lifted bodily by a fungus. In old wine vaults gaily coloured fungi may be seen, often suspended from the roof, growing amidst the dust and cobwebs.

H. Bastin.

THE STINKHORN

Some fungi advertise themselves most unpleasantly. Here is a British fungus which has earned the name of Stinkhorn, but it is nothing like so unpleasant as some of its tropical cousins.

THE ORCHID HUNTERS

ON one occasion the late King George VI, visiting a flower show, stopped to admire a most lovely little rock plant with crinkled green leaves and waxy white flowers on short red stems. He asked where it came from, and was told from the Falkland Islands, and that it was brought from there by Mr. Clarence Elliott, who had travelled all that distance simply to look for rock plants.

The plant grows among moss and rocks on the mountain side and it took many days to find it. The climate was very wet and every day the rain poured down. Mr. Elliott found another rock plant which goes by the pretty name of " Pale Maidens," and a third, which the great Charles Darwin called " The Living Stone." This extraordinary plant grows in a great cushion 8 feet or 10 feet in diameter, making it very difficult to move. But Mr. Elliott managed to get three of these to the ship and brought two home safely. One of them is at Kew Gardens, and one was sold to the late Sir Frank Crisp, who had a rockery at his place near Henley-on-Thames, built in the shape of the Matterhorn, and covered with the most wonderful collection of rock plants in England.

Mr. Elliott had great difficulty in keeping his rock plants alive on the 8,000-mile voyage home to England. He made a special little garden on the ship's deck, with an awning over it so as to keep off the hot sun while they were crossing the Equator, and he watered his collection with fresh water every day.

The Romance of Orchid Hunting

Every big firm of seedsmen sends its travellers to scour the wilds of the world on a search for new plants. There is no part of the universe in which these travellers have not been busy, from the forests of Central America to the barren steppes and tundras of Siberia, for on the latter wastes many beautiful flowers grow in the spring and summer.

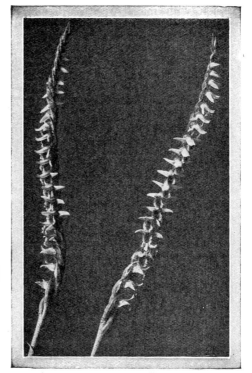

James's Press Agency.

LADY'S TRESSES

It is easy to see how this odd-shaped orchid has gained its name. The flowers are small, but of lovely colour. One great advantage of the orchid as an ornament is that the blooms will remain fresh in water for a very long period, some as much as two months.

The most exciting adventures are those of the orchid seekers. Orchids are the strangest of flowers, for as a rule they do not root in soil at all, but are " epiphytal," that is, they grow like mistletoe, attaching themselves to tree trunks. They need a very damp atmosphere and great heat, so are found only in the depths of tropical forests. The finest specimens are gathered in the heart of the forests of northern South America, Borneo and the other great islands of Polynesia and Melanesia.

The family is a very numerous one, several thousand varieties being known already, and their beauty and marvellous colouring have caused them to be valued above all other flowers. Since the middle of the last century the cultivation of the orchid has become a passion with many wealthy people in Britain and America, and great firms have specialised in their collection.

Fabulous Prices

No price seems too great to be paid for a really rare orchid. Years ago £365 was given for a single small plant of *Cypripedium stonei*, and more recently 1,150 guineas was paid for a little gem with the very long name of *Odontoglossum crispum pittianum.* On another occasion a poor collector attending a sale paid half a crown each for some outcast, unnamed plants, and one of these turned out such a novelty that two years later he sold it for £500.

With such prices it is not wonderful that many men spend years in the hothouse-like atmosphere of tropical jungles, searching for new orchids, and whole books might be written —indeed have been written—of their adventures.

Gems of the South American Forest

One of the best of stamping grounds for the orchid hunter is British Guiana. Imagine yourself one of a party paddling a canoe up the smooth, dark waters of the Demerara River. The canoe turns into a tributary deep and narrow. You see trees covered with golden spikes of flowers, others tinted with rose, a third with blooms of rich crimson. Great swarms of yellow butterflies flaunt in the hot sunshine, and humming birds, living jewels of every imaginable colour, dart to and fro, their wings beating at such a rate that each makes a sound like a giant bumble bee.

Unforeseen Difficulties

But where are the orchids ? It takes a trained eye to discern them, and even when pointed out to you, the wealth of foliage and the mass of vines and " bush ropes " make them very difficult to see. But wait! Here is one which no one

James's Press Agency.   *James's Press Agency.*
THE LADY'S SLIPPER ORCHID
These two pictures represent the same orchid, that on the left the back view, on the right the front. The flower is one of the Lady's Slipper orchids, called Cypripedium. Cypripediums are not difficult to grow, but require to be planted in very small pots in a mixture of peat loam and sphagnum moss. They need a lot of moisture, but the pot must be carefully drained, for these plants will rot in stagnant water.

THE "BABY-IN-A-CRADLE" ORCHID

This quaint and gaily-coloured flower, whose curious form reminds one of an infant just sitting up in a very beautiful cradle with a canopy, belongs to the Anguloa section of orchids. This group takes its name from Angulo, a Spanish collector, and will only live in a greenhouse that is well heated during the winter months. There are nearly a score of separate families of orchids, each family embracing a great many distinct varieties.

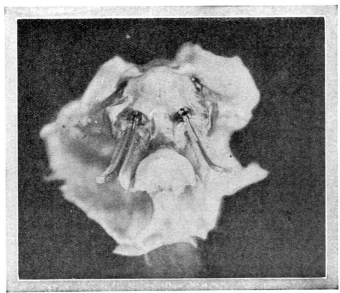

AN " OLD MAN'S FACE "

H. Bastin.

The petals of this flower have been cut away so as to show the extraordinary resemblance of its interior to the face of an old man. The plant is *Schubertia grandiflora*, and is native to Brazil, but frequently cultivated in English hothouses.

can miss. A magnificent mass of pale yellow flowers covering stalks many feet in length. The whole plant is more than a yard in thickness and at least 10 feet in height. It is *Oncidium Altissimum*, not very rare, but such a splendid specimen that the collector vows he must have it.

So the canoe is paddled to the bank and one of the negroes starts to climb after it. But he does not get far. Down he comes shrieking with pain.

" Too much antses," he explains, rubbing his bare legs.

True enough, big black ants have settled on him by the score, and the plant itself is black with the insects all in battle array. It is no use, and the collector reluctantly gives it up and goes on in the hope of finding another less strongly guarded.

Ah! there is one on a branch hanging right over the stream. A cutlass is tied to the end of a bamboo, the whole branch is hacked off and dropped into the water. This drowns the ants and the spendid plant is got aboard.

Hidden Dangers

Further on are many more, Gorgoras, Stanhopeas, Brassias. The Gorgoras' blooms are a purplish-brown, but just beside it hangs the paper-like nest of a swarm of " maribunta," a kind of wasp that stings almost as badly as a hornet. The collector raises his gun and as he pulls the trigger the nest flies to pieces and its remains fall into the river. There are many similar dangers. On one branch close to a very lovely plant a small spotted snake is coiled, and again the gun has to be used before the prize can be secured.

The scenery is entrancing. In places great white water lilies nearly choke the stream; birds, insects, and flowers give every exquisite colour, great fish swim just below the surface, enormous air plants hang in the branches, and if taken hold of deluge the unwary meddler with a quart or so of water which lies in the central cup. But we must not stay too long, for as dusk comes on swarms of mosquitoes bite viciously. A night spent on the river would mean a bad attack of fever, so we turn and paddle back the boat loaded with plants which, if they could be transported straight to London or New York, would fetch many pounds.

Orchid hunters have the strangest adventures. One explorer named Roebelin was sent to the Philippines to find what he could, and was sleeping as the guest of a savage chief in a house built out of reach of wild beasts in a big tree. In the small hours of the morning he was wakened by a deep roaring sound and felt the tree swinging as if in a

AN ORCHID FROM COLOMBIA

James's Press Agency.

Some orchids grow to a very large size and throw out long sprays of bloom. There is one of this type found in Colombia, South America, where it grows in a comparatively limited region around Bogota. This orchid, known as *Odontoglossum crispum*, is seen in this photograph, and is very popular with growers. Orchids are grown in baskets or pots filled with peat and sphagnum moss, with plenty of charcoal and porous crocks so as to ensure good drainage. Very few species require earth around their roots, and some will grow on a bare block of wood.

H. Bastin.

A LOVELY ORCHID

Orchids are the most varied and beautiful flowers in the world. One of the largest families is the Cypripedium, to which this flower belongs. It is a hybrid, that is, a cross between two other orchids, and is called Sir Redvers Buller. Our common Lady's Slipper, shown on page 363, is a Cypripedium.

mighty gale. An earthquake had rent the forest, flung all his companions to the ground, demolished the ladder and left him alone in the tree top. When dawn came he saw through a hole in the broken roof of the tree-house some gigantic flowers of pink, yellow and crimson growing in that very tree, and at once climbed after them. They belonged to a new species which was named *Vanda Sanderiana*, and is said to be the stateliest of all the orchid family.

Another explorer ventured into the wilds of New Guinea, where he found a new orchid growing among the skulls in a cemetery close to a cannibal village. They

were "tabu"—*forbidden*—but he risked his life to get some specimens, and after desperate adventures reached the coast in safety with his prize. Another rare orchid, the purple Phalænopsis, was first seen with the blooms twisted grotesquely in and out among the feather head-dresses of a party of Papuan head-hunters.

Orchids are beautiful, but not particularly useful. Yet there is one exception. Vanilla, so well-known as a flavouring, especially for ices, is made from the seed-pod of a species of orchid which flourishes in Central and South America, and also in the East Indies. The seed-pods grow to a length of fully 6 inches, and a curious point is that the flowers themselves are green or else green and white.

SLIPPER ORCHID   *H. Bastin.*

This is another orchid of the Cypripedium family, and is called the Slipper Orchid. Baron Schroeder, the well-known collector of orchids, once sold a small plant of *Cypripedium stonei* for £365. Another collector bought a batch of these orchids for 3s. 6d. each and sold one for £200.

THE PLANTS WE VALUE MOST

Canadian National Film Board.

HARVESTING CANADA'S WHEAT CROP

Wheat has through many centuries been a foremost plant in its usefulness to man as a staple food. Scientists and engineers have given their aid in producing better grain and in the invention of machines to plough, sow, reap and harvest the crop. Our photograph shows the scene on a big Canadian farm, with three machines known as "combines" harvesting the wheat.

PLANTS AS FOOD

THE origin of wheat as food for man and beast is lost in the mists of antiquity. So far as history goes back man has been growing wheat and grinding its kernels into flour. We cannot even tell from what wild grass wheat was first evolved. Wheat was cultivated in China five thousand years ago; it is found in prehistoric lake dwellings and was the main crop of Egypt in the days of Moses.

The most important Food Grain

Yet it is only in modern times that wheat has been used extensively for bread. In the eighth century the monks of Bury St. Edmund's ate barley bread because they could not afford wheaten bread. In those days, and for long after, wheat produced only fivefold as against fortyfold nowadays. Even so lately as one hundred years ago wheaten bread was only eaten by the better-off, and it is on record that a labourer going into Carlisle market in the year 1825 and wishing to treat himself to a penny roll of wheaten bread, could not find such a thing in the town. There was nothing but oat cake. In 1812 wheat was one hundred and twenty-six shillings a quarter; in 1892 the price had fallen to twenty-eight shillings.

To-day wheat is grown in every part of the world where the climate allows, in India, Australia, the Argentine, Canada, and in every part of Europe, and is the most important of food grains.

Maize or "Indian Corn"

Wheat will not grow in the tropics, and there its place is taken by Maize or Indian Corn. In old days, before Columbus reached America, maize was

Camera Press.

TRANSPLANTING RICE

Rice is the principal crop of the East and requires flooded ground for its growth. The grain is broadcasted thickly in the first place, and after it is sown water is allowed to cover the land. When the young plants are about 6 inches high they have to be transplanted, and our photograph shows this work in progress. Rice is grown in Spain and Italy as well as in the East, and the best of all comes from the American State of South Carolina.

known in England as Turkey wheat and was imported from the Eastern Mediterranean. The name Indian Corn was given to it by the early settlers in America who found the Red Indians growing it. Columbus himself was the first to import maize from America, and to-day the American crop exceeds two thousand million bushels yearly.

Maize is a plant with many uses. The green ears are boiled and eaten as a vegetable, the ripe grains, when roasted, are made into popcorn, and the plant is one of the chief sources of starch manufacture. The stalks are used for thatching and fuel and the green leaves as fodder for cattle.

Glucose, a kind of sugar, is made from maize, and the juice of the stems of sugar corn is fermented into a kind of beer. One more interesting use is the making of pipe bowls out of the *cobs*. Corn cob pipes are cheap and much used by farmers in America.

Maize is more nourishing than either barley or rye, though not so feeding as good wheat. It is a most beautiful plant, growing much larger than any other grain. In rich soil it will stand 6 feet to 8 feet high, and its broad green leaves and graceful tassels of bloom make a field of maize a joy to the eyes of one who sees it for the first time.

All About Rice

In one way rice is the most important of all food plants because a greater number of people live on it than on either wheat or maize. Nearly half the world's population depends mainly on rice for food, and even a country like Great Britain uses enormous quantities of rice. In India and Pakistan sixty million acres are under rice, in Ceylon nearly a million, while China, Japan and the Philippines grow a quantity that can hardly be imagined. Oddly enough the best rice in the world is grown in Carolina, one of the United States, where the cultivation began about two hundred years ago.

Rice is a wet plant; it must have a moist soil or the seed will not germinate. *Paddy* fields, as they are called in the East, are usually so arranged that they can be flooded. The worst of this

GRACEFUL COCONUT PALMS

The coconut is the most valuable to man of all the palms, and will grow in almost any part of the tropics, but thrives best near the sea. This grove is on a South Sea island.

is that fevers are caused by the swampy state of the ground, so that rice-growing is anything but a healthy occupation.

Rice has been grown for such an immense length of time that a very great number of different varieties have been evolved. At an exhibition in Calcutta four thousand distinct sorts of rice were shown.

The chief objection to rice is that one cannot make bread from the grain because it has so little *gluten*. So as a rule it is eaten boiled. The straw is used for hat making, but the rice plant has fewer uses than maize.

The Invaluable Potato

The first known use of potatoes in Europe was in 1572, when they were being grown at Seville, in Spain, but it was not until 1586 that the first potato was planted in England in a garden in London. Sir Walter Raleigh then obtained some tubers from a herbalist

A HUMAN MONKEY

A coconut palm runs up to a height of 40 feet to 60 feet, yet the black boy trained to the work thinks little of climbing the tall, straight stem to reach the mass of nuts hanging among the feathery leaves. The trunk is rough, and his feet are as good for gripping as those of any ape.

R. A. Malby.

A SPROUT

You may not recognise this coconut because it is still covered with its outer coat or husk, whereas the nuts sold in the shops have had this peeled off. This nut has evidently been lying on the ground for some months; for, as you will notice, it has begun to sprout.

and cultivated them at Youghal in Eire. To-day the potato forms one-quarter of the food of Europeans and English-speaking peoples, and has become not only the most popular of vegetables, but by far the most important.

It is a wonderful happening that a few tubers brought across the ocean from one continent to another should become the parents of such a widely-grown staple food. Clever hybridists, however, working mostly on the rich soil of Lowland Scotland, are constantly producing new and better varieties of potatoes. Thus as the older sorts weaken and become literally worn-out, there are vigorous young kinds to take their places, so that evolution continues all the time.

Besides its value as a vegetable, the potato yields spirit, glucose for confectionery, flour for cooking and great quantities of starch.

The Coconut Palm

Let us turn to trees. Of these the most useful to man is without doubt the coconut palm, of which about thirty separate sorts are known, and which is grown in every part of the tropics, Africa, Asia, America and the islands of the South Seas. Plantations have also been established in Northern Australia. This beautiful palm begins to produce fruit at seven or eight years of age and goes on bearing for seventy or eighty years. Immense numbers of natives live on the kernel of the nut, but the principal value of the coconut to the world is the quantity of valuable oil, or coconut butter, which it contains, and which is used for making margarine, cold cream and for many other purposes.

But every part of the coconut is useful in one way or another. The rough fibres from the outside of the nut are used for stuffing mattresses and cushions, and for making coconut matting; the dried leaves are used for thatch; toddy and sugar are made from the palm *cabbage* or bud. The wood, too, is valuable, for it takes a high polish, and is imported into England under the queer name of *porcupine* wood. Even the roots are good for something, for a narcotic drug (sleeping draught) can be made from them. The shells of the nut itself burn with a nice clear flame and make excellent fuel.

Date Palms

If it were not for the date palm, the people of North Africa, Arabia and Persia would suffer seriously, for the dried fruit is their principal food. Cakes of dates pounded and kneaded together form the fare provided by caravans on their journeys through the Sahara, and no wonder they are feeding, for fifty-eight parts in every hundred of the date fruit is pure sugar.

In each oasis throughout the desert you may see great groves of date palms which grow to a height of sixty feet and produce immense crops of fruit.

Three hundred to six hundred pounds per tree is the crop of a palm in full bearing so that the amount of food produced per acre is twelve times as much as if the ground were sown with wheat. The trees begin to bear at eight years old and will go on for a century.

Like the coconut palm, the date has a dozen uses. It produces *jaggery*, which is a kind of sugar, toddy, bags and mats, baskets, walking sticks, fans, as well as cattle-food and oil. No other fruit tree, not even the apple, is as important to man as the date palm.

The Cinchona Tree

Before the year 1820 mankind had no drug with which to fight that terrible scourge, malarial fever, so that life in

Will F. Taylor.

AN AVENUE OF PALMS

We could not have an avenue like this in London or New York, because palms grow only in tropical climates. These beautiful palms in the Hawaiian Islands are only twenty-five years old.

a tropical country was most dangerous to any white man. In that year quinine was extracted from the dried bark of the cinchona tree, and was found to have a marvellous effect in cases of fever. The cinchona from which quinine is obtained is not just one sort of tree, but a whole family, all of which are native to South America. The trees are evergreens with laurel-like leaves, and the best varieties are found in the mountains about five thousand feet above sea-level.

In olden days the bark was collected by Indians, who felled the trees and peeled off all the bark, a wasteful way of doing things which nearly ended in exterminating the tree. However, in 1848, the botanist Weddell brought cinchona seeds to Europe, and these were sprouted at the Botanical Gardens in Paris, and the young shrubs sent to Algiers. Later, the great English explorer, Sir Clements R. Markham, collected a quantity of seeds and started

Sport & General.

CLIMBING FOR A DRINK

This is an Indian picture. The man is climbing a palm in order to get the sweet juice from the crown. Notice the calabash slung at his waist, and observe the rope which he uses to help him. At each step he pulls the loop up a couple of feet.

Paul Popper.

FRUIT FARMING IN AUSTRALIA

Here we have a Victorian fruit farm at Warandite, near Melbourne. In these orchards the trees are kept below 10 feet in height to ensure easier picking of the fruit and more rapid cultivation of the trees. The owner's house can be seen on the crest of the hill.

new plantations in India where quinine was badly needed. The growing of quinine is now an important industry all through the East, and the medicine is distributed by the Government of India in every part of that huge country.

Bamboos and their Uses

You have probably never eaten bamboo asparagus, but the writer can assure you that the dish is a very good one. The little green shoots, if boiled in milk, are delicious. But that is only one fancy use of a family of huge grasses which grow in almost all warm parts of the world and are perhaps more useful to man than any other sort of reed.

China would not be China without the bamboo, which is used there for almost every imaginable purpose. It is made into furniture, ladders, masts for boats, spear shafts, drinking cups, spade and hoe handles, and many other useful articles. The stems are split and worked into mats, ropes, and even sails for boats. Immense quantities of bamboo are imported into England and used for making fishing rods, stakes for tying up plants, walking sticks, wicker work, etc.

The bamboos are really huge grasses with stems that are jointed and hollow. The wood is intensely hard, very light and elastic. Those small bamboos which are grown in English gardens come from a height of 12,000 feet in the Himalayas, but the larger sorts grow only in hot climates. The rate at which these big plants grow is perfectly amazing. The writer has measured a shoot to lengthen 8 inches in twenty-four hours.

The Banana

If the Arab depends for food on the date, so does the negro of Central Africa on the banana, and this fruit is also the main food of millions in Central America and in the islands of the Pacific. Sixty years ago a banana was a rarity in England, but to-day it shares with the apple and orange the position of being

WORK ON A BANANA PLANTATION

This is a view on a Jamaica banana plantation. Bananas were used for human food before history was written, yet it was not till 1890 that they were known in Britain.

When harvesting the banana the " cutter " nicks the trunk with his long-handled knife while the " backer " stands ready to receive the bunch on his shoulder as the plant bends over.

Photos: Elders & Fyffes Ltd.

The banana plant grows up from a " stool " and a shoot takes about eighteen months to grow, bloom and bear fruit. The fruit is cut while it is still green, and where the bananas grow close to the main railway, dumps of freshly-cut bunches are formed, then later loaded direct into railway trucks for transport to the wharf where they are shipped aboard special banana steamers.

N.S.W. Government.

A STRINGYBARK

The bark of this Australian eucalyptus tree yields a tough, springy fibre, some times used for stuffing furniture. The wood is used for building, fencing and railway sleepers. The best varieties grow in Tasmania.

one of the three most popular fruits.

In one respect it is the most wonderful of all plants, for no other fruit bears so heavily. The crop from an acre of bananas is actually one hundred and thirty-three times greater than the weight of wheat which could be raised on a similar area of land. There are dozens of different sorts of bananas, from the great coarse plantain down to the delicate little "lady's finger," but since these dainty small fruits will not travel we rarely see them in England.

WHAT FORESTS MEAN TO MAN

LOOK at the map of North Africa. See how the desert comes up to the very shores of the Mediterranean. If you landed on that coast you would observe great stretches of yellow sand or shingle running away to the horizon. A few bunches of harsh grass, here and there a small patch of desert scrub, but no other vegetation. Hardly

any life except a few lizards, no fresh water, no crops, no birds. All day the sun blazes down with furious heat, but at night, owing to radiation of heat into the cloudless air, the cold is intense.

How the Desert came

It is hard to believe that this dismal land was once a vast forest, with rich black soil lying thick under the shade of tall trees, and pleasant streams pouring seawards from the inland hills. Yet if you could go back twenty-five centuries that is what you would find.

It was the needs of the fast-growing Roman Empire which were the first cause of the disaster. The people required corn, and this North African coast was cleared of trees and turned into farms and wheat fields. That was all very well, for it was merely changing one sort of vegetation for another. The country remained green, the springs still flowed, people lived on the land.

But then the great wave of northern barbarism crushed the Roman Empire and the Mohammedan power arose in the East. There was no market for the corn, there were no ships to fetch it. The farms were abandoned, and since there were no trees to stop it, the desert crept in. Sand choked the springs, it covered the cities and farmhouses, and by degrees changed the country into a dreary waste.

Camera Press.

A VALUABLE FIBRE

The sisal is grown in tropical regions throughout the world. It yields a strong fibre used for making coarse ropes. See picture opposite.

The Other Side of the Shield

Facing the Bay of Biscay is the maritime province of Landes, which up to the eighteenth century was the French desert. All along the seventy-five miles of coast huge sand dunes 300 feet high had driven inland, so that most of the department, an area larger than Yorkshire, was completely barren. The only industry was sheep farming, and the shepherds crossed the great plains and marshes on stilts.

In 1787 the planting of trees began along the dunes. It was found that pines would root in the sand, and that as soon as they rooted the sweep of the sand before the sea winds was stopped. As they grew up they formed a complete barrier to the gales and enabled other vegetation to grow behind them. To-day the visitor sees 225,000 acres of pine with cork and oak trees from which the Government draws a large revenue in resin, charcoal and cut timber. The population has increased from a few thousand to more than a quarter of a million, the rainfall also has increased and the soil is enormously improved. Farmers grow rye, maize and wheat.

The World's Forests

Trees cover about a fifth of the land surface of our planet, an area equal to 100 times that of the British Isles, or twelve million square miles. You might think that was plenty to go on with, but apart from those we cut, a vast number of trees is destroyed every year. Fire is the great enemy of the world's forests. The average area of forest cut for lumber yearly in the United States of America is $3\frac{3}{4}$ million acres. The average area burned out is $7\frac{1}{2}$ millions, or twice as much as is cut.

Forest Fires

There are 50,000 forest fires a year, 200 or 300 a day during the drier months, and that is in the United States alone. Fires do equal damage in Canada and Australia and cause very serious losses in Europe also.

Some of these fires are colossal. In 1871 the Peshtigo fire in Wisconsin burned 1,200,000 acres, and 1,500 unfortunate people lost their lives. Four hundred people were burned to death in the great Hinckley forest fire in Minnesota in 1924, and 150,000 acres

Camera Press.

THE SISAL PLANT

Here, the sisal has run to seed, sending up a tall " pole " like a tree. You would hardly believe it is related to the daffodil, yet such is the case!

N.S.W. Government.

AUSTRALIAN PINES

Great forests of these pine trees have been planted in Australia to maintain the supply of native softwoods. This plantation is being thinned.

of fine forest were reduced to ashes. Another forest fire in Minnesota in 1918 destroyed 1,000 lives and £10,000,000 worth of timber. You may put it that the waste of timber caused by fire amounts to £8,000,000 yearly in the United States alone.

Other Destroyers

Insects of various kinds work havoc in the forests. In 1883 white pine butterflies descended upon the forests of the State of Washington in such hosts that springs and pools had to be skimmed of their floating bodies before cattle could be watered. The caterpillar completely stripped the pines. Wood boring beetles destroy miles upon miles of sugar pine in California, and lodge-pole pines on the Pacific coast. The spruce bud worm is another terrible pest which attacks the spruce trees in Quebec and elsewhere. Two hundred million cords of spruce, enough to supply paper for the whole

civilised world for twenty years, have been destroyed by this one insect.

Cattle and sheep rank next to insects as destroyers of timber. They not only bite the grown trees, but actually eat the young seedlings just as they come above the ground. A thousand years ago all Dartmoor, up to about the 1,200 foot level, was a real forest. The tinners cut the grown trees for fuel to smelt their ore, then the cattle and ponies ate the young trees that came up instead of the old ones, and the result is a barren waste with heather and gorse instead of oak and ash.

We must have Trees

Trees are as necessary to man as air and water. We require timber for all kinds of purposes, for building our houses, making our furniture, pit props for use in mines, boat building, etc. This book itself depends on timber, for practically all our paper is made from wood pulp.

But forests do more for man than supply his material needs; they have a profound effect upon climate and soil. Rainfall is always heavier and more regular in a wooded than in a desert country. Since the central States of North America were first settled and planted about 150 years ago the rainfall has increased by 2 to 4 inches yearly.

Another point of value is that the roots of trees interlacing through the ground save it from being scoured, that is washed away by heavy rainfall. An open country is washed and pitted in every direction by storms which sweep the soil away from the hillsides leaving them bare and barren. Take the case of the island of St. Helena, which was once thickly wooded. Goats were imported and ran wild upon the island. A goat will eat almost anything, and these goats browsed upon the trees until they died, and ate the young seedlings. Then the heavy rains cut away the exposed soil and washed it into the valleys so that to-day the higher parts of the island are a scene of stark desolation. The

FROM NIGERIA TO—
In comparatively recent times the tall Iroko tree of Nigeria has become a popular hardwood for street and park " furniture," including benches, chairs and lamp standards.

—A BRITISH SEASIDE TOWN
This handsome Iroko lamp standard is one of many along the front at Sidmouth in Devonshire. It is 21 feet high, 9 inches in diameter at the base and 6 inches at the top.

large island of Mauritius in the Indian Ocean has suffered in similar fashion.

Trees improve the soil. The leaves fall and turn into leaf mould. Year by year they heap up, rotting during the winter, until within a comparatively short time the whole surface is covered with rich loam.

Bringing New Trees to Britain

The British Isles are the largest importers of timber in the world and until fairly recently only about 5 per cent. of our needs was produced in our own country. It was the war of 1914–18 which brought home the realisation of the need to cultivate trees in Britain. Then in 1919 the Forestry Commission began the task of planting and cultivating new forest areas.

The new forests of Britain are being planted with many trees which were formerly unknown in this country. It has been found that many Asiatic and

Will F. Taylor.

A CAMPHOR TREE

Camphor comes from a tree which belongs to the laurel family, and is grown largely in the East, especially in Formosa and Japan. The wood is cut into chips and distilled with water, the vapour being collected in the head of the still. Camphor is much used in medicine.

also American trees flourish in this country. Among the best are the Douglas Fir, the Sitka Spruce and the Canadian Hemlock. Immense quantities of seeds of these and other Canadian trees are shipped each year from the Dominion to England, and quite a profitable trade was started in British Columbia in collecting these seeds for the market.

The seeds are milled before being packed for export and sown in nurseries when they arrive in England. New Zealand and Australia have also bought tree seeds from British Columbia, and the export of such seeds is growing.

Australia takes seeds and even growing trees from England. In 1927, when King George VI and Queen Elizabeth (then Duke and Duchess of York) opened the Commonwealth Parliament

at Canberra, a number of English trees, sent out for the occasion, were specially planted on the day of the ceremony. They included beeches, oaks, alders, elms and cricket-bat willows.

The great difficulty is not in making English trees grow in Australia, but in getting trees from a temperate zone safely through the tropics. On this occasion the trees were packed in boxes with their roots in wet moss, and the boxes kept in cold storage at a temperature of not more than 40 degrees. Most of them came through quite safely and are now growing in Australia's capital.

But Australia has her own native trees and nearly 70 million acres of forest lands. They consist chiefly of hardwood trees, the family of Eucalypts, popularly known as gum trees. The soft woods have to be imported. The tropical forests of New South Wales and

Will F. Taylor

IN THE DESERT OF SINAI

One of the few trees which will grow freely in the bleak desert of Sinai is the cypress. This row of tall, slender trees with their strange dark foliage may be seen on the south-west side of the mountain called Gebel Musa. The name of the place is Wadi-al-Lajaon.

PINES ON A SURREY HILLSIDE

J .Dixon-Scott.

Anyone who knows the county of Surrey will recognise this beauty spot. It is Crooksbury Hill, overlooking the village of Waverley. Much of Surrey is sandy soil in which conifer trees flourish. The shape of trees and the height to which they grow tell us much of the nature of the soil beneath. A layer of rock a few feet below the surface prevents the tap root from striking downwards and dwarfs or stunts the trees growing above it. From the height and straightness of these trees we can tell at once that the soil, though poor, has plenty of depth.

SPRUCE CONES SIX INCHES LONG

Reginald A. Malby.

The whole world has been ransacked for ornamental trees for British gardens and parks, and scores of different sorts of conifers (cone bearing trees) have been brought from North America, Asia and elsewhere, and found to do well in Great Britain. The Cedar of Lebanon was one of the first to be imported, and more recently the Wellingtonia, a giant from the Pacific coast of America, was planted in large numbers, and some specimens have already reached a height of 80 feet. Our illustration represents one of these conifers brought from the Himalayas to England and known as the Himalayan Spruce.

United States Information Service.

These giant sequoia trees, which make up the famous redwood forests of Mariposa Grove, California, are often called " the oldest living things." Some of them were already old at the time when Christ was born, and many of them tower to a height of 300 feet or more. The trunks of the trees are often wide enough to permit a full-sized car to pass through arches cut through them. Many of these trees were felled in the early days of Californian settlement, but now they are protected by law, and most carefully guarded, not only from the axe of the lumberman, but also from fire.

Queensland supply many beautiful cabinet timbers which are in great demand, such as black bean, silky oak, maple, walnut, rosewood and red cedar. West Australian jarrah has gained a high reputation for its wide range of uses. Karri, which also comes from Western Australia, is another fine timber, while Victoria is famed for its white mountain ash, which is widely used for house construction, decoration and fencing.

Giants of the Plant World

The biggest tree in the world —what is it and where is it? These are interesting questions, not altogether simple to answer. Years ago a well-known

Will F. Taylor.

A ONE-TREE FOREST

The banyan has the remarkable habit of dropping suckers from its branches, which, on meeting the ground, take root and spring up afresh so that one tree may eventually form a small forest. The banyan is common in India and the tropical East.

CEDARS OF LEBANON *Will F. Taylor.*

Here are cedars of Lebanon growing in their native mountains. This tree in the foreground is over 80 feet in height. The cedar of Lebanon grows well in England, but is brittle and apt to break down under heavy snow.

American millionaire made a bet that he would have a table made, a cross-section of one trunk, which would seat forty people. The piece of wood sent him from America was 52 feet in circumference, and he won his wager.

This was a section from a Californian redwood, but if he had been allowed to cut down one of the really big trees he could have made a table 90 feet round. The so-called " Mother of the Forest " was 321 feet high and 30 feet through the trunk.

BUNYAN PREACHED BENEATH THIS OAK

John Bunyan was born at Elstow, near Bedford, in 1628, and this is the great oak at Harlington under which he preached. Old more than two centuries ago, this tree is now but a ruin of its former self. The trunk is hollow, and some of the largest branches are decayed, yet others are still vigorous and full of leaf each spring, and the ancient tree may well go on living for another century or more. We have oaks in England believed to be 1,000 years old.

A GIANT OF THE TROPICS   *Sport & General.*

With its squat trunk and enormous buttresses or ribs, the Cotton Tree of Jamaica is able to
defy even the worst cyclones and to live through centuries to an age of 1,000 years or more.
This photograph shows the great cotton tree known as Tom Cringle's, at New Spanish Town, in
the West Indian island of Jamaica. No one knows its age, but it figures in old records of three
centuries ago. There is said to be room for more than 1,000 people to stand beneath its shade.

The "Grizzly Giant"

Some of these Californian giants were
old when Christ was born. Of the
" Mother " only the bark remains, but
" The Grizzly Giant," which still stands,
is 93 feet in circumference at the ground
and 275 feet high. It rises 200 feet
before it throws out a single branch,
and is reckoned to be 4,680 years old.
The Mariposa Grove, containing 700 of
these tremendous trees, is set apart as
a National Park and carefully preserved
by the Government.

All along the Western coast of
America are found trees of enormous
size. A flag-pole cut for the Panama-
Pacific Exhibition was 246 feet long
and weighed over 45 tons. It was hewn
in the Nehalem Valley of Oregon from
a Douglas fir.

New Zealand has kauri pines of
immense size. In 1922 one was discovered in the Northern forest, which
was 69 feet in girth and reckoned to be
over 200 feet high and more than 2,000
years old. It is from dead forests of
kauri timber that they dig a beautiful
gum which looks so like amber.

Oldest in the World

Nassau, capital of the Bahama
Islands, has a silk-cotton tree in its
main square which ranks among the
wonders of the world. It literally fills
the square, and casts its shade over the
surrounding buildings. It is of no
great height, but its trunk is tremendous,
being surrounded by great wing-like
buttresses which brace the tree against
all attack. It is called the hurricane tree
because the hurricanes which devastate
these islands, though they may strip off

the leaves, have never harmed it. There is said to be room for 3,000 people in its shade.

But even this giant is surpassed by a tree of the cypress family which grows near the famous ruins of Mitla in Mexico. Its circumference 6 feet from the ground is 154 feet 2 inches. Men of science say that this may very well be the oldest living thing in the world, and reckon its age at approximately 6,150 years.

Huge British Trees

In our own Northern climate trees do not grow to such a giant size as in warmer, wetter countries. The tallest English tree is believed to have been the Queen beech in Ashridge Park, less than 30 miles from London, but now blown down. It was 135 feet in height and stood up beautifully straight. It was, however, slim compared with some of the great oaks found in different parts of the country. The famous Damory's oak which grew near Blandford in Dorset was 68 feet round at ground level. It must have reached its prime about the date of Edward III. By Cromwell's time it had become hollow and its trunk was turned into an ale shop.

The Cowthorpe oak near Wetherby, Yorkshire, is about 1,600 years old, and at the close of the seventeenth century was 54 feet in circumference, though now only a stump. On Jubilee Day, 1887, the vicar of the parish with the

Sport & General.

CLIPPED YEW

The bole of the yew is short and massive. The tree is very slow growing, but lives to an immense age. There are yews alive in England which were trees when William the Conqueror landed. The wood is hard, compact and elastic, and was the material used for the old English long-bow. Also it is so durable that a post of yew will outlast one of iron. The tree was often planted to shade the dairy of old farmhouses, and will withstand any amount of clipping.

HEALING PLANTS

I N an old book on medicine published in 1618 the preparations include pearls, snails, vipers, and the thigh bone of a hanged man among the remedies. But besides these marvellous and horrible substances many herbal remedies are mentioned, and at the present time chemists still procure by far the greater part of their medicines from the plant world.

Wayside Plants as Medicine

In the early days every monastery and most large private houses had each its own " physick " garden where useful herbs and plants were grown, but this practice died out, and at one period we imported nearly all the raw material which we needed for medicine making.

Most of it came from the Continent,

OAK-APPLES   III II I Dunn In

We call them oak-apples, but the proper name is oak galls. They are formed by an insect which lays its egg upon the twig and causes the tree to throw out an abnormal growth. Gall-nuts of this kind have their value because they contain tannic acid used in making ink.

two churchwardens and ninety-five Sunday School scholars got inside the tree and sang the National Anthem. Another famous tree is the Fairlop oak in Hainault Forest, which has, however, been largely destroyed by the fires of careless picnic parties.

Scotland has some fine trees. There is a black poplar at Luss, in Dumbartonshire, which is 105 feet high, and a silver fir of similar height at the same place. The best beeches in Scotland are at Daldowie House, in Lanarkshire. These trees were planted in the year 1720, and, though more than 200 years old, are still growing steadily.

The size of a tree depends largely on the *depth* of soil beneath it. No tree can grow to a great size if its tap root strikes rock at only a few feet below the surface. Tall, straight trees are proof of deep soil and a good supply of moisture for their roots.

M. H. Crawford.

SWEET CHESTNUT

The deeply grooved bark of the chestnut often gives the trunk a twisted appearance. It yields an extract used in tanning. In some countries the nuts form an important article of food. The young trees grown in coppices are split for making barrel-hoops and palings.

especially Germany, Austria and Hungary. In time of war Britain has twice found a great shortage of many necessary drugs, and high prices were paid for plants which had for long been considered worthless weeds. Dandelion roots, for instance, fetched £6 10s. per hundredweight, and the leaves of the deadly nightshade as much as 2s. a pound.

A very large number of common wayside plants are used in making medicines. They include wood sage, balm, pennyroyal, rue, tansy, mullein, horehound, centaury, feverfew and the beautiful buckbean which grows in marshy spots. Of some plants the leaves are used and of others the roots. The latter include valerian, comfrey, mugwort, marshmallow, burdock and many others.

TANSY   *A. W. Dennis.*

This yellow-flowered weed flourishes in soil too dry and barren for other plants to grow. Tansy was used in old days by herbalists for making Tansy tea. Tansy cakes and puddings were also made for Easter. The plant is one of the same family as that to which wormwood belongs.

A. W. Dennis.

A BOG PLANT

Buckbean is one of the most beautiful of British wild flowers, yet at the same time one of the least known, for it is very local. It grows only in peat bogs, and may be found in quantities on Dartmoor. But one requires waders in order to pick these lovely blooms.

Oak apples powdered are made into an ointment for boils, a preparation of mistletoe is good for epileptic fits, hops are made into a tonic, foxgloves are used as a heart stimulant; and there are hundreds of plants which will cure or help to cure various illnesses.

At Kew Gardens may be seen a wonderful collection of plants used in medicine. They are " crab's eyes " (the seeds of a plant called jequirity, which are used in certain eye troubles), fruits of cedron good for curing snake bite; bullock's heart or custard apple, a cure for dysentery; winter's bark, a medicine for scurvy; and chinchina (cinchona), the cure for malarial fever.

If you visit the London Docks you will perhaps see quantities of medicine plants being landed. Here are bundles of thin, dry looking twigs which seem as if they might be meant for making

W. Pedersen.

THE COOLIBAH TREE

This is one of the many kinds of Eucalyptus trees which grow in Australia. It is found in the semi-desert interior, and indicates that there is water not far away.

brooms, but are really the creeping roots of a prickly shrub growing in the West Indies called Sarsaparilla. The medicine made from them is famous as a blood purifier. Other twiggy bundles are ipecacuanha, which comes from the moist forests of Northern Brazil. They are packed in sacks and give off a throat-irritating dust; the medicine made from them is on sale in every chemist's shop.

Australia's Eucalypts

One of the first natural raw products used by the earliest British settlers in Australia was eucalyptus oil. The surgeon-general to the new settlement was John White, and in his " Journal of a Voyage to New South Wales," published in London in 1790, there is a statement about the medicinal value of eucalyptus oil, which he had found much more efficacious for certain complaints than English peppermint. Surgeon-General White had made an important

discovery, though it was not until more than half a century later that the first factory for the commercial distillation of eucalyptus oil was founded in Victoria.

A Most Valuable Tree

To-day eucalyptus oil is used largely in medicinal preparations; it is also important in the perfumery industry and is used in soap-making, the preparation of disinfectants, and in certain processes for the separation of metallic sulphides by the mining industry. All these uses are in addition to the value of the many varieties of Eucalypts as timber, a factor which was recognised in the very early days when the first ships to bring settlers to New South Wales returned with valuable cargoes of timber cut from the Australian forests.

Eucalyptus trees belong to Australia and were unknown in any other part of the world a century and a half ago. Since then they have been planted in many other countries where the climate is similar to Australia—in many parts of North America and in North, West and South Africa especially. Russia, too, has planted large numbers of Eucalypts, while Italy has also introduced them with good results. Australia still imports soft woods but has given to other continents one of the most valuable hardwood trees in the world.

Oils and Gums

Castor oil is hard to recognise in the little polished brown beans which arrive in bags from India. The juice of the aloe comes pressed into cakes which are often sewn up in monkey skins. Gums of many kinds are used by druggists, and most of these come from Smyrna or Bussorah. There is Gum Arabic, Gum Senegal, Gum Benjamin, Gum Myrrh, and Gum Tragacanth, all of them extracted from various trees and shrubs; while liquorice, a juice pressed from the root of a plant grown in Yorkshire, is used in making " Pontefract cakes." Much of the world's liquorice is now grown in Italy.

The Work
of the
Scientist

Improving
the Fruits
of the Earth

A. W. Dennis.

SEED-VESSELS OF THE PANSY

The pansy differs from the other members of its family (the violas) in having the two upper petals very erect instead of leaning forward. The flowers vary from white through yellow to purple. Its name is *Viola tricolor* (three-coloured). There are several varieties of wild pansy from which the garden sorts have come. Our photograph shows the seed vessels both closed and open, with the ripe seeds.

THE WAYS OF NATURE AND OF MAN

THE BIRTH OF PLANTS

FISHING one day on Dartmoor, the writer noticed in a little dip of ground by a pool half a dozen tiny beech trees pushing their heads above the turf. Now the nearest beech trees were on a tributary stream a long way away, and he realised that these little trees came from beech nuts washed down all this distance by a winter flood and cast up just where they would have their chance to sprout when spring came.

How Seeds Travel

An enormous number of seeds are water-borne, carried by rivers or by the sea. In the year 1883 happened the biggest explosion ever known. The island of Krakatoa in the East Indies blew up, and torrents of lava and blasts of burning gas destroyed every trace of life on the island. It was three years

before any one dared to land and explore. Already tiny algæ were breaking up the lava, a dozen sorts of ferns were growing and fifteen other kinds of plants.

By 1897 the whole of that barren waste was covered afresh with vegetation. Sixty-two species of plants were counted, including even orchids. It was noticed that the variety of plants was much greater near the sea than inland, and it was reckoned that more than half the plants growing came from seed washed up by the waves, that one-third were probably borne there by the wind and the rest carried by birds.

When Seeds Cross Seas

Among important seeds that travel by water are those of the coconut, which often drift great distances in the open sea, and may have colonised the thousands of Pacific and Indian Ocean islands where they are found growing wild. While most seeds would be spoiled by sea water, the strong shell of the coconut may protect it from the brine. Another way in which seeds are carried by water is on ice. Huge glaciers run down to the coast of Alaska and icebergs break off and float away. On these are soil, stones, plants and seeds, which may be carried to very great distances.

Migrating birds and animals carry seeds, and many feathered visitors, as we may well imagine, take seeds across stretches of sea. Ducks and other water birds distribute seeds all over the globe. A wild duck or goose or swan wading along in the mud at the edge of a lake or river picks up a certain amount of earth on its feet and legs in which seeds may be contained,

and next night may drop that earth and those seeds at another spot hundreds of miles distant. A botanist who has been inquiring into this matter examined the mud scraped from the legs of a number of wading birds and found seeds of grasses, sedges and rushes numbering in all no fewer than thirty-one different species. This is the reason why certain mud and marsh plants are found in almost every quarter of the globe, both north and south.

Rooks, as we know, are fond of acorns, and jackdaws of walnuts. These birds and others are responsible for the birth of many of our finest English trees.

Animals as Seed Carriers

The red squirrel, now so sadly scarce

H. Bastin.

HOOKED SEEDS

Plants adopt many methods of spreading their seeds. One of the most useful, from the plant's point of view, is the means to provide hooks which catch upon the fur of passing animals and so carry the seeds to considerable distances. Our photograph gives examples of the seeds of several of these inventive plants, such as burdock and clivers. Often after a country ramble you will find your dog's coat matted with burdock seed which is most difficult to comb out.

in England, is a great tree planter. He collects stores of acorns, beech mast, hazel nuts and other seeds, and buries them as winter provender. But he is a scatter-brained creature, and half the time forgets where his hoards are hidden. So the seeds remain until spring, and sprout. Rats, voles, dormice, and lemmings all have similar habits of hoarding, and are likewise responsible for spreading the seeds and kernels which they collect.

In the section " How Plants Protect Themselves " we have mentioned the seed of the grapple plant which sometimes kills lions. A great many other seeds are provided with hooks and spines, by means of which they catch in the coats of deer, antelope, buffalo and other animals, and are thus distributed. We all know how " burrs " stick to our own clothes after a walk through the fields, but perhaps it has not occurred to you

H. Bastin.

VEGETABLE CANNON

Sit among broom bushes on a hot day in summer and you will hear the snap, snap of fairy artillery going on the whole time as the black seed pods curl, burst open and fling the small, dry seeds far and wide over the soil. Gorse has the same habit.

that the real reason for their " stickiness " is merely their desire to be spread abroad and grow into new plants. Burdock, forget-me-not, goosegrass, and many other British plants have sticky or clinging seeds.

This sort of thing may develop into a pest. There is a plant called the " Xanthium " which belongs to the daisy family. The head of the flower and the seed pod are covered with small but strong curved hooks. This plant appeared in the Russian Crimea about a century ago and soon became a fearful pest. By 1860 it had covered the whole peninsula, and, sticking in the wool of the sheep, fretted and matted it so that it was almost valueless. Carried in fleeces, it reached South America and Australia, where the loss which it has caused to sheep-farmers has amounted to millions of pounds.

Vegetable Guns

Have you ever stood among broom

H. Bastin.

" TOUCH-ME-NOT "

This is the yellow balsam, a native of Europe and found wild in Britain, which gets its touch-me-not name from the fact that the ripe seed capsules burst at the slightest touch and fling forth their seeds like shot from a gun. The balsam belongs to the geranium family.

plants on a hot July day and listened to the little snap-snap of the black seed pods ? One by one they explode, each flinging out its seeds to a distance of several feet. There are other plants which have even stronger " guns."

The pod of *Acanthus Mollis* goes off with such a bang that the seeds fly as much as 10 yards, while *Hura Crepitans* is a regular cannon, shooting its seeds to a distance of no less than 54 feet. The wild geranium has perfected an even stranger trick for distributing its seeds. The seeds lie at the end of long springs and when ripe these fly up and toss the seeds into the air. The common vetch works on a catapult-like principle, for when its pod splits each half instantly rolls up into a spiral with such energy as to fling its seeds far and wide.

Fairy Parachutes

You must have watched thistledown, as we call it, sailing through the air, borne by even the gentlest of breezes. The thistle and the dandelion both provide their seeds with feathery parachutes which, if the wind is strong, may carry them many miles. Another weed, with the queer name of " goat's beard," builds up a parachute of such beauty and perfection as is unmatched by any other plant. The yellow seed which contains the young plant is the weight which balances the parachute, and the parachute itself is made of light and soft feathery material.

M. H. Crawford.

A DANDELION " CLOCK "

The dandelion has no stem, and the leaves spring directly from the long tough root. The flower-heads rise from amid the leaves on hollow stalks which, if broken, exude a milky fluid. While the flower is still blooming you may see that the corolla is invested with a " pappus " of soft silky hairs which will eventually form the fluffy ball of down. The seed itself is barbed and pointed so that when it falls to the ground it will stick into the soil and germinate.

THE END OF THE JOURNEY   *J. J. Ward.*

Blown by the wind from a head like the Dandelion " clock " opposite, these seeds of the common yellow Goat's Beard are landing by parachute upon a piece of bare soil. Probably not more than one seed in fifty is lucky enough to do this, and so get a chance of sprouting and making a new plant. The rest are caught on trees, or fall in thick grass and so perish. But those which do fall on moist ground are almost sure to sprout, so that new Goat's Beards grow each year.

Winged Seeds

Other plants or trees, instead of parachutes, provide their seeds with wings. The most familiar of these is the ordinary English elm, each seed of which is held in the centre of a leaf-like wing.

The useful result is that the seeds, instead of dropping straight to the ground, as do the acorns of an oak, go gyrating and twisting through the air, often landing at a very considerable distance from the parent tree. The elm produces an immense number of seeds, which is necessary, for hardly one in a thousand reaches a spot where it can root, and not one in a million makes a new tree.

The sycamore is another tree with winged seeds. The wing is rather like an aeroplane in shape, being double, with the seed in the centre. The pine fruit is also equipped with a wing, and each seed of the Ailanthus or " Tree of Heaven " has double wings, oddly twisted so that they spin like arrows in travelling through the air, and in a strong wind cover very great distances. The ash and the hornbeam are other examples of English trees whose seeds possess wings. When a tree seed sprouts it is the root that first creeps out of the seed case. The leaves do not start until the root has taken firm hold in the ground.

Millions of Seeds

The number of seeds produced by a single plant is often amazing. The common red poppy may have a hundred seed vessels each containing 500 seeds, so it is no wonder that a cornfield is soon scarlet with the bright blooms. Another poppy produces no fewer than

H. *Bastin.*

(1) STORK'S BILL

The stork's bill has a flower similar to that of the geranium, and is in fact a geranium, especially near the coast. But the odd part of the plant is its seed. Each of the five capsules in which the seed is enclosed is provided with a long, spiral, twisted stalk.

60,000 seeds, and the common spear thistle has 24,000. The burdock has over 600 seed vessels with 40 seeds in each, and the wild chamomile contains 300 seeds in each of its 150 seed capsules. Many other common plants produce seed by the thousand, so that it is no wonder that weeds increase and multiply. Many of these seeds are amazingly small. The Bible quotes the mustard seed as the smallest, but tobacco plant seed is smaller, and the poppy is another very tiny seed.

The Life of Seeds

After examining and testing the seeds of 289 different cultivated plants, the curator of the Oxford Botanic Gardens came to the conclusion that very few of them retained the power to sprout for more than eight years. Some, like that of the parsnip, will not germinate if more than one year old.

The oily seeds last longest. Melon seed, for instance, has been known to grow after forty years, and haricot beans are said to hold the life principle for as long as a century. The wild raspberry is a very long-lived seed, and it is said that the pips of this plant have sprouted after a period of no less than 1,700 years.

Stories are often told of mummy wheat taken from Egyptian tombs being sown and sprouting, but most of such stories must be accepted with a grain of salt. The majority of such seeds have been substitutes palmed off on travellers by dishonest natives. Yet there certainly are cases of seeds keeping their life for very long periods, and the fact that newly made railway embankments often grow plants quite unknown in the neighbourhood seems to argue that seeds buried deeply in the ground for centuries have still the power to sprout.

H. *Bastin.*

(2) THE SEED SOWER

Here is a second picture of the seed of the stork's bill, showing the tail. This twisted tail is alternately lengthened by moisture and shortened by dryness, so that it acts as a kind of auger by which the pointed, hairy seed is gradually driven into the ground.

PLANTS MADE BY MAN

LUTHER BURBANK of California once pulled up 65,200 seedling berry bushes and burned them in one big bonfire and during the same season had fourteen other bonfires of similar size, each consisting of fine-looking young trees. *And each of those trees, it must be remembered, was a new sort, one that had never been produced before!*

It sounds a crazy proceeding, does it not, but these trees were not *up to the desired quality.*

Luther Burbank, greatest of American plant inventors, went to California over seventy years ago, took up land and started not merely to grow plants, but to *invent new plants.* He did not do it for money. Indeed, he spent all the profit he made out of his large nursery garden on his work.

Before explaining how he laboured, we must go back to early days. From the time when man first turned farmer it has always been his desire to get bigger and better crops. The farmer soon discovered that there were two ways of doing this. The first was by skilful cultivation of the earth and the use of manures; the second by keeping on year after year sowing the soundest and best seed obtainable.

What "Sports" Are

After a time the farmer discovered a third way. Now and then in a field of grain he would notice, if his eyes were sharp, a head of wheat or oats or barley which looked different from the rest. Such a thing appears now and then at long intervals and is called a "sport." It may occur not only in grain plants, but in any plant, and the "sport" may be either worse or better than the average plant. If it is better the farmer saves the seed, sows it with

MAPLE SEEDS

H. Bastin.

The seeds of the Norway Maple are winged. Each, as you see from this photograph, has two wings shaped like those of a bird. The result is that when the ripe seed breaks off it does not fall straight to the ground, but may flutter to a considerable distance.

great care and, with luck, may in this way discover a new and valuable variety.

In the year 1819 a Scots farmer named Sheriff observed a branching wheat plant in one of his fields. It yielded sixty-three ears with 2,500 kernels or grains. He saved and sowed it, and it became famous as "Mungoswell's Wheat."

Major Hallett discovered in similar fashion a head of wheat which was red in colour. The first ear had only forty-seven kernels, but by careful cultivation he worked it up to ninety kernels to each ear, and "Hallett's Red Wheat" became a recognised variety. "Bearded Red Wheat," "Bearded White," and

" Pringles' Wheat " all started from natural variations or sports.

For many hundreds of years these were the only methods known to man of improving his crops. It was not until the nineteenth century that the discovery was made that plants could be *artificially crossed*. This is what gave to men like Luther Burbank and John Garton the opportunity to change the whole face of Nature and literally to invent new food plants.

A Simple Secret

Here are two plants, one from Australia perhaps, the other from Siberia. Each has its own structure, habits and characteristics, and has preserved its identity for thousands or tens of thousands of years, but now these two plants are growing in the same garden. Pollen from the blossoms of one is taken out on a watch glass and dusted carefully into the bloom of the other. That bloom is marked and protected by a cap from insects, and in course of time bears seed. The seeds are sown, and a year later there appear new plants—plants different from anything that ever grew before.

These may be absolute monstrosities, grotesque and useless and in that case they are destroyed. But on the other hand, there may be a seedling which has the best characteristics of both of its parents, and this, of course, is carefully preserved, and may form the start of a new and valuable variety.

Thorns off Thistles

Mr. Burbank performed the apparent

H. J. Shepstone.

THE PLANT WIZARD

Greatest of American plant inventors, the late Mr. Luther Burbank produced scores of new plants. Apples, peaches, plums and nuts he made larger, more delicate and valuable. He propagated walnuts with paper-thin shells, plums without stones and rhubarb that is ready for the table at all seasons of the year. But his greatest triumph was depriving the prickly pear of its thorns and changing the tasteless fruit into a delicious foodstuff with a peach-like flavour.

H. J. Shepstone.

THE NEW BLACKBERRY

One of the plants on which Mr. Burbank worked for years was the blackberry. He crossed all kinds of varieties to produce fresh ones. The greater number of his new seedlings were freaks with queer-shaped leaves and still queerer fruit, and these were remorselessly burned, but out of each batch a few were kept, and presently he arrived at a blackberry briar that had no thorns at all and produced a large white, or rather yellow, fruit of excellent flavour. Here we see some of his experimental plants.

miracle of inducing a thistle to give up its thorns ; he also produced roses, blackberries, raspberries and gooseberries which were free from thorns, but his greatest achievement was the reformation of that very tough character, the prickly pear cactus.

The cactus is a desert plant which, in order to protect itself from many enemies, grows the most formidable spines on its leaves and fruit. Burbank not only took away its thorns, but bred its fruit to a perfection hitherto undreamed of. The flavour is delicious, something between a pineapple, a melon and an apricot.

Some Other Miracles

Burbank took the American wild plum, the Japanese plum and the apricot, and out of the three produced a fruit he called the " plumcot," delicate in flavour and beautiful in colour; he created a chestnut which bears nuts at eighteen months old, and

a walnut which in thirteen years was six times as big as an ordinary walnut at double that age.

He grew rhubarb which bears all the year round, is of rare quality and enormous size. He perfected plums without stones, and a prune four times as big as the old sort and very rich in sugar. One of his oddest inventions was the " pomato," a tomato growing on a potato with a white fragrant, succulent fruit. At one time he had in his grounds at Santa Rosa 300,000 distinct varieties of plums, 60,000 peaches and nectarines all different, 5,000 different almonds, 3,000 apples, 2,000 pears, 5,000 walnuts and a huge variety of berry-bearing plants of all kinds.

The Price of Fame

After 1893, when he sold his large and flourishing nursery business in order to give his whole time to plant breeding, Burbank suffered terribly. He often

H. J. Shepstone.

ALL FROM ONE PLANT

This picture gives an interesting example of what happens when the scientific gardener, like Mr. Burbank, begins experimenting. These are leaves of hybrid blackberries, *all produced from one plant*. The blooms were touched with pollen from other plants, the seeds saved and sown, and the picture of the leaves of these hybrids gives some idea of the marvellous changes which hybridisation produces. Of these many leaves no two are alike. Most of the plants were destroyed as useless.

for information. But no patent rights can be obtained for any improvement in plants. The only reward is in the joy of having done good work.

Another Plant Wizard

What Burbank did in America, John Garton carried out in England, but Garton's life work was devoted almost entirely to improving the wheat plant, and has been of greater value to the world at large than that of the American inventor. Talk of making two blades of grass grow where one grew before! Garton in many cases made a hundred grains of wheat grow where only one grew before.

John Garton and his brother were Lancashire seed merchants; but, as in Burbank's case, their business was only a means to an end. By degrees the Gartons collected seeds of grain plants from all over the world, and when these were growing in their grounds at Warrington John Garton set to work to cross them and breed new grains.

had not money to buy proper food, and when he was ill with fever he could not afford a doctor or medicines. He denied himself all the luxuries of life and many of the necessities. He was denounced as a charlatan, and certain "unco guid" persons called him a "foe to God." When at last fame came he was an old and tired man. Then he received a grant of £2,000 a year, and during the latter part of his life his garden was crowded with visitors. Six thousand came in one year, and he received 30,000 letters in twelve months asking

The wheats grown in England before Garton's time had three defects. They had not enough gluten—what bakers call "strength"—to make a big loaf, so the flour had to be mixed with imported flour from Canada, and the English farmer received less money for his wheat than was paid for "Manitoba Hard." The second fault of the British wheat plant was that it ripened slowly; and the third that it was apt to shed its grain before the crop could be harvested.

John Garton took a wild wheat from Southern Asia and crossed it with one of our best cultivated wheats and produced a seed wheat which ripens early, has great strength, and does not shed its grain.

Barley loses its Beard

In growing its well-known beard, the barley plant wastes a lot of useful energy which might be better used in making grain. John Garton found a barley from Nepal which has a loose skin and no beard, but the grain of which is very small. He crossed this with English barleys, and finally produced a splendid type of barley with no beard and big plump grains.

He also worked wonders with the oat. For improving this, he finally selected the Chinese oat grass. This grass has seeds far too small to be of

any use in themselves, but there are more of them than in an ear of the cultivated oat. Also it is tremendously hardy. After long experimenting, Garton perfected a brand-new variety of oat which produces ten to twenty grains in each of its spikelets instead of the two or three yielded by its tame parent. Shortly before Garton died Edinburgh University made him LL.D., i.e., Doctor of Laws.

Wheat for the Arctic

As you all know, a great part of the world's wheat comes from Canada, and especially from Western Canada. The prairie soil there is particularly good for wheat growing, and the hot summer sun ripens the grain rapidly. Wheat growing in Canada has been pushing north, but the difficulty has been that early August frosts may spoil the crop.

H. J. Shepstone.

HYBRID POPPIES

In one season Mr. Burbank produced no fewer than 2,000 poppy hybrids. Of them all, no two were exactly alike, and our photograph shows the extraordinary difference between some of the plants. Mr. Burbank worked for years on poppies, getting plants from all parts of the world, wild and cultivated. In the end he produced a new range of poppies of lovely colour. with large blooms and of great lasting quality.

Then came the discovery of "Marquis" wheat, a sort which ripened more quickly than any yet known, and this enabled the wheat-growing belt to be pushed quite a long way north.

But this was not the end, for another variety, called "Garnet," has been invented which will ripen from five to ten days quicker than "Marquis." The result will be that millions of acres which have so far been barren will now be ploughed, and the growers will be able to house their crops before the autumn frosts come.

Every year pioneer farmers push their way farther toward the Arctic Circle. Wheat is now being grown on the Churchill River 500 miles northwest of Winnipeg. The wheat belt is advancing into the land of the Midnight Sun.

Wheat in Australia

Another country where agriculture owes much to thought and scientific is

Australia, which is to-day one of the world's great food producers and comes third in the list of the world's wheat exporters. The aborigines of Australia had no agriculture and until the arrival of the First Fleet, the good Australian earth had never been turned by spade or plough. It was very old earth, too, and it did not take kindly to the European ways of farming brought by the white men. The first wheat farm was a failure and although wheat was successfully grown at Parramatta a year later, Australia was not able to grow enough for her people until many years had passed.

Once a way across the Blue Mountains had been found, there was naturally a great increase in the amount of wheat grown and in the acreage of land sown to this crop. But it proved very difficult to increase the amount of wheat harvested from each acre ; indeed, there was a serious fall in yield—the result of growing wheat crop after wheat crop on

DESERT CACTI

H. J. Shepstone.

Here we see a collection of wild cacti of various sorts grown under desert conditions. Each one of them is a mass of thorns and spikes produced by the plant to protect itself against grazing animals and extremely efficient for that purpose. Without its thorns, the desert cactus would soon be extinct. Mr. Burbank took some of these spiky plants into his garden and persuaded them that there was no need to be thorny. We shall see the result in the next picture.

the same land. The earth had become exhausted.

But an answer to the problem was found in superphosphate which was used as a fertiliser to correct the balance of things in the soil. In 1885, the average yield of wheat per acre had been 5·4 bushels ; by 1900, it had risen to 9·5 bushels and in 1951–52 it was 15·47 bushels.

It would be wrong to say that this great improvement was due entirely to the introduction of artificial manures such as " super." More important was the discovery that strains of wheat brought in from abroad were not suited to Australian conditions and attempts were made by pioneer plant breeders to develop new and more suitable varieties. That such varieties were found was largely due to the painstaking experiments of William Farrer, who ranks as the father of Australian wheat.

H. J. Shepstone.

A CONTRAST

The cactus in the foreground is the ordinary wild, prickly pear impossible to touch on account of its hard needle-like spines. Behind it are the plants which Mr. Burbank induced to abandon their defences. They are as safe to handle as beetroot and equally good for cattle. They produce more food to the acre with less care and less water than any other plant on earth, and excel even the banana in their bountiful crops of fruit.

Farrer was an Englishman who had settled in Australia as a tutor. His experiments in wheat-breeding were carried out on a small plot of ground near Canberra, and by 1898 had resulted in a strain that would grow well in the low-rainfall areas of the country. His famous " Federation " wheat was not only high-yielding but was also resistant to rust disease, which was the chief scourge of wheat farmers at that time. " Federation " increased Australian wheat production by 16 per cent., and the development of this and other strains made wheat-farming possible in the drier lands of Australia. " Farrer's genius," it has been said, " paved the way for the breeders who followed him. His ideal has not yet been, and perhaps never will be, attained, but it serves as the inspiration of wheat-breeders throughout the world."

438   THE WAYS OF NATURE AND OF MAN

SCIENCE AIDS THE FARMER

ALTHOUGH English history records the work of pioneer agriculturalists such as Sir Richard Weston (1591–1652), Jethro Tull, Lord Townshend and Coke of Holkham, new ideas in farming have always made slow progress, and in no branch of industry has the principle of " what was good enough for my father is good enough for me " been more stubbornly followed. It is only in the last century that any continuous effort has been made to gain knowledge of the chemical composition of our foodstuffs and not only to improve the quality and quantity produced but to understand scientifically the methods of improving crops and livestock. Superphosphates were manufactured from phosphate rock and sulphuric acid from 1842 ; potassium salts were first used about 1860, though they were practically unknown in this country until 1890, when soda nitrate also began to be used.

To show how the use of chemical fertilisers has increased since the beginning of the present century it may be noted that in 1903 the total quantity of nitrogenous fertiliser used in that year throughout the world was 370,000 tons; in 1938 it was over 5,000,000 tons. In the growing of our food the chemist is playing an increasingly important part as it is through his knowledge that the exhausted soil can be restored.

Wheat, Barley and Beet

In other directions the scientist began

John Topham.

FLOWER CULTURE WITHOUT SOIL IN CORNWALL
Flowers have received a good deal of attention from the scientist working in conjunction with the horticulturist. In this photograph carnations have just been planted in coarse sand. The beds are about 7 inches deep and are made of cement. Nutrient is piped along the centre allowing the liquid to drip through the whole length of the beds. This is carried out twice a week for about four hours. The result is a wonderful crop of early first-class blooms.

Fox Photos.

AT BRITAIN'S PIONEER EXPERIMENTAL STATION

The first agricultural experimental station in this country was founded at Rothamsted, near Harpenden, Herts, by John Bennet Lawes in 1843. He was assisted by his partner, a young chemist named Joseph Henry Gilbert. The two worked together until Lawes' death in 1900, but the research work has been carried on ever since. Our photograph shows work in progress in the Insectary as it is to-day.

to aid the farmer. Following the ideas of Gregor Mendel (1822–1884) research workers discovered thread-like bodies, which they called chromosomes, present in all plants and were able to prove that these were responsible for the production of more plants of the same kind. Based on this discovery it has been possible to produce better plants by scientific crossing of different species. Thus in Russia the wheat and barley crops have been greatly improved, while as an example in our own country the sugar beet has been made to increase its sugar content from 9% to nearly 20%, and larger roots are also grown.

In the breeding of better animals more progress has been made during this past century than in all the years before. In Queen Victoria's reign livestock societies were formed and flock and herd books were published ; no other country in the world could show such yields of corn and root crops as in Britain, while people came from all over the world to buy British livestock to improve their own herds.

How Rothamsted Began

One young man, J. B. Lawes (1814–1900), who inherited an estate at Rothamsted, Herts., began experiments about 1838 to try the effects of various substances on plant growth. A young chemist, J. H. Gilbert (1817–1901), joined him in 1843, and together the two made many valuable discoveries both in the feeding of crops by fertilisers and in the right feeding of animals.

Rothamsted became world famous and Lawes eventually set up a trust, endowed with £100,000, for the continuation of agricultural experiments. With Government support the work still goes on, particularly in relation to the right composition of soil for different crops and the proper use of fertilisers.

All this progress was largely the outcome of individual efforts in the nineteenth century. It was not until 1889 that a Board of Agriculture was established and in 1903 they took over the supervision of all British fisheries. The war of 1914–18 wakened the country generally to the tremendous importance of our home-produced food supplies and in 1919 the Board became the Ministry of Agriculture and Fisheries. Since then another war has made it increasingly important that the growing of food as well as the breeding of livestock shall be encouraged and helped in every way by the Government of the country.

Agricultural Research Institutes, financed wholly or in part by the Ministry, have increased in number. These cover a wide range from the large experimental stations such as Rothamsted to special research units which have their own laboratories in one or other of the Universities. There are stations, such as the John Innes Horticultural Institution, which specialise in fruit culture, as does the East Malling Station in Kent, though other work is carried out.

At other stations problems connected with pests and diseases which attack crops are studied and remedies sought.

Storage of Meat and Fruit

Farmers, market gardeners, fruit growers, and anyone with a practical interest in agriculture or horticulture can obtain advice and help on problems which arise in their work. Most counties now have a staff of general advisers and instructors in agriculture, horticulture, dairying and poultry-keeping.

It is no longer a haphazard matter. Science has come to the aid of all who produce the fruits of the earth and an organised and continual effort is made by specially-trained chemists, working under the Agricultural Research Council, to improve upon Nature and to limit

Fox Photos.

A THREAT TO OUR FOOD CROPS

One of the diseases which may damage wheat is known as " Eyespot," which attacks the base of the straw, weakening it and so making it fall or " lodge " before harvest. Its complete cure would be of immense value and experiments which have been made in recent years are designed to that end. Here we see workers studying the effect on different species and counting the infected plants.

the ravages which may be inflicted when pests and disease threaten our supplies of food. Then, too, the Department of Scientific and Industrial Research carries out a good deal of work which is helpful to the agricultural industry.

Thus great strides have been made in recent years in the problems of cold storage, gas storage, drying, etc., of meat, milk, vegetables and fruit. There is a special pest laboratory where pests which attack growing crops and livestock are dealt with. There are special officers, trained in their own branches of science and having sound knowledge of other languages, whose task it is to keep in touch with other countries where agriculture is being studied scientifically.

Helicopters for Crop-spraying

At the same time there have been great changes in the tools used in agriculture. Although you can still see horses at work on many British farms, Britain now has the most highly-mechanised agriculture in the world. The horse has been largely replaced by the tractor, harvest time sees a growing number of combine-harvesting machines at work in the cornfields, while the almost impossible ground task of spraying growing crops to prevent disease is now being carried out by specially-equipped aircraft.

Killing Weeds and Pests

You can read in another volume of two important insecticides developed by chemists. They are D.D.T. and "Gammexane." D.D.T., B.H.C. (benzene

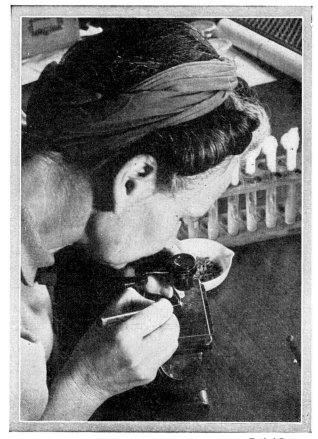

Topical Press.

HASTENING THE GROWTH OF SEEDS

Vernalisation is the term applied to a method of hastening the earing of cereals and other plants and is being extensively studied in Britain, Russia and America. Important experiments are being made at East Malling Research Station and our photograph shows a scientific worker carrying out a delicate task with the embryo from the grain.

hexa-chloride), and another new substance called 2,4-D or Crag Herbicide 1, have been widely used by farmers in Great Britain.

The new chemical, 2,4-D is a remarkable herbicide. That is to say, it will kill off weeds and other noxious growths. But it does not affect valuable grasses, and because it is not a poison it is not a danger to livestock. But it will rapidly kill weed seedlings and plant pests.

Developments of this kind are most important. At the present time, Britain loses £50 million worth of crops every year as a result of diseases, pests and

IN MARKET GARDENS AND ORCHARDS

It was in France that glass bells were first used by gardeners and these " cloches " were later adopted by many other countries. The bell-shaped type has now been largely replaced by the hand-lights seen above. Small portable frames of glass, joined by metal strips, are placed over the plants to protect them from the weather or to encourage early maturity. Many hundreds of these hand-lights are in constant use on a large market-gardener's holding.

Photos: John Topham.

At East Malling in Kent there is a Government research station mainly concerned with fruit culture and the problems of soil management for the benefit of British fruit-growers. In this picture fruit-growers from a wide area have gathered while one of the scientists explains the various experiments which have been carried out in the orchard and indicates the results attained.

FIGHTING FROST AND A DREADED PEST

When the blossom is on the trees with the promise of setting well, late frosts are a serious threat to the fruit-grower. The whole crop may be lost in a night. Various methods have been adopted to ward off the ill-effects of such a frost. In this picture two of the latest type " blowers " are ready for action on a night when frost has been forecast. They will cover the orchards with a warm cloud to nullify the frost.

Photos: John Topham.

One of the most dreaded enemies of the potato crop is the Colorado beetle, a native of the U.S.A., which appeared as a menace in England in 1934. Entire crops in large areas have been ruined by this pest. In recent years the helicopter has been used to spray growing crops with an insecticide which renders the crop immune or kills off any larvæ or beetles that may be already there.

weeds. These enemies of the farmer rob us of the produce of some two million acres.

Although scientists are now the valuable allies of all those who get their living from the land, farmers in all parts of the world still face hard struggles against Nature. In Britain, for example, we have still to discover a sure way of preventing blight on our potato crops and of countering the wheat bulb fly, which is a menace to our wheat. The terrible foot-and-mouth disease, which over the years has led to the destruction of thousands of pounds' worth of valuable cattle in its more serious outbreaks, cannot yet be prevented or even cured quickly.

Sometimes crops or livestock raised by the farmer himself have proved not the blessing that he had hoped, but a scourge beyond control. An example of this is the prickly pear, or American cactus, which was once used by Australian farmers to form hedges round their properties, but which later spread across the country and devastated 60 million acres of good land. " Thus prickly pear, pride of many a station homestead garden in the early days, had become a national disaster."

An answer to this " pest plant " was eventually found in the larvæ of the South American Cactoblastis cactorum moth. The eggs of this insect were imported and reared, and they provided nearly $2\frac{1}{2}$ million egg sticks, each containing from seventy to a hundred eggs. These sticks were then " liberated," that is, gummed to a small piece of paper and fixed to the prickly pear plants so that the larvæ from the eggs would enter

John Topham.

A GAS ATTACK ON AN OLD ENEMY

Most plants and vegetables have their own particular enemies and each needs its own special remedy. The aphis of the Cabbage Butterfly can ruin a field of green vegetables, causing a heavy loss to the grower. In this picture, taken in Kent, a huge canopy, larger than the size of a tennis court, is being dragged very slowly over cabbages, while nicotine gas is pumped beneath to kill off the aphis.

John Topham.

WATERING THE THIRSTY ORCHARDS

Nature sends " the breezes and the sunshine, and soft refreshing rain," but does not always send them at the right time for everybody. The owner of the orchard seen above has sunk a deep artesian well which supplies the water, as required, for this artificial " rainer " to provide the fruit trees with moisture in times of drought.

the plants. During the period 1925–1931, 2,750 million egg sticks were " liberated " in this way.

The immense effort was amazingly successful. Vast areas of prickly pear died as the larvæ ate their way deep into the pest plants. Dense barriers of prickly pear collapsed under their assault, and fertile lands that had been held in bondage for twenty years were freed. That is why you can see at Boonarga, on the western rim of the Darling Downs in Queensland, the Cactoblastis Memorial Hall, which commemorates the wonderful work done by the Cactoblastis cactorum moth.

Reclaiming Flooded Land

Science is ready to help the farmer when disaster overtakes him. In February 1953 when thousands of acres of good farmland on the East Coast of Britain were flooded by the sea, it was the soil scientists who were able to tell the farmers how they could bring this land back to fertility by using gypsum. Holland and France were also hard hit by these floods and needed the advice of scientists on how the salt could be removed from the soil and good crops made to grow again.

Gypsum, incidentally, is now considered by many scientists to be a very good soil conditioner for certain types of land. Tests carried out during 1953 and 1954 have shown that gypsum can often miraculously improve the land, making it easier to work and giving it an almost permanently improved soil structure. Chemists have also produced a remarkable soil conditioner which goes under the name of Krilium. It improves the quality and texture of the soil, but is at present rather expensive.

Many a British farmer has the scientists to thank for the cheap roads he has been able to build on and about his farm, using for the purpose his ordinary farming implements and, perhaps, a steamroller hired from the County Council. He can build good roads cheaply because the scientists have shown him how to stabilise, i.e., make firm, ordinary soil by mixing cement or certain other material with it. And he usually starts his roadmaking by asking the scientists to analyse his soil so that he can use the correct amount of cement and moisture in its stabilisation.

This method of road-making is also being used on a larger scale by many local authorities in Britain. At Dartford, Kent, making roads by the soil stabilization method has saved the borough £24,000 since 1945, because the method is cheaper and quicker. This saving of £4,000 on every mile of 14 feet wide

road built on the new housing estates there represented a saving of £12 on every new house built.

Science, then, is doing much for our farmers. In fact, it could be argued that farming is itself becoming a science. The country yokel, who used to be a favourite subject for the humorous artist, has disappeared. In his place is the trained mechanic, who understands as much about internal combustion engines as he does about superphosphates and other chemical fertilisers.

All this means that the farmer of the future will need theoretical as well as practical training, and agricultural education is now very important. There are a good many Agricultural Colleges where every branch of farming science can be studied and degrees taken: B.Sc.(Agric.) and B.Sc.(Hort.) are granted at the Universities of London and Reading. At Durham University a degree course can be taken in Agricultural Engineering.

Fox Photos.

FOR FRUIT FARMERS AND MARKET GARDENERS

Courses in agricultural subjects are held at some universities, at agricultural colleges, and at farm institutes. Modern developments make it very necessary that some knowledge of the theoretical as well as the practical side should be gained by those engaged in horticultural work. Our picture gives a scene in the laboratories at Swanley Horticultural College.

EXPERIMENTS IN PLANT GROWTH

In this picture the effect of inoculating sainfoin with a beneficial strain of nodule culture is seen. The plant on the right shows normal growth and on the left is the inocul ted plant.

Careful check is kept on all plants on which experiments are being made. Here we see a research worker at Rothamsted examining symptoms in sugar beets in the glass houses.

Fox Photos:

Growing plants in water solutions is not an entirely new idea, but it is now being carefully studied and the best methods discovered by experiment. Here we have a picture showing lettuces planted at weekly intervals; the youngest plants are in the front and are graded up to nearly full-grown plants at the back.

Diplomas in Agriculture, Dairying and Poultry Husbandry are also given. Most agriculturists are engaged in practical work, but there are to-day many posts for those who have been trained in the theoretical and practical sides. Those who consider adopting any form of agricultural career are advised to pay special attention to scientific subjects, especially biology, whilst they are at school, and to work on farms during part of their school holidays.

There are many difficulties facing the farmer in Britain owing to the vagaries of our climate. Methods such as vernalisation, one of the more recent discoveries which scientists are now engaged in testing, may prove a means of overcoming or at least minimising some of our weather handicaps besides increasing the certainty of better crops.

The care and cure of sick animals is the task of the veterinary surgeon and here, too, great strides have been made in recent years, coinciding with the advance made in medical science generally. Training for this work takes five years at one of the recognised schools, after which the final examination is taken. The successful student is given the Diploma of the Royal College of Veterinary Surgeons and is entitled to use the letters M.R.C.V.S.

Nature Still Dominant

For this work a keen love of animals is one of the first essentials. It is equally essential that for practical work on the land a love of the country and a real desire for farming life should be inborn. Science may bring about a revolution in methods and machinery may rob the work of much of its heavy drudgery, but Nature remains the dominant factor even though we have progressed in our efforts to counterbalance her more difficult moods.

John Topham.

MODERN SPRAYING METHODS FOR FRUIT TREES

The spraying of fruit trees with some preparation which will ward off the blight that may ruin the crop has long been practised. Even the amateur may use his syringe and bucket, but on a large fruit farm more modern methods are necessary. Here we see a motor-driven sprayer at work in a large English orchard.